People and politics in Britain

D041744S

People and politics in Britain

Lynton Robins
Tom Brennan
John Sutton

MACMILLAN
EDUCATION

First published 1985
Reprinted 1987, 1988

Published by
MACMILLAN EDUCATION LTD
Houndmills, Basingstoke, Hampshire RG21 2XS
and London
Companies and representatives
throughout the world

Printed in Hong Kong

British Library Cataloguing in Publication Data
Robins, Lynton
People and politics in Britain.
1. Civics, British
I. Title   II. Brennan, Tom
III. Sutton, John
320.441   JN906
ISBN 0-333-27834-8

Contents

PART FIVE
Policies and issues

199

PART ONE

Government and people

1

Government and politics

Why does a society need government and politics? In this chapter we consider the advantages and disadvantages of government and look at the main types of government that exist. The growth of government over the last hundred years is examined in some detail. Governments are said to provide for our welfare 'from the cradle to the grave', and we tend to expect them to solve problems of all kinds, even those without an easy solution. Difficulties which have faced successive Labour and Conservative governments since the end of the Second World War and are still unresolved, are becoming more severe. Some people have lost confidence in government and are turning to violence. This adds to the problems as government works best when it is based on the general consent of the people. Politics is the process by which society attempts to cope with disagreement and conflict. It involves the use of power and does not always produce just or fair results.

The role of government

All societies try to influence the behaviour of their citizens by establishing rules. In advanced societies, people's behaviour is governed by (i) rules which have the force of law, and (ii) customs, which are not law but which suggest acceptable ways of behaving. This book is about *politics* in Britain, and so it is primarily concerned with the rules and regulations made by government. By contrast a book on sociology would be more concerned with the customs and manners which influence the way people live. Government both influences and is influenced by the kind of society we live in.

Having to obey rules made by governments can be inconvenient or annoying for people, but without those rules their lives would be in turmoil. If there were no rules to govern what people did, all our lives would be chaotic and disorderly. For example, can you imagine how difficult and dangerous driving a car would be if there was no Highway Code?

Sometimes the fact that a rule exists is more important than its actual details. Let us consider driving a car once again. In the USA it is the rule that vehicles must be driven on the *right*-hand side of the road: in Britain the rule is that we drive on the *left*-hand side. It does not really matter whether we drive on the right or left in any one country so long as there is a rule that everyone does the same thing.

All rules, of course, limit our freedom to act as we choose. The rule which says cars must be driven on the left-hand side of the road takes away the freedom to drive just anywhere on the road. If car drivers had the freedom to drive wherever they wanted, this would result in accidents which would involve other people. Other drivers and pedestrians might be injured or killed as the price for the freedom to drive anywhere. So although the rules of the Highway Code limit the freedom of drivers, those rules result in quicker journeys and far fewer accidents. It is a fact of life that the freedom of the individual must be limited in the interests of society as a whole.

We use the word **anarchy** to describe a situation in which there are few or no rules. Anarchists believe that living in a society without a government would be better for people. They think that people should be free to make their own decisions rather than always do as the government demands.

However the lack of government would have many disadvantages. We have seen this already with something as simple as riding a bike or driving a car on our roads. But what are the other benefits of living in a society which is governed by a small group of politicians and civil servants? Figure 1.1 shows the most important responsibi-

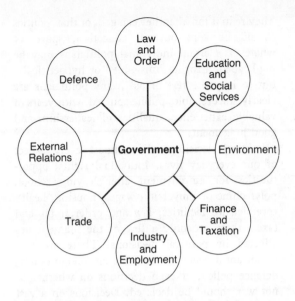

Fig. 1.1 The responsibilities of government

lities of government in Britain, which can be summarised as:

(a) government helps to protect life and property by the establishment of law and order
(b) government can organise armed forces to protect its citizens from attack by foreign countries
(c) government can regulate the financial and economic affairs of society
(d) government can provide for the welfare of citizens through education and social services

What we must not forget in this study of government in Britain is that different societies are governed in different ways. Some societies have **authoritarian** governments which pay little respect to the wishes of individuals. Such governments tend to obtain and keep power by the use of armed force. Authoritarian governments go to great lengths, frequently relying on secret police, to make sure that the rules they make are obeyed.

Other societies have more **democratic** government where citizens have at least some influence in the way the country is run. Democratic governments obtain power through being freely elected by their citizens. A democratic government will resign peacefully if elections show that the voters would prefer to be governed by another party.

There are many varieties in the type of government which can exist, and many differences in the way power can be used. Although we shall be mainly concerned with government in Britain, it is always necessary to remember that this is only one of the many ways in which countries are ruled.

The nature of politics

People are all different. They hold different opinions, have different lifestyles, and want the government to follow different policies. Therefore there is bound to be disagreement and conflict in society. But somehow or other, most of these conflicts and disagreements must be solved. In some societies they are solved by violence, but it is clearly better if they can be solved in a peaceful way.

This is where politics comes in because politics is the process through which society tries to cope with disagreement and conflict. Politics is about 'who gets what'. Of course, what any individual or group gets depends mainly on how powerful that individual or group is. The most powerful voices in society tend to get the most. In coping with society's conflicts, politics does not guarantee that everybody will be properly or fairly treated.

Professor Bernard Crick said that government is 'the organisation of men in a given community for survival'. But he also reminded us that 'political rule must be preceded by public order'. Serious problems can occur for government if individuals or groups refuse to accept official decisions or policies. Government in Britain, as in many other countries, faced increasing disorder during the 1970s and 1980s. Terrorism posed problems for the governing of Northern Ireland, and inner-city rioting and violent picketing at factories posed problems in governing mainland Britain. In all of these cases, groups of individuals felt that their views were being ignored, and so turned to violence as an expression of their frustration. But violence brings with it misery and tragedy. The wise government takes account of all views in society, so that no sizeable group feels 'left out' or ignored.

In a society where all the people agree with the way politics is run (even if they do not agree with all the policies of a particular government) we say that political rule is based on **consensus**. Consensus means that there is general agreement within society on how government and politics are to be organised. It means agreement on how new governments are to be chosen and how they are to be got rid of. It means agreement on the general way in which government is carried out. Political consensus means a willingness by people to obey laws which are passed, even if they do not like those laws.

Clearly no society in the world has *total* consensus. In Britain the great majority of people agree that we should be governed by Parliament, but there are minorities who oppose parliamentary government.

In politics, consensus and conflict go hand in hand. Within society there are those who support having elections to choose the MPs who will represent and govern us, but there are also those who would rather have some other system.

Within the political parties there is widespread consensus on how government should behave. Labour, Conservative and Liberal/SDP (Social Democratic Party) MPs will all agree that the government should allow free speech, not lock up opposition MPs in prison, hold regular elections, and so on. However those same MPs would disagree markedly about the policies a government should follow - nationalisation or privatisation, private education or comprehensive education, leaving or staying in the European Economic Community (EEC), and so on. Even within *each* party there is agreement that it would form a better government than its rivals, but conflict about which are the best policies. Inside the Labour party, for example, there is disagreement over Britain having nuclear weapons and, inside the Conservative party, there are conflicts about economic policy. So consensus exists on the basic ways in which Britain should be governed but there is endless conflict about the particular policies to be pursued.

Politics and everyday life

Many people have a low opinion of politics and politicians. We have all heard views such as

'they're in it for what they can get', or that 'politics should be kept out of' education, sport, or whatever. Certain individual politicians may be pig-headed, arrogant, misguided or hypocritical - but so may the rest of us! Many politicians are clearly sincere, able, public-spirited, with years of valuable experience, qualities of leadership, and good judgement.

Political decisions affect almost every aspect of our everyday lives. Individual rights; opportunities for employment after leaving school, polytechnic or university; wages; housing; health care; leisure facilities; law and order; rates and taxes; these are only a few of the many issues affected by political decisions. There are also important decisions to be made on foreign policy, defence policy, or even decisions on whether or not war should be declared. Decisions on a vast range of matters from membership of the EEC to setting up a micro-chip industry in Britain have important consequences for our everyday lives - and all of these decisions are political.

In these circumstances it is hard to understand why some people find politics boring. Politics may be complicated and worrying, but democratic politics is vital in keeping our freedom and way of life. Could it be that many of us are not interested in politics because we do not have the knowledge and skills needed to put our views across? It is often said that people 'get the government they deserve'. Like most sayings, it contains a germ of truth although it is not absolutely correct. What it does do, however, is make us see that we must have political knowledge and information if we are to have any influence on what governments do.

The scope of government action

The range of matters which governments control has grown and grown in the last hundred years. A number of factors have led to the increasing scope of government. As reforms gave more and more people the right to vote, so governments became more interested in the issues which concerned ordinary voters. The rise of the political parties in Britain meant that more issues were debated in public. Finally, the experience of Britain in two world wars has led governments to take control ▷ p.13

All the people shown below are applying rules in their jobs. Which of them are applying rules which come from the authority of government?

referee

policeman

health inspector

teacher

ticket inspector

magistrate

This cartoon is about the uncertain future of Britain and the rest of the world. Discuss the issues which make our future so uncertain. Are there any issues that you think ought to be added to those shown on the bus?

'Good luck, kid – and by the way, there don't seem to be any brakes'

Guardian, 31 December 1979

over many aspects of daily life which previously they had left alone.

This expanding area of activity in which government has become involved can be seen in the growth of the civil service. In 1868 there were only 16 000 civil servants; by 1900 the number had grown to 28 000. By the end of the First World War in 1918 there were 380 000, and by 1945, the end of the Second World War, there were 575 000. In 1984 there were 630 000 civil servants and, in addition, local government employed some 2¼ million people despite recent efforts to cut back the number. If we include all the people who work in the **public sector** - this includes civil servants, local government workers, teachers, police, armed forces, workers in nationalised industries, water and health authorities, and other government bodies - then there is a total of 8 million public employees. And all of them are working on things in which the government is now involved. The total number of employees in Britain is about 20 million.

In the 1880s a prime minister needed only to appoint about 36 ministers and junior ministers in the House of Commons. By the 1980s the number has risen to nearer 100. A hundred years ago acts of Parliament tended to be short and fairly simple. Today they are likely to be long and complex. Many new government departments have been set up to administer these growing responsibilities.

In contrast to the many commitments of government in the 1980s, the much more limited responsibilities which existed at the end of the nineteenth century have been examined by Professor John Mackintosh in *The Government and Politics of Britain*. He explained that:

The small, largely propertied electorate of the 1850s and 1860s had accepted that the government's task was confined to foreign affairs, defence, internal law and order and raising the very limited amount of money needed to pay for these services. A certain degree of regulation of social and industrial practices was also possible, such as specifying a minimum age for children or maximum hours for women who were working in difficult conditions, and some elementary services could be provided, such as free primary education. But it was not thought proper to extend regulations to cover

the hours of work of adult men; they were best left to look after themselves - a view taken by the Trades Union Congress until the late 1880s. Nor was it considered proper or possible for the government to act in any way which influenced the activity of industry or the rates of wages that were paid. When Keir Hardie was elected in 1892 as the first independent Labour member he was deeply offended, not so much by political attacks, as by the assumption on all sides that unemployment and poverty were not issues which should concern Parliament.

The reforms introduced by the Liberal government at the beginning of this century gave to government new responsibilities, especially in the fields of social welfare and control of the conditions in which people worked. The importance of government then increased further during the First World War when it introduced conscription, food rationing and made decisions about what and how much industry should produce. In the Second World War the responsibilities of government were greater still. Government policies touched upon almost all aspects of life, and included managing the whole economy.

Many of the strict government controls were lifted at the end of the Second World War, but the Labour government's policies between 1945 and 1951 brought many new responsibilities. The basic industries were nationalised, the National Health Service was established, education was reorganised, and a comprehensive scheme of social services was introduced. What surprised many people was that these new responsibilities were retained with little change when a Conservative government was elected in 1951.

More and more, government was expected to tackle every problem as it arose. Professor Mackintosh commented:

By the end of the 1950s or early 1960s the government was being asked to do even more in providing higher education, in building motorways, protecting the countryside, stopping the congestion of the cities and supporting the regions of Britain which had lower rates of growth, lower wages and higher rates of unemployment and emigration than the rest of the country.... Thus, in the period under consideration, a combination of the problems to be tackled and the demands of a mass electorate, an electorate uninhibited by any notions that governmental action was inherently undesirable or inappropriate, all led in the direction of greater government involvement in the life of the community.

By the 1970s government had accepted responsibility for investment in industry and for deciding wage rises and price rises. At the same time people expected the government to solve more and more problems. When Court Line, an airline and shipping firm which sold 'package' holidays, went bankrupt, the disappointed customers looked to the government for help. When there was a shortage of sugar in the shops, the public looked to the government to solve the problem. Whenever there was a flood or some other natural disaster, the government was expected to take action and provide help.

In the 1980s the feeling grew that governments had become too involved in people's lives and were now expected to do too much. A Conservative government, led by Mrs Thatcher, tried to be less involved in running the economy but found this very difficult to do. For example, some Conservative ministers said it was wrong for government to get involved with the level of prices and incomes. They thought that the economy should be left to run itself without government interference. Despite this, other Conservative ministers found that they were spending much time in trying to lower the rate of inflation and limit price rises. Also they were urging workers to settle for lower wage increases and were setting limits for pay rises in the public sector. Therefore, although the Conservative government did not want a prices and incomes policy, it found that it had to have policies for price rises and wage rises.

Is Britain becoming harder to govern?

The problems of governing Britain became more complicated during the 1970s. In the early 1980s there was serious rioting in a number of major towns. It seemed that laws passed by Parliament and decisions made by government were being ignored by a growing number of people. In a book, *Why is Britain Becoming Harder to Govern?*, edited by Professor Anthony King, he wrote:

It was once thought that Britain was an unusually easy country to govern, its politicians wise, its parties responsible, its administration efficient, its people docile. Now we wonder whether Britain is not perhaps an unusually difficult country to govern, its problems intractable [difficult to deal with], its people bloody-minded. What has happened? What has gone wrong?

He concluded that:

The reason it has become harder to govern is that, at one and the same time, the range of problems that government is expected to deal with has vastly increased, and its capacity to deal with problems, even the ones it had before, has decreased. It is not the increase in the number of problems alone that matters, or the reduction in capacity. It is the two coming together.

Since the end of the Second World War big changes have taken place in society, and these have had an effect in the world of politics. The economic boom of the 1950s and 1960s slowed down and was finally replaced by recession. Inflation became a major problem in Britain and other industrialised countries. The Organisation of Oil Producing and Exporting Countries (**OPEC**) introduced a steep rise in oil prices which led to price rises across the economy. Fewer goods were bought and fewer workers were needed to make them. Unemployment became a major problem. The two economic ills of stagnation and inflation coincided during the 1970s to produce a situation which was termed 'stagflation'.

Governments have attempted to solve these problems with a number of very different policies. Labour attempted to plan the economy, drew up a 'National Plan' for recovery, and put money into industry through a National Enterprise Board. Both Labour and Conservative governments have tried to cure inflation with prices and incomes policies. Both have tried to solve unemployment with schemes to attract new factories into poorer areas and with 'job creation' schemes designed to give young people 'work experience'. Both Labour and Conservatives hoped that Britain's membership of the EEC would bring economic benefits, but in vain. Although both Labour and Conservative governments have thought that Britain's poor productivity was partly caused by trade union activities, only the Conservatives have attempted to control the unions through the Industrial Relations Act and the Employment Act. Finally, the Conservatives reduced inflation by following monetarist policies and cutting back on government spending. However, these policies contributed to massive unemployment.

In fact, none of the remedies or policies tried so far have solved Britain's problems. The gloomy prospects not only for Britain but also for the wider world, shown in the *Guardian* cartoon, are still with us. What sort of position Britain will be in at the end of the 1980s is hard to imagine. Whatever happens, we hope that the following chapters will help you understand government and politics better. We will be considering (i) political ideas, such as democracy, (ii) how institutions like Parliament work, and (iii) the working of political processes such as the selection of our leaders. Hopefully, this will encourage a more informed approach to the study of the relationship between government and the governed in a democratic society.

Terms used

Anarchy The absence of established government.

Authoritarian Favouring obedience to authority rather than individual liberty.

Consensus The existence of widespread agreement about how governments should act.

Democratic A form of government involving representation and/or participation of citizens.

OPEC The Organisation of Oil Producing and Exporting Countries. Industrial countries like Britain use up vast amounts of energy, such as oil. For a long time oil was very cheap for Britain to buy, but in 1973-4 OPEC increased the price of oil by over four hundred per cent. This caused problems in all industrial countries. The oil price rises caused rises in the price of many other products.

Public sector Organisations and activities which are directly or indirectly accountable to government.

Summary

1 All societies have some form of government for regulating the behaviour of their members. The necessity for rules means that the freedom of the individual is limited in the interest of the general good.

2 Government is expected to provide for the protection of personal life and property; protect society from outside aggression; regulate economic affairs and provide for the welfare of its citizens.

3 Politics is the process which has been developed to reconcile the differing demands of individuals and groups.

4 The range of matters with which government concerns itself has increased a great deal in the last hundred years, and the size of the government machine has grown correspondingly.

5 Britain is becoming more difficult to govern, because people expect much more from government just at the time when government cannot do so much.

Questions for discussion

1 Examine the ways in which politics affects our everyday lives.

2 Give reasons for the growth in the responsibilities of government.

3 Do you agree that Britain is becoming harder to govern? Give reasons for the view you hold.

4 Many people dislike or distrust politicians. Why do you think this is so?

5 In William Golding's book, *Lord of the Flies*, we can read a story about a group of schoolboys marooned on a tropical island. The boys soon argue about how they should behave towards each other. Despite the fact the boys all come from a middle-class background, we see how quickly civilisation breaks down. Imagine your class was shipwrecked. Discuss how you would set about governing yourselves.

2

The social context

In this chapter we examine some aspects of the political, social and economic environment. We also consider how political messages are communicated from one section of society to another. First, however, we must consider the influence historical and geographical factors have had on shaping our outlook on the world. But outlook on the world also differs according to a person's upbringing and social class. We examine some of the ways in which social class affects politics. Do the mass media affect the different attitudes and outlooks found in different social classes? Do people buy newspapers which fit in with their own political views? The chapter concludes by considering how fair the mass media are in reporting politics to viewers and readers.*

Society and politics

Every person is influenced to a great extent by the way in which he or she is brought up and by the type of environment in which he or she lives. Family, friends and neighbourhood help shape the way a person understands society. **Sociologists** use the term **socialisation** to describe the process through which an individual's attitudes are shaped or influenced. Socialisation affects a person's political views as well as his or her general outlook on life. Although every person is socialised into living in society, it is a process which can vary a lot from person to person. For example, a child born to wealthy parents is likely to have a different education, meet different people, and be prepared for a different type of job from a child born to much poorer parents. The rich child will grow up expecting different treatment from society than the poorer child. The child from the wealthy background will have a different view of himself and his future role in society from the child from the poorer family. The rich child will even develop a different view of society.

The political system to a large extent mirrors the society of which it is part. If society is stable, then its politics will be stable. The outstanding features of the British political system are said to be its **continuity** and **stability**. This does not mean that there is not change or instability in Britain. Indeed, Britain's political institutions have been extremely flexible in adapting to changes which have sometimes been sparked off by increasing levels of **conflict** in society. Nevertheless, Britain's political institutions have developed over a long period of time and they have not been through the kind of sudden change experienced in other countries. A number of factors contribute to this.

Britain's geography

First, there is the geographical fact that Britain is an island. Partly because of this Britain has not been invaded successfully for nearly a thousand years. Even Hitler's armies, which overran the rest of Europe, found the English Channel a formidable obstacle to invasion.

Britain's island position and its former role as centre of the greatest empire the world has ever known helped to produce an outlook different from that of our European neighbours. The empire has long disappeared and Britain is now a member of the EEC. But it is frequently said that Britain is still out of step with the thinking of her continental partners in the Common Market. Britain's **imperial** past and her clear geographical boundaries have helped form a strong sense of national identity. Scotland and Wales have strong regional identities but there is relatively little support for the idea of these areas breaking away from England and forming their own governments. Northern Ireland formerly had its own

Parliament for domestic affairs but this was abolished and 'direct rule' was re-established in 1972.

Our geographical position has other consequences. Because half the food we eat has to be imported along with many raw materials needed by industry, Britain has to export goods and services to pay for them. Britain's foreign policy is shaped in part by our trading relations with other countries. Because Britain is an island it has developed a strong naval tradition in its defence policy. Finally, Britain's position on the 'north-west corner' of Europe makes it an important NATO (North Atlantic Treaty Organisation) partner and ally of the USA.

Population and industry

Britain is densely populated and has become increasingly **urbanised**. Most Britons live in or close to towns. The total population has grown from 38.2 million in 1901 to an estimated 55.8 million in 1979. Although the overall density or concentration of the population is high, it is unevenly distributed. The south is more densely populated than the north with about 7 million living in Greater London alone. Nearly 40% of the total population is crowded into seven **conurbations** of Greater London, South-East Lancashire, West Midlands, West Yorkshire, Merseyside, Tyneside, and Clydeside. The more wealthy sections of the population have moved out from the city centres to the suburbs. The housing areas which remain in the inner cities are likely (outside London) to be occupied by ethnic groups and the poorest groups in the community.

In the period from 1950 to 1962 there was an appreciable level of immigration from the new Commonwealth countries, especially the West Indies, India and Pakistan. The immigrant groups tend to be concentrated in the larger cities especially in London, the midlands, the north-west and the north-east. This has brought about a significant change in the social structure and one which has political consequences. A recent study showed that twelve constituencies had over 12 000 voters who had been born in countries of the new Commonwealth and a further 20 included groups of about 10 000 or more. The report concluded that these ethnic minorities 'played a significant part in determining the outcome of the election' in October 1974. In the 1980s an increasing number of coloured citizens are born in Britain rather than being immigrants.

Of a total working population of about 24 million in Britain, only about 1.5 million are engaged in agriculture, forestry and fishing, and this number is declining. Most post-war governments have tried to keep unemployment low, but the numbers of people unemployed have risen sharply in the 1980s. In 1969 the number of people without jobs passed 900 000. By 1982 it was 3.4 million and still rising. These totals include considerable numbers of school-leavers and higher education graduates unable to find employment. The figures may even underestimate the real position, for they do not include many women who are out of work but who have not registered as unemployed. Finally, there are marked regional differences in levels of unemployment with Scotland, the north of England, Wales and Northern Ireland suffering the worst. In some of these areas as many as 40% of the workforce is unemployed.

Social Class

Social class is a difficult and complex subject. It is also a controversial one. It involves placing people in different groups or categories and, understandably, some people object to being labelled in this way. Social class categories are, nevertheless, used increasingly in many types of social research.

In analysing early industrial society Karl Marx identified two classes; the 'bourgeoisie' and the 'proletariat'. These classes were based on what they each owned. The bourgeoisie owned capital, which enabled them to construct factories, railways and the like for profit or to build property which would provide rent. The proletariat owned only muscle and skill in the form of labour and earned wages by selling their labour to the bourgeoisie. Marx saw the whole of history in terms of a class struggle between these two forces. The bourgeoisie attempted to control and exploit the proletariat, and the proletariat worked towards the eventual overthrow of the bourgeoisie. The **capitalist** economy has changed a great deal from the time when Marx was studying society. As a result of these changes, social divisions have become less clearly marked. But it is still possible to see society as being made up of different social classes.

The most important factor which distinguishes the members of different social classes from each other is that of occupation or type of job. Although social class involves many aspects of life, from what a person eats to how he talks and what he does with his spare time, the main pattern we use to identify the class of an individual is his occupation. In conversation we often name people by the jobs they do - nurses, miners, teachers, steel-workers, and so on.

Of course a person's occupation is closely connected with other aspects of social class including education, income and status. The sociologist, Salvador Giner, suggests that a number of individuals may be said to belong to the same class 'when they share a similar set of life chances, that is, the same degree of likelihood that they will enjoy a certain type of education, income, status, standard of living, private property, position in the political structure, and the like'.

In everyday life we tend to think in terms of there being an upper, middle, and working class. For the purposes of research much more precise divisions are made. There are basically three different ways in which society can be measured:

(i) The Registrar General's classification

The Registrar General's classification, which is used in the census, distinguishes between the following groups:

Class I *Professional*
  e.g. chartered accountants, senior civil servants
Class II *Intermediate*
  e.g. bank cashier, pharmacist
Class III *Skilled*
  e.g. (N) non-manual - foreman, meter reader
      (M) manual - skilled plumber, electrician
Class IV *Semi-skilled*
  e.g. machine operators, storemen

Class V *Unskilled*
  e.g. farm labourers, building labourers.

(ii) The Hall-Jones Index

The Hall-Jones Index distinguishes between seven groups. Sociologists tend to use this index in their research. (The information collected by Professor Halsey contained in Tables 2.2 and 2.3 is based on a rather similar index which has one additional category for self-employed persons.)

Class I *Professional and high administrative*
  chartered accountant, business executive, senior civil servant
Class II *Managerial and executive*
  e.g. pharmacist, departmental manager, substantial farmer
Class III *Inspectional, supervisory and other non-manual higher grade*
  e.g. wages clerk, draughtsman, commercial traveller
Class IV *Inspectional, supervisory and other non-manual lower grade*
  e.g. foreman, shop assistant, door-to-door salesmen
Class V *Skilled manual and routine grades of non-manual*
  e.g. workers who have served an apprenticeship or equivalent
Class VI *Semi-skilled manual*
  e.g. painters and decorators, drivers
Class VII *Unskilled manual*
  e.g. farm labourer, dustman

(iii) Market research

Market research and public opinion polls have developed a great deal in recent years. There are now a number of commercial organisations including Gallup, National Opinion Polls (NOP), Marplan and Market and Opinion Research International (MORI). A number of these organisations now classify social classes in the following way:

A Higher managerial, professional, administrative

B   Lower managerial, professional, adminis-
    trative
C1 Skilled, supervisory or lower managerial
C2 Skilled manual
D   Semi- and unskilled manual
E   Residual, including state pensioners.

In presenting the results of surveys the top three and bottom two categories are each combined to simplify the data in many cases. Table 2.1, which shows voting by social class, uses this method. You can see from the top line of figures that this method roughly divides the population into thirds.

Table 2.1 Voting by social class in the 1983 general election (%)

	ABC1	C2	DE
% of voters	41	30	29
Conservative	55	40	33
Labour	16	32	41
Liberal/SDP Alliance	28	26	24

Source: Peter Kellner, 'Anatomy of a landslide' *New Statesman* 17 June 1983

We shall be examining the links between social class and voting in chapter 12. At this stage you can use the statistics to see how far the major political parties represent different social classes.

Social class, education and politics

The findings of numerous research reports indicate that there is a close link between social class and education. Generally it can be said that the educational system works to the advantage of middle-class children and, despite many reforms, to the disadvantage of working-class children.

A recent survey of nearly 10 000 males revealed the influence of social class on education. Table 2.2 shows that 5.8% of the male population went to **private** primary schools, and 6.5% to private secondary schools. However, there are great differences between the social classes in the numbers who were privately educated. You can see, for example, that approximately a third of class I males had a private education. In contrast, only one-third of one per cent of class VIII had a private primary education and just over one per cent had a private secondary education.

Housing conditions differ according to social class. The poorest usually have the most over-crowded surroundings. The social classes also enjoy different levels of health care, with the poorest receiving least. It is not at all surprising that children from different social classes vary in success. Table 2.3 shows what happened to males from different social classes after they left school. You can see, for example, that just over 20% of classes I and II went to university, compared with 1.8% from classes VI, VII and VIII. Other studies have shown that working-class children are similarly disadvantaged when considering health, employment opportunities, social status and political powers.

A number of other studies have shown that the influence of social class and socialisation is important in political life. Richard Rose writes: 'Those in national politics are better born, better educated and better employed than the average Englishman. As one goes up the ladder of office-

Table 2.2 Percentages of males who had a private education, according to social class

Type of schooling	Social class of father								
	I	II	III	IV	V	VI	VII	VIII	All
Private primary	32.7	14.3	6.9	10.3	2.4	1.1	0.9	0.3	5.8
Private secondary	35.7	15.6	7.2	11.2	3.1	1.5	0.9	1.1	6.5

Source: A. H. Halsey *et al. Origins and Destinations*

Table 2.3 Social class and education beyond secondary school (%)

Father's social class	No post-secondary education	Part-time further education	College of education	University
I, II	29.6	47.6	2.7	20.1
III, IV, V	43.8	49.8	1.7	4.6
VI, VII, VIII	55.4	41.8	0.9	1.8
All	48.4	45.1	1.4	5.1

Source: ibid.

Table 2.4 The occupational background of politicians (%)

Occupation	Councillors	MPs Con.	MPs Lab.	Ministers Con.	Ministers Lab.	Nation
Professional	16	41	54	50	55	8
Managers	29	35	10	22	5	11
Lower middle class	12	2	5	0	0	16
Manual workers	19	1	26	0	41	56
Farmers	15	9	0	6	0	4
Armed forces	2	7	0	11	0	1
Other	7	49	24	11	0	4

Source: R. Rose, *Politics in England Today*

holders from voter to councillor, MP, senior civil servant and minister, the social differences between governors and governed increase.' Table 2.4 shows some details which illustrate this point and it is worth careful examination. Attention should be paid not only to the overall pattern but also to the similarities and differences in this respect between the two major parties. We shall consider other influences of social class on political participation in chapter 6.

Class differences in political office-holding become even more apparent when we examine the part played by those who attended public schools and the ancient universities of Oxford and Cambridge. The percentage from these groups in the top levels of government is out of all proportion to their actual numbers in society. A recent study of the educational background of 'top decision-makers' found that 50% of government ministers, 19% of the senior civil servants and 66% of Bank of England directors had been educated at major public schools. Seventy-one per

cent of the ministers and 68% of the civil servants had studied at Oxford or Cambridge. This proportion is staggering when one refers back to Tables 2.2 and 2.3 and sees how few receive a private education or go to university.

These findings suggest that only a small section of the population is socialised into political participation. In other words, very few people are brought up expecting to play an important part in Britain's politics. The vast majority, on the other hand, are socialised in a way that makes only slight involvement in politics likely. It is clear that political power and influence in Britain is very unevenly divided between the different social classes.

The mass media

The mass media include television, radio and the newspapers. These together provide the main means of communicating political news and comment to the general public. There is evidence that television provides the most popular medium for learning the political facts of national life. Although individuals do not always take notice of what they see on television or read in the paper, the mass media are a major influence in the way we understand politics. Perhaps the media's most powerful role in political communication is that they select the issues which receive most attention in politics. For example, the media may give considerable coverage to news of social security 'scroungers' while more or less ignoring the numerous court cases of those charged with tax evasion. As a consequence we may come to see 'scroungers' as a growing problem. But we may have no such views on tax evasion because, since it is rarely in the news, we do not believe it to be much of a problem.

Whether or not the media actually change people's political views is uncertain, but it is true that the media can largely determine the 'political climate' in which arguments, discussions and decisions take place.

One important difference between broadcasting (both television and radio) and newspapers is that, whereas the former are legally required to preserve a political balance, the latter are free to do as they wish. The majority of newspapers are unashamedly **partisan**. In other words, television and radio are politically 'neutral' whereas each newspaper tends to support a particular political party or view. The British Broadcasting Corporation at present provides two national television services (BBC 1 and BBC 2) and four radio channels. The four radio channels each have a distinctive character with the main news and information services being provided by Radio 4. The Independent Broadcasting Authority presides over the relatively new Channel 4 and grants licences to 15 television companies operating in the regions, with two companies sharing the contract for London. The BBC provides 20 local radio stations in England and there are 19 independent stations scattered over Britain. The number of BBC and IBA local radio stations will expand rapidly in the near future.

The governing bodies of both the BBC and IBA are appointed by the government but both authorities are independent so far as the day-to-day operation of services, including the nature and content of programmes, is concerned. Both bodies are, however, required by law to preserve a balance and impartiality in the presentation of political programmes. Thus in Britain we have broadcasting systems half-way between the state-controlled systems which reflect government policy and the independent systems which are guided by commercial considerations.

Since 1978 the proceedings of Parliament have been broadcast on radio but Parliament has so far resisted pressure for the televising of its debates. In 1983, however, the possibility came much closer when the Lords voted by 3 to 1 in favour of televising their debates. This put pressure on MPs to support a Private Member's Bill to televise the Commons. It was argued that all the technical problems could be overcome. Small wall-mounted cameras could be used which would not involve camera crews. The lighting in the Commons would not have to be much stronger than it is now. Only the MP speaking would be filmed; there would be no shots of empty benches or sleeping backbenchers. Some occasions, such as the Budget, are broadcast 'live', and recorded sound extracts may be included in both radio and television news and current affairs programmes.

Television and industrial relations

The general public sees the presentation of political news and current affairs on television as impartial but this is not the view of political parties, trade unions and some academic researchers. A frequent complaint is that political matters are 'trivialised' or 'personalised' in a sensational way which leaves the complex underlying issues ignored or oversimplified. For example, the arguments between Tony Benn and Labour's then leader, Michael Foot, or between Edward Heath and the prime minister, Mrs Thatcher, were shown as personality clashes involving personal hostility, old grudges or jealousy. Rarely were the arguments explained in terms of the different policies and priorities which divided them.

There is also the serious criticism that television gives a narrow, one-sided and biased view of industrial relations. Since 20 million people watch the main television news bulletins each night, and the majority of them assume that the news is free from bias, this is a serious accusation. It is one, however, which is supported by evidence from the Glasgow University Media Group. The Glasgow researchers argue that in reporting industrial relations the view of industry transmitted to the public is one in which managers are sensible people who are being frustrated by the antics of irresponsible workers. A famous case-study illustrates this. A speech by the then prime minister, Harold Wilson, had its meaning and content carefully changed by the media. The speech covered a number of topics including government policy on industry and investment, and carried a plea to management and trade unions to work together. The BBC reported the speech mainly in terms of a warning to workers and ITN presented it in terms of a warning applying *only* to the workforce.

In response to the Glasgow Group's charge of bias in the news, television reporters argue that when presenting a speech politicians often run through several themes but then come to the major one which they know will get reported in the news. In this case, it was argued, Mr Wilson did make a wide-ranging speech but the section reported in the news was clearly the section that Mr Wilson wanted them to report. The Annan Report on broadcasting, published in 1977, took the view that 'the broadcasters were not guilty of deliberate and calculated bias. But that the coverage of industrial affairs is in some respects inadequate and unsatisfactory is not in doubt.' It stated:

> They too often forget that to represent the management at their desks, apparently the calm and collected representatives of order, and to represent shop stewards and picket lines stopping production, apparently the agents of disruption, gives a false picture of what strikes are about. The broadcasters have fallen into the professional error of putting compelling camera work before news.

This, understandably, is a matter of great concern to the trade unions, who feel that they are given a raw deal by the media. It is a problem which they are likely to keep under continuing review.

The press

In Britain, unlike many other countries, it is the *national* daily and Sunday newspapers which have most influence. National newspapers have a total circulation of about 15 million on weekdays and 18 million on Sundays although, of course, the *total* readership is much greater than this (see Table 2.5). Despite a slow but continuous decline in national newspaper sales, nearly three out of four adults read a national newspaper every day.

Over the last thirty years there have been two trends in the organisation of Britain's newspapers. First, the number of national newspapers available has declined. Secondly, the ownership of newspapers has become concentrated in fewer and fewer hands.

Daily and Sunday newspapers can be divided

Table 2.5 The circulation of national newspapers in Britain in 1980

DAILY PAPERS

Popular	*circulation*
Daily Express	2 405 609
Daily Mail	1 943 793
Daily Mirror	3 623 039
Daily Star	937 866
Sun	3 793 007
Morning Star	34 558
Quality	
Daily Telegraph	1 476 887
Financial Times	206 360
Guardian	379 429
The Times	293 989

SUNDAY PAPERS

Popular	
News of the World	4 708 575
Sunday People	3 930 849
Sunday Express	3 257 728
Sunday Mirror	3 888 651
Mail on Sunday (1982)	1 450 000
Quality	
Observer	1 124 018
Sunday Telegraph	1 278 894
The Sunday Times	1 409 296

Source: Based on a table in *Britain 1980*, HMSO, p. 409

into two broad categories which have been described as the 'naughties' and the 'haughties'. First there are the 'popular' newspapers, such as the *Daily Mirror* and *Sun*, which are **tabloid** in form. Secondly, there are the 'quality' papers, such as *The Times* and the *Guardian*, which are larger and more traditional in their appearance. Political news in the popular tabloid press is dealt with in a simplified, direct and often biased manner. Detailed analysis and comment is restricted in the main to the quality press although this, too, is often politically biased. Table 2.6 shows that the 'populars' have a predominantly working-class readership and the quality newspapers a largely middle-class readership.

Overall the press has a Conservative bias although it does not always support the official Conservative policies (see Table 2.6). Until 1964 the former *Daily Herald* was partly owned by the Labour party and Trades Union Congress (TUC) and it was regarded as 'Labour's own newspaper'. Currently the *Daily Mirror* is most sympathetic to Labour policies and some support is given by the *Guardian*. The *Daily Mail, Sun, Daily Telegraph, The Times* and *The Financial Times* are predominantly Conservative. The only newspaper which has direct links with a political party is the *Morning Star*, which supports the Communist party. A detailed study of the press in *The British Election of 1979* (edited by D. Butler and D. Kavanagh) concluded:

The strongest impression of Fleet Street's role during the campaign was the extent of bias among the popular dailies. The uncommitted voter could not have relied for informed election coverage on any one of the tabloids – rather he needed to have turned to the quality dailies for a balanced judgement.

The extent to which the press directly affects the shaping of political views amongst its readers is unknown. The fact that newspapers are predominantly Conservative in outlook prevents a full debate of Labour or Liberal/SDP viewpoints. What is, perhaps, surprising is that many readers appear to be unaware of the political bias of the newspaper they buy. In a survey undertaken by MORI on the eve of the 1979 general election readers were asked whether the newspaper they read was biased towards Conservative or Labour, or whether it was unbiased. In each case about 50% or more felt their paper was unbiased or did not know. Only 19% saw the *Daily Mirror* as a Labour newspaper as against 24% who saw it as Conservative.

Labour politicians and trade unionists have been extremely critical of the press. They believe that it is biased and guilty of unfair reporting. A Royal Commission on the Press stated:

Many people and organisations have complained to us of bias against the left on the part of the press as a whole. We have no doubt that, over most of this century, the press has treated the beliefs and activities of the Labour movement with hostility. Such evidence as we have indicates that today it may be less partisan than ▷ p.27

Table 2.6 The political leaning and readership of national daily newspapers (1980)

Paper	Political leaning	Readership by social class (%)			
		AB	C1	C2	DE
Daily Mirror	Labour	6	17	41	35
Daily Express	Conservative	18	27	32	24
Sun	Conservative	6	16	42	35
Daily Mail	Conservative	21	30	29	21
Daily Telegraph	Conservative	51	29	13	8
Guardian	Independent/reformist	54	30	10	6
The Financial Times	Conservative	54	27	13	6

Source: Based on a table in Butler and Kavanagh, *op. cit.*

TASKPAGE 2.1

This quiz is taken from the *Commonwealth and Empire Annual 1956*. There is a chance that this annual was read by your parents (or their elder brothers or sisters) when they were about your age. How many of the twenty 'simple' questions can you answer? The annual and the quiz both show how the outlook of Britain has changed since 1956. It would be hard to imagine such an annual being published today. Write your own quiz, with five questions which are based on Britain's role in today's world.

A COMMONWEALTH AND EMPIRE QUIZ

What Do You Know?

Here are 20 simple questions relating to the British Commonwealth of Nations. How many of them can you answer?

1. What is the capital of Sierra Leone ?

2. What three British territories in Central Africa have recently been federated ?

3. Who first discovered Jamaica, and what did he call it ?

4. Of what state is Brisbane the capital ?

5. Can you name an African School and University established in the Gold Coast ?

6. Is Kenya a Colony or a Protectorate ?

7. When is Dominion Day in Canada celebrated ?

8. Edinburgh is the capital of Scotland. But do you know another capital also named Edinburgh ?

9. Where is Bathurst ?

10. What Colony possesses a remarkable lake of asphalt ?

11. Are there any British possessions in South America ?

12. What Colony supplies the world with the greater part of its cocoa ?

13. By what famous treaty was Gibraltar ceded to Britain ?

14. What is the largest British Colonial Territory ?

15. What Crown Colony was administered by a Chartered Company until as recently as 1942 ?

16. After whom was the island of Mauritius named ?

17. What is the capital of the Australian Commonwealth ?

18. In what part of the Empire and Commonwealth did the Emperor Napoleon I die ?

19. Where is Mt. Kilimanjaro (19,320 ft.) ?

20. What is the largest lake in the Commonwealth ?

TASKPAGE 2.2

This map shows the population density of the British Isles in 1968–70. Large urban areas and individual towns are marked. Use your atlas to identify the seven conurbations referred to on page 17. Also name those areas with the lowest population densities.

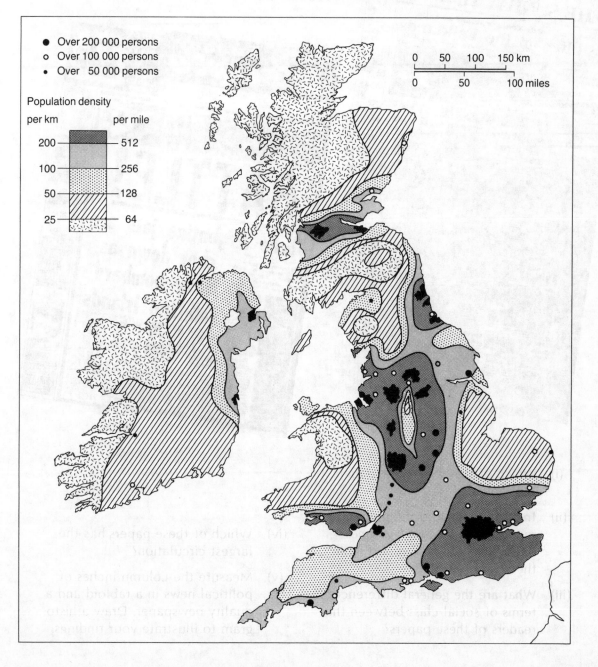

- ● Over 200 000 persons
- ○ Over 100 000 persons
- • Over 50 000 persons

Population density

per km		per mile
200		512
100		256
50		128
25		64

0   50   100   150 km

0   50   100 miles

(i) Which of the above newspapers is a tabloid?

(ii) In what ways does the political reporting in *The Sunday Times* differ from political reporting in the *Sunday People*?

(iii) What are the general differences in terms of social class between the readers of these papers?

(iv) Which of these papers has the largest circulation?

(v) Measure the column inches of political news in a tabloid and a quality newspaper. Draw a histogram to illustrate your findings.

its left-wing critics believe. It is certainly the case that some newspapers of the right persistently seek for discreditable material which can be used to damage the reputation of Labour ministers or those connected with the Party or trade unions.

The mass media have been the focus of considerable attention in recent years and various proposals for the reform of both television and the press have been put forward, especially with regard to political matters. For the moment many of the major problems, including those of partisanship and poor treatment of politics, remain. They must, therefore, be taken into account when considering the social context of the political system.

Terms used

Capitalism An economy based on private property, private enterprise and the profit motive. It is very different from **collectivism** which is based on state ownership and state control. Britain has a 'mixed economy', which steers a middle course between capitalism and collectivism.

Conflict Struggle between groups wanting to achieve different goals.

Continuity Lasting through time.

Conurbations Large urban areas resulting from separate towns growing and merging together. Associated with 'urbanisation' and 'rural depopulation'.

Imperial Of or belonging to an empire.

Partisan biased towards a party.

Private education Fee-paying education outside the state school provision.

Socialisation The process through which a person's attitudes and outlook on life is determined.

Sociologist A 'social scientist' who examines how society works.

Stability Not subject to disruptive change. A stable society will experience change but not revolutions.

Tabloid Newspaper printed on a small page. Tabloids are about half the size of the quality papers.

Urbanised Britain is an urban society. Most people live in or close to towns.

Summary

1 The British political system adapts to change, and is characterised by stability and continuity.

2 Britain's island position has been instrumental in preventing foreign invasion. It may also have assisted in developing a sense of national identity.

3 Britain is a densely populated and heavily urbanised country. Nearly 40% of the population live in seven conurbations. The north is less densely populated than the south and has higher levels of unemployment.

4 A social class is a group of people with similar occupations, status and life-style. A person with a middle-class background is much more likely to be educationally successful, to vote Conservative, to take an interest in politics and to become actively involved in politics than a person from a working-class background.

5 As one moves up the various levels in politics from councillors to government ministers and senior civil servants, the social differences between governors and the people they govern increase. Individuals from the public schools and the ancient universities dominate the upper levels of government in a way which is out of all proportion to their numbers in the population as a whole.

6 Television is the main medium of political news. Some individual programmes on politics and current affairs are outstanding, but there is criticism of the tendency to 'personalise' and 'trivialise' politics. There is some evidence that television presents a view of industrial relations which is unfair to trade unions.

7 The number of national newspapers has decreased over the last thirty years and ownership is in fewer hands. The majority of national newspapers have a Conservative bias.

8 This bias in the mass media influences our perception of politics. The views of minority parties are poorly represented in the media.

Questions for discussion

1 How has Britain's island position affected its political development?

2 In what ways is a person's social class likely to affect his or her political attitudes and viewpoint?

3 In what ways can television contribute to political awareness and political understanding?

4 Does the Conservative bias in the majority of newspapers work against democracy in Britain?

5 Are trade unions treated fairly by the press?

Either (i) discuss this in class or (ii) collect cuttings about trade unions from tabloid papers for any one week. Draw a graph which shows the number of articles which present unions in a favourable way, and the number which show the unions unfavourably.

6 Try to design the front page of a newspaper which is not politically biased. Include two stories about current political issues. What type of photograph might you include? Can photographs be politically biased?

3

Relationships between the government and the governed

The aim of this chapter is to examine ways in which we can understand the links between government and the people in a democratic society. We look at this relationship between the rulers and the ruled in two ways. First, we think of government dealing with what is called 'input'

and 'output'. Input comes from sources such as political parties or pressure groups. They ask the government to do (or not to do) certain things. The output is what the government actually does – it may either say 'yes' or 'no' to such requests. The second way of looking at government and the governed is in terms of twelve 'concepts' – power, force, authority, order, law, justice, representation, pressure, rights, individuality, freedom and welfare. Some of these concepts help us to understand government, some help us understand people, and some to understand the links between government and people. Finally, we illustrate the use of these concepts by applying them in an effort to make some sense of the complex politics of Northern Ireland.

Representative and responsible government

People expect government to do certain things for them. They expect government to protect them from foreign aggression, to maintain law and order, and to provide them with welfare. In order to do all these things, government needs the help of many different organisations such as the civil service, the nationalised industries, and local councils.

We, as citizens, make use of many services provided by the government. When you visit your doctor or dentist, attend school, play in a park or leisure centre, post a letter, or watch BBC TV, you are 'consuming' services that government has provided. This, however, is only one aspect of the relationship between government and the governed.

Another aspect of the link between government and the governed can be seen at election time. Through elections, representatives are chosen to sit in Parliament or on local councils. Sometimes general elections do not produce clear-cut winners and we may be governed by **coalition** or **minority** governments. Usually, however, one party is the clear winner and it forms the

government and has responsibility for running the country until the next election. Because the representatives who take office are chosen by the electorate, they are also answerable to them. This is why we speak of Britain having 'representative' and 'responsible' government.

The existence of this type of government from one generation to the next depends on people agreeing that this is the type of government that they want. We have already referred to this as 'consensus' about government and politics.

Britain's system depends upon Government and **Opposition** in Parliament, which compete with each other to win the support of the electorate. The government will always hope to stay in power by winning the next election. The Opposition – which people see as the alternative government – hopes that it will win the next election and replace the existing government. In this way government and the governed are linked through the electoral system – and this forms the basis of democratic government.

Inputs and outputs

Our first examination of the links between

29

government and the governed looks at 'inputs' to and 'outputs' from government. Inputs and outputs are about politics. And politics is the way government deals with disagreements and conflicts amongst its citizens. We consider briefly the flow of demands made upon the government and the responses which the government makes. These are the inputs and outputs of government.

By himself or herself, an ordinary citizen is unlikely to have much influence on government. People who share the same ideas or interests often join together so that they may carry more weight with government. They may try to influence government through joining a political party or **pressure group**. The demands that they make on government are referred to as 'input'.

People who share broadly similar ideas may be members of a political party. A political party usually stands for a particular philosophy or view of society. Each party has a wide range of policies dealing with all aspects of life from economic affairs, technology, and social services to foreign policy. Members of one political party face rivals

in other parties who hold different opinions and philosophies. These rival parties also have a different range of policies.

Pressure groups, on the other hand, are usually concerned with a particular issue and are joined by people who share an interest in that issue. For example, animal lovers join the RSPCA, and expect it to try to influence government decisions about blood sports, the export of live animals, the protection of animals in the wild, and so on. Members of the **RSPCA** would not expect it to have views on economic policy or to try to influence government economic policy. Whereas there are only a few major political parties, there are thousands of pressure groups in Britain. They are concerned with a vast range of issues, from nuclear weapons (**CND**), children's welfare (**CPAG**), old people's welfare (Age Concern), to care of the environment (Friends of the Earth).

In addition to parties and pressure groups, other input which attempts to influence government comes from the mass media. Views given coverage on television, radio and in the newspapers

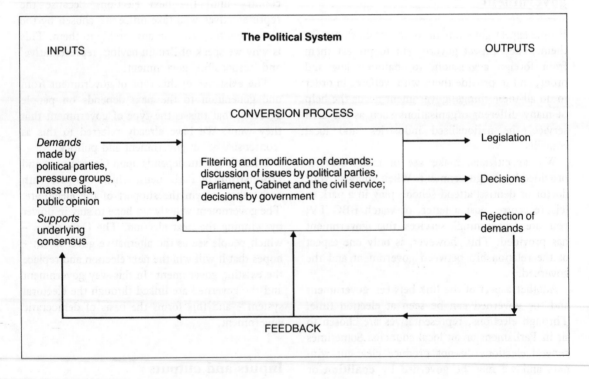

Fig. 3.1 Inputs and outputs of the political system (based on David Easton's 'dynamic response' model in *A Framework for Political Analysis*, Prentice Hall, 1965)

obviously influence government more than those views which are rarely heard.

Not all the input demands carry equal weight in the eyes of the government. Powerful organisations such as the **TUC** or **CBI** are listened to carefully by government. Input demands made by less powerful groups receive less attention, especially if such groups have little public support. For example, 'Exit' which supports suicide and 'Gay Lib' which promotes homosexual rights are not popular groups and consequently find it harder to make the government consider their suggestions.

Finally, public opinion can be a very powerful input influence on government. In the early 1960s a pressure group inside the Labour party called 'Labour Committee for Europe' wanted the party to support the idea of Britain joining the EEC. They made little impression on Labour's leaders and the party was generally against membership of the EEC. At the time opinion polls showed that only a quarter of the public supported Britain's entry into the EEC. But by 1967 over two-thirds of the public were in support of Britain's entry. Partly because of this change in public opinion, a Labour government headed by Harold Wilson applied to join the EEC.

You can see from Fig. 3.1 that the inputs, which are demands and support for the government to do particular things, go through a kind of 'conversion' process. Eventually 'outputs' from government are produced in the shape of laws and decisions. But government decisions may be 'no' rather than 'yes' to particular demands. For example, despite large support for CND, no British government has yet agreed to give up nuclear weapons.

Governments are thus receiving inputs and giving outputs. The 'feedback' loop in Fig. 3.1 is the way in which a government can find out how well the electorate thinks it is doing. If voters are satisfied, the government will be doing well in public opinion polls, and doing well in local government elections and **by-elections**. In this case, government would be receiving 'positive' feedback and continue without much change. If, on the other hand, the government is not successful in the polls and doing poorly in local and by-elections, it will be getting 'negative' feedback. Governments receiving negative feedback

often change policies or appoint new ministers in an attempt to win back support.

Political concepts

The understanding of the links between government and the governed may be helped by examining some political **concepts**. When we argue with friends or relatives about politics, we use ideas and concepts. For example, 'democracy', 'liberalism' or 'socialism' are concepts. When we are considering the ways in which government and people are linked, a number of other concepts are useful in helping us understand the system.

Professor Bernard Crick has listed twelve basic concepts, and they are shown in Fig. 3.2. Concepts which help us to understand the role of citizens are natural rights, individuality, freedom and welfare. Concepts which help us to understand the role of government are power, force, authority and order. Finally, the concepts which help us to understand the relationship between the government and the governed are law, justice, representation and pressure.

GOVERNMENT
power force authority order
RELATIONSHIPS
law justice representation pressure
PEOPLE
natural rights individuality freedom welfare

Fig. 3.2 The basic concepts for political understanding (based on Bernard Crick, 'Basic concepts for political education', *Teaching Politics*, vol. 4, September 1975)

(i) Governing concepts

The first group of concepts is about the role of government. *Power* and *authority* are closely linked concepts, but they are not the same. Having power is being able to get people to do things that they would not do unless made to. Exercising power may require the use of *force*, or at least the threat that force will be used in the last resort. A person who has authority can get people to do things because they think that person has a right to give them orders. Sometimes people obey the authority of 'charismatic' leaders. This type of authority is held by exceptional men and women who have the ability to inspire and lead others. Although very different individuals, both Jesus and Hitler had charismatic authority.

The difference between power and authority can be illustrated with two examples. An armed hijacker on a plane might get the pilot to fly miles from the proper route; the hijacker has power, but not authority. On the other hand, a young teacher might find it impossible to control a class of rowdy pupils; he or she has authority, but no power.

The concept of *order* means that our lives follow a pattern and are fairly predictable. Imagine how difficult it would be for us if we could not count on things taking place every day, such as meals being served, buses running, classes being held at school, or shops being open. We rarely stop to think what life would be like if these things did not happen regularly. There is also order in the world of politics. *Disorder* is when we do not know what will happen next. There must be order before there can be government.

(ii) Popular concepts

Professor Crick describes natural rights, individuality, freedom and welfare as popular concepts. They are 'popular' not in the ordinary sense that they are generally liked, but in the sense that they are about the people. The first concept to consider in this group is that of *natural rights*.

One of the most famous statements about human rights was issued on 4 July 1776. It is *The Declaration of Independence* of the United States of America. Part of it reads:

We hold these truths to be self-evident, that all men are created equal, that they are endowed by their creator with certain inalienable [cannot be taken away] rights, that among these are life, liberty, and the pursuit of happiness. That to secure these rights, governments are instituted among men, deriving their just powers from the consent of the governed, that whenever any form of government becomes destructive of these ends, it is the right of the people to alter or abolish it, and to institute new government, laying its foundation on such principles, and organising its powers in such form, as to them shall seem most likely to effect their safety and happiness.

The Declaration was written by Thomas Jefferson and it reflects the respect that he thought government ought to have for individual citizens.

Individuality refers to the value of each human being, and the respect which this entails. Government makes many demands on us but there are still areas of our lives untouched by government, which remain private. For example, we have the right to keep our political views private if we want to. A terrible abuse of individuality was the treatment of people in the concentration camps of Nazi Germany.

Freedom has positive and negative aspects; sometimes mentioned as 'freedom to' and 'freedom from'. For example, we have the freedom to vote for the candidate of our choice at an election. That is positive freedom. If the elected government makes sure that our lives are free from hunger, then that is negative freedom.

The concept of *welfare* involves the idea that government should provide for the happiness and well-being of its people over and above their mere survival. After all, cavemen survived from day to day without government. So government is concerned with the welfare of its people above and beyond their physical survival. Ideas on the scope of welfare have been enlarged with the passing of time. Early ideas were that welfare was limited to food and shelter. Later ideas of welfare included health, education and social security.

The distinction between *welfare* and *right* is important. Rights refer only to the basic requirements for human dignity. But welfare goes beyond this and is concerned with many things which contribute to human happiness.

(iii) Relating concepts

The concepts of law, justice, representation and pressure are all concerned with relating government to the governed.

Law is the collection of rules made by government which most people agree to obey. ▷ p.

These pictures are about government and its policies for running the economy. Which one shows 'input' and which shows 'output'?

A

B

These pictures are concerned with two of the political concepts we have discussed.

Which concept does this illustrate? Why do people join demonstrations instead of staying at home and writing to their MPs to let them know of their views?

Which concept does this illustrate? What sort of problems do soldiers face when they patrol communities which are split into two hostile sides?

There are frequently people who think that a particular law is so unjust that they refuse to accept it. For example, a law making motor cyclists wear crash helmets was thought unfair by the Sikhs. They objected to it because their religion required them to wear turbans, which was not possible under a crash helmet. If a particular law is so unpopular that many people refuse to obey it, then it becomes difficult to enforce. When the Conservative Industrial Relations Act became law in 1971, it was ignored by many thousands of trade unionists. Clearly it would have been unrealistic to think of arresting all those who broke the law. Such laws are often said to be 'bad laws', and the law on industrial relations was repealed in 1974.

Law and *justice* are not the same thing. In fact, laws often result in injustice. Laws which gave men alone the right to vote were clearly unjust and unfair to women. Professor Crick said that justice is 'what is right'. Of course we may disagree on what is right, and each one of us will have his or her own view of what is just.

The British system of government rests on the principle of *representation*. Government claims authority over us because it represents us. In what ways are citizens represented in the House of Commons? Despite the fact that over half the population is female, there are few women MPs. Despite the fact that people over the age of 18 have the right to vote, relatively few young people are MPs. Despite the fact that the working class is the largest social class, most MPs come from the middle class. Does this mean that Parliament does not really represent the people? The answer to this question is 'no'. This is because Parliament is representative, because it represents us on a geographical basis. The United Kingdom is divided into over 650 geographical areas – called constituencies – and each sends one MP to Parliament to represent the people who live within its boundary. In this way Parliament is representative.

Some people criticise Parliament for not accurately reflecting the views and opinions that exist in society. They argue that Parliament, and therefore government, would be more representative if elections were held by a different method. What most of them have in mind is changing the present system for one based on proportional representation (often referred to as 'PR'; see chapter 10).

Pressure is often defined as the action of groups which are trying to influence government. However, pressure may be applied by government to the people. For example, the TUC may use pressure to get the government to create new jobs in the economy. But the government may use the pressure of high unemployment on the unions in order to keep wage increases low.

Applications

These are the basic concepts we use when we study the relationship between government and the governed.

The purpose of discussing these concepts is, of course, so that we can use them to help us understand political events. Take the problem of Northern Ireland as an example. Northern Ireland had two forms of *representation*; representatives of the people of Northern Ireland sat in the Parliament in Belfast (Stormont) and also elected MPs to the House of Commons in London. However, some of the minority Catholic community still felt that they were inadequately represented because Protestants so dominated affairs in the province and the representation in West minster. They felt that their basic *rights* were not being upheld and that they were being *unjustly* treated.

Such feelings led to protest from the Catholic community. *Pressure* groups were formed, civil rights marchers clashed with the police and there were outbreaks of violence from terrorist groups. The *authority* of government was challenged and central government in London used its *powers*. Troops were sent to Northern Ireland and *force* was used in an effort to establish *law and order*.

The troops were only partially successful in restoring *order* because terrorism continues. The troubled history of Northern Ireland has seriously limited the *rights* and *freedom* of its citizens. Finally, the 'troubles' have reduced the quality of people's lives in Northern Ireland, thus cutting back on their *welfare*.

Terms used

By-election An election which is caused by the death or resignation of an MP, and is held on a day when there is not a general election.

CBI Confederation of British Industry.

CND Campaign for Nuclear Disarmament.

Coalition government A government formed from members of more than one party. Usually bargains and compromises are made by each party so that they can work together in government. Asquith and Lloyd George led coalition governments during the First World War.

Concept A way of organising our ideas about a topic which helps our understanding of it.

CPAG Child Poverty Action Group.

Minority government The party forming a minority government has less than half the MPs in the House of Commons. This happened to a Labour government in early 1977 as a result of MPs dying and Labour losing the by-elections. However, a 'pact' was formed with the Liberals, and a minority Labour government survived until May 1978.

Opposition The second largest party in the House of Commons forms the opposition to the government. Since 1937 the Leader of Her Majesty's Opposition has been paid a salary greater than that of an ordinary MP. The opposition parties also receive some financial assistance to help their work in Parliament.

Pressure group An organisation formed to influence but not to replace government.

RSPCA Royal Society for the Prevention of Cruelty to Animals.

TUC Trades Union Congress – sometimes called the 'Parliament of British trade unions'. The TUC meets once a year and elects a 'General Council' to deal with union affairs during the rest of the year.

Summary

1 British politics works on the principle of 'representative and responsible' government. The party with the majority of seats in the House of Commons forms the government which is responsible to Parliament for running the country.

At the next General Election the government is either returned to office or an alternative government is elected.

2 Inputs to the working of government include both 'supports' and 'demands'. Support includes general political consensus as well as support for particular policies. Demands stem mainly from the suggestions and proposals of political parties, pressure groups and the mass media.

3 The demands made are discussed by the parties, Parliament, the Cabinet and the civil service. Demands may be accepted, rejected or changed. The outputs of government appear as legislation, administrative decisions and decisions not to act on an issue.

4 Professor Bernard Crick has published a framework of basic political concepts to help us understand links between government and the people. Government is concerned with *power* and *authority*; it must maintain law and *order*. It can use *force* to win people's obedience. The governed can be studied in terms of *natural rights*, *individuality*, *freedom* and *welfare*. The relationship between government and the governed can be discussed in terms of *law*, *justice*, *representation* and *pressure*.

Questions for discussion

1 What is the basis of 'representative and responsible' government in Britain? To what extent is this system fully 'representative'?

2 Making use of the concepts outlined in this chapter, examine from two different viewpoints:
(a) the right of trade unions to 'picket'
(b) the grievances of the Catholic community in Northern Ireland.

3 Imagine that there is a major demonstration planned to take place near your school. Many local shops are closing early because the shopkeepers fear theft and vandalism. The cost of policing will be high because many extra policeman are being brought in from a neighbouring force to help deal with the crowds.

Organise a class debate on the problem. One side must argue against the demonstration taking place. The other side must support the right of the demonstrators to express their views. Remember that you may be asked to argue on the side that privately you do not agree with.

4

Political democracy

This chapter examines some aspects of the type of government we call 'democracy'. In basic terms democracy means 'government by the people'. But there is more than one variety of democracy. The type of democracy which existed in ancient Greece is not the type which will work in industrialised societies with large populations. We explore the differences between the direct democracy of ancient Greece and the indirect democracy of industrial countries. Most governments claim to be democratic. We shall consider what governments must do in order to be described as liberal-democratic.

Democracy is not free from problems. The idea of majority rule seems fair, but it can lead to difficulties. We look at some of the odd circumstances which are caused by majority rule in Britain. Finally we consider the idea of democracy reflecting the wishes of the people. This means that a healthy democracy depends on having a well-informed and interested electorate.

What is democracy?

Greece is the birthplace of democracy; democracy is a word which comes from the Greek language and means 'rule by the people'. Democracy existed in Greece in the fifth century BC. In 431 BC Pericles stated:

> We are called a democracy because the city is administered not for the few, but for the majority.... Liberty is a principle of our public life ... we are prevented from breaking the laws by respect for them; we obey both the magistrates and the laws, especially those which are for the protection of the injured and those unwritten laws which have the support of public opinion.

The system of government in ancient Athens is called *direct* democracy because *all* citizens were expected to take part in making decisions. In other words, the ancient Greeks did not elect people to represent them and take decisions on their behalf. They were expected to participate themselves and take decisions.

Greek democracy was not quite as democratic as it would seem, for slavery existed in Greece alongside democracy. Probably as few as 10% of the Greek population had the right to participate in their democracy.

Despite the shortcomings of Greek democracy, the ideas from those times still influence the way we think about government. Abraham Lincoln had Greek democracy in mind when he described democracy as government 'of the people, by the people, for the people'. New countries in the Third World promise their people 'one person, one vote'. Even communist countries in Eastern Europe claim to be 'people's democracies'.

When we try to decide whether countries such as the USA, Tanzania or East Germany are democratic or not, we must ask certain questions. How is the government of each country chosen? How are political decisions made in each country? What type of society is each government trying to set up? For the idea of democracy is concerned with (i) values, (ii) the type of government, (iii) the methods that governments employ, and (iv) the goals they are trying to achieve.

Democratic values

The types of government found in Britain and the West are in the *liberal-democratic* tradition. We are concerned mainly with government in Britain. The liberal-democratic tradition of government involves (i) free elections, (ii) two or more political parties, and (iii) a government which, through

Parliament, is responsible to the electorate. The *authority* of government in a democracy comes from the agreement of its citizens to obey the government. The liberal-democratic tradition involves values of human dignity, rights, representation, majority rule, responsibility, political equality, freedom and justice. Liberal-democratic governments should govern in a way which is influenced by these values.

Types of government

There are many different types of government. A liberal-democratic government will be expected to behave differently from a **dictatorship** or **totalitarian** type of government. Table 4.1 sums up the main features of liberal democracies and totalitarian regimes. In order to decide whether or not a country can be called a liberal democracy, it is necessary to question:

(a) *the way in which the government is chosen*. Does it come into being by lawful means, such as elections? Does it govern with the agreement of the people?
(b) *the areas of life over which the government has control*. Does it leave many aspects of our lives outside its control?
(c) *the extent to which opposition to the govern-ment is allowed or encouraged*. Is there more than one party? Are people who oppose the government free and not in prison? Are pressure groups allowed? Are books, newspapers, radio and television allowed to criticise the government?
(d) *the extent to which the actions of government can be freely examined*. Are only a few decisions, such as defence, made in secret? Is the government accountable to Parliament for its actions?

If it is possible to answer 'yes' to these questions, then the government being examined can be called 'liberal-democratic'.

Representative government

The democracy of ancient Greece operated in small 'city-states' of only a few thousand inhabitants. Today the population of some industrialised countries is counted in hundreds of millions. The *direct* democracy of Greece would be impossible for a modern industrial society. It is not possible for millions of people to participate actively in making society's decisions. Therefore, *indirect* or *representative* democracy has been established in the West.

What is the difference between *direct* and *indirect*

Table 4.1 Western views of democracy and totalitarianism

Western view of democracy	Western view of totalitarianism
A variety of viewpoints are openly and vigorously expressed.	Existence of dominant view of society which is fostered by government to exclusions of others.
Two or more political parties compete in free elections.	Only one political party. No competing parties allowed.
An independent judiciary. Judges and courts are free from government control.	Judges and courts subject to government interference or control.
Civil liberties protected by government.	Civil liberties open to abuse by government.
Mass media free of government control.	Mass media not free of government control.

democracy? Let us imagine a school in which the headmaster wants the pupils to decide whether or not there should be a 'tuck shop' at breaktime. The pupils have strong views. Some of them believe that selling biscuits and sweets is wrong because it goes against their dentists' advice. They say pupils can look after their teeth by eating less sugar. Other pupils disagree. They point out that the school minibus will need to be replaced in two years' time, and profit from the tuck shop could go towards buying a new bus.

Under *direct* democracy, all the pupils would meet and debate the issue. Under *indirect* democracy, each class in the school would vote for a pupil to represent them. All the representatives would then meet, debate the issue, and vote. If a 'school council' made up of representatives already existed, then it might debate and vote on the issue. The key difference is that under direct democracy, every individual participates in making all decisions. Under indirect democracy, every individual participates in electing representatives. But it is the representatives who make the decisions.

In the British system of government, the representatives in national government are the Members of Parliament chosen by the voters. The leader of the party which obtains the greatest number of seats in Parliament forms a government which is accountable to Parliament. One of the main jobs of the electorate is to choose a government from among the parties which are competing for their votes at general elections. At the following general election the voters can either get rid of the government, or vote it back into office for another term. This is how 'the **sovereignty** of the people' works in a liberal democracy. It is important to remember that Parliament gets its authority from the people and is answerable to them. As we will see, similar arrangements and conditions apply in the case of local government.

Only on rare occasions have the voters been consulted *directly* in Britain. The first ever official national **referendum** was held on 5 June 1975, to decide whether or not Britain should stay in the EEC. The question put to the electorate was: 'Do you think that the United Kingdom should stay in the European Community (the Common Market)?' The earlier decision reached by Parliament to join the EEC was confirmed with 26 million people voting 'Yes' and 17 million voting 'No'. In 1979 the referendum was used once again to settle the **devolution** question for Wales and Scotland (see chapter 25). For some time there had been demands that Wales and Scotland should have a degree of self-government. In the referenda, this was rejected by both Welsh and Scottish voters.

Majority rule

The idea of majority rule plays an important part in liberal-democratic government. Majorities, however, may not always be what they seem. In a parliamentary election, the candidate who receives most votes wins and becomes the MP. This seems fair. Yet because of the way the system works in Britain, there are some surprising results. For example, in the 1979 general election:

Conservatives received 13.7 million votes which elected 339 MPs
Labour received 11.5 million votes which elected 269 MPs
Liberals won 4.3 million votes which elected 11 MPs

In 1979, therefore, the Conservative party had more MPs than Labour and Liberal added together even though the Conservative party had received far fewer votes than the Labour and Liberal total.

We shall be examining the British system of 'majority rule' in a later chapter. At this point we can note that since 1945 the winning party in a general election has never obtained more than 50% of the votes cast. Indeed, there have been some amazing results. It has happened that the party which won an election received fewer votes overall than the party which came second.

Problems of democracy

Democracy is an 'in' word, but neither majority rule nor democracy guarantee superior government. There are dangers in majority rule and, indeed, in democracy itself. Lord Hailsham has ▷ p.42

TASKPAGE 4.1

At the end of the Second World War, Berlin was divided among the victorious allies. The Russian sector was known as East Berlin. On 13 August 1961 the East Germans built a wire fence to seal off West Berlin. Four days later they began to build a wall. The thirty-mile boundary between West and East Berlin now had only four crossing points. There were shooting incidents. Not only the city, but families and friends were divided. Many people did manage to cross to West Berlin, however.

The photograph shows part of the Berlin Wall. Little more than a hundred metres separate a 'liberal' democracy from a 'people's' democracy. Imagine that you have a penfriend called Ulrike who lives in East Berlin. Write her a letter explaining how democracy works in Britain.

argued that the government's majority in the House of Commons has resulted in an 'elective dictatorship'. Nowadays, he has argued, the power of the Cabinet has increased while that of backbench MPs, the Opposition, and of Parliament has been reduced.

Democracy does not always produce good or moral government. People might be manipulated into voting for parties which represent evil forces in society. Anti-democratic parties can use democracy to gain power. Hitler's Germany was born in a democracy where more and more people were turning out to vote in elections. If democracy reflects the wishes of the people, then an unwise electorate may vote in an unwise government. Democracy relies on having informed and interested people to enable it to work towards creating a better world.

Terms used

Devolution Giving some of the powers and responsibilities of central government to other bodies.

Dictatorship A government dominated by one leader who demands strict obedience from the people. The people have no real opportunities to put their views forward.

Referendum A vote in which the electorate decides on the policy a government should follow on a particular issue.

Sovereignty Supremacy.

Totalitarian A type of government which allows no rival parties, and which tries to control all aspects of people's lives.

Summary

1 Democracy means 'rule of the people'.

2 There was a form of *direct* democracy in Athens in the fifth century BC. Modern industrialised societies in the West have an *indirect* form of democracy.

3 The term 'democracy' may refer to the methods of government, the goals of government, or both.

4 The countries of Western Europe, the USA, the USSR, and the countries of Eastern Europe all claim to be 'democracies'.

5 The liberal-democratic idea of government involves free elections with two or more political parties. Also the government, through Parliament, is responsible to the electorate.

6 Majority rule plays an important part in the working of a democracy, and this in itself can lead to problems.

7 The referendum was used in Britain in 1975 and 1979 over issues of fundamental constitutional importance.

8 A healthy democracy depends on an informed and interested electorate.

Questions for discussion

1 How does the western view of democracy differ from that of communist countries?

2 Should the principle of majority rule always apply in a democratic society? Does it matter if minorities are overruled by the majority?

3 Should more use be made of the referendum in Britain?

4 What do you regard as the strengths and weaknesses of democratic government?

5 Imagine that there is to be a referendum on whether or not Britain should ban fox-hunting. Design a campaign poster which tries to persuade voters to support your view.

5

The individual and government

In this chapter we consider the problems for citizens of having 'big government' in Britain. As government has become more complex, so the danger of citizens' rights being ignored has increased. This chapter examines different ways in which disputes between the government and the individual·may be settled. In recent years officials, popularly known as ombudsmen, have been appointed to safeguard the rights of citizens in many spheres of government. We now have Parliamentary, Local Government and Health Service Commissioners. But are the Parliamentary Commissioner for Administration and the other ombudsmen really effective? What is the role of administrative tribunals in settling disputes and disagreements? Are the decisions made by these tribunals fair? Finally, the chapter examines the arguments for and against having a Bill of Rights in Britain. Although our rights are protected in many acts of Parliament, should there be one document which contains all our rights?

The complexity of government

The machinery of government in a modern industrialised society such as Britain is vast and complex. It includes many different kinds of organisations. They range from the nationalised industries, like British Rail, to public bodies such as the health authorities, water boards, and 'quangos' such as the Commission for Racial Equality. The machinery of government includes the courts, public corporations like the Post Office, and government departments such as the Inland Revenue or Department of Health and Social Security (DHSS). Government touches almost every aspect of our lives from birth to death.

Government in a democracy is there for the benefit of its citizens. But many people have fallen foul of government. They may complain about rude treatment by civil servants. They may be annoyed to find that they have been paying too much tax, or angry not to obtain a social security benefit they feel entitled to.

How can our individuality, freedom, rights and welfare be protected within the vast sprawl of government in Britain? We have MPs to represent us, but are they a sufficient safeguard? Many other democracies have **ombudsmen** who look into complaints against the government. Also, many other countries have a Bill of Rights to protect citizens against big government.

The ombudsman system in Britain

The first ombudsman was appointed in Sweden 170 years ago, but it was not until 1967 that Britain appointed one. Here he is known as the Parliamentary Commissioner for Administration (PCA). The PCA is concerned with citizens obtaining **redress of grievance** which results from **maladministration**. This means that the PCA investigates citizens' complaints. If he agrees with them, he recommends that the complaint be put right. Maladministration occurs when government officials make mistakes in doing their jobs – they may give the wrong advice, take too long in dealing with affairs, be biased when making a decision, or fail to keep promises they have made.

The PCA exists to protect the citizen against maladministration. Strictly speaking, he is not there to protect people against bad laws. This distinction can be made clearer by a far-fetched example. Let us imagine that Parliament decided that all people with red hair should pay more tax than other people. This would be a 'bad' law. For people cannot help what colour their hair is, and it would be unfair to treat redheads differently from people with fair or dark hair. But the PCA would not be entitled to investigate complaints by redheads who felt that the law was wrong. Only if the government officials who carried out the Act were accused of maladministration could he investigate. If the officials gave the wrong advice to red-headed people who dyed their hair a different colour, then the PCA could investigate and recommend changes.

Has the PCA been successful in protecting the individual in cases where the government has been acting wrongly? Some people believe that the PCA has a good record in this respect. One of his early successes is known as the 'Sachsenhausen case'. It involved British soldiers imprisoned by the Nazis in a special cell block at Sachsenhausen, and not in the main camp. After the war, the Foreign Office refused to pay these men compensation. Civil servants argued that conditions in the special cell block were not as bad as in the main camp. Therefore they felt that the ex-prisoners should not get compensation. The case was referred to the PCA. He studied all the documents and found evidence to show that conditions in the cell block were worse than in the main camp. The PCA then recommended that the ex-prisoners should receive compensation.

This case showed that the PCA could be effective. Although he cannot order the government to correct mistakes that have been made, he can usually persuade ministers to do so. The PCA had more success in the Sachsenhausen case than MPs because he was in a position to study all the documents himself. MPs could only ask questions in Parliament and had to rely on the accuracy of the answers they received. MPs were not allowed to study the documents.

Other people claim that the ombudsman has failed to protect citizens against bad government. They say he should be renamed the 'ombudsmouse'. This is because the PCA here is less powerful than the ombudsmen in other countries. In Britain, people with complaints about the government have to go first to an MP. The MP will pass the case on to the PCA. In other countries, the public can go *direct* to the ombudsman. Having to go through an MP probably limits the number of complaints the PCA

receives. The first PCA, Sir Edmund Compton, expected to get about 7000 complaints a year. Sweden, for example, has a much smaller population than Britain and the Swedish ombudsman receives about 3000 complaints a year. In fact, the British PCA receives on average only 800 complaints a year.

Critics of the PCA also argue that there are too many areas he is not allowed to investigate. Public complaints about the police, armed forces or nationalised industries are not the concern of the PCA. However, a Health Service Commissioner has now been appointed to investigate complaints about the National Health Service. Also there are Commissioners for Local Administration to investigate complaints about local government although critics of local government ombudsmen speak of them as 'toothless commissioners'. Taskpage 21.2 in chapter 21 examines this criticism in detail.

The most common complaints received by the PCA are about the Inland Revenue. The complaints received by the Commission for Local Administration are mainly about planning permission. This reflects the type of person most likely to complain to the ombudsmen. A recent survey showed that middle-class people knew more about the PCA and how to use him than did working-class people. If the ombudsman system in Britain is to provide effective safeguards against maladministration, then all citizens must learn how the system works. Some people say it is time to reform the ombudsman system. They would like the Commissioners' findings to be enforceable by law rather than relying on persuasion as at present.

Administrative tribunals

As the scope of government has increased, so the possibilities of disagreement between citizens and the state have grown. People may feel that they are being refused a social security benefit to which they are entitled, or they may feel that they are being taxed unfairly. Administrative tribunals were established to settle disputes such as these.

These are over 2000 tribunals in Britain dealing with many different issues. For in addition to settling disagreements between the individual and the state, they also settle disagreements between individuals. Administrative tribunals are rather like courts, but less formal. A person without a legal training may preside over a tribunal; courts are presided over by judges or magistrates.

The advantage of administrative tribunals is that they are cheaper for all concerned than going to court. They deal with business quickly, and they are said to be efficient in settling disagreements. The disadvantage is that the members of tribunals are appointed by government ministers. Also if an individual appeals against a tribunal's decision, the minister's decision is final. This means that when an individual has a disagreement with government, the government or persons appointed by the government are both 'judge and jury'. Consequently, the powers of government are massive. The citizen who challenges the authority of government is usually taking part in a very uneven contest.

Does Britain need a Bill of Rights?

Lord Hailsham has spoken in favour of Britain having a written constitution which contains a Bill of Rights. Britain has signed the European Convention on Human Rights, and yet is one of the few democracies without a Bill of Rights.

The idea of having a Bill of Rights is that it would protect citizens' rights. At present certain rights are protected in various Acts of Parliament. For example, there are laws protecting people against unfair **discrimination** in terms of their gender or race. The advantage of having a Bill of Rights is that it would bring all these rights together in one document.

Are individual rights neglected in Britain? There have been some cases in which the authorities have not been aware that they have been acting wrongly. For example, in Northern Ireland the army put hoods on suspected terrorists and used noise machines before interrogation. The army authorities knew this was a tough way to treat people, but believed it was necessary in order to maintain law and order. But in this case the European Court of Justice found that the army was acting illegally.

A second example of the neglect of individual rights is more general. It involves the use of 'social security snoopers'. Investigators employed by the government may check that a single woman who is receiving a widow's pension or supplementary benefit is not living with a man. The investigators may observe a woman's house to see who goes in and comes out. They might question neighbours about the woman. The woman concerned may never learn what is contained in the report written about her by the investigators. This strikes many people as a gross infringement on privacy. There are politicians in all political parties who are unhappy about the use of government 'snoopers'.

Would drawing up a Bill of Rights be easy? In fact a Bill of Rights was introduced into Parliament in 1970 but it failed to make progress and become law. Subsequent attempts in the Commons and Lords also failed. The problem in drawing up a Bill of Rights is in dealing with *conflicting rights*. For example, a law which *protects* female rights to be treated fairly when applying for a job *limits* an employer's right to employ whomever he wants. Giving citizens the right to free speech can also cause problems. In order to protect people's reputations against lies, free speech has to be limited by the law of **defamation**. In order to protect national security, free speech about defence matters has to be limited by the **Official Secrets Act**. Drawing a line between these conflicting rights in a Bill of Rights is very tricky. You may wish to discuss this further in class, and attempt to complete the mock constitution on the Taskpage.

As we have seen, Lord Hailsham is in favour of having a Bill of Rights. Harold Laski took a different view. He argued that if citizens' rights were really protected in a country, there was no need for a Bill of Rights. If, on the other hand, citizens' rights are not protected, then a Bill of Rights will not be of any use. A Bill of Rights is included in the Constitution of the USA, but there are many citizens who feel that this does not adequately protect them.

Terms used

Defamation Things said which damage a person's character or reputation. There are two ▷ p.48

45

YOUR LOCAL OMBUDSMAN

There are three Local Ombudsmen (LO) in England. They are independent people who investigate complaints against local authorities, water authorities and police authorities. There is no charge for the service and investigations are made in private.

The LO cannot question what an Authority have done just because someone does not agree with it. There must be a complaint that something went wrong and caused injustice to the person who has complained.

HOW TO COMPLAIN

If you feel you have been unjustly treated, for example, by something a council have done (or not done):

(i) first go or write to the Council office and ask them to do something about it;

(ii) if you are still not satisfied, contact a Councillor and ask him or her to take up your complaint;

(iii) if that does not settle the matter, put your complaint in writing and ask a Councillor to send it to the LO.

The LO cannot normally consider a complaint unless it is sent through a Councillor. But if a Councillor does not send your complaint on in a reasonable time, you can send it direct to the LO.

Complaints can be made about most Council activities housing, planning, education, social services, highways, public health, etc. But there are some things the LO cannot investigate including:

A complaint about something that happened before 1 April 1974.

A complaint about which you could go to court or appeal to a tribunal or a Government Minister.

A complaint affecting all or most of the inhabitants of a Council's area, for instance a complaint that the rates have gone up.

A complaint about court proceedings or about the investigation or prevention of crime.

A complaint about a police officer.

A complaint about personnel matters, including appointments, dismissals, pay, pensions and discipline.

A complaint about contractual and commercial transactions, although complaints about land and property transactions can be investigated.

A complaint about public passenger transport, docks, harbours, entertainment, industrial establishments and markets.

HOW WE INVESTIGATE

The investigation is thorough and the LO has power to examine files and to interview anyone concerned with the complaint. At the end the LO issues a report which will not usually mention people's names If the report finds that you have been unjustly treated the Authority have to consider it and tell the LO what they are going to do about it. The LO cannot force them to act but in most cases the Authority remedy the grievance of the person who complained. Authorities have power to pay money if necessary to do that.

This leaflet briefly describes the LO service. If you need advice, or our fuller "YOUR LOCAL OMBUDSMAN" booklet, please contact your nearest Citizens' Advice Bureau or an LO office:

Local Ombudsman
21 Queen Anne's Gate
London SW1H 9BU

Telephone (01) 222 5622

Local Ombudsman
29 Castlegate
York YO1 1RN

Telephone York (0904) 30151

(10095)

Here is a leaflet giving information about the local government ombudsman and is available at your town hall. Imagine you live in the corner house near a busy road junction. The street light outside your house has not worked for two years. You have made many requests to the council for it to be repaired, but so far your requests seem to have been ignored. In fact, you have reached stage (h) (iii) on the leaflet. Write a letter for your councillor to pass on to the local government ombudsman outlining your complaint. Give an account of the efforts you have made to get the lamp repaired. Explain how important it is that the lamp should be repaired.

TASKPAGE 5.2   Here is an imaginary constitution for Britain. It includes a Bill of Rights.

THE BRITISH CONSTITUTION

incorporating

A BILL OF RIGHTS

Preamble

The British people by this constitution wish to clarify the principles concerning the relationship between the state and citizen in order to protect and promote the dignity, freedom and equality of man, and to give the necessary authority to government for this end. These principles being:

1 **All persons regardless of race, gender, religion or class should have equal consideration in the processes of government and law.**

To exercise this right fully will involve protection of the following rights:

(i)   Freedom of speech and expression.

(ii) Freedom of belief and of the right to exercise it.

(iii) Freedom of person and property from arbitrary interference without due process of law defined here as (a) no person to be detained unnecessarily, and no longer than twenty-four hours without a warrant, (b) right to an impartial hearing, (c) right to defence, (d) right to a fair and speedy decision.

(iv) Freedom of association.

(v)   No person to be prevented by inadequate means from exercising these rights. To this end (a) right to a reasonable standard of living and health, (b) right to education, (c) right to free justice, are deemed essential.

2 **Sovereignty is vested in the people, who hereby delegate the power to govern to elected Members of Parliament who are answerable to the electorate in the following ways.**

(i)   All people over the age of eighteen years to have the right to vote except the following . . . .

Discuss what other rights could be added.

forms of defamation. If the offending words are in written or recorded form (this includes TV and radio) they are said to be libellous. If the words are not in written form, they are referred to as slander.

Discrimination To treat differently. Discrimination 'against' a person usually means that he is being treated unfairly. 'Positive discrimination' means he is being given preferential treatment.

Maladministration Occurs when government officials show bias in dealing with citizens, or fail to advise them correctly, give misleading information, or take too long in answering questions.

Official Secrets Act Originally passed by Parliament to protect national security. Some people are now concerned that governments use the Act to limit debate on issues which are not concerned with security.

Ombudsman The first Scandinavian 'watch-dog' on the activities of government.

Redress of grievance To put right a case of hardship resulting from maladministration.

Summary

1 The machinery of government in modern society is vast and complex.

2 The Parliamentary Commissioner for Administration was established in 1967 to investigate cases of maladministration forwarded to him by MPs.

3 Although some people feel that the PCA was never given enough power, he has nevertheless been successful in changing many government decisions.

4 Disagreements between the citizen and the state may be settled by administrative tribunals. Some people feel this is an unfair method because tribunals are a part of government and therefore will always favour government.

5 From time to time it is suggested that Britain should have a Bill of Rights to protect citizens against abuse of power by government. Protecting the rights of some citizens often results in limiting the rights of other citizens.

Questions for discussion

1 Should Britain's ombudsmen be given more powers?

2 Assess the advantages and disadvantages of administrative tribunals.

3 Does Britain need a Bill of Rights?

4 Should there be a new Commissioner appointed to investigate complaints against the police?

5 Design a simple leaflet which provides information about all the ombudsmen. Decide what information is vital for inclusion. How can the leaflet be made attractive so that people are tempted to read it?

PART TWO

Participation in politics: parties and pressure groups

6

Political participation

Democracy depends on at least a fair degree of participation by its citizens. In this chapter we examine how much people know about politics and the ways in which they can participate. Only a minority of Britain's population is involved deeply in politics. Half the population is not interested, and a third of the electorate has not voted in recent general elections. There are general differences in political awareness and behaviour between men and women, and between different social classes. Survey evidence shows that young people have a poor knowledge of politics in Britain. Many people are worried about this political ignorance among the young and the population at large. The chapter concludes by considering political education in schools as a way to improve the people's political knowledge and skills.

The idea of participation

Political **participation** has been defined by G. Parry as the involvement of citizens 'taking part in the formulation, passage, or implementation of public policies'. Therefore an individual who participates in politics has more power than one who does not. Participation has become an 'in' idea in recent years. The Skeffington Report recommended greater participation by people in the planning of their environment. The Bullock Report urged that workers should participate more in the running of their firms. The Taylor Report proposed that there should be greater participation and pupil involvement in the governing of schools. Sherry Arnstein commented that participation was like spinach; nobody is against it because it is good for you.

The ladder of participation

Democracy and participation are closely linked. As we saw in chapter 4 there are two basic types of democracy: direct and indirect. There are also different ways of participating. Various political scientists have devised 'ladders of participation' to help us understand the different ways in which people can participate. Figure 6.1 shows a typical ladder. It is like a real ladder in that a person who has reached a certain 'rung' is likely to have climbed all those rungs below. In other words, a person who is an active member of a pressure group will have participated at meetings, discussed politics, and voted.

At the bottom of the ladder are those people who do not participate at all. They may be **apathetic** ▷ p.5

Holding political office
Seeking political office
Active membership of a political organisation
Passive membership of a political organisation
Participation in public meetings or demonstrations
General interest in politics, such as discussing politics with other people
Voting
Total apathy or alienation

Fig. 6.1 The ladder of participation

POLITICAL KNOWLEDGE QUESTIONNAIRE

Test your political knowledge with this questionnaire. You can mark it yourself once your teacher has provided the answers. Each correct answer scores you one point. What total score is 'average' in your class? Work out what scores will show 'poor', 'good' and 'excellent' political knowledge.

1   What is the name of the Prime Minister?
2   What is the name of the Chancellor of the Exchequer?
3   Which party forms the government?
4   What is the name of your MP?
5   Who is the Secretary of State for Education?
6   What is the name of the Leader of the Opposition?
7   Which political party is the main opposition in Parliament?
8   Name two political parties in Parliament in addition to the two main parties [no point if only one can be named].
9   What is the name of the President of the United States?
10 What is NATO?
11 Who is the Secretary General of the United Nations?
12 Where is your local town hall?
13 What type of state schools exist in your county?
14 What is the TUC?
15 How would you contact your MP?
16 How do you forward a complaint to the Parliamentary Commissioner?
17 At what age do people have the right to vote?
18 Name one pressure group which is concerned with children's welfare.
19 Do you put a tick or a cross on a ballot paper when you vote?
20 What is a referendum?

Bicycle Sheds

POLITICAL THEORY

Times Educational Supplement, 9 December 1977

This cartoon shows a group of boys reading a book about politics. They are in the bike sheds, which are usually out of sight of the teachers. Is politics out of place in school?

Imagine that you have been asked to organise a 'council' in your school. How would you set about the task? Would you suggest that each class votes for one representative on the council? Or would each class have one representative for the boys and another for the girls? Would teachers vote for one or more representatives? Would the council raise money to spend on the school? Would pupils be expected to pay a small sum into the school fund each term? How would the council let the rest of the school know what was going on? Discuss these and other issues in class.

or **alienated**. If they are apathetic, it may simply be that they are not interested in politics. Or they may be quite happy with the way in which the country is governed, and not bother to vote. Alienation is more serious than this. Those who are alienated may be disillusioned with politics, or they may feel that government is too remote and bureaucratic. Turn back to Taskpage 4.1 on page 41. Which piece of graffiti on the Berlin Wall reflects the feeling of alienation?

It is interesting to note how low voting is on the ladder of participation. This is because voting is an act which requires little skill or knowledge and only happens rarely. Individuals are participating more if they discuss politics with other people, or if they attend demonstrations.

Further up the ladder of participation are people who are active members of pressure groups which have 'political' aims. Such pressure groups would be CND or trade unions. The next rung up involves joining a political party. The top rungs of the ladder involve being a candidate for political office, and getting elected for political office. Councillors and MPs are participating on the top rung.

Different types of participation

People who are participating near the top of the ladder are participating in a different way from people who do no more than vote. People near the top of the ladder have more power and influence in making decisions than people who only vote from time to time.

Political scientists have also written about the difference between *real* participation and *false* participation. Real participation happens when those people who participate actually affect the decisions that are made. False participation happens when people think they are participating but in fact they are not influencing decisions. False participation occurs in the following example. Imagine that local people have been invited to a meeting to decide what trees and shrubs should be planted around a new community centre that is being planned. They will not be asked whether there is a need for the community centre, or where it should be built. They will not be asked to decide what

facilities it should have, or how it ought to be designed. These important decisions have already been made. Since the people have only the opportunity to influence small decisions, this would be a case of false participation.

Political awareness

The results of surveys suggest that levels of political interest and knowledge are low in Britain. In a survey conducted by Mark Abrams the question was asked: 'How would you describe your interest in politics?' The replies were:

very interested	15%
interested	37%
not really interested	33%
not at all interested	15%

If this sample of people reflects the attitudes of the general population, then only half of Britain's electorate is interested in politics. A survey for the Redcliffe Maud Report on the Reorganisation of Local Government confirmed this view, revealing that few people take an interest in what goes on in their town halls. Only 13% of the sample had ever contacted a local councillor and only 7% had ever attended a council meeting.

Other surveys have provided more details on political awareness. Generally, it appears that women are slightly less interested in politics than men. Also they are less well informed about politics and less likely to vote than men. Middle-class people are better informed and more involved in politics than working-class people. It must be stressed that these are generalisations and there will be many exceptions. For example, there will be some working-class females who are better informed and more active in politics than most middle-class males.

A survey of 15- and 16-year-olds was conducted by Dr Robert Stradling. One of its findings was that young people are more likely to know the names of political leaders than the names of their local MPs. These are the percentages of those who knew the:

name of Prime Minister	94%
name of Leader of Opposition	82%
name of Liberal Leader	86%

| name of Foreign Secretary | 47% |
| name of local MP | 52% |

Dr Stradling's survey showed that young people were confused about many political issues. For example, they misunderstood the situation in Northern Ireland and a quarter thought that the Conservatives approved of nationalisation. Almost a half could not name a single pressure group. Test your own knowledge of politics on the Taskpage questionnaire.

Political education

The results from the surveys which have investigated political awareness are depressing. They are depressing because a political democracy depends on having well-informed citizens. Dr Stradling remarked: 'There is something essentially paradoxical [contradictory or odd] about a democracy in which some eighty or ninety per cent of the future citizens are insufficiently well informed about politics to know not only what is happening but also how they are affected by it and what they can do about it. Most of the political knowledge they have is of little use to them either as political consumers or political actors.'

People who believe that more citizens should participate in politics recognise the problems that have to be overcome. Citizens can only participate effectively if they have the necessary political knowledge and skills. Therefore greater political participation may depend on more political education.

Some educational experts believe that schools should teach all pupils about politics. Political education in school should prepare pupils for 'informed and responsible' participation in politics when they leave school. It has been argued that 'political education might also do something to restore a respect for political activity and attitudes, and rescue them from the worrying trend of current cynicism about the place of politics in society.'

It is generally agreed that schools should help pupils understand society. At the same time, some people are worried about bringing 'politics into school'. They fear that some teachers may try to indoctrinate their pupils. Other people believe that teaching politics would help pupils to be informed and reasonable in their approach to politics.

In what ways could schools teach politics? Political education could result from doing lessons on politics and using books such as this one. Also it could be learnt from 'doing' politics at school. Some schools already have 'councils' or 'moots' where issues which concern pupils and teachers are discussed. Learning about politics by a combination of both methods might be most successful. Any improvement in the political knowledge and skills of its citizens would be 'good news' for democracy in Britain.

Terms used

Alienation To feel like a stranger or 'alien' in one's own country.
Apathy Lack of interest.
Indoctrination An attempt to force views on other people.
Participation Being involved, taking part.

Summary

1 People participate at different levels on the 'ladder of participation'. Those who are apathetic or alienated do not participate at all. Only a small minority of the population participate fully in politics.

2 British people take relatively little interest in politics at local or national level. This is particularly true of young people.

3 One way of tackling political ignorance is to teach politics to all pupils in school.

Questions for discussion

1 In what ways can people participate in politics?

2 'Democracy depends on well-informed citizens.' Discuss.

3 What are the arguments for and against political education in schools?

4 Contrast the styles of language (simple or complex sentences and short or long words) used in a 'quality' and a 'tabloid' newspaper. Make a poster for your classroom to illustrate the different ways in which one story or item about politics is reported.

7

Political parties: structure and organisation

This is the first of two chapters which look at political parties in Britain. Here we are concerned with how the different parts of the parties, inside

and outside Parliament, link together. Each wing of a political party has a different job to do. But which wing of the party has the power to make policy is often argued about. The position inside the Conservative party is easier to understand than the position inside the Labour party. Recent changes in the Labour party constitution have been controversial. We examine why. Finally, we consider the Liberal party and the Social Democratic party, and the alliance between them.

The political system

Political parties dominate British politics. Parliament and local councils are organised along strict party lines. So too is the European Assembly to which Britain elects representatives. At elections, people vote for parties rather than the personalities of the candidates. Much of the news about political affairs that we read in papers or see on TV is about what the political parties are saying or doing. It would indeed be difficult to understand British politics without some knowledge of the aims and activities of political parties.

It is the parties, more than any other political organisations, which focus attention on political ideas, issues or problems. In the British system of representative democracy, the parties are the main link between government and the governed. This is because government gets its authority from the people's vote, and the people's vote is cast for political parties.

A political party is an organisation which has policies it wants to put into practice *by gaining political power*. Unlike pressure groups parties do not try simply to influence government on particular issues but to provide government. If a party does not win an election, it will criticise and oppose the governing party on a wide range of issues.

In Britain we refer to 'major' and 'minor' parties. The difference between the two is based on factors such as the number of MPs a party has, its support from voters, its actual membership, and its finances. In Britain the major parties are

the Conservative and Labour parties. Either Conservative or Labour has formed every government since 1945. Some people would include the Liberal party as a major party because of its importance in the past and its role today. If there is almost the same number of Labour and Conservative MPs in the Commons, then the Liberals hold the 'balance of power' in Parliament. When this happens, Liberals become more important and influential. Similar considerations apply to the relatively new Social Democratic Party.

The minor parties in Britain include the Scottish National party (SNP), Plaid Cymru (Welsh nationalists), the Ulster Unionists, the Communist Party, the Socialist Workers Party, the National Front and the Ecology Party. Liberal, Social Democratic Party (SDP) and Scots and Welsh national parties have been successful in gaining some seats in Parliament.

The major parties changed and developed as more and more people were given the right to vote. As the electorate grew in size, so the parties had to make changes in order to win the support of the new voters. It is interesting to note the different origins of the major parties. The Conservative and Liberal parties grew up within Parliament, but the Labour party grew up outside Parliament. As we shall see, these differences still affect the parties.

On the surface, however, the Conservative, Labour, Liberal and Social Democratic parties look much the same. Each has a head office in London which maintains records, manages party finances, publishes party literature and organises national campaigns. Since all parties are trying to do the same thing (win support and gain office) they tend to use the same methods. But under the surface there are big differences which reflect the distinct ideas and different history of each party.

Structure of the Conservative party

Figure 7.1 shows the way the Conservative party is organised. It is best understood by thinking of it in terms of two basic units, each having links throughout the party. One unit is the National Union of Conservative and Unionist Associations; this links together Constituency Associations and the Area Councils into which the constituencies are grouped. The other unit is the Conservative party proper, which consists of the party leader and the parliamentary party. The leader is elected by Conservative MPs, and it is the leader who appoints the Chairman of the Party Organisation and who has control of the Central Office.

The Central Council is the governing body of the National Union. It is made up of Conservative peers, MPs and prospective parliamentary candidates, and four representatives from each Constituency Association. Because this council is so large, it usually meets only once a year. The day-to-day work is carried out by an Executive Committee and a General Purposes sub-committee. Conservative MPs and senior officials of the Central Office are represented on each of these bodies.

The Party Conference is made up of all members of the Central Council of the National Union together with three representatives plus the treasurer and agent from each constituency association. This adds up to a total of around 6500 people, of whom about 5000 are likely to attend.

It can be seen that the two halves which make up the Conservative organisation are closely linked at each level. Now it is necessary to look more closely at the way in which this organisation works.

Constituency Associations and Area Councils

Each Constituency Association elects its own

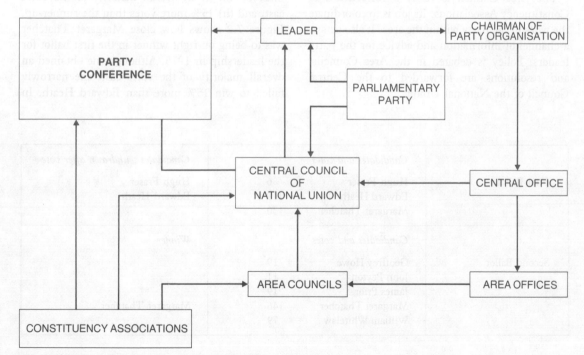

Fig. 7.1 Outline of Conservative party organisation

officers (chairman, secretary, treasurer, etc.) and appoints its own agent. The agent is usually a full-time officer who is responsible for organising election campaigns. He or she also has the task of keeping the constituency organisation in good working shape. The day-to-day work of each constituency organisation is controlled by an Executive Council, which is made up of constituency officers, representatives from local branches, Young Conservatives, Conservative Clubs, and a few **co-opted** members. Each Constituency Association raises its own funds and has considerable freedom in the way it conducts its affairs. Constituency Associations select the candidates for parliamentary and local elections, and are generally responsible for promoting the Conservative cause locally.

The Constituency Associations recognise that their most important tasks are to maintain a strong body of Conservative MPs in Parliament and to provide support for the party leadership. This is not to say that they always agree with what Conservative MPs or the party leadership does. Sometimes they are critical about the performance of the Conservatives in Parliament.

The Area Council is really a **federation** of Constituency Associations. Its job is to co-ordinate the work of the party within the area. It also acts as a channel of information and advice for the party leaders. Policy is debated in the Area Councils, and resolutions are forwarded to the Central Council of the National Union.

The Conservative party leader

Today the leader of the Conservative party is elected by Tory MPs. However, this method for choosing a leader is relatively new; the first leader to have been elected by Conservative MPs was Edward Heath in 1965. Before this, the leader was said to 'emerge'. Lord Home was the last Conservative leader to 'emerge', in 1963. That is to say, he was not elected by the party but appointed after long private discussions among Conservative MPs and 'elder statesmen' in the House of Lords. Apart from not being democratic, this method of getting a new leader had disadvantages. At times it let in leaders who were least opposed rather than most supported. In other words, top Conservative figures who might well be in line for the leader's job obviously had their opponents in the party. Less well-known figures naturally had fewer opponents. But for a less well-known figure to emerge as leader had obvious political snags for the party.

The present method for electing the party leader may involve a number of stages. In order to be elected party leader in the first ballot, a candidate must obtain (i) an overall majority of the votes cast, and (ii) 15% more votes than the runner-up. Figure 7.2 shows how close Margaret Thatcher was to being outright winner in the first ballot for the leadership in 1975. Although she obtained an overall majority of the votes cast, she narrowly failed to win 15% more than Edward Heath. In

First Ballot	*Candidates and votes*		*Candidates withdrawn after vote*
	Hugh Fraser	6	Hugh Fraser
	Edward Heath	119	Edward Heath
	Margaret Thatcher	130	
Second Ballot	*Candidates and votes*		*Winner*
	Geoffrey Howe	19	
	John Peyton	11	
	James Prior	19	
	Margaret Thatcher	146	Margaret Thatcher
	William Whitelaw	79	

Fig. 7.2 The election of the Conservative leader: 1975

these circumstances a second ballot is held. The candidates in the first ballot are renominated unless they withdraw, and nominations can be accepted for new candidates. In the second ballot an overall majority is sufficient to become party leader. If necessary a third ballot is held in which nominations are limited to the three candidates who obtained most votes in the second ballot.

When the voting for party leader is over, the winner is confirmed in office at a special meeting of Conservative MPs, peers, prospective parliamentary candidates and the Executive Committee of the National Union.

In the Conservative party, policy-making is the **prerogative** of the leader and not, as in the case of the Labour party, of the Party Conference. The Conservative Party Conference receives reports from the National Union and debates policy resolutions. Conference decisions on policy are taken into account by the leader, but they are not regarded as **binding**. The Conference provides an opportunity to show the solidarity of the party and to raise the morale of party members. As a result of this, the atmosphere at Conservative Conferences tends to be far more social than at Labour Conferences.

In the past the relatively unimportant role of the Conference in the Conservative party organisation was reflected in its links with the leader. Before Edward Heath was leader, it was the custom for the leader to miss most of the conference and arrive in the closing stages. Now it is usual for the leader to be present throughout the Conference.

When the Conservative party is in opposition, the members of the 'Shadow Cabinet' are personally chosen by the leader. This is unlike the position in the Labour party, where the most important members of the 'Shadow Cabinet' are elected by Labour MPs. Again this reflects differences between Conservative tradition of respect for firm leadership, and Labour's tradition of party democracy.

Conservative party resources

The Conservative party is by far the richest of all British political parties. It has an income at least twice the size of Labour's income and about twelve times the size of Liberal income. Almost all the money is donated by industrial and commercial firms. Only a small proportion is received from Constituency Associations and investment income.

This wealth provides for a high degree of professionalism: the Central Office is well-staffed and most constituencies have a full-time agent. Professional fund-raisers are employed in each of the areas into which the party is divided.

No detailed figures of Conservative party membership are available. The total is estimated to be 700 000, although this includes many 'nominal' members who are not really involved in Conservative politics. These nominal members are in Conservative clubs, which are social in nature and not political. Nevertheless, compared with the Labour party's active mass membership of 359 000 it is high. It is also high when compared with the membership of European right-wing parties. But it must be remembered that membership of the Conservative and Labour parties has been declining for the last thirty years. In the Conservative party, membership is about half of what it was when it was led by Sir Winston Churchill while membership of the Labour party is about a third of what it was at its post-war peak.

Structure of the Labour party

The Labour party has a history, traditions and beliefs very different from those of the Conservative party. But on the surface, its organisation looks remarkably similar. It is important to understand that the Labour party is a federal or fragmented organisation made up of different parts. The Labour Party links together (i) the Parliamentary Labour Party; that is, Labour MPs in the Commons, (ii) Constituency Labour Parties, (iii) trade unions and (iv) Co-operative organisations and socialist societies such as the **Fabian Society**.

Figure 7.3 shows the general structure of Labour organisation. It can be seen that trade unions, Co-operative bodies and socialist societies are represented at all levels. The trade unions have played an important part in the growth of the Labour party. The links between the unions and party are close, although at times they become strained. A

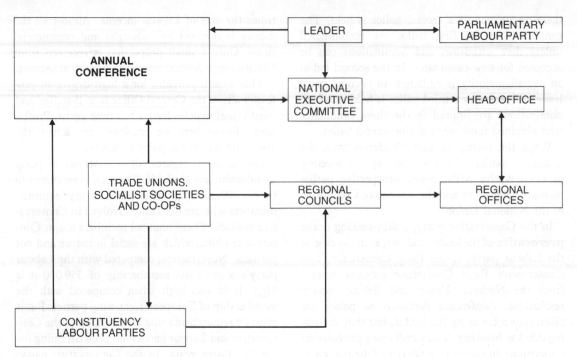

Fig. 7.3 Outline of Labour party organisation

common mistake is to think that the TUC is part of the Labour party. It is true that the TUC called a conference in 1900 which set up the Labour party (or Labour Representation Committee as it was then called). But it is the individual trade unions, such as the **TGWU**, **GMWU** or **NUPE**, which are **affiliated** to the Labour party. There are many unions in the TUC which are not in the Labour party. Also trade union leaders who sit on the General Council of the TUC cannot sit on the National Executive Committee (NEC) of the Labour party.

Each Constituency Labour Party is made up of delegates from ward parties, Young Socialist branches, trade union branches and socialist societies within the constituency. The Constituency Labour Party selects a parliamentary candidate and is responsible for waging the election campaign. It also accepts responsibility for the day-to-day work of the party within the constituency. At present only a small minority of constituencies have a full-time agent, but where one exists he or she usually acts as secretary to the constituency party. Constituency parties take an active interest in policy matters, making their

views known from time to time to the NEC or Labour MPs. Also they submit resolutions for consideration at both the Regional Conference and the Annual Conference.

The Regional Councils (which are roughly the equivalent bodies to the Conservative Area Councils) are attended by delegates from constituency parties, trade unions and socialist societies in the region. The Regional Conference is held annually. It elects an Executive Committee which in turn elects its own chairman and vice-chairman. The secretary of the Regional Council is also the regional organiser, and he is appointed by the NEC. The Regional Councils have little influence in Labour policy-making, but they provide important links between the constituencies. They arrange a variety of rallies and conferences.

The Labour Party Conference

The Annual Conference of the Labour party is made up of about 1000 delegates appointed by constituency parties, trade unions, socialist societies and Co-operative bodies. The number and voting strength of a particular group of delegates depends on the size of membership of the group being represented. For example, some trade union delegates have over a million votes whereas delegates from a constituency have only 5000.

Labour MPs, prospective parliamentary candidates, regional organisers and party agents may attend conference as observers. They may vote or stand for election to the NEC only if they are official delegates representing a constituency, trade union, etc.

Voting on important matters is done by a 'card' vote; each card representing the number of members in the organisation for which the holder is delegate. It is sometimes said that the Labour party is in 'the hands of the unions'. It is certainly true that if the six largest trade unions were to vote together, they would cast around half the votes at conference. You can see from Table 7.1 that if the twelve biggest trade unions voted together, they would cast well over two-thirds of conference votes. But the unions are divided into 'left-wing' and 'right-wing' unions, and rarely vote together on the same side. It is never a case of all the unions versus all the constituency parties in a vote. Inevitably some unions and some constituencies will line up against other unions and constituency parties.

The conference elects the National Executive Committee which is responsible for seeing to party affairs when conference is not in session. Since conference only meets for one week each year, the NEC deals with matters as they arise during the rest of the year at its monthly meetings. The NEC has 28 members. Seven are elected by the Constituency Labour Parties; 12 by the trade unions. The socialist societies and Co-operative bodies elect one member to the NEC. Five women members and the party treasurer are elected by the

Table 7.1 How Labour Conference votes are shared out

The big 12 unions	5 030 000
Smaller unions	1 391 000
Constituency parties	631 000
Socialist societies	39 000
Co-operative organisations	29 000
Total vote at Conference	7 120 000

whole conference. The leader and deputy leader of the Parliamentary Labour Party are **ex-officio** members of the NEC. Block votes of the large unions influence 18 of the 28 members elected on to the NEC.

Who makes Labour policy?

There has been much disagreement over who has the power to decide Labour party policy. Professor Robert McKenzie wrote about the issue in his well-known book, *British Political Parties*. He argued that power to make party policy was concentrated in the hands of the leader and the Parliamentary Labour Party. The Labour MPs in Parliament, he argued, were **autonomous** and not controlled by the Annual Conference. In fact, the Labour conference was as powerless as the Conservative conference. Professor Samuel Beer disagreed with this. In his book *Modern British Politics*, he argued that power was spread throughout the Labour party. Both the Parliamentary Labour Party and the Annual Conference had power.

What light does the Labour party constitution throw on this disagreement? The constitution states that the prerogative for policy-making lies with the Annual Conference, not with the leader of the party. The relevant clause reads:

No proposal shall be included in the Party Programme unless it has been adopted by the Party Conference by a majority of not less than two-thirds of the votes recorded on a card vote.

This means that it is possible for different parts of the Labour party to have different policies. For example, a special Labour conference in 1975 voted for Britain pulling out of the EEC. The vote for leaving the Common Market was 3 724 000; the vote for staying in was 1 986 000. Thus the votes for Britain leaving the EEC fell just short of a two-thirds majority. Nevertheless, a sizeable majority of the Conference was for Britain pulling out of the EEC. The NEC was also against continued membership, and in Parliament 145 MPs voted against the EEC and 137 voted in favour. Only inside the Labour cabinet was there a majority in favour of Britain staying in the EEC.

This kind of split between different parts of the Labour party has occurred frequently in the history of the party. There were bitter clashes between Clement Attlee when he was prime minister and Harold Laski who was chairman of the NEC. When Hugh Gaitskell was party leader he made it clear in 1960 that Labour MPs would not be bound by a conference vote in favour of Britain giving up nuclear weapons. When Labour is in power, the party leader becomes the prime minister. Labour prime ministers have all taken the view that the leader of the party and the Parliamentary Labour Party must be responsible to parliament and not the NEC. It is a view which causes unease within some sections of the party.

The NEC is responsible to the Annual Conference. Naturally it feels that policy decisions made by conference ought to be carried out by a Labour government. Two changes were made to Labour's constitution in 1980. It was hoped that these changes would close the gap between the different parts of the party. They were:

1 The leader of the party is no longer elected by Labour MPs only. Now trade unions and constituency parties are involved. Trade unions have 40% of the votes for leader, Labour MPs have 20%, and the constituency parties have 30%.
2 Labour MPs now have to be 're-selected' before each general election. Re-selection involves the MP being considered along with other candidates who would like to represent Labour in that constituency. Even if a constituency wants to have the same MP at the next election, he or she will still have to be re-selected.

These changes give more power to the unions and constituency parties, and less power to Labour MPs. Debate on these issues caused much bitterness in the party. They were one of the reasons why some Labour MPs broke away to form a new political party.

The Liberal party

Since the 1920s, the Liberal party has been replaced by the Labour party as the main rival to the Conservative party. Liberals are now more strongly represented in local government than in central government. Of the total number of votes cast in general elections since 1945, the Liberal party has polled between 25% (in 1951) and 19.3% (in February 1974). Despite this, the party has never had more than 14 MPs in Parliament during this period.

Many Liberals argue that the support they have in the country is not fairly reflected in Parliament. There is much truth in this. For even when the Liberals won nearly a fifth of all the votes cast in the February 1974 general election, only 2.2% of MPs in Parliament were Liberal.

Despite its problems, the Liberal party is proudly conscious of its long history and hopes to regain its old importance. There have been promising developments for the party. Liberal MPs wielded much influence during the 'Lib-Lab' pact of 1977–8. They made bargains with a minority Labour government. The Liberal MPs supported Labour, and in return Labour carried out some Liberal policies. In 1981 a milestone was reached in Liberal history when an alliance was formed with the Social Democratic Party (SDP).

The Liberal party meets each year in a conference which is known as the 'Assembly'. As in the Conservative and Labour parties, the Liberal party has constituency and regional organisations. At the national level there is a Council, which is made up of representatives from the parliamentary party, national and regional parties, and other bodies recognised by Liberals. There is also a National Executive Committee and a number of other smaller committees.

The Liberal party was the first of the major parties to involve the party outside Parliament in the election of its leader. Only Liberal MPs may be nominated for the post of leader. The number of votes cast by each constituency party in the election of the leader is 'weighted' to take account of the number of Liberal voters. The exact method is spelled out in the Liberal party constitution. It states: 'Each affiliated Constituency Association shall be entitled to exercise ten votes if it was affiliated for the previous year, plus one further vote for each 500 votes or part thereof cast for the officially nominated Liberal candidate in that constituency at the previous General Election....' ▷ p.

(i) Identify these party leaders, and (ii) state which party they led. Find out which party has had most leaders since 1945.

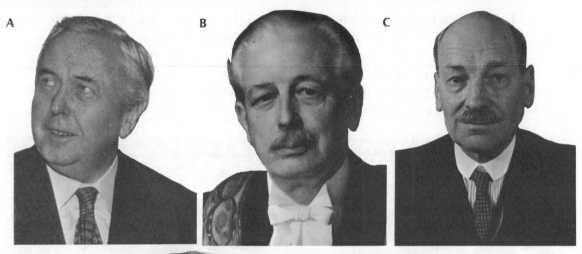

A

B

C

D

E

F

G

H

63

This photograph was taken at an Annual Conference of the Labour party. Who are the people on the platform and who do they represent? Who do the delegates in the hall represent? How do they vote? The conferences are shown on television. How else might you find out what speeches were made and what policies were decided at conference?

In 1982 Roy Jenkins and David Steel both attended the Liberal Assembly. Who was leader of the SDP and who was leader of the Liberals? Mr Jenkins told Liberals that the Alliance's strongest appeal was that it could bring the nation together and rise above the bogus bitterness of out-of-date class politics. He added: 'But these points won't seem valid if we quarrel over spoils before they had even been won, or if we cannot bring ourselves together.' Why is the alliance difficult to keep together? What sort of issues do Social Democrats and Liberals argue about?

The new system was first used in 1976 when David Steel was elected as leader.

The Social Democratic Party

Early in 1981 a new 'centre' party was formed in Britain. Its aims were spelled out by the 'Council for Social Democracy' which was formed in February. The Social Democratic Party was formed in March, and it entered into an alliance with the Liberals in June. This meant that they would agree which constituencies their candidates would stand for in a general election, so that they would not compete against each other for votes. It also meant that they would act together in Parliament and, if they won enough seats, jointly form a government which would pursue agreed policies.

For some time senior Labour politicians had been worrying about changes inside the Conservative and Labour parties. The Tories had become much more right-wing, and Labour had become much more left-wing. The politicians concerned with what was happening were all respected national figures. They were Roy Jenkins (who had been deputy-leader of the Labour party and had held office as Chancellor and Home Secretary); David Owen (who had been Labour's Foreign Secretary); Shirley Williams (who had been Education minister) and William Rodgers (who had been a Labour Transport minister).

New parties usually find it hard to win support from the public, but the SDP made a good start. The SDP was joined by many individuals who left the Labour party and some who left the Conservative party. Surprisingly, they were also joined by some who left the Liberal party, even though the parties were in alliance. The SDP/Liberal Alliance won some spectacular victories at by-elections. At the end of 1981, the SDP had 75 000 paid-up members.

In 1982 a postal ballot of these members elected Roy Jenkins as leader of the SDP, and Shirley Williams as president. During the year the SDP published a number of policy statements which made clearer to the public what the party stood for.

There was much talk in the newspapers of the SDP/Liberal Alliance 'breaking the mould' of British politics. It is true to say that the Alliance enjoyed a 'honeymoon' period when everything seemed to go right for it. But only time will tell if the Alliance will become an important part of British politics.

The Alliance faces a number of problems. (i) Liberals tend to make important decisions at constituency level, whereas the SDP expects its leaders to make important decisions. This has and will lead to tensions between the two. (ii) If the public sees the SDP and Liberals disagreeing, then this may lead to a loss of support. For many supported the Alliance because it gave hope of a new kind of politics in Britain based on moderation. If members of the Alliance disagree bitterly with each other, they will not look a great deal different from the squabbling Tory and Labour parties. (iii) The idea of a moderate political party between the extremes of 'Thatcherism' and 'Bennery' is attractive to many voters. But what would happen if both Conservative and Labour moved back from their extremes to adopt more moderate policies? Is there a danger that the SDP and Alliance would become politically redundant? Shirley Williams, the President of the SDP, argues that the 'moderate' members of the Conservative and Labour parties have more in common with each other than with the 'extremists' inside their own parties. She adds, however, that both the major parties have policies which are out of date. (iv) There is disagreement about the purpose of the Alliance. Some say that the Alliance is a temporary coalition formed to promote electoral change. Once this has been achieved the Alliance will be disbanded and the two parties will compete against each other. Others say that the Liberals and SDP should merge together and that the Alliance should become permanent.

Terms used

Affiliated members When one organisation (e.g. a trade union) has organisational links with another (e.g. the Labour party) it is said to be 'affiliated'. Usually there is a financial contribution made to the organisation which are 'affiliation' fees.

Autonomy The right of self-government; freedom from outside interference.

Binding When decisions taken must be carried out.

Co-option When individuals are invited to become non-elected members of a committee.

Ex-officio By virtue of the office held.

Fabian Society A socialist society which concentrates on the study of political, social and economic issues, and publishes its findings for the consideration of the Labour movement.

Federation The grouping together of separate organisations in order to achieve a common goal more effectively.

GMWU General and Municipal Workers Union.

NUPE National Union of Public Employees.

Prerogative The possession of a special right or privilege.

TGWU Transport and General Workers Union.

Summary

1 Political parties are organisations which seek power in order to put their policies into practice.

2 Parties dominate British politics at all levels. They focus attention on political issues and problems.

3 Parties developed hand in hand with extensions of the franchise. The Conservative and Liberal parties grew from within Parliament; the Labour party was born outside Parliament. The differing histories of the two major parties are reflected in the way they are organised and the way they make decisions.

4 In the Conservative party, the leader makes policy. The finances of the party are heavily dependent on donations from industrial and commercial firms.

5 The Labour party has close links with the trade union movement and receives much of its income from the unions. Policy is decided by the Annual Conference, but this produces tensions between the Parliamentary Labour Party and the NEC.

6 The individual membership of both major parties has fallen drastically in the last thirty years.

7 The SDP/Liberal Alliance was formed as a moderate alternative to the Labour and Tory parties.

Questions for discussion

1 In what ways do political parties dominate British politics?

2 What are the important differences between the Conservative and Labour parties in terms of (a) organisational structure, (b) responsibility for policy-making, (c) finance?

3 What are the main problems which face the major parties at the present time?

4 How successful has the SDP/Liberal Alliance been in 'breaking the mould' of British politics?

5 Imagine that there are three major issues which divide your school.
(a) School uniform. Some pupils want school uniform to be compulsory. Others want to ban it altogether.
(b) Smoking. Some pupils want all over sixteen to have the right to smoke during breaks even though it is harmful to health. Others want to ban smoking in school. Among other things, they object to smoke-filled rooms and the increased fire risk.
(c) Physical Education. Some want PE to be replaced by 'Leisure Studies' which include activities such as chess, snooker, darts and video-games. Others want all students to be involved in physical sports such as rugby, soccer, hockey, tennis and athletics.
Some pupils will feel strongly about some issues but not have a strong opinion on others. Some will feel strongly about all the issues. How many 'political parties' would have to be formed in your class to represent all the pupils? How many pupils are in each party? How many pupils would not be represented by the two largest parties?

8

Political parties: aims and activities

This chapter continues the examination of political parties. Having looked at the origins, structure and leadership of the main parties, we shall now consider the political beliefs held by each party and the types of activity in which they engage. Members of the same political party often disagree about policy. But if they share the same beliefs, how can they disagree? This chapter outlines the differences between groups or factions inside the Conservative and Labour parties. We also consider the beliefs held by members of the Liberal party and SDP.

What are the main jobs that constituency parties do? The most important activities include selecting the next party candidate for Parliament, and organising the election campaign. But have parties in Britain enough resources and money to do these jobs well? The chapter ends with a look at the question of giving state aid to British political parties.

Political parties are coalitions

Members of a political party do not all hold the same beliefs or opinions. Within each party there will be general agreement on some beliefs, and disagreement on others.

Disagreement within a party is often misunderstood by people. You may hear someone say that a party is unfit to govern because 'they can't even agree amongst themselves'. But there is nothing alarming about disagreement within a party. Because parties are **coalitions** of different views, disagreement should be expected. Members agree broadly on the ends to achieve but disagree on the way to achieve them.

Of course, from the point of view of the parties, it is important that internal disagreements do not get out of hand. Differences of view must not be so great that they split the party into pieces. A united party appeals to the electorate as a strong party. This is why party leaders call for party unity as a general election gets closer.

Beliefs and policies

Beliefs come from views people hold about the nature of society. Political policies are based on these beliefs. You will often hear the terms 'left-wing' and 'right-wing' used to describe the views held by politicians. Basically, right-wing politicians prefer society to be based on the individual's right to own private property. Their policies will promote competition and protect private property. Left-wing politicians prefer society to be based on public ownership. Their policies will promote co-operation and the growth of public ownership. Table 8.1 is part of a chart compiled by Dr Bill Jones. It shows which policies are supported by various groups inside parties as well as the differences between parties.

The policies of parties when they are in opposition are rarely those followed when they are in government. This can lead to tensions in the party because party members become disappointed in what their government is achieving. When a party gains office, it faces harsh realities, and policies adopted in opposition may be difficult to implement. It is hard for a government to make policy which will please all the party. Lord Hailsham has commented that:

> The actual situation which a new government is confronted with is often vastly different from what it was imagined to be in opposition, and the measures proposed in the manifesto often include the impossible, the irrelevant, and the inappropriate.

Table 8.1 Policies and the political spectrum

| | | Labour | | Social Democratic Party (SDP) | Liberal | Conservative | |
		Left	Right			'Wet'	Radical right-wing
1	**Structure of the economy**	Extension of state control to reduce private sector. Intervention to stimulate growth. (Neo-Marxist)	Mixed economy with some intervention in private sector to control and stimulate growth. Some control of money supply. Not keen on further nationalisation.	Mixed economy with state investment to stimulate growth. Decentralised enterprises. (Keynesian)	Mixed economy with state intervention but less enthusiastic about economic growth. Concerned about 'post industrial society'. Decentralised enterprises.	Mixed economy with intervention where absolutely necessary. Encourage private sector especially small industries.	Ideally a market economy unfettered by government controls. Tight control of money supply. Denationalisation wherever possible.
2	**Employment**	Full employment. Extensive training programmes. Import controls to protect ailing industries from foreign competition.	Some unemployment inevitable if productivity and competitiveness decline. Extensive training programmes.	Maximise employment through stimulating economic growth. Reshaping and expansion of training and apprenticeship programmes. Grants to employers who take on long term unemployed.	Stimulate economic growth. Expand training especially for 16- to 19-year-olds.	Some reflation of economy. Unemployment unfortunate product of poor economic performance. Expand training for young.	Acceptance of unemployment in present until economy becomes competitive enough to expand. Government schemes no substitute for 'real' jobs, but necessary to alleviate hardship. Opposed to import controls.
3	**Education**	Abolish private sector. Universal comprehensive education.	In theory against private sector but in practice reluctant to move against it. Pro-comprehensive.	Withdraw support for private sector but do not abolish. Mrs Williams favours abolition. Reform examination system.	Pro-comprehensive. Opposed to privileged private sector but would not abolish. (Private sector of minor importance in Liberal view.)	Anti-comprehensive but will not abolish. Pro-private sector.	Staunch defenders of private sector and maintenance of 'excellence' in educational system.
4	**Law and order and civil rights**	Opposed to extension of police powers. Pro-civil rights. Tendency to see criminal as victim. Against immigration controls.	Cautious about police powers but firm on need for order. In favour of some immigration controls.	Cautious about police powers, liberal on penal reform.	In favour of penal reform. Very pro-individual liberties.	Favours strong police force, sees society as criminals' victim. Some controls on immigration.	Very pro-police and anti-criminal. In favour of harsh sentences. Not so sympathetic to race relations legislation, in favour of controls on immigration if not repatriation.
5	**Social services**	High spending on social services. Increase benefits and index link them to inflation.	High spending on social services but cut if economy declines. Increase benefits: index linked to inflation.	High spending on social services.	High spending on social services.	Favour private welfare sector, e.g. 'pay beds' but support efficient welfare state.	Encouragement of private welfare schemes as possible substitute for state system but in favour of welfare 'safety net'. Opposed index linkage. Unemployment pay too high in some cases.
6	**Housing and local government**	Big programme of housebuilding and improvement. Opposed to sale of council houses.	Expand housing programme. Anti-council house sales. Give important services back to non-metropolitan districts.	New minister for regional policy. Reform rates system. More power to local government.	Expand housing programme, especially housing co-operatives. Pro-decentralised 'community' politics. Single tier local government.	Supports sale of council houses. Some cuts inevitable. Reform rates system.	Local government must take big share of cuts. Protect councils from over-spending. Stronger central controls.
7	**Trade unions**	No legal restrictions on activities. Government to consult closely on wide range of policies.	Some legal restrictions on trade union activities. Close co-operation when in government.	New consensus of employers and unions but union reform a priority: legal framework giving statutory rights to trade unions in exchange for defined limits on industrial action.	Emphasis on co-operation between employers and trade unions.	Some legal restraints but emphasis on voluntary agreements and building of consensus.	Tough legislation to restrict picketing, ban closed shop and remove trade union immunities.

Source: Based on tables in Bill Jones, 'Realignment on the Left', Teaching Politics, vol. 11, May 1982

We must also remember that a government has to listen to advice from pressure groups, foreign governments, and civil servants. Such advice is likely to influence government policy. Opposition parties tend to listen only to their party supporters. Government action is restricted by the very real problems it is faced with in office. Opposition parties do not have to tackle these problems directly since they are not in office. They must, however, remember that they are offering themselves as an alternative government, and the public reaction to their policies matters.

Sometimes Labour and Conservative governments may adopt very similar policies. They follow the same policy because they face the same problems. **Bi-partisanship** occurs when government and opposition agree on a policy. Labour and Conservative governments have generally had a bi-partisan approach to the problems of Northern Ireland and to threats from foreign countries.

Conservative beliefs

It has been written that Conservatism is 'less a political doctrine than a habit of mind, a mode [way] of feeling, a way of living'. This suggests that Conservatives prefer to solve problems in a practical way rather than in a way based on some abstract theory. Lord Hailsham has argued that Conservatives are not opposed to change. However, they believe that 'a living society can only change healthily when it changes naturally'. As we shall see, many of these views are no longer as accurate about the Conservative party as they once were. For the modern Conservative party contains two **factions**. That means that there are two groups of Conservatives who disagree about what the party stands for and what policies it should have.

The radical right wing of the Conservative party

This wing of the Conservative party has been called a variety of names. 'Diehards', 'dries', or 'monetarists' usually refers to the group of MPs and party members on the radical right wing of the party. The radical right are found on the far right of the Conservative party.

The radical right believe in what is called a **free market economy**. This implies the government leaving the economy alone and not influencing the way it works. They believe that the working of a free market best protects individualism. For example, they would like to see taxation greatly reduced. This is because taxation limits the freedom of individuals to spend all the money they earn. Taxation interferes with the free market because, through taxes, the government takes money away from the individuals who earned it; the government, not the individual, spends money taken away in taxation.

The radical right oppose many aspects of the welfare state. They do not agree with people receiving welfare (social security, education, housing) as a right. From the radical right's point of view, welfare should only be provided to those in need.

The radical right believe in an economic policy called **monetarism**, and in cutting back government spending. Monetarism involves controlling the supply of money in the economy. This is done by using methods such as high interest rates to discourage borrowing. Monetarists argue that less money in the economy will lead to a fall in inflation. Groups on the right wing of the Conservative party include the Monday Club. In 1983 the Young Conservatives published a report which claimed that racist individuals were infiltrating the right wing of the Tory party at constituency level.

The 'One-Nation' Tories

'One-Nation' Conservatives are also known as 'wets' or 'progressive' Conservatives. They support the sort of policies forwarded by 'Rab' Butler and Harold Macmillan in the 1950s and 1960s. They do not have the same faith in the 'free market' as those of the more extreme radical right. They believe that the free market causes social problems (such as poverty) which it cannot solve.

'One-Nation' Tories are concerned with the wellbeing of all the people. Sir Ian Gilmour is a 'wet' MP who has made this clear. In his book, *Inside Right*, he wrote that the welfare state 'is a thoroughly Conservative institution'. Generally speaking, Tory 'wets' want a bigger welfare state in Britain.

Groups on this wing of the Conservative party

include the Bow Group and the Tory Reform Group.

Labour beliefs

The British Labour party sees itself as a socialist party. Members believe in the brotherhood of man, equality of opportunity and the idea of a just society. They do not believe that private enterprise and the free market will ever bring about the sort of society that they seek. In order to reform society, they have attempted to plan industry. This means controlling where firms are set up, and what goods are produced. Sometimes control of industry is obtained by bringing it under public ownership. Some socialists would like to see more of the economy brought into public ownership.

Clause IV of the Labour party constitution is the clause which gives Labour the right to claim that it is a socialist party. The relevant part states that one of the party's general aims is:

> To secure for workers by hand or brain the full fruits of their industry and the most equitable distribution thereof that may be possible upon the basis of the common ownership of the means of production, distribution and exchange, and the best obtainable system of popular administration and control of each industry and service.

The Labour left

The Labour left believe that the party's policies should be truly socialist ones. The left wing of the party would like to see the banks and many more industries **nationalised**. When an industry or firm is nationalised it becomes part of the public sector. It is then owned by the state.

The left would like a Labour government to follow **pacifist** policies. This would mean Britain giving up nuclear weapons. They would also like to abolish public schools and bring about more **equality** in society.

During the 1970s and 1980s the left grew in size. Trotskyite groups such as Militant Tendency and the Socialist Organiser Alliance entered the Labour party and joined its left wing. This was known as 'entryism' and it worried many members

of the party. Moves were taken by Conference and the NEC to reduce the influence of these groups. A typical left-wing group which has been in the Labour party for many years is the Tribune Group. Groups such as Militant Tendency are often referred to as the 'hard' left. The Tribune Group is on the 'soft' left of the Labour party.

Labour's right wing

Labour believes strongly in equality in the **mixed economy**. They argue that the Britain of today is very different from Britain in the days when the party was born in 1900. The problems of today's economy will not be solved by more public ownership or nationalisation. The right believe that the main problem with the economy is that it has not grown fast enough. Thus, the Labour right support policies which will bring about faster economic growth.

Labour's right wing believe in **equality of opportunity**. In other words, people should be given the chance to do well in their lives regardless of whatever background they come from. The right of the Labour party believe that more equality can be obtained through extending and improving the welfare state.

The right support Britain's membership of the EEC and NATO. Right-wing Labour MPs also believe that Britain should keep her nuclear weapons.

Anthony Crosland has argued the views of the Labour right in a book called *The Future of Socialism*. The Manifesto Group of Labour MPs is a right-wing body.

Liberal party beliefs

The Liberal party accepts the existence of free enterprise. However, Liberals believe that wealth should be more fairly shared out. They also believe in greater participation by ordinary people in decisions which affect their lives.

Liberals claim to represent all people in society, and not one particular group. They criticise Labour for its ties with the unions and the Conservatives for their ties with big business. The Liberal leader, David Steel, wrote that 'we must set aside class conflict, the endless debates about capitalism versus socialism and the policies that divide and weaken us as a nation'. He rejected the view that Liberals are simply 'half-way between Labour and Tory'. He argued that Liberals had their own identity. He continued by pointing out that 'the Liberal party is a classless party, dedicated to pursuing the maximum of freedom and power for the individual consistent with his responsibilities to the community'.

Social Democratic Party beliefs

The Social Democratic Party is a 'left-of-centre' party. There are similarities between SDP and Liberal beliefs, and this enabled both parties to form the 'Alliance'. Social Democrats reject rigid control of political or economic organisation. They do not favour more nationalisation. They do not like the existence of huge firms or companies.

They support the idea of people becoming more involved in decision-making. Social Democrats believe in the community becoming more involved in local government, and in workers becoming more involved in making decisions in their factories, offices, shops, etc. Social Democrats support **industrial democracy**.

Party activity

General election campaigns generate much political activity in the constituency parties. Members and supporters who do not normally go to constituency meetings will turn out to help the party during a campaign. Under the direction of the party agent they will do the many jobs that need doing – canvassing from door to door, addressing envelopes, and so on.

In between general elections constituency parties spend time holding meetings, raising money, and fighting local government elections. It is sometimes said that parties spend most time organising fund-raising activities. This means that the time spent on discussing politics is limited. Nevertheless, a small minority of the electorate do these jobs and the parties depend heavily on them.

Members of constituency parties who are elected

as officials and delegates will attend meetings at a variety of levels – local constituency, regional and national. At the annual party conference they will meet members from other constituency parties. Also they may meet prominent politicians in their party. Annual conferences – particularly the Conservative conference – are 'stage-managed'. This means that the debates are carefully controlled so that the conference gives a good impression to the public. But there are opportunities for constituency members to voice their opposition to official party policy at 'fringe' meetings. These are usually held in hotels, halls or public houses near the conference hall. In the past, Tory 'wets' have held fringe meetings at conferences to oppose the policies of the Conservative government. The Militant Tendency has organised fringe meetings at Labour conferences in order to promote their policies.

State aid for political parties?

In the nineteenth century a wealthy person could 'buy' a seat in the House of Commons. Until the passing of the Corrupt Practices Act of 1883, the wealthy could bribe voters into supporting them. In the 1980s, money is still a vital necessity for a party which wants to fight election campaigns.

In its first year, the SDP did quite well in raising party funds. You can see from Table 8.2 that it ▷ p.74

Table 8.2 Political party finances

LABOUR

Central income	£2.6 million
Union contributions (1980)	approx. £4.1 million
Individual membership	250 000

CONSERVATIVE

Central income	£3.2 million
Company contributions (1980)	approx. £2.7 million
Individual membership	1¼–1½ million

SDP

Central income	£750 000
Individual membership	78 000

The following extracts are taken from two of the major parties' manifestoes for the general election, 1983. Identify the two manifestoes concerned. Consult table 8.1 for preliminary guidance if necessary. How do the extracts given fit in with the approaches in the table? Obtain copies of the manifestoes and examine carefully the full statements of policy on these and other issues.

A

We face three major challenges: the defence of our country, the employment of our people, and the prosperity of our economy.

• How to defend Britain's traditional liberties and distinctive way of life is the most vital decision that faces the people in this election.

The Western Alliance can keep the peace only if we can convince any potential aggressor that he would have to pay an unacceptable price. To do so, NATO must have strong conventional forces backed by a nuclear deterrent. And we in Britain must maintain our own nuclear contribution to British and European defence. At the same time we shall continue to support all realistic efforts to reach balanced and verifiable agreements with the Soviet Union on arms control and disarmament.

• The universal problem of our time, and the most intractable, is unemployment.

The answer is not bogus social contracts and government overspending. Both, in the end, destroy jobs. The only way to a lasting reduction in unemployment is to make the right products at the right prices, supported by good services. The Government's role is to keep inflation down and offer real incentives for enterprise.

Reform of the nationalised industries is central to economic recovery. ... ... Nationalisation does not improve job satisfaction, job security or labour relations – almost all the serious strikes in recent years have been in state industries and services. ...

... We shall transfer more state-owned businesses to independent ownership.... Those nationalised industries which cannot be privatised or organised as smaller and more efficient units will be given top-quality management and required to work to clear guidelines.

• We have a duty to protect the most vulnerable members of our society, many of whom contributed to the heritage we now enjoy. We are proud of the way we have shielded the pensioner and the National Health Service from the recession.

We welcome the growth in private health insurance in recent years. This has both made more health care available, and lightened the load on the NHS. ... We shall continue to encourage this valuable supplement to state care.

B

... ... things crying out to be done in our country today.

To get Britain back to work. To rebuild our shattered industries. To get rid of the ever-growing dole queues. To protect and enlarge our National Health Service and other great social services. To help stop the nuclear arms race.

This is what we plan to do. We will:

Launch a massive programme for expansion. We will:

Provide a major increase in public investment, including transport, housing and energy conservation.

Begin a huge programme of construction, so that we can build our way out of the slump ...

Increase investment in industry, especially in new technology – with public enterprise taking the lead. And we will steer new industry and jobs to the regions and the inner cities.

Begin to rebuild British industry, working within a new framework for planning and industrial democracy. We will:

Agree a new national economic assessment, setting out the prospects for growth in the economy.

Prepare a five-year national plan, in consultation with unions and employers.

Back up these steps with a new National Investment Bank, new industrial powers, and a new Department for Economic and Industrial Planning Repeal ... legislation on industrial relations and make provision for introducing industrial democracy....

Start to create a fairer Britain, with decent social services for all. We will:

... Provide more resources for the health service with an increase of at least 3 per cent a year in real terms....

In international policy, we shall take new initiatives to promote peace and development. We will:

Cancel the Trident programme, refuse to deploy Cruise missiles and begin discussions for the removal of nuclear bases from Britain ....

We will also open immediate negotiations with our EEC partners, and introduce the necessary legislation, to prepare for *Britain's withdrawal from the EEC* ....

raised £750 000 from its 78 000 members. But the Social Democrats feel that the present system of financing parties is unfair. For the Labour party is supported by the trade unions, and the Conservative party relies on money from big business.

In fact, most of the money from the unions and big business is not spent on campaigning. It is spent on maintaining the Labour and Conservative headquarters and their regional organisations. However, the value of donations by big business to the Conservative party has dropped by a third in the last twenty years. Despite union money, Labour has gone into debt.

This is not a healthy situation for politics in Britain. If the parties are crucial for democracy to work, then the parties should be financially secure. As we have seen, the individual membership of both the major parties has declined drastically in the last thirty years. Although the parties have a vital role to play in Britain's democracy, they do not always seem strong enough to succeed. Some people argue that the parties are not independent enough to be truly democratic. They refer to the old saying that 'he who pays the piper calls the tune'. There is the same danger facing both parties. Because Labour depends on the unions for money, it may become too much under their influence. Similarly the Conservatives will be tempted to put big business first so that the money from companies and firms will keep coming in to the party.

In many countries, including West Germany, Austria, Sweden, Finland, Denmark, Norway, Italy and Canada, the parties receive financial help from the government. In Britain the parties receive some help in the form of free time on radio and TV for party political broadcasts. They also get free postage for election material. But there is no direct or large-scale state subsidy for the parties. In this respect, Britain is the odd man out.

In 1975 the government set up a committee to 'consider whether, in the interests of Parliamentary democracy, provision should be made from public funds to assist political parties in carrying out their functions outside Parliament'. The committee was chaired by Lord Houghton. A majority on the committee felt that some financial help should be given to the parties at both central and local levels. Generally speaking, the Labour party agreed with this conclusion and the Conservatives opposed it. The Houghton Committee's recommendation that limited support should be given to the parties has not yet been put into effect. In the meantime, the parties face increasing financial problems.

Terms used

Bi-partisanship A similar approach to particular problems by two political parties.

Coalition A grouping or coming together of individuals holding different views in order to increase their chances of success in politics.

Equality and **equality of opportunity** The idea that individuals have the same worth. People born into poorer circumstances may be held back through being disadvantaged. Equality of opportunity attempts to compensate for such disadvantage through the welfare state.

Faction A group of people who hold similar views organised inside a political party.

Free market economy This is central to a capitalist economy. A market in which supply and demand are not subject to government interference.

Industrial democracy The idea that all those who work for a firm or company should be represented when decisions are made. It involves the idea of 'worker directors'.

Mixed economy An economy in which there is private and public enterprise.

Monetarism An economic policy which is aimed at 'squeezing' inflation out of the economy. Monetarists want to see less public spending by government. Monetarist policy is associated with high levels of unemployment.

Nationalisation A form of public ownership. British Rail is a nationalised industry.

Pacifism An attitude which opposes the use of military force as a way of settling international disputes.

Summary

1 Political parties are coalitions of individuals who hold different beliefs.

2 All governments are faced by difficulties when

making policy. These difficulties are not shared to the same extent by opposition parties. This is likely to result in a gap between what the party wants and what the government actually does.

3 The Conservative party believes in minimum government and maximum personal freedom. It places great emphasis on private enterprise. The Conservative party contains factions. The Labour party believes in equality of opportunity, public ownership and planning. It is a strong supporter of the welfare state. It also contains factions.

4 Prospective parliamentary candidates are chosen by the party organisations in the constituencies. Their decisions are subject to approval by the party at national level. Parties in 'safe' seats are, in effect, choosing an MP.

5 The governments of nearly all political democracies in Western Europe provide financial support for their political parties. A scheme for limited state aid to the parties was proposed by the Houghton Committee, but so far it has not been implemented.

Questions for discussion

1 Argue the case for either Conservatism, Socialism, Liberalism or the Social Democratic viewpoint. Justify your choice.

2 In what sense are all parties coalitions? What problem does this produce for party leaders?

3 Argue the case for or against the government giving financial aid to political parties.

4 Devise a questionnaire which measures a person's political beliefs. Set our ten questions in this way:

'The welfare state should be abolished as soon as possible.' Do you agree strongly? ... agree slightly? ... disagree slightly? ... disagree strongly? *or* Don't know.

Try out the questionnaire in your class. Mark answers from 4 to 0, with 'Don't know' answers scoring zero. Right-wing opinions should have high scores, and left-wing opinions low scores.

9

Pressure Groups

In this chapter we examine one of the ways in which many people participate in politics - as members of pressure groups. Pressure groups try to influence political decisions at local, national and international level. At local level, a pressure group might contain only a handful of people. At national level the most powerful groups are wealthy and employ large staffs. We examine the differences between pressure groups and political parties, and see how groups are linked with parties. There are two main types of groups - protective and promotional groups. Some groups work directly with government. Others try to influence government indirectly through campaigning to win public support. Some people think pressure groups strengthen democracy in Britain, whilst others feel that pressure groups work to undermine democracy. The chapter concludes by considering the arguments on both sides.

Organisational society

Britain can be described as an *organisational society*. Whatever a person is interested in, there is almost sure to be an organisation he can join to meet other people who share the same interest. For example, there are organisations for people who are interested in conserving the environment, looking after old people, playing table tennis, singing folk songs, restoring old steam engines, and so on.

Any one person may belong to several organisations, each one representing a particular interest or need. For example, one man may be a member of the local branch of his trade union in order to protect his job, wages and working conditions. He may also be in the Automobile Association (AA) to protect his interest as a motorist. Finally, he may be in the Ramblers' Association because of his love for the countryside. Another man may be a member of the Conservative party, the Rotary Club and the local golf club.

Some of the organisations mentioned so far are not political at all. Others are political because they attempt to influence government at local or national level. A table tennis club is unlikely to want to influence government at any level. But a conservation group will always be trying to persuade government to make decisions which safeguard the environment. When groups act in a political manner they are known as *pressure groups*. In other words the conservation group is a pressure group because it is trying to exert pressure on government and influence political decisions. Table 9.1 gives examples of some pressure groups in Britain and indicates what the groups are trying to achieve.

It has been estimated that there are between five and six thousand pressure groups seeking to influence central government. It is important to note, therefore, that political interest and activity is not confined to the political parties. There are many people active in politics who are members of pressure groups, but they are not members of political parties. Some pressure groups are very big. For example, it has been estimated that more people support CND than there are active members of the Labour party.

In addition to the pressure groups trying to influence central government, there are countless small groups trying to influence local government. These may range from a group of parents who are trying to save a village school or a group of mothers who are campaigning for a zebra crossing outside a school to a civic trust which is trying to save old buildings from demolition.

Pressure groups are not a new type of political organisation. The Committee for the Abolition of the Slave Trade, the Anti-Corn Law League and the **suffragette** movement are examples of pressure groups from Britain's past. In recent years, pressure group activity has become more

Table 9.1 Different types of pressure group organisation

Type	Organisation	Function
Political	Electoral Reform Society	To secure adoption of STV (Single Transferrable Voting) system in all elections.
	Committee for Democratic Regional Government in North of England	To press for elected assembly in the region with delegated powers.
Employers and business	Confederation of British Industry	To promote interests of British business and uphold market system and profit motive.
	Institute of Directors	To advance the interests of company directors.
Labour and professional	Trades Union Congress	To promote interests of affiliated trade unions and improve economic and social conditions of workers.
	National Union of Journalists	To promote and protect interest of journalists.
Consumers	Consumers' Association	To offer impartial testing of consumer goods and services.
	Telephone Users' Association	To campaign for improved telephone service.
Educational and cultural	Confederation for the Advancement of State Education	To secure improvement in quality and scope of education services.
	British Association for the Advancement of Science	To promote understanding and interest in science.
Religious	Catholic Truth Society	To disseminate knowledge of the Catholic faith.
	Lord's Day Observance Society	To preserve Sunday as the Christian Sabbath.
Health and medical	Disablement Income Group	To promote welfare of disabled.
	Mind (National Association for Mental Health)	To draw attention to problems of mental health and remove social stigma of mental illness.
Social welfare	Shelter	To provide assistance to homeless and those in poor housing and to influence policy in this field.
	Child Poverty Action Group	To campaign for better conditions for low income families.
Animal welfare	International League for the Protection of Horses	To prevent cruelty to horses and promote welfare legislation.
	The Royal Society for the Protection of Birds	To work for the better protection of birds by developing public interest in them.
Environmental	Anti-Concorde Project	To oppose development, manufacture and operation of supersonic transport.
	British Naturalists Association	To support all schemes for the protection of wildlife and the preservation of the countryside.

common as a means of participating in politics. There are many more pressure groups in Britain now than there were twenty years ago.

Pressure groups and political parties

Political parties and pressure groups are similar in some ways. For example, both types of organisation have political aims. But they differ in other important ways.

First, political parties are interested in a *broad* range of issues. Pressure groups, on the other hand, are normally interested in a *single* or a *narrow* range of issues. Secondly, political parties put much energy and many resources into getting their representatives elected to Parliament, local councils or the European Assembly. Political parties want to be the government. Pressure groups only want to influence the government. Consequently pressure groups do not usually try to get representatives elected at local, national or European level. The Ecology Party is in some respects like a pressure group but it functions as a party and puts up candidates.

There are, however, close links between political parties and pressure groups. The best known link of this kind is that between many trade unions and the Labour party (see chapter 7). As we have seen, the Labour party receives about three-quarters of its annual income from the trade unions. Trade unions are represented at all levels of the Labour party, and they **sponsor** their members as would-be MPs. Trade unions exist to improve the lives and working conditions of their members. They believe this can be done best under a Labour government.

There are no formal links between any pressure groups and the Conservative party. However, groups such as the Confederation of British Industry (CBI), the Institute of Directors, and Aims of Industry, have attitudes similar to those of the Conservatives. They all believe there would be more freedom and prosperity in society if the economy was based more securely on private enterprise. A large number of firms in industry, commerce and finance make contributions to the Conservative party. About three-quarters of Con-servative party income comes from these sources.

We also noted in chapter 8 that the Conservative and Labour parties were split into factions. Members of these factions join together in a particular kind of pressure group. They are sometimes known as 'ginger' groups. Figure 9.1 shows these groups as well as the other pressure groups which compete to influence the policies of the main parties.

Protective and promotional groups

Pressure groups can be divided into two main types. Protective groups, sometimes called interest groups, are organised to safeguard aspects of people's lives. For example, a trade union exists to protect people's jobs, wages and working conditions. The British Road Federation campaigns for more and better roads, but this is in the self-interest of firms which build vehicles and make concrete and cement. Promotional groups, sometimes called 'cause' groups, are concerned to gain support for a principle or idea. Promotional groups include the National Council for Civil Liberties which campaigns for human rights, and the Electoral Reform Society which is campaigning to change the way we vote. Other promotional groups include the Noise Abatement Society, the RSPCA, the Conservation Society, Action for the Crippled Child, and the Thalidomide Parents Committee.

The division between protective and promotional groups is not hard and fast. Members of CND, for example, might argue that they are a protective group because they have a self-interest in trying to save the world from nuclear disaster. On the other hand, it could be argued that CND is a promotional group because it is trying to win support for the idea of giving up nuclear weapons. Read about the action group shown on Task-page 9.1 and attempt to decide what type of group it is.

Generally speaking, protective groups tend to be permanent, and find it easier to communicate *directly* with government than promotional groups. Promotional groups may disband once they have achieved their goals. Also promotional groups tend ▷ p.81

OAPs say "SAVE OUR WAY OF LIFE!"

The *Eastleigh Weekly News*

Here is a demonstration by a small community action group. The members are photographed with the Mayor on the steps of the local Town Hall. The issue concerned old age pensioners who were being evicted from their allotments at Ham Farm. The Council had offered them another site at Knowle Hill. But the men felt Knowle Hill was unsatisfactory because the land was poor. Younger allotment gardeners who sympathised with their plight organised an action group. There was much publicity about the issue in local newspapers, and also on radio and television. The campaign ended with a march to the Town Hall, with men pushing wheelbarrows of vegetables from the threatened allotments. Two men carry bags of soil – the rich soil of Ham Farm and the stony soil from Knowle Hill. After much bargaining between the action group and council officials, some allotments were kept for pensioners when the Ham Farm site was redeveloped.

How would you describe this pressure group? Was it a *promotional* group which was concerned with the welfare of old people? Or was it a *protective* group trying to keep a hold on fertile land which produced valuable crops? Discuss this in class, and read your local newspapers for reports of small pressure groups working in your community.

WHO?

- sorts out people's problems at work?
- campaigns for higher pay and better working conditions for everyone?
- wants a better deal for pensioners, for families, for children and for the unemployed?
- has 11 million members?
- stands for the future?

- is the Minister responsible for 3 million registered unemployed?
- believes cutting wages will create jobs?
- thinks the unemployed should get on their bikes and look for work — which doesn't exist?
- intends to deprive millions of people of their rights?
- stands for the past?

THE UNIONS | MR TEBBIT

Leaflet distributed on the TUC 'day of action'

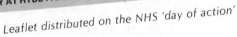

Leaflet distributed on the NHS 'day of action'

At most 'days of action' or demonstrations, leaflets such as these are handed out. Design a leaflet for a pressure group which is now in the news or has been recently. Make sure that the message you are trying to communicate is clear and easily understood. Remember that any illustrations must help communicate, and not confuse or distract.

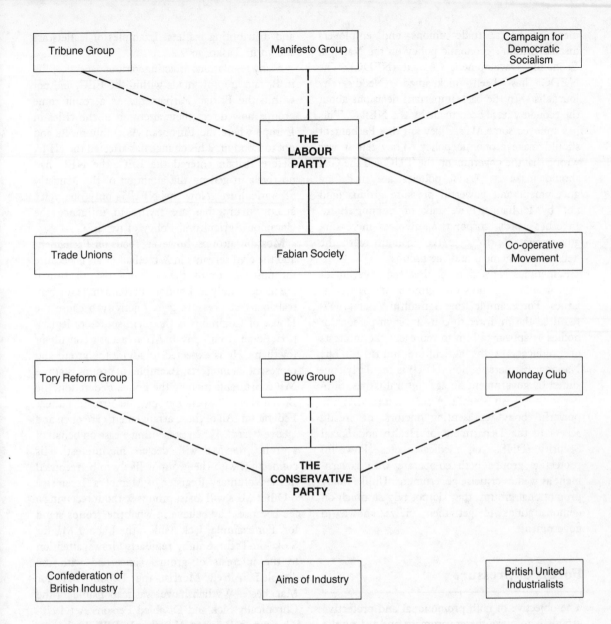

Fig. 9.1 Parties and pressure groups

to rely on *indirect* methods to gain support for their cause. For example, they may try to influence public opinion and hope that this affects government policy.

The reason that protective groups have easier access to government is because government depends on the information they can give. Although the government has the civil service to help provide information and advice, protective groups often have **expertise** which is not found elsewhere. Since the civil service only provides information for the government, opposition parties depend on information from protective groups.

Part of the work of government is to settle disagreements between particular groups. It is for this reason that the CBI, representing thousands of firms, and the TUC, representing millions of workers, are consulted by government. Government ministers, trade unions and employers discuss Britain's economic policy on the National Economic Development Council (NEDC). The NEDC has been nicknamed 'Neddy' by journalists. In the past, important decisions about the economy have been made by the NEDC. This has annoyed some MPs. They felt that Parliament should make economic policy. They felt it was wrong that the government, the TUC and the CBI should make it. When policies are made by government and powerful pressure groups (and not by Parliament) we talk of **corporatism**. In other words, corporatism involves increasing government control over the economy with the help of management and the unions.

Sometimes legislation requires the government to consult with pressure groups on particular issues. For example, the Agriculture Act (1947) required the minister to consult 'such persons or bodies as appear to him to represent the interests of producers in the agriculture industry.' The National Farmers' Union (NFU) is regularly consulted by government on agricultural issues. Similarly the British Medical Association (BMA), the powerful body representing doctors, has ready access to the Department of Health and Social Security (DHSS) on medical issues. Powerful protective groups both co-operate with government as well as criticise government. Unlike many promotional groups, they do not rely so much on demonstrations to get their views known to government.

Forms of pressure

The objective of both promotional and protective groups is to make the government and the public aware of their views. Groups believe that this will increase the chances of getting decisions made in their favour. The methods used by groups vary according to (i) the aims being pursued, (ii) the place where decisions are made and (iii) the skills and resources available to the group concerned. Methods include lobbying MPs and using Parliament, making informal contact with ministers and civil servants, and providing data and evidence. Methods can also include organising demonstrations, using the media, paying for advertisements

and distributing leaflets. Examples of leaflets are shown in Taskpage 9.2.

Many regulations affecting various aspects of life in Britain are now made within the EEC, and not within the British Parliament. As a result some groups now direct their attention to the cities in Europe where the European Assembly meets and not to London. This change has affected the NFU. Before Britain entered the EEC, the NFU had no rivals in getting the attention of the Ministry of Agriculture. Now the NFU is only one voice among many that are trying to influence the Common Agricultural Policy of the EEC.

Most big groups, however, focus on Parliament and the civil servants in Whitehall. This is because for most big groups, the decisions that affect them are made mainly in London. Parliament is the central focus of pressure group activity because the House of Commons is the main source of legislation. Some groups pay an MP to act as a consultant for them. He is expected to advise the group and represent its interests. Examples of groups that use MP consultants include the Police Federation, the Bookmakers' Association and the British Timber Federation. All of these arrangements are open and 'above-board'. When presenting a case on behalf of a group, the MP will 'declare his interest'. His connection with the group is likely to be recorded in the Voluntary Register of Members' Interests.

Other MPs will assist groups without receiving a fee because they believe in what the groups stand for. For example, Jack Ashley, the Labour MP for Stoke-on-Trent South, regularly draws attention to the interests of groups concerned with the disabled. Alfred Morris, the Labour MP for Manchester Wythenshawe, was responsible for the Chronically Sick and Disabled Persons Act 1970. This was a **Private Member's Bill**. To have a chance of putting a Private Member's Bill before Parliament, MPs have to win a place in a ballot. When Alfred Morris won a place, he was offered 450 ready-made bills from a variety of pressure groups.

MPs who support pressure groups can make a considerable impact on the House of Commons. In addition to steering Private Member's legislation, they can make a contribution at Question Time, in Adjournment Debates and debates on government bills. They can make a contribution in the various committees of the Commons. All these settings provide opportunities for 'politics by pressure'.

Pressure groups may also attempt to contact ministers and senior civil servants directly to discuss their interests. Some pressure groups will be consulted by government in need of advice before legislation is passed. Groups often send documents, reports and circulars to MPs in order to draw attention to their aims. The opposition parties, who are eager to attack the government's record, rely a great deal on the information provided by pressure groups.

Newspapers and television play an important role in publicising the aims and activities of pressure groups. Large demonstrations often get filmed for TV news programmes. In order to attract TV cameras, some pressure groups do a 'stunt' or have a 'gimmick'. For example, farmers might ride their tractors to Parliament or a famous film star might appear at a conservation meeting. Occasionally a film or TV play has helped a pressure group to publicise its cause. *The China Syndrome* was a film about the risks of nuclear power stations. The Friends of the Earth had argued some of the same points at the **Windscale Inquiry**. The TV play, *Cathy Come Home*, was about the terrible plight of homeless families, and helped Shelter to publicise the problem. In order to get publicity, groups have organised 'sit-ins', 'work-ins' and 'teach-ins'.

Some groups go beyond the law in order to draw attention to their causes. For example, one small group dug up the wicket and poured oil on the turf during a Test Match. Groups are sometimes tempted to go this far because publicity is seen as all-important. They feel that the worst thing that can happen so far as their group is concerned is to be ignored.

Some causes arouse controversy and, for every group that exists with one set of aims, there is another group with an opposing viewpoint. During the period when the government was making up its mind about Britain joining the EEC, there were pro and anti-Common Market groups at work. The Abortion Law Reform Association does not agree with the Society for the Protection of the Unborn Child. The Lord's Day Observance Society is opposed by the Sunday Freedom Association.

Assessment of pressure group politics

For good or ill, pressure groups are part of modern political democracy. But are they, on balance, helpful or harmful to democracy?

We have seen that pressure groups have been successful in providing people with a better life. Old age pensioners have kept their allotments because of pressure group activity. Many disadvantaged groups – the disabled, the mentally handicapped, the homeless – have all benefited from the activities of pressure groups. But do pressure groups represent *all* the interests and ideas in society? For example, the TUC and the CBI represent workers and managers, but who represents the unemployed? The trade union movement and the CBI are wealthy. But those who are unemployed do not have the resources to organise a powerful pressure group.

In other words, groups which represent the most powerful people in society have a great advantage over other groups. Pressure group politics tends to make powerful people even more powerful. The CBI has a staff of 400 full-time employees; the TUC has over 100 employees. The questions arise: do the weaker people in society get left out of pressure group politics? Or if they do take part in pressure group politics, are their interests adequately represented?

Some people are suspicious of pressure groups because much of their work is done in secrecy. These critics do not like the idea of powerful pressure goups and government ministers making deals in private. It is argued that the floor of the House of Commons is where debates should take place, not 'behind closed doors'. Critics of pressure groups feel that pressure group politics has undermined parliamentary democracy in Britain.

Terms used

Corporatism A state in which policy comes from bargains made between government and the major business and labour pressure groups. Parliament would have no policy-making role in a corporatist state.

Expertise Expert opinion or knowledge.

Private Member's Bill Most parliamentary bills originate from government departments. If a backbench MP is one of twenty names drawn in a ballot, he can guide his own legislation through Parliament. Only a small percentage of Private Member's Bills successfully reach the Statute Book.

Sponsored MPs Trade unions affiliated to the Labour party may sponsor candidates for Parliament. If their candidates are selected to represent Labour, the unions will pay up to 80% of the candidates' election expenses. Trade union sponsored MPs meet from time to time to discuss problems and issues related to their unions.

Suffragette movement An organisation of women which had the aim of winning for women the right to vote. The Suffragettes were led by Emmeline Pankhurst and became increasingly militant in the years leading up to the First World War.

Windscale Inquiry The Windscale Local Public Inquiry took place in 1977 when British Nuclear Fuels Limited requested planning permission to build plant in Cumbria to reprocess nuclear waste. The inquiry was chaired by Mr Justice Parker, and it turned into a great national debate about Britain's future energy policy. Interests representing the nuclear industry clashed with Friends of the Earth.

Summary

1 Pressure groups are organisations which seek to influence the decisions of government at local, national and international level.

2 Pressure groups differ from political parties in that their objectives are much narrower and they do not normally seek election to governmental office.

3 Some groups may have close links with political parties, such as the trade unions and the Labour party: others may share similar attitudes and goals, such as the CBI and the Conservative party.

4 There are two main categories of pressure groups:

(a) *Protective* groups. These are mainly concerned with the protection and advancement of sectional interests.

(b) *Promotional* groups. These seek support for a particular cause.

5 There is a tradition of consultation between government and certain well-established groups, e.g. the CBI, BMA and TUC.

6 Groups may attempt to influence political decision-making in a variety of ways:

(a) *directly* through interviews with or deputations to ministers, MPs, and civil servants. Some groups have spokesmen to represent their interests in Parliament.

(b) *indirectly* by demonstrations, meetings, advertisements and publicity through the news media.

7 Pressure groups play an increasingly prominent role in British political democracy. On the one hand, it is argued that they give people an additional voice and help them represent interests which are important to them. On the other hand, it can be argued that the voice of the least powerful groups does not have a fair hearing in pressure group politics.

Questions for discussion

1 In what ways are pressure groups (a) similar to, and (b) different from the major political parties?

2 Examine the various ways in which pressure groups attempt to influence political decisions.

3 Do pressure groups help or hinder the working of democracy in Britain? Are they a useful way in which views can be expressed, or do they give more power to the already powerful groups in society?

4 Collect information about a pressure group currently in the news. You will be able to collect material from newspapers, from weekly journals such as the *New Statesman*, *The Economist* and the *Spectator*, and from TV and radio programmes. Design a poster for your classroom which (i) explains the aims of the pressure group concerned,

and (ii) shows the ways in which the group is trying to change government policy.

5   Design a board game which is based on pressure group politics. 'Snakes and Ladders' or 'Monopoly' might provide you with some ideas which you can adapt. You will probably find it useful to base your game on throwing dice. Depending on where players land they might pick up 'good luck' cards (your group is invited to meet an interested MP – move on 3 places) or 'bad luck' cards (a rival group has appeared on TV – move back 6 places). Can you think of any better ideas for your game? Also you will need to think of an appropriate name for it.

PART THREE

Participation in politics: elections, voting and public opinion

10

The electoral system

In this chapter we examine the political developments that have led to our present situation in which all men and women in Britain over the age of 18 have the right to vote. However, 'one person, one vote' does not necessarily lead to representative government. We consider the arguments of those who say the British electoral system is inefficient and unfair. Is it true that many votes cast in an election are 'wasted'? Does the present system give the Labour and Conservative parties too many MPs in Parliament, and the Liberals and SDP too few? There are many calls to change the present system. This chapter discusses some of the alternatives to Britain's 'first past the post' method. One change that has taken place in British politics is the increasing use of referenda. We examine in detail how these referenda have worked in practice. Finally, we examine what happens on election day, and how the winner of an election will represent the people.

The growth of democracy

As early as Anglo-Saxon times, kings were expected to take the advice of their most important lords. This consultation was continued after the Norman Conquest, when the word 'council' was used to describe the meeting where the king took the advice of his barons. By the thirteenth century, however, kings found it useful to seek advice from a wider range of people from different parts of the country. So in addition to the barons, the king summoned knights from each shire (county) and burgesses (citizens) from each major town to his 'talking session' or 'parliament'.

By the middle of the fourteenth century the representatives of these sections of the community were important enough to meet separately from the lords. The Norman-French word for communities is 'communes'. And so the 'House of Communes', or 'House of Commons', was born. It is important to note two things about the early days of Parliament. First, the House of Commons represented distinct classes of people who were elected on a *geographical* basis. Secondly, each community chose its representatives. The king did not have the right to choose them.

Parliament gradually gained in power and influence. It became so strong that it could control the king's finances, influence his policy and limit his freedom to choose his ministers. But as Britain entered the Industrial Revolution, Parliament became less effective in representing the geographical communities. The Industrial Revolution created entirely new communities and gave rise to a new class of wealthy men. Also, some of the communities that had flourished in the Middle Ages had declined or even disappeared during the eighteenth century.

Pressure grew to change the system. You can see from Fig. 10.1 that in 1800 only 3% of the population had the right to vote. The Reform Act of 1832 increased this to 5% and **redistributed seats** to take into account changes in where people lived. Until 1867 only people who owned a considerable amount of land and property had the right to vote. The Reform Act of 1867 gave most householders in towns the right to vote. In 1884 householders in rural areas were given the right to vote.

It seems incredible to us today that women were rated as 'second class citizens' who did not have the right to vote. In the last chapter we referred to the Suffragette movement which campaigned in the early part of this century for 'votes for women'. The Representation of the People Act of 1918 was a major step forward since it gave all women over 30 the right to vote. But it was not until 1928 that the voting age for women was lowered to be the same as for men. In 1971, the voting age for both men and women was lowered to 18. These developments, giving the right to vote to more and

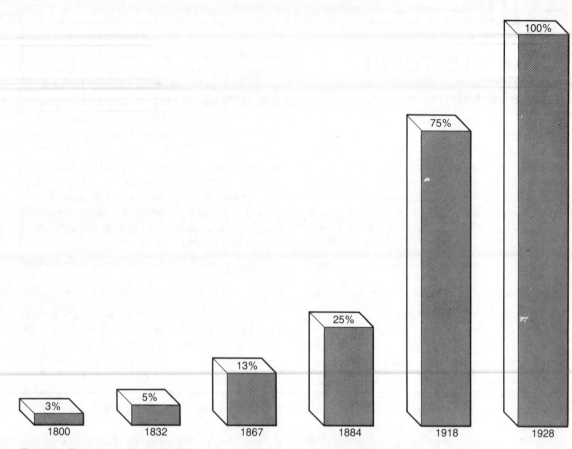

Fig. 10.1 Percentages of population over 21 years in age entitled to vote, 1800–1928

more people, are stages in the **extension of the franchise**.

Is our electoral system fair?

Elections play an important role in democratic government. You will remember from chapter 3 that elections are an 'input' to government as well as providing government with 'feedback'. Also elections are vital to the concept of 'representation' which links government and the governed. In chapter 4 we saw how the representative democracy in modern Britain differed from the direct democracy of ancient Athens. Since elections play such a key role in democratic politics, it is vital that they should be fair. In this section we shall

examine the strengths and weaknesses of Britain's electoral system.

An election is a way of gathering together people's preferences or choices about who they would like to represent them. Elections are an important input to government which will influence the type of policies that will be followed. Our electoral system is called the 'simple majority' or 'first past the post' system. The winner of an election for Parliament or local government is the candidate who gets most votes. The successful candidate does not have to gain a fixed proportion of the votes cast. One more vote than his nearest rival is enough to win. Supporters of Britain's electoral system argue that although it is a fairly crude method for getting MPs or councillors, it has a number of advantages. These advantages are:

(i) It is a straightforward system that everybody understands. The complicated systems used in some countries probably confuse many voters.

(ii) It provides a clear result with an outright winner.

(iii) In most general elections it produces strong government with good **working majorities** in the House of Commons. This leads to stable government in Britain. In contrast many other countries with different systems, notably Italy, suffer from weak and unstable government.

Opponents of Britain's 'first past the post' system disagree with these arguments. They say that the arguments are misleading because:

(i) Other systems vary in their complexity. The different voting system used to elect members to the Northern Ireland Assembly in 1982 did not confuse voters. American and Australian electoral systems are more complicated than Britain's and yet the voters in these countries are not at all confused.

(ii) The results are not clear and often the winner is not an outright winner. Often the winner in Britain's elections has fewer votes than the votes of rival parties added together. In other words, there are many constituencies where more people voted against the winner than voted for him.

(iii) Britain has not had a history of strong and stable government. For almost half of this century, Britain has had **coalition or minority governments**. Often governments have been elected with very small majorities (e.g. Labour's majority in 1964). Britain had a **hung** Parliament after the February 1974 general election. In 1977-8 there was a 'Lib-Lab' pact formed to keep Labour in power.

Critics of Britain's 'first past the post' system argue that there are other disadvantages. First, they suggest that parties can win seats and even form the government without doing particularly well in terms of total votes cast. A computer test showed that Labour could be an outright winner of a general election with a majority of seats in Parliament, and yet only win 34% of the vote. You can see from Table 10.1 that recently no party forming the government has won more than 50% of the **popular vote**. In fact, no party has won more than half the vote since 1935.

Second, it is argued that Britain's electoral system does more than over-reward the party which is 'first past the post'. It also over-rewards the party which comes second, whilst under-rewarding all other parties. The results of the 1983 general election in Table 10.2 show how well Labour did in winning seats bearing in mind their share of the vote. On the other hand, the Alliance with 26.0% of the vote won only 3.5% of the seats. Even in the February 1974 general election when the Liberals had won 19.3% of the vote, they still only won 2.2% of the seats.

The final criticism of the present electoral system is that it is creating two Britains. The Conservatives are strong and getting stronger in the south, with Labour strong and getting stronger in the north. As a result, Conservative cabinets contain very few ministers from northern constituencies and Labour cabinets have few ministers representing southern constituencies. It is argued that such a split cannot be in the interests of the country as a whole.

The statistics in Tables 10.1 and 10.2 show that the share of seats won by the various parties does not accurately reflect national support for those parties. Indeed, on two occasions since the Second World War a party has formed the government be- ▷ p.92

Table 10.1 Percentage of voters supporting the government party

	Percentage of voters who got the government they voted for
1951	48.0
1955	49.7
1959	49.4
1964	44.1
1966	48.0
1970	46.4
1974 February	37.2
1974 October	39.2
1979	43.9
1983	43.5

The results of the last general election for three adjoining constituencies in this imaginary part of England were as follows:

BRENNANSBY

Basil Burham (C)	26 074
Harry Parkhouse (Lab)	10 921
Ernest Berridge (SDP/All.)	16 004

ROBINSTOWN

Denis Gardner (C)	8 494
Barbara Jones (Lab)	18 990
Stephen Matthews (SDP/All.)	15 426

SUTTON-BY-THE-SEA

Peter Swish (C)	19 420
Dick Scrivens (Lab)	24 077
Michael West (Lib/All.)	22 558

Under the 'first past the post' system these three constituencies returned one Conservative and two Labour MPs. Was this an accurate reflection of political opinion in the whole area?

Calculate the vote for each party and suggest what result would have been more accurate. Name the candidates who you think should be the MPs for the area.

Performance of the Labour and Conservative parties in recent general elections

	Percentage of seats won in the Commons by Labour and Conservative	Percentage of the popular vote won by Labour and Conservative	Percentage of the total electorate voting Labour or Conservative
1951	98.5	96.8	79.9
1955	98.8	96.1	73.8
1959	98.9	93.2	73.4
1964	98.6	87.5	67.4
1966	97.9	89.9	68.1
1970	98.0	89.5	64.4
1974 February	94.2	75.1	59.2
1974 October	93.8	75.0	54.7
1979	95.8	80.8	61.4
1983	93.2	71.8	52.2

These statistics show the number of seats that Labour and Conservative have won between them in each general election since 1951. You can see the percentage of the popular vote that the two parties obtained between them in each election. Also you can see the support the two parties received from the electorate as a whole. For example, in 1979 Labour and Conservative won 95.8% of the seats in the Commons. They obtained 80.8% of the popular vote between them. Finally, Labour and Conservative were supported by 61.4% of the electorate who were entitled to vote in 1979.

(i)   In which general election did Labour and Conservative win least support from those who were entitled to vote and those who actually voted?

(ii) Do these statistics suggest that we have a two-party system in Britain, or a multi-party system?

(iii) In what ways do these figures support the case for electoral reform? In what ways do these figures support the case for keeping the 'first past the post' system?

Table 10.2 Results of the 1983 general election under simple majority and true proportional representation

Party	Vote	Actual allocation		Allocation under true proportional representation	
		No. of seats	Seats (%)	No. of seats	Seats (%)
Conservative	12 991 377	397	61	283	43.5
Labour	8 437 120	209	32	184	28.3
Liberal/SDP Alliance	7 775 048	23*	3.5	169	26.0

*Liberals 17 seats, SDP 6 seats

cause it had a majority of seats even though more people voted for the main opposition party. There have been many calls for the reform of our electoral system – especially from the minority parties which feel they are treated unfairly. It is however understandable that the major parties who benefit under the present system oppose change.

The alternative systems

In the elections to the European Assembly in 1979, Britain was the 'odd man out'. All other countries of the EEC used a system of **proportional representation** (PR) to vote for their Euro-MPs. Britain kept to the 'first past the post' system. There are many alternative electoral systems to the one used in Britain. Many of them differ from each other in some detail. There are, however, five main alternatives. These are:

(i) Second ballot

This system involves two elections, one a week after the other. It is used in France. If, in the first election, no candidate has more votes than all the others put together, a second election is necessary. In between elections, some of the lesser candidates may withdraw (or be forced to do so). They may advise their supporters who to vote for in the second election. The second election will have fewer candidates and the winner may well have an overall majority. This system allows the expression of second choices by those voters whose first

choice did badly. Its use in France was a deliberate and largely successful attempt to reduce the number of seats won by the more extreme parties.

(ii) Single Transferable Vote (STV)

This is a complicated system which requires large constituencies represented by a number of members. In the election, voters have to place the candidates in order of preference. The counting of votes takes longer than in our present system. But it enables second, third and subsequent choices to be taken into account in determining the final result. Under STV Britain might be divided into approximately 130 constituencies, and each constituency might have 5 MPs. In any constituency a candidate would need one fifth of the votes in order to be elected. If he won more than a fifth of the votes, the 'surplus' would be transferred to other choices of candidates. In this way, few votes are wasted under STV. Also the final result of the election reflects closely the division of opinion in the electorate. Under our present system many votes are 'wasted'. For example, in a safe seat the winner may receive a majority of several thousands. Those votes above and beyond the number required to win are in a sense 'wasted'. In a rather different way all the votes cast for the losers are wasted. The votes cast for parties or individuals other than the one who wins get nothing at all.

A disadvantage of the STV system is that the counting of votes is very complex and some express the worry that it may confuse some voters.

However, it seems to work effectively in countries where it is used, such as the Irish Republic.

(iii) Alternative Vote

This system uses a single-member constituency similar to our present system. But the voters have to number the candidates in order of preference. If a candidate gets more than 50% of the votes cast, he is elected. If no candidate reaches this figure, the candidate with the fewest votes is eliminated. All the votes of those who chose him first are transferred to their second preference. If this still fails to produce a figure over 50%, the next lowest candidate is eliminated and the process is repeated until a clear result is achieved. This method of voting is used in Australia.

(iv) Proportional Representation by lists

This system also involves the country being divided into large constituencies. In each constituency the parties put forward a list of candidates. The voters then vote for the *parties* of their choice and the seats are won in proportion to the votes. For example, if there are twenty seats in a constituency and party *A* wins 50% of the votes, the first ten names on its list will be elected. If party *B* has 5% of the votes, then only the first name on its list will be elected. As there will always be some odd votes left over, the system can be made even more logical by having a national list to allocate seats using up all the remainders. This system is very accurate in arithmetical terms but it has disadvantages. It removes the identification of a member from his constituency. Voters vote for parties, not for individuals. It makes life difficult for independent candidates who are not in the political parties. Finally, PR tends to encourage the growth of small break-away parties which are likely to be more successful under this system than under 'first past the post'.

(v) The Additional Member system

This method is the one that the Hansard Society Commission on Electoral Reform would like to see in Britain. It combines elements of both the PR list system and the traditional 'first past the post'

system. The Hansard Commission recommended that there should be a House of Commons with 640 MPs. Three-quarters of these should be elected in single-member constituencies, with the other quarter being 'additional' members. Each elector would have only one vote but this would count for both the election of the candidate in the constituency and for the *party* to which the candidate belongs. The 480 single-member constituency seats would be decided by the existing 'simply majority' method. But the 'additional' seats would be shared nationally in proportion to the total share of the vote won by each party and the number of seats won in the constituencies. For example, if the share of the total vote showed that a party was entitled to 150 seats but it had only won 140, it would be allocated an additional 10 seats. Sharing out the additional seats helps to correct the imbalance or unfairness produced by the election in the constituencies under the simple majority rule.

Referenda

In a representative democracy, important decisions are taken by those who are elected to office. However, some people feel that, on really important issues, the people themselves should be asked to decide directly. Putting a question directly to the electorate is known as a **referendum**. Holding a referendum is fairly common in some states of the USA and in some European countries. In Britain the referendum has been used on a national scale only once. It has also been used once only on a regional scale, although referenda have been held on a local level on several occasions.

The only national referendum in Britain was held on 5 June 1975, when the electorate was asked whether or not Britain should stay in the EEC. A total of 63.2% of the electorate voted with 17 378 581 wishing Britain to remain in the EEC and 8 470 073 wishing to withdraw. One body of opinion felt that it was right to hold a referendum on this issue. Britain's membership of the EEC had led to major constitutional changes. Britain had given up sovereignty over many issues. Important decisions were now made in Europe and not in Parliament. It was felt that these issues were important enough for the people to have the final say. But other people felt that the referendum was unnecessary. They argued that there had been no referendum in 1972 when Britain joined the EEC, and holding one in 1975 seemed irrelevant. Some argued that the referendum was a fraud since it was not a fair test of people's views. The government wanted Britain to stay in the EEC and used its resources to persuade people to vote 'yes'. Opponents of EEC membership did not have the same resources as the government and many felt that the issue was not debated on equal terms.

The second important constitutional issue which was settled by referenda was **devolution**. It had been proposed that Assemblies in Scotland and Wales should be empowered to make decisions on certain policies affecting their own countries, instead of having these matters dealt with in Parliament. Before these proposals could go ahead, however, it was decided that 40% of registered electors in Scotland and Wales must support the principle of devolution. A simple majority was not sufficient. When the Scots voted on 1 March 1979, 62.9% **turned out**. Of these, 51.6% said 'yes' to devolution and 48.3% said 'no'. Although more Scots said 'yes' than 'no', only 32.5% of all those entitled to vote said 'yes'. This was not enough support for the devolution proposals to be put into practice. In Wales the turnout was 58.3% with three-quarters voting against devolution. In fact, only 11.8% of registered voters in Wales wanted to see devolution.

Referenda have been held on a local scale in Wales to decide whether the people of a district wished alcohol to be sold within their area on Sundays. Sunday closing was imposed on Wales in 1881, and in 1961 the first referenda were held on the issue. They have been held every seven years since. After the most recent referenda held in 1982, only two districts remain 'dry' on Sundays.

Another local referendum was organised by Coventry City Council in 1981. The electorate were asked to choose between spending cuts amounting to £2 million or a one-third increase in rates. Only a quarter of Coventry's electorate turned out to vote in the referendum (or 'Public Consultation Process' as it was called). Voters supported spending cuts by a majority of seven to one.

The British experience with referenda is not altogether successful. But the fact that they have been used recently will encourage suggestions that they should be used again. Would more use of referenda strengthen direct democracy in Britain? Some people worry that they are not as useful in a democracy as they might seem. For example, did those people who voted in the EEC referendum really understand the issues involved? Did the Coventry voters who chose spending cuts have any idea which services would be lost? It is always easy to get people to vote for 'lower rates' or 'less taxes'. But would the same people refuse to vote for 'poorer schools', 'fewer ambulances' or 'lower pensions'?

Finally, some people are concerned about the effect that holding more referenda would have on Parliament. If the electorate are consulted on more and more issues, what role would MPs have? If people present their own views directly, MPs become less important. If MPs become less important, then Parliament becomes less important. The very basis of a representative system of government would be called into question.

Elections and representatives

The conduct of elections is tightly controlled to ensure total fairness. For example, the use of TV and radio is regulated. The political parties have an agreement with the BBC and ITA which gives equal time to the two main parties. The smaller parties get a share of time related to the number of candidates they put forward.

On election day, polling stations are set up. These are often in schools or local halls. Each polling station is supervised by two clerks and often there is a police officer in attendance. Each voter must give his name which is checked against the electoral register. Each voter is then issued with a ballot paper. He or she must then record the vote on the ballot paper, fold the ballot paper, and put it in the sealed ballot box on the clerk's table.

There are heavy penalties for **personation**. In other words, it is against the law to vote in the name of someone else. It is also illegal to attempt to vote more than once.

When the polling station has closed, the sealed boxes are taken to a central hall. Here the boxes are opened, and the counting of votes takes place. The candidates are entitled to watch this taking place and can challenge anything they believe to be unfair. Ballot papers which have been spoilt or incorrectly completed may be discounted. If the result of the counting is close, it may be necessary to have a recount. Sometimes three or four recounts are necessary before the winner of the election is finally declared.

The winner of an election becomes the councillor, MP or Euro-MP. But who is he or she representing? For example, do MPs represent only those people who voted for him? The answer is a definite 'no'. An MP represents *all* his constituents regardless of who they voted for or whether they voted at all. But how can he represent all of the thousands of views held by his constituents? He represents them by voicing what he believes to be in their interests. He represents them by supporting policies which he believes will improve their welfare. Of course, some of the constituents that an MP represents may not agree with his actions. It is important to understand that MPs are not delegates. They are not instructed how to vote in Parliament by the people they represent.

Terms used

Coalition and minority governments A coalition government is formed when two or more parties join together to form a government. Asquith led a coalition government of Liberals, Unionists and Labour from May 1915 to December 1916. He was followed by Lloyd George who led a more successful coalition government. A minority government can be outvoted and defeated if all other parties unite against it. The first Labour governments led by Ramsay MacDonald were minority governments.

Devolution The delegation or passing down of power to take decisions from Parliament to other bodies. The Kilbrandon Report of 1973 recommended legislative devolution to Wales and Scotland.

Extension of the franchise The process of giving more and more people the right to vote.

Hung parliament This would exist after a general election in which there is deadlock because no party or parties are clearly able to form a government.

Personation This occurs when someone pretends to be someone else when voting.

Popular vote The share of the vote that a party gets nationally.

Proportional representation A system of voting in which the number of seats a party wins closely corresponds with the support it receives.

Redistribution of seats This involves the drawing up of boundaries for new constituency areas. This task is done by the Boundary Commission.

Referendum Putting a specific question or questions directly to the electorate for a decision.

Turnout The percentage of the electorate entitled to vote who actually do vote in an election.

Working majority Held by a governing party with a substantial majority of seats in the House of Commons. A small majority puts a government at risk. The death of one or two older MPs could cause a crisis for the government. The majority of the Labour government elected in 1964 fell to one. After the 1966 general election the Labour government had a working majority of 97.

Summary

1 Men and women over the age of 21 had the right to vote in 1928. In 1971 the voting age was lowered to 18.

2 Britain's electoral system is often referred to as 'first past the post' or 'simple majority' system. It is a system which favours the large parties which win elections or come second. It works to the disadvantage of smaller parties.

3 The main alternative methods to 'first past the post' are (i) second ballot, (ii) single transferable vote, (iii) alternative vote, (iv) proportional representation by lists, and (v) the additional member system.

4 The referendum has been used once on a national level in Britain, and once on a regional level. It has been used at local level on several occasions.

The increasing use of referenda has advantages and disadvantages.

5 Councillors, MPs and Euro-MPs represent all their constituents. But they are not delegates.

Questions for discussion

1 What are the advantages and disadvantages of Britain's electoral system?

2 Why do small political parties frequently campaign for electoral reform? Outline one alternative electoral system, giving its advantages and disadvantages.

3 Argue the case for or against further use of referenda at national and local level.

4 Divide your class into three groups. One group must prepare a three-minute 'party political programme' in favour of electoral reform. Another group must prepare a programme in favour of 'first past the post'. These programmes may be recorded if equipment is available, or presented 'live'. The final group must assess the performance of the other two groups. Outline the strengths and weaknesses of the arguments and comment on the way in which they were presented to you. Which group was most persuasive? And why?

11

Voting behaviour

In this chapter we explore recent patterns of voting in Britain. After each general election many statistics are published on how people voted and these help us to understand changes in the way the electorate supports different parties. What do people actually vote for in an election? Do they support a particular candidate, a set of policies, or something else? We examine the idea of 'swing' which enables us to measure changes in voting patterns. More people seem to be voting in ways which are in conflict with their own interests; in recent years voting has not been determined solely by social class. We examine why many workers vote Conservative and why a considerable number in the middle class vote Labour. What leads people to hold particular political opinions or to support a particular party? We explore possible answers to this question by looking at the agencies of political socialisation. We consider why voting in general elections is so different from voting in other types of elections. Finally we must ask why people often vote for parties which they do not fully support.

General trends

After a general election a great deal of information is published about how the electorate voted. The ballot is secret and we can not know exactly which individuals voted or **abstained**, or how they voted. It is nevertheless possible to gain a great deal of information about general voting trends.

(i) Voting for parties

Election studies show that people vote for political parties rather than individual candidates. The party seems more important to voters than the party leader. For example, in 1979 Mr Callaghan (Labour leader) was more popular than Mrs Thatcher (Conservative leader), and yet the Conservatives won the election. At that time Mrs Shirley Williams was a leading member of the Labour government and was generally popular. But when the tide of opinion turned against Labour in the general election, she lost her seat.

Independent candidates who do not have the backing of a major party usually do very badly in elections. There have been a number of exceptions to this rule. For example, in a by-election in 1973, Dick Taverne stood as an independent candidate in Lincoln and defeated the official Labour party candidate. Dick Taverne won the seat again in the February 1974 general election but lost it in the October 1974 general election. Eddie Milne won at Blyth as an Independent Labour candidate in the February 1974 election. But he too lost to the official Labour candidate in the October election.

(ii) Voting for policies or images?

The detailed policies presented by the political parties seem to have little influence on the way people vote. One survey showed that 21% of Labour supporters agreed more with Conservative policies than they did with Labour policies. The figure was not so startling for Conservative supporters. Only 7% of them preferred Labour policies to Conservative ones. On many issues, such as law and order and immigration, Conservative and Labour supporters have similar views.

If people are not clear in their minds about the policies of various parties, what is it that they support? People seem to have a general image of what the parties stand for. These images are built up over many years and express what people think the parties have done and will do. **Political images** do contain much that is true, but they are also vague and may be inaccurate on some points.

Labour's image tends to be that it is 'for the working class' and 'for the trade unions'. Labour is seen as the party which is 'for the social services and welfare state'. Some of this image is accurate. But Labour governments have ended free collective bargaining, attempted to control union activity by law, and raised many National Health Service charges. The Conservative image is that it is 'for the middle and upper classes' and is 'for big business'. Conservatives are seen as taking a tough line on law and order and immigration. This image has persisted even though crime rates rose to their highest levels under a Conservative government. Conservative policies, which have enabled many Commonwealth citizens to become British passport holders, also seem to depart from the traditional image. No matter how vague or inaccurate these images are, they seem to influence many voters.

(iii) The 'swing'

General patterns of turnout and 'swing' are shown in Table 11.1. The swing between the two major parties has been relatively small. Under our present electoral system a swing of 3% can cause thirty or forty seats to go to another party in the Commons. The swing is a measurement of support as it moves from one party to others in two successive elections. It is expressed in percentage terms, and calculated by averaging the percentage gain by one party and the percentage loss by

Table 11.1 Turnout and 'swing' in general elections 1950–79

Year	Turnout (%)	Swing (%)
1950	84.0	Con. 2.8
1951	82.5	Con. 0.9
1955	76.8	Con. 2.1
1959	78.7	Con. 1.1
1964	77.1	Lab. 3.1
1966	75.8	Lab. 2.6
1970	72.0	Con. 4.7
1974 February	78.1	Lab. 1.3
1974 October	72.8	Lab. 2.1
1979	76.0	Con. 5.2
1983*	72.7	Con. 6.0

Source: Based on a table in Butler and Kavanagh, *op. cit.*

* Comparison between 1979 and 1983 in terms of swing is complicated by the decline of the two-party system and by the major redistribution of constituency boundaries which took place between the two general elections. Major changes affected 526 of the 635 1979 constituencies.

others. For example, if the Conservatives polled 47% of the vote in one election compared with 42% in an earlier election there is a gain of 5%. If the corresponding votes for Labour were 48% and 44%, there is a loss of 4%. Averaging the two results is a swing to the Conservatives of 4.5%. The idea of swing is most useful when only two major parties are involved in elections. Now the two-party system in Britain has given way to a multi-party system, swing is harder to calculate and less helpful in showing general trends.

The swing can be used to compare results of individual constituencies as well as the country as a whole. In any one election the swing is likely to be in a similar direction; that is, towards Labour, towards Conservative or towards the Liberal/SDP Alliance. At the same time there will be regional variations. There is a different pattern north of a line drawn between the Mersey and the Humber, and the southern part of the country. In 1979 the swing to the Conservatives was nearly twice as high in the south as it was in the north. The northern swing averaged 4.2%, whereas in the south it averaged 7.7%.

Some people think that swing is a misleading way of looking at election results. For example, imagine an inner-city constituency which is being redeveloped. Many people living in poor accommodation who voted Labour in the last election are rehoused on a new estate in another constituency. The following election will record a 'swing to the Conservatives' in the inner-city constituency. The constituency with the new housing estate will show a 'swing to Labour'. Yet nobody need have changed the way he voted. All that has really happened is that people have moved.

The idea of 'swing' can also give a false view of the 'floating voter'. Swing encourages the idea that floating voters are a group of people who keep changing their vote from one election to the next. For example, a swing of 6% to Labour might be interpreted as being made up of 6% of voters who now vote for Labour but previously voted for other parties. In reality, some of the 6% swing to Labour will be caused by (i) people who did not vote in the previous election but who now vote Labour, and (ii) people who voted for other parties in the previous election but who do not vote in the current election.

Voters are not as strongly rooted in the habit of voting for one party as in the past. Recent election studies show that the electorate is more **volatile** than it was.

Social class and voting for the major parties

You can see from the statistics below that a large majority of the middle class voted Conservative and a majority of the working class voted Labour in the years following the last war.

	AB (%)	C1 (%)	C2 (%)	DE (%)
Conservative				
1945–58	85	70	35	30
Labour				
1945–58	10	25	60	65

Source: M. Abrams, 'Class, Distractions in Britain' in *The Future of the Welfare State*, Conservative Political Centre, 1958.

But by the 1970s neither majority was so large as it was before. Labour and Conservative got almost equal support from social class C2. Conservatives do much better than Labour with ABC1 voters, and Labour does better than Conservatives with DE voters. Only half of trade unionist voters supported the Labour party despite Labour's links with the trade union movement.

The link between social class and voting was not easy to explain. Why do so many middle-class voters support the Conservative party? It might be said, for example, that the majority of the middle class had a 'good' education, and many have secure and well-paid jobs. They will not rely on the welfare state to the same extent as the working class; many will purchase a private education for their children, will pay for private health care, and will contribute to a private pension scheme. The middle class will therefore tend to be satisfied with society as it is. The middle class did not see any great need for change. Middle-class voters supported a party which wanted society to remain as it is. They supported a party which wanted less state intervention, which invests less in the wel-

Table 11.2 How Britain Voted in 1983

		Con. %	Lab. %	Alliance %
Gender	Men	42	47	55
	Women	31	27	16
Age	18–24 years	25	24	28
	55 + years	46	31	40
Trade Union	Members	26	39	32
	unemployed	27	29	26

		Percentage of electorate	Con. %	Lab. %	Alliance %
Social Class	A/B/C1 Middle class	41	42	30	33
	C2 Skilled workers	30	33	45	41
	D/E Semi-skilled; unskilled; casual workers; pensioners	29	22	26	24

fare state, and which wanted greater individual prosperity.

Many in the working class had an inadequate education. Their jobs tended to be insecure and boring. Many members of the working class depended upon the social services provided by the state to maintain a basic standard of living. Many in the working class therefore wanted to see society changed in a way which will help poorer people. They supported a party which would strengthen the welfare state and which would reform society in order to increase equality.

In many ways these explanations why people vote the way they do are too simple, as well as being misleading. For example, some people have pointed out that the Conservative party is not a party which wants society to stay as it is. As we saw in chapter 8 many Conservatives want to see **radical** change in Britain. In other words, many Conservatives want policies which will alter the economy, the welfare state, law and order, etc., a great deal. On the other hand, Labour governments have never produced conditions of greater equality between the different social classes. In addition, the arguments themselves are too simple, for there are many people whose voting habits are not governed by these general ideas.

(i) Middle-class socialists

Someone who has a middle-class job and lives in a middle-class area, but whose parents are working-class is more likely to vote Labour than someone with a completely middle-class background. Some middle-class people have jobs which bring them into contact with liberal ideas. Teachers and lecturers tend to vote Labour more than other middle-class occupations. You can see from the table in Taskpage 11.2 that school teachers gave greater support in 1974 to Conservatives than to Labour. But the amount of support Labour receives from teachers is greater than the support received from the legal or banking professions. There are also middle-class people, like doctors or social workers, whose jobs take them into working-class areas where they have direct experience of working-class problems. These people are more likely to vote Labour than middle-class people with no experience of working-class conditions.

There is also a new 'middle class' that has grown in numbers since the last war. It is made up mainly from people who work in administering the public sector. In other words, this new class includes social workers, health service administrators, local government officers, teachers, lecturers, civil servants, and office workers in the water authorities and other government bodies. Most of these people feel that they have a strong interest in protecting the public sector. They will tend, therefore, to support political parties which favour a strong public sector. For this reason there is considerable support in this new middle class for the Labour party and the SDP.

(ii) Working-class Tories

Since Labour 'is the party of the working class', it seems odd that in successive elections a third or more of the working class have voted Conservative. Researchers have felt there is a need to explain why so many working-class people do not appear to vote in their own interests. The main explanations are:

The 'deferential' Tory voter There are some working-class Tories who are **deferential**. This means that they see Conservative leaders, many of whom have an upper-class background, as 'born rulers'. They believe that Conservative leaders have the right education and 'breeding' which makes them fit to govern. Labour leaders are not thought to have this sort of background, and therefore are seen as less fit to govern. Deferential voters see the Conservative party as the 'natural' governing party.

The 'secular' Tory voter Professor Robert McKenzie and Alan Silver conducted a study in which they identified **secular** Tory voters in the working class. Secular voters support the Conservatives because they agree with their policies. They also see Conservative governments as more likely to increase their standard of living than Labour governments. At the end of the Second World War a Labour government was faced with the task of rebuilding Britain. The standard of living was quite low, and many items of food and clothing remained rationed until the early 1950s. During the period of Conservative government from 1951 to 1964 Britain experienced an **economic boom**. ▷ p.1

TASKPAGE 11.1

Here are two contrasting accounts of the 'floating voter'.

Floating voters may play a crucial part in the British system of government. But they do not seem to be aware of their responsibilities. They do not seem to be drawn from the most politically conscious section of the community. The reasons for their change of allegiance are often trivial. They seem to be less committed, not because of any genuine independence of mind, but more out of apathy.

J. Blondel, *Voters, Parties and Leaders,* Penguin, 1963

What we ... seek to challenge is the inference [impression] that is sometimes drawn that the electorate in Britain is ... somewhat irrational, with two large blocks of voters motivated by unthinking loyalty to their parties and a handful of floating voters whose arbitrary and perhaps capricious [guided by whim and not serious] decisions hold the balance. ... A substantial proportion of the floating voters were well informed and interested in politics.

R. Benewick, A. H. Birch, J. G. Blumler and A. Ewbank, 'The floating voter and the liberal view of representation', *Political Studies,* vol. 17, 1969

(i) Write one paragraph which describes and contrasts these two viewpoints, and one paragraph which evaluates them.

(ii) Are there any students in your class who would describe themselves as being the 'floating voters' of the future? Discuss their reasons for not being committed to one particular party.

TASKPAGE 11.2

Voting intentions of teachers and lecturers in the October 1974 election

Institution	Conservative (%)	Labour (%)	Liberal (%)	Nationalist (%)	Other (%)	Total (%)
Primary school	44	23	27	5	0	100
Secondary school	35	28	28	8	0	100
FE college	34	45	15	6	1	100
Coll. of education	28	32	36	0	0	100
Polytechnic	24	47	29	0	0	100
University	23	44	31	1	0	100
TOTAL SAMPLE	37	30	27	6	0	100

Voting intentions of teachers and lecturers by gender

Gender	Conservative (%)	Labour (%)	Liberal (%)	Nationalist (%)	Other (%)	Total (%)
Male	31	36	27	5	1	100
Female	44	22	27	6	0	100
TOTAL SAMPLE	37	30	27	6	0	100

Voting intentions of teachers and lecturers by age

Age	Conservative (%)	Labour (%)	Liberal (%)	Nationalist (%)	Other (%)	Total (%)
Up to 25	35	29	28	8	0	100
26–29	28	34	30	7	0	100
30–34	25	42	25	8	0	100
35–44	42	28	25	5	0	100
45–54	38	25	33	4	0	100
55 +	64	19	11	3	3	100

Source: Times Educational Supplement and Times Higher Educational Supplement, 1974

(i) In which type of educational institution is there greatest support for Labour?

(ii) In which type of institution is there greatest suport for Conservatives?

(iii) If you were a member of the 'Alliance', why might you be pleased with the statistics shown in these tables?

(iv) In what ways do the second and third tables help you understand the top table? What information is missing from the lower tables which would give you an even greater understanding of the top table?

(i) Using the information given in this chapter, try to describe the 'typical supporter' who might attend each of these two meetings.

(ii) Which of these meetings would be most likely to attract a 'floating voter'? Give reasons for your answer.

(iii) Design a leaflet advertising a meeting of the Conservative party in your village, town or constituency.

(iv) In what ways does the 'image' of the Young Socialists differ from the 'image' of the SDP? In what ways the image of the Conservative party differ from that of the SDP?

(v) To what extent is it true to say that Labour is the party of the working class?

(vi) Why do working-class voters support the Conservative party?

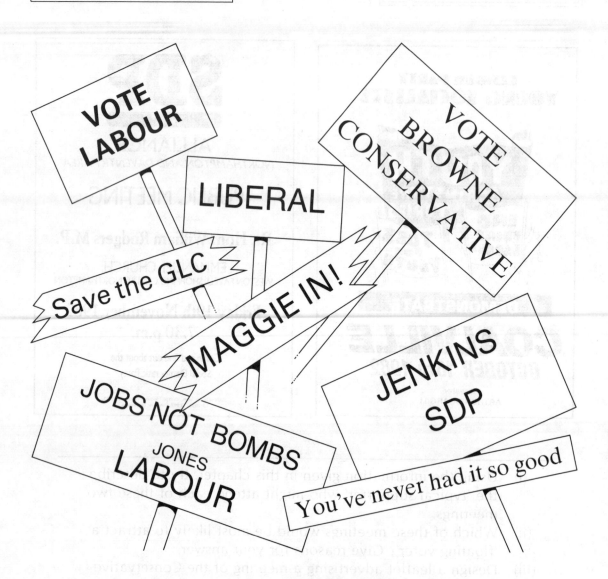

Write a short article for an Australian newspaper giving an account of the last general election in Britain. Make sure that you:
  (i)   describe the main issues in the election campaign
  (ii) provide the results of the election
  (iii) comment on the new government
  (iv) explain any unusual developments, such as the success of a third party, the exceptional accuracy of opinion polls, or the influence of a particular event on the campaign.

The standard of living for all people rose quickly. The Labour governments of 1964–70 experienced some prosperity, but after devaluation of the pound in 1967 the standard of living began to fall slowly. Therefore over a long period, Conservative government was linked in people's minds with prosperity. Labour governments were linked with economic hardship. Secular voters in the working class see this link, and vote Tory in the hope that their standard of living will be improved.

Embourgeoisement thesis This ugly phrase is linked in some ways to the idea of secular voters. During the 1950s, 1960s, and 1970s, many workers improved their life styles. They enjoyed a standard of living which was beyond the wildest dreams of their fathers and grandfathers. The 'new' working class bought their own homes instead of renting them. They bought many consumer goods, such as cars, TVs, fridges, and so on, and enjoyed holidays abroad. Although their jobs were still working-class jobs, away from work they enjoyed middle-class life styles. Some argued that these workers would now see themselves as middle-class and vote Conservative. This **self-image**, it was said, would weaken traditional support for Labour, but it was shown that their support for Labour remained strong. It was no longer based on traditional loyalties, however, but on what they saw as their own best interest.

Social class and the SDP

A survey of the initial support for the SDP was published in March 1981. It suggested that in terms of age and social class, SDP supporters reflected society as a whole. Geographically, SDP support was even throughout the country with the exception of Scotland. Here it was weaker but, despite this, Roy Jenkins won Glasgow Hillhead in a by-election in 1982 for the SDP/Liberal Alliance. Some researchers feel that support for the SDP will come from the 'new' middle class. In terms of individual party membership, the SDP recruits from the professional and managerial middle classes. Fifty-seven per cent of members come from the middle class as opposed to seven per cent from the working class.

Dealignment and realignment

The changes that have taken place in voting behaviour have been described as *dealignment* and *realignment* by political scientists. Dealignment refers to the way support for the political parties is rooted in social class. As we have seen, in the past it could be said that Labour was the party of the working class and the Conservatives were the party of the middle class. Table 11.2 shows that by 1983 there was considerable dealignment between political party and social class. Most dealignment occurred between Labour and its traditional supporters, the working class. Only 32% of skilled workers and 41% of semi-skilled and unskilled workers voted for the Labour party.

Why has dealignment occurred between political party and social class? This is a difficult question to answer. However, it seems clear that the class structure itself has changed considerably in the last

Table 11.3 The 'new' and 'old' working classes

	New working class			Old working class		
	Owner occupier %	Works in private sector %	Lives in South %	Council tenant %	Works in public sector %	Lives in Scotland or North %
Con.	47	36	42	19	29	32
Lab.	25	37	26	57	46	42
Alliance	28	27	32	24	25	26

Source: Guardian 13.6.83

thirty years. In their book, *The Fragmentary Class Structure*, K. Roberts and his colleagues argue that the working class has changed. Many working-class people now see themselves as being middle-class. Since they see themselves as middle-class, they vote the way middle-class people vote. The authors suggest that the mass media are biased against the working class and the trade unions, and that this has undermined the confidence of working-class people in themselves and in working-class organisations. In addition, the working class has become split into (i) those people who are members of strong trade unions and who earn relatively high wages, and those who are members of weak trade unions and who earn low wages, and (ii) those who own their own homes, and those who rent their homes. Added together, all these changes have weakened the links between the working class and the Labour party.

As we have seen, the major change in the middle class has been the growth of a 'new' middle class alongside the old. The new middle class is one which is largely based on people who work in the public sector – such as health authority workers, social workers, teachers and civil servants. Erik Olin Wright has studied this class and argued that it is in a 'contradictory class location'. The contradictory class location of this group can be illustrated with the example of university lecturers. They work in the public sector. There is a very small minority of Marxist lecturers, with the overwhelming majority being middle-class in outlook. Yet, as the recent education cuts have shown, lecturers are not much safer from the threat of redundancy than factory workers. In other words, a 'contradiction' exists between the political views of lecturers (which are middle-class) and their job security (which is similar to working-class conditions).

The two-party system does not fit in with these changes in the class structure. For example, the policies of the Labour party on issues such as nationalisation and council house sales no longer reflect what many working-class people want. The contradictions of the new middle class mean that neither Conservative nor Labour will necessarily win its support. Although its members are middle-class in outlook, they will not favour Tory policies aimed at cutting back the public sector. This is because their jobs depend on a large public sector. Although Labour supports the public sector, its hard-left extremist image will stop many of the new middle class from voting Labour.

The second process which political scientists have been studying for a decade or more is referred to as realignment. This concerns changes in the line-up of the political parties. From 1950 onwards there has been a steady decay in the two-party system. We saw in Taskpage 10.2, for example, that in 1955 96% of the voters voted Labour or Tory. This represented nearly 74% of the total electorate. In October 1974 only 75% of the voters voted Labour or Tory. This figure represented almost 55% of the total electorate. In 1974 there were over 40 MPs who were neither Labour or Conservative. Political scientists talked of 'multi-party' Britain.

The major realignment appeared to occur in March 1981 when the SDP was launched. The SDP formed its alliance with the Liberals in the following June. There was a series of spectacular by-election victories, but by-elections are not a good guide to what happens in general elections.

Political socialisation and voting

We discussed the effects of socialisation in chapter 2. Political socialisation is that part of the general socialisation experience which is concerned with learning about politics and power. Political socialisation occurs when people learn about their political role in society. Like general socialisation, political socialisation differs from one individual to another. The political ideas and values which are passed on to some people are quite different from those passed on to others. Long before a child starts to think about political issues, he or she will hear about law and order, strikes, education, etc. from parents. The sources of political learning are sometimes called the **agencies of political socialisation**. The main ones are:

(i) The family

Fifteen or twenty years ago it was true to say that when a person reached voting age, he or she would almost certainly vote for the same party as the parents. Parents do not usually **indoctrinate** their children. In other words, parents very rarely try to force their own views on their children, or try to force them to support the same party. Political socialisation happens without people really being aware of it. Political socialisation is something which is normal in families. A survey published in 1971 showed that 90% of young people whose parents voted Conservative also supported the Conservative party. And 75% of the young people whose parents voted Labour also supported the Labour party.

These strong political links between parents and children can be explained in a commonsense way. For example, a child born into an upper middle-class Conservative voting family is likely to go to an independent school. He or she is likely to follow a professional career, in law for example, and is likely to vote Tory. The Conservative political values obtained from the family are reinforced by the type of education and the choice of job. Such a person is likely to remain a loyal supporter of the Conservative party. In contrast, a child from a working-class Labour-voting family who leaves school at 16, takes a manual job and joins the TGWU is likely to vote Labour. His education, job and union membership reinforce his support for Labour.

However some socialisation experiences can conflict with each other. This can be seen in the case of a boy from a working-class Labour-voting family, who wins a scholarship to Oxford and who becomes a senior officer in the army. His socialisation will be complicated since some experiences conflict with others. His education and job will bring him into contact with political attitudes which are very different from those he learnt in his family. These new attitudes may be strong enough to change his early support for the Labour party into support for another party.

(ii) Social groups

The group of people we mix with influence our views. In turn, we influence the views of others in the group. The influence of a person's neighbourhood was shown to be small in a survey conducted in Luton. Seventy-nine per cent of affluent workers who lived on council estates voted Labour. Seventy-two per cent of workers who lived on private lower-middle-class housing estates voted Labour. In this case, having lower-middle-class neighbours seemed to have some influence on working-class voters. Several surveys showed a strong link between membership of a trade union and voting Labour. The Luton survey showed that, in 1964, 79% of working-class Labour supporters were trade union members. Table 11.2 shows how the trade union link with support for Labour had weakened by 1983.

(iii) Mass media

The research of Joseph Trenaman and Denis McQuail showed that television seemed to make little impact during an election campaign. They found that TV did not increase people's understanding of issues to any extent. According to Trenaman and McQuail, newspapers simply reinforced the political views of the people who bought them. For example, 89% of Tory voters read a newspaper which supported the Conservative party. Only 11% of Tory voters read a paper which supported Labour. Sixty-seven per cent of Labour voters read a Labour paper and 33% read a Conservative paper.

Past studies have shown that election campaigns appear to have little influence on the way people vote. A survey in 1959 showed that over 80% of the voters had decided which party to vote for before the campaign began. But is this the situation today? The electorate of the 1980s is far more changeable and support for the parties can alter a great deal during a campaign. Professional advertising agents are able to create impressive **propaganda**. Propaganda is political information which usually contains an element of truth, but which also distorts the truth. Politicians are amateurs in the field of advertising, and generally they produce less effective party political broadcasts than advertising agents. In 1979 a firm called Saatchi and Saatchi handled Conservative publicity. One of their most successful posters was of a string of actors in a dole queue, with the slogan 'Labour isn't working'.

(iv) Religion

In *Politics in England*, Richard Rose concluded that '... the chief significance of religion for political socialisation today is its absence of influence'. It is certainly true that research into the influence of religion has produced confusing results. For example, one study showed that more Anglicans voted Conservative than non-Anglicans; another study showed that fewer Anglicans voted Conservative than church-going Protestants.

A study in Dundee conducted by J. M. Bochel and D. T. Denver was published in 1970. The two researchers noted how difficult it is to measure 'religion'. For example, a person can say he is 'Church of England' yet never go to church or even think about religious issues. Another person can say he is 'Church of England' and be a committed Christian who goes to church regularly and may be a sidesman. Clearly these two people would have widely differing views on religious behaviour. Taking this into account, Bochel and Denver found that religious denomination was fairly closely linked with party support. Table 11.4 shows that the Church of Scotland was closely associated with support for the Conservative party. Support for Labour was very closely linked with Roman Catholicism.

Voting in local government elections

Turnout in local government elections is lower on average than turnout in general elections. Turnout has varied from 14% to 89% in local elections. A high proportion of candidates are elected unopposed, that is to say, they face no rival candidates. Table 11.5 shows the turnout and percentage of councillors returned unopposed in recent local government elections.

Voting in the elections to the European Parliament

The first elections to the European Parliament in June 1979 had the second largest electorate in the world. (The largest electorate is in India.) Nine countries voted in Europe at the same time. Britain voted to elect 81 MEPs. The results of Britain's results are shown in Table 11.6.

Alan Brier's study of the European elections in

Table 11.4 The Scottish vote in the 1966 general election, by denomination

	Conservative	Labour
None (%)	21	79
Church of Scotland	59	41
Roman Catholic	7	93
Other	52	48

Source: J. M. Bochel and D. T. Denver, 'Religion and Voting: a critical review and a new analysis', *Political Studies*, vol. 18, 1970.

Table 11.5 Turnout and unopposed candidates in local government elections

	Year	Councillors returned unopposed (%)	Poll (%)
English metropolitan counties	1973	4	37.1
	1977	1	40.2
Non-metropolitan counties	1973	12	42.6
	1977	12	42.3
English metropolitan districts	1973	3	33.4
	1978	1	36.1
English non-metropolitan districts	1973	12	38.6
	1978	7	42.3

Source: T. Byrne, *Local Government in Britain*

Table 11.6 UK result of direct elections to the European Parliament (excluding Northern Ireland)

	Votes	% of total votes	Seats	% of seats
Conservative	6 508 481	50.6	60	76.9
Labour	4 253 210	33.0	17	21.8
Liberal	1 690 600	13.1	0	0
Nationalist	331 235	2.5	1	1.3
Others	90 318	0.7	0	0

Source: Alan Brier, 'The direct elections to the European Parliament 7 June 1979', *Teaching Politics*, vol. 9, January 1980

Britain showed the low turnout of only 32.1%, with the lowest in Liverpool (23.7%) and East London (20.4%). Apart from two London seats, all Labour's 16 seats were won in South Wales, the North of England and Clydeside. The responses of the media, electorate and parties to these elections were unenthusiastic. As usual, the Liberals were disappointed. They gained 13.2% of the votes but failed to win a single seat.

Voting in by-elections

There are very few general points that can be made about by-elections. They can produce 'freak' results. Often by-elections record a massive 'anti-government' protest vote. Third parties, such as the Liberals, can do well in them. Calculations after one by-election in 1981 showed that if the same swing occurred in a general election, the House of Commons would be made up of 501 SDP/Liberal MPs, 113 Labour MPs and one Conservative.

Tactical voting

We normally assume that a person votes for the party he supports. On the surface, it seems unreasonable for a person to do otherwise. Yet a person may have a good reason for voting for a party which he does not really support. For example, a Labour supporter in a Conservative constituency may feel that Labour has no chance of winning in the coming election, but he wants the Conservatives to lose. He knows that the Liberal/SDP candidate has much more support than the Labour candidate so he eventually votes for the Alliance, believing this to be the best chance of beating the Conservatives. Tactical voting involves switching a vote from one party to another in order to stop a third party winning. In this example, the person's vote for the Alliance would have been a tactical vote.

Terms used

Abstain To decide not to vote.
Agencies of political socialisation The social sources of most of our political learning. The family and school are seen as the most influential agencies of political socialisation.
Deferential Having respect for what is seen as the superiority of another person or group. Belief that these superior people are 'born to govern'.
Economic boom A period of high economic growth, low unemployment and rising living standards.
Indoctrinate Attempt to teach a particular idea (or doctrine).
Political image A politician or a political party may project a political image. The image is made up from (i) information, and (ii) the way people react to this information.
Propaganda The passing on to the people of information which favours a particular party or country. If propaganda is to be successful, it must be believed by the people. Therefore it must contain some truth, even if many of the 'facts' are slanted or distorted.
Radical Wanting major changes or reforms.
Secular In the political sense, this word refers to a voter who calculates which party will do most for him before he registers his vote. His vote therefore is based on this calculation and not on habit or deference.
Self-image How a person sees himself or herself.
Volatile Changes quickly.

Summary

1 Most of the electorate vote for political parties rather than individual candidates.

2 The 'swing' is a measurement of the movement of support from one major party to others in successive elections. Some people criticise 'swing' for giving a misleading view of how support for the parties changes.

3 Patterns of social class and voting behaviour are becoming less clear-cut. Many working-class people vote Conservative, and a smaller but still considerable number of the middle-class vote for Labour or Liberal/SDP.

4 The way people vote is influenced to some extent by their political socialisation. A person's family, friends, religion and the mass media are likely to influence the way in which he or she understands politics. Political socialisation experiences do not necessarily reinforce one another and determine which political party will be supported. Such experiences may conflict with each other.

5 Voting in by-elections, local government elections and the elections to the European Parliament is not an accurate guide to the way the electorate will vote in the next general election.

6 Tactical voting is likely to take place on a large scale when a third party looks strong enough to break up the two-party system.

Questions for discussion

1 'Women vote Conservative to a greater extent than men do.' What evidence is there for this statement? See Table 11.2 and Taskpage 11.2 for information to use in your answer.

2 Is 'swing' a useful guide for understanding the mood of the electorate?

3 'A person's family, education and job will determine the way he will vote.' How true is this view of political socialisation?

4 Discuss experiences which may have influenced the way you think about politics. Your outlook may have been influenced by such things as living abroad for a period, knowing someone who is active in politics, seeing a film or TV programme, or by your own reaction to a political decision.

5 Local government affects all our lives and yet relatively few people vote in local government elections. Discuss why this might be. Why do we tend to treat national politics as important but local politics as unimportant?

6 'Since the election of MEPs to the European Assembly was such a flop, Britain should abandon them in the future and save a great deal of money. MEPs could be appointed by the parties in proportion to each party's strength in the Commons'; 'Voting in the European elections will gradually build up our identity of being "Europeans". Future generations will see themselves as not only being British, but also being citizens of Europe. This can only cause good.' Discuss these conflicting viewpoints. Attempt to argue for one side even if you do not really support that point of view.

7 Examine the relevant tables in this chapter and comment on links between the age of voters and party support.

12

Public opinion

This chapter examines the nature and measurement of public opinion. Public opinion polls, based on the results of a small sample of the electorate, measure what the whole electorate thinks. Polls measure opinion in a scientific way. Recent polls have been very accurate in predicting general election results but on other occasions they have been wrong. What sort of things can go wrong and cause the polls to predict an inaccurate result? We examine some of the errors that can arise. Some countries ban opinion polls during election campaigns because of the influence they might have over the voters. We examine these possible effects, and identify elections which may have been influenced by the polls. Finally, we consider the influence of opinion polls on government.

What is public opinion?

Some MPs feel that they can measure public opinion simply by meeting and talking to people. They feel that they can sense the mood of their constituents and build up a reliable picture of public opinion. Other MPs may feel that public opinion is expressed clearly in the many letters they receive in the post from the public. Newspaper editors often feel that they reflect public opinion in their papers. **Editorials** give opinions on issues in the news. Also the editor of a paper will receive many letters from readers, some of which will be published.

Political opinion polls also claim to measure the public's attitudes. Usually opinion polls give us information about people's **voting intentions**; that is, about the way people think they will vote. Polls also provide information about the popularity of various politicians, and about public reaction to political issues.

How accurate are opinion polls?

Public opinion polls were first used in the USA. In one famous case, an opinion poll made a big mistake in predicting the winner of the 1936 presidential election. The *Literary Digest* magazine sent over 10 000 000 **questionnaires** to people whose names were taken from telephone directories or car registration lists. The result predicted by the poll was that Republican Alf Landon would become America's next President. George Gallup, who set up the American Institute of Public Opinion, interviewed only 3000 people and correctly predicted that the Democrat Franklin D. Roosevelt would remain President. How could a **survey** of 10 million be less accurate than one of three thousand?

The *Literary Digest*'s **sample** was biased. Since it was based on people who owned telephones or cars, it reflected the opinions of the more wealthy individuals. The views of poorer people who were less likely to have phones or cars were not included. But poorer people would, of course, be voting in the election. Gallup's sample was small but it was **representative**. In other words, the 3000 people interviewed by Gallup was a fair cross-section of the whole electorate. It included rich as well as poor voters. Because Gallup's sample was representative, it did not matter that it was small.

Opinion polls had a good record of success in Britain until the 1970 general election. They had correctly predicted the winner of each election since the war. In 1970 nearly all the polls predicted that Labour would win, and Marplan gave Labour an 8.7% lead over the Conservatives. Only the ORC poll gave the Conservatives a 1.5% lead over Labour. In the event, the Conservatives won the election with a 2.4% lead over Labour. How could Marplan, Gallup, Harris and NOP get the 'wrong' result when measuring public opinion? In the following sections we will examine some of the problems which pollsters face.

The science of polling

There are about 40 million people entitled to vote in Britain but some polls interview only a thousand people in order to predict how the 40 million will vote. The opinion polls can get a representative sample by a number of methods:

(i) Random sample

People are interviewed at random in the street. This is a fairly simple way of sampling. It is not biased because everyone stands the same chance of being interviewed.

(ii) Stratified sample

This method tries to account for differences in the electorate. For example, interviews might take place in towns and villages to take account of urban and rural differences.

(iii) Quota sample

This is probably the most accurate type of sample. The proportion of men and women, middle-class and working-class, young and old, etc., is the same as in the electorate as a whole.

The problem of bias

Even if a poll is conducted carefully, the results can still be biased. All pollsters recognise that their results might be a little inaccurate because of sampling error. The difference between the average answer in the sample of people interviewed and the average answer in the whole population is known as the sampling error. If Labour and Conservative were running neck and neck in an election campaign, a small sampling error could lead to predicting the wrong result.

The questions that are asked of the public have to be carefully worded. They must not be too complex or abstract. For example, in *Political Opinion Polls*, Frank Teer and James Spence gave an illustration of a question which was not always understood. When asked whether Britain should stand under America's nuclear umbrella, some people thought it was a question about a new type of weather protection. The questions that are asked must not be biased themselves. Teer and Spence point out that if you ask people 'Did you fulfil your civic duty by voting in the last general election or not?', you will get a biased answer. Most people want to appear respectable, and so answer 'yes'.

It is possible to ask 'leading' questions. These are questions which tend to lead people towards giving a certain answer. For example, a leading question would be 'Are you in favour of the Government keeping troops in Northern Ireland?' There is no mention in the question of alternative policies. Thus people are guided into agreeing with the policy mentioned in the question. On the other hand, if you were to ask 'Should the Government interfere with the running of the economy' you would have introduced another type of bias. The word 'interfere' is biased. Generally speaking, we do not like people who 'interfere' with things. Even if the questions are free from bias, they can produce the wrong results if they are not asked correctly. It is important that interviewers used by the polling organisations are given a full training.

Finally, the polls can appear wrong even if they are right. This is because the electorate can change its mind fairly quickly. The polls might be right on the day that they interviewed their samples, but opinion may have changed within the next few days. If there is a last-minute change of opinion during an election campaign, it may occur after the last poll was taken. Generally speaking the nearer a poll is taken to the actual time of voting the more accurate it is likely to be.

The influence of polls on voters

In some countries opinion polls are banned during election campaigns. This is because it is thought that polls have an influence on the way people vote. The 1967 Speaker's Conference on Electoral Reform recommended that polls should be banned in the 72 hours running up to election day. This suggestion was not accepted by the government and polls are still free to publish their results throughout the campaign. If polls do influence voters, what are the effects?

▷ p 1

TASKPAGE 12.1 — Ranking the importance of certain problems facing Britain, 1969–72

Q: What do you think is the single most important problem facing Britain today?

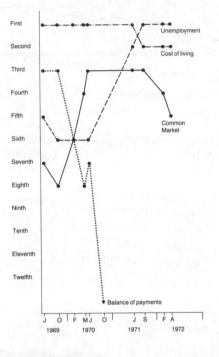

Source: F. Teer and J. Spence, *Political Opinion Polls*

Opinion polls sometimes measure the public's attitudes towards issues. In this graph you can see what the public thought was the most important problem facing Britain from 1969 to 1972. What issue do you think the public would see as the most important problem today? Collect the opinions of your teachers and parents to see what answers they give, but bear in mind that the views of your teachers and parents may not be the same as the public at large. Why is this?

(i)   What was the exact question people were asked in the survey conducted between 1969 and 1972?

(ii) Which issues did the public feel fell from importance during the survey?

(iii) Why did the Common Market move from being the seventh and eighth most important issue in 1969 to the third most important issue for much of 1970 and 1971? The answer to this question can be found in this chapter.

TASKPAGE 12.2

Final poll predictions in the 1983 general election campaign

Fieldwork	Publication Date	Place	Poll	Con. %	Lab. %	Alliance %	Con. lead %	Sample size
6-7 June	9 June	D. Express	Mori	47	26	25	21	867
7 June	9 June	Sun	Audience	45	23	29	16	1100
			Selection				18	2003
7-8 June	9 June	D. Telegraph	Gallup	45	27	26	21	567
7-8 June	9 June	Observer	Marris	47	25	26	20	1335
8 June	9 June	Guardian	Marplan	46	26	26	21	1082
8 June	9 June	Northcliffe	NOP	47	25	26	16	1101
8 June	9 June	Standard	Mori	44	28	26	15	
				43	28	26	15	

(Adapted from The Economist 11.6.83)

(i) Which poll or polls would you say were most accurate in predicting the election result?

(ii) Did the size of sample influence the accuracy of the various polls?

(iii) In what ways might opinion polls influence a Prime Minister's decision to call a general election?

(iv) In what ways might opinion polls influence the results of a general election?

(v) How can public opinion be expressed other than in opinion polls?

(i) The bandwagon effect

Opinion polls show which party is the most popular. This information might encourage some more people to vote for it and, as the party increases in popularity, still more people decide to support it. If people like being on the 'winning side', then polls might produce this bandwagon effect. The early popularity of the SDP and the spectacular by-election victories of the Alliance may have been caused by the bandwagon effect.

(ii) The boomerang effect

This works in the opposite direction to the bandwagon effect. If the polls show that one party is going to be the clear winner, then some voters will feel sorry for the 'underdog' and switch support away from the winning party to one of the other parties. Other people see that their party is winning in the polls, and become so confident that their party is going to win that they do not bother to vote. The loss of the 1970 General Election by Labour could have been because the polls gave Labour a good lead over the Conservatives. Many Labour voters thought the result of the election was a foregone conclusion and felt it was not worthwhile voting.

The influence of polls on government

Polls get mentioned a good deal in the mass media and in Parliament. Does this mean that they influence government? Certainly the polls reflect public opinion and could act as a useful means of communication between the people and government.

However, the record of government shows that polls have little influence. For example, public opinion did not seem to influence the policies of various governments wanting Britain to join the EEC. A low-point of 36% in favour of British entry in 1962 did not alter the government's application for British membership. A low-point of 40% in favour did not seem to affect the government's application in 1967. The 70% who opposed entry in 1971 did not seem to influence the government's determination to take Britain into the EEC.

Politicians tend to quote opinion polls only when they are in agreement. Richard Hodder-Williams reported that Richard Crossman's view was: 'I am only completely convinced of the findings of the Gallup Poll when they confirm my own impression of what the public is thinking.' If the polls contradict what a politician believes, he will tend to ignore them.

On the other hand there is a moral argument which says that the government should sometimes ignore public opinion. A government which simply reacted to public opinion might well be failing in its responsibilities. A former Prime Minister, Sir Harold Wilson, once observed: 'If a Government has embarked upon a policy it believes to be right, it should stick to it despite hostile, short-term reactions.'

It is important to note that a public opinion poll is not the same as a referendum. Governments do not treat polls as referenda. Before voting in a referendum people will have given the issue considerable thought and may have discussed it with others. The answers people give to an interviewer in the street may not be thought-out or informed. This is an important reason why polls have little influence on government decision-making.

Terms used

Editorials You will find the editorial towards the centre pages of most newspapers. The editorial will give the paper's view on three or four current issues. If there is one important issue in the news, the whole of the editorial may be taken up with it.

Questionnaires These are forms which ask a series of questions and record the answers given. The questionnaire may be completed by an interviewer in the street. The questionnaire is sometimes referred to as the 'interview schedule'. Some questionnaires are sent through the post and are filled in directly by the person who is answering the questions.

Representative sample We may want information about the millions of people who make up Britain's population. But it is not practical to interview them all in order to get this information. It is possible to interview a small percentage of the population in order to find out about all of them. However, the small percentage must be representative of the total population. The opinions and beliefs of this representative sample will reflect the opinions and beliefs of the population at large.

Survey A study to get certain information either about the whole population or particular parts of the population. In chapter 6 we looked at a survey conducted by Dr Robert Stradling into the political awareness of school leavers. Surveys such as this will include only a small percentage of the population that is being studied.

Voting intention This is the way a person thinks he or she will vote at the next election. It is possible, however, that the voting intention is never carried out. By the time the next election comes the person may have decided to support a different party or have decided not to vote at all.

Summary

1 Public opinion can be measured in a number of ways. The most scientific way of measuring public opinion is by the use of public opinion polls.

2 In order for polls to be accurate measures of public opinion, pollsters must interview a representative sample of the electorate.

3 Polls will give biased results if the questions are worded wrongly or if the interviewers are poorly trained.

4 Polls might influence voters in different ways. The 'bandwagon effect' encourages people to vote for the party shown as winning in the polls. The 'boomerang effect' encourages people not to support the winning party.

5 Polls are used arbitrarily by politicians. There is little evidence to show that government is influenced by public opinion polls when making policy.

Questions for discussion

1 Do you agree or disagree with the proposal to ban opinion polls during the last three days of an election campaign? Give reasons for your view.

2 In what ways does the public opinion poll result on an issue differ from a referendum on that issue?

3 Should government make a greater effort to take public opinion into account when making policy? What are the advantages and disadvantages of more responsive government?

4 Devise your own questionnaire in class which measures support for the political parties or views about an issue. Poll the opinions of pupils during lunch break. Analyse the results. Discuss the problems you faced in writing the questionnaire and conducting the poll. Assess how accurate the results of your poll are likely to be.

PART FOUR

The machinery of government

13

The prime minister

In this chapter we examine the office of prime minister. The prime minister is the most important politician in Britain, and much of the reporting in newspapers and on television is concerned with what the prime minister has done or said. Many politicians may wish to become prime minister, but very few achieve their ambition. Those who do get right to the top in politics are a select group, and yet they have little else in common. The personalities of prime ministers have differed a great deal, and that has influenced the way they have approached their work. As leader of a political party and leader of the country, their responsibilities and powers are extensive. They have to choose who will be in the Cabinet, decide what the Cabinet will discuss, and declare what the Cabinet has agreed on. To accomplish all this the prime minister has a surprisingly small staff of civil servants. The chapter concludes by considering the case for and against the establishment of a separate Prime Minister's Department, which would assist in keeping an overall view of government.

Head of government

The prime minister is the head of government. In many countries the head of government is directly elected by the people but this is not the case in Britain. Here the prime minister is a Member of Parliament and depends on the support of the majority in the House of Commons. This means that the prime minister is the elected leader of the party which has obtained a majority of seats in a general election. As we have seen, sometimes general elections do not produce an overall winning party. In these cases, the prime minister leads a coalition or minority government.

Prime ministers face very similar problems in government, yet the office has been held by very different types of people. Whilst Lloyd George dominated his Cabinet, Baldwin frequently fell asleep during his Cabinet meetings. A similar contrast in personalities can be found in post-war prime ministers. The Labour prime minister from 1945–51 was Clement Attlee. He was a very mild and quietly-spoken man who was less dominant than some of his Cabinet colleagues such as Stafford Cripps or Ernest Bevin. He was a skilful prime minister who conducted Cabinet meetings efficiently despite the presence of these strong-minded ministers. Winston Churchill became prime minister once again in 1951. Having been Britain's wartime leader, he had a tough 'bulldog' image. He was followed by Anthony Eden who had a glamorous image rather like a film star. In spite of his long experience as Foreign Secretary, he did not enjoy success as prime minister. After Eden retired through ill health, he was replaced as Conservative prime minister by Harold Macmillan. Macmillan took a great personal interest in foreign policy. He was a rather aloof prime minister who dominated his Cabinet. He was a leader who had personal charm but could also be politically ruthless. He was followed by Sir Alec Douglas-Home, a man from an aristocratic background who was not a dominant force in his Cabinet.

Labour's election victory in 1964 brought to office a man from a different background. Harold Wilson was younger than his predecessors, had a modern, efficient image and was interested in technology. He was a skilful politician who could normally outwit his opponents with ease. In 1970 Edward Heath, another young prime minister, was appointed. Heath was associated with Britain joining the EEC, a policy close to his heart. On other issues, his government did 'U-turns' and changed policies. When Harold Wilson retired in 1976, he was replaced by James Callaghan. Callaghan was a jovial, down-to-earth prime minister who was nicknamed 'Sunny Jim'. Britain's first female prime minister was Margaret Thatcher. ▷ p.1

The decision to build Concorde

The first Cabinet meeting:
One of those present (favourable to Concorde) describes the line-up as follows: the Treasury was solidly opposed; so, broadly speaking, were the 'social' ministers, who resented the order of priorities which massive expenditure on Concorde seemed to imply. On the other side were ranged the 'Europeans' (i.e. the Foreign Office ministers and Christopher Soames, Minister of Agriculture), and the 'technologically-minded' – Sandys, Thorneycroft, Marples (Transport) . . . .

The second Cabinet meeting:

The story of the second and final Cabinet has passed into Whitehall folklore. The Prime Minister was in reminiscent mood. He told his colleagues about his great aunt's Daimler, which travelled at the 'sensible speed of thirty miles an hour', and was sufficiently spacious to enable one to descend from it without removing one's top hat. Nowadays, alas! people had a mania for dashing around. But that being so Britain ought to 'cater for this profitable modern eccentricity' [odd habit]. He thought they all really agreed. No one seriously dissented. It was all over in a few minutes.

Jock Bruce-Gardyne and Nigel Lawson, *The Power Game*, Macmillan, 1976

The Defeat of In Place of Strife

The meeting of the full Cabinet began with the Prime Minister reporting on all that had passed with the TUC. He gave it as his judgement that the credibility of the Government required it to legislate if the TUC would not legislate through its own rules. He proposed that he should inform the TUC of the Cabinet's decision to this effect the next day. Barbara Castle followed in total support. The Prime Minister then moved to consult his Cabinet colleagues in the usual fashion. But for once he was cut short. The Chief Whip is not a member of the Cabinet although he attends its meetings. Normally he does not speak unless spoken to or requested by the Prime Minister to make a contribution. But Robert Mellish is not a man to stand on constitutional formality. . . . 'Prime Minister, before you consult your colleagues of the Cabinet I feel you and they should hear what your Chief Whip has to say. . . .' He went on to speak the blunt truth as he saw it. There was not a hope of this measure passing, the party would not stand for it, the loyalists were in revolt. . . . His unscheduled intervention had a powerful effect. Several Ministers began their contributions: 'In view of what the Chief Whip has said. . . .' Harold Wilson watched his Cabinet crumble before his eyes. . . . At the end Wilson and Castle were virtually isolated. Harold Wilson was quiet in the way that he is when he is really angry. The Cabinet was refusing to authorise him to threaten the TUC with legislation. It wanted him to settle on whatever terms he could obtain from the General Council the next day.

Peter Jenkins, *The Battle of Downing Street*, Charles Knight, 1970

(i) Describe the differences between the Cabinet meetings chaired by Harold Macmillan and Harold Wilson on the occasions detailed above.

(ii) In what ways might the personalities of these two prime ministers account for the differences you have described?

(iii) Discuss in class whether or not the examples above were 'typical' Cabinet meetings.

Thatcher names her special defence adviser

The appointment of a civil servant from the Ministry of Defence with special responsibility for defence within the Prime Minister's Office was announced by 10 Downing Street yesterday.

The creation of the post, to which Mr Roger Jackling has been appointed, immediately fuelled further speculation about the development of Mrs Thatcher's office to give her greater personal power.

The announcement about Mr Jackling, a 39-year-old assistant secretary who was intimately involved in the Falklands operation – and was awarded the CBE in the Falklands Honours List – was made at the same time as the official confirmation of the appointment of Sir Anthony Parsons as adviser on foreign affairs.

Sir Anthony is the former UK Ambassador to the United Nations who retired in July and who is said to have made a great impression on Mrs Thatcher, in particular during the critical discussions surrounding the handling of the war with Argentina.

It was the news of this intended appointment which led to rumours earlier this month that Mrs Thatcher was planning to establish a Prime Minister's department at No. 10. This is a suggestion that she has firmly rejected, asserting that she has a private office but that this does not represent a separate department.

She has, however, expressed recognition of the need for her to strengthen the personal advice she receives about foreign affairs and about defence.

In choosing an adviser on defence Mrs Thatcher is demonstrating again her concern about the growth in the degree of support for unilateral disarmament in Britain and in Europe. Significantly, Mr Jackling, who is an expert in nuclear policy and something called crisis management, had been dealing with non-NATO defence policy at the Ministry of Defence.

There were rumours recently that the former Permanent Secretary at the Ministry of Defence, Sir Frank Cooper, was to be appointed to Downing Street, and some of Mrs Thatcher's ministers began to express private disquiet.

The Foreign Secretary, Mr Francis Pym, said in public that in his view the creation of a Prime Minister's department would be unconstitutional.

It was emphasised yesterday that the appointment of Sir Anthony had been made in consultation with Mr Pym and was designed to facilitate and reinforce contact between Downing Street and the Foreign Office.

It is repeatedly emphasised that Mrs Thatcher has no intention of downgrading the authority of individual departments, or of the civil servants who work in Downing Street. It is an open secret in Whitehall that relations between No. 10 and the Foreign Office are strained, and it seems likely that the two new jobs could exacerbate this.

It is pointed out that the payroll at No. 10 has not increased significantly under Mrs Thatcher's occupancy. When he left office in May 1979, Mr James Callaghan had 65 civil servants and four special advisers working there. When Sir Anthony and Mr Jackling join in January there will be 68 civil servants and five special advisers.

Sir Anthony Kershaw, chairman of the Commons Select Committee on Foreign Affairs and Conservative MP for Stroud, said last night that he was writing to Mrs Thatcher to ask that Sir Anthony should appear before his committee to give evidence.

'This is a new development. The committee, which has a general oversight for foreign affairs, would like to know exactly what is Sir Anthony's role and how he will work with the Foreign Office.'

Guardian, 25 November 1982

(i) What are the names of the two advisers appointed to help Mrs Thatcher, the prime minister?

(ii) On what types of policies will they offer advice?

(iii) Does the prime minister agree that these two posts are the beginning of a Prime Minister's Department?

(iv) Why do other ministers oppose the creation of a Prime Minister's Department?

(v) Give two reasons why the prime minister should be served by a separate department.

(vi) Argue the case against setting up a Prime Minister's Department.

She has a dominant personality, which looked even tougher after her Falklands victory. She is sometimes known as the 'Iron Lady'. Some journalists nicknamed her 'Tina' (There Is No Alternative) because of her refusal to change policies.

Despite their differences, all prime ministers have similar responsibilities. They may vary very much in how well they perform as prime minister, but they all start with similar opportunities. Their powers are very great, yet even they cannot control every aspect of government.

The tasks of the prime minister

The prime minister cannot possibly know what is going on in every department of government, let alone control it. The prime minister's overriding concern is, first, to decide which problems and policies have top priority, and then to ensure that the work of each department is in accordance with the general policies the government is following. In addition to this, the prime minister has a number of specific tasks:

(i) The power of appointment The prime minister's first task on taking office is to appoint the other members of the government. These are drawn mainly from the House of Commons, possibly with a few from the House of Lords. As ministers must answer to Parliament for their actions, it is not practicable to appoint outsiders to ministerial positions. When this is done they have to be found seats in the House of Commons or become members of the House of Lords.

The right to appoint ministers is one which gives the prime minister considerable power. But this power does not mean that the prime minister has complete freedom in choosing the cabinet. As leader of a political party, the prime minister must remember that the party includes people of various shades of opinion. These shades of opinion must be represented in the Cabinet to reassure the party factions that their views will not be ignored. Also there will be a number of important people in the party who will have to be included in the Cabinet. They will either be very able, very popular, very loyal or too powerful to be left out of the Cabinet.

The prime minister has little choice but to invite them to become ministers.

Some senior politicians in the party may have been rivals for the post of party leader, and may still have hopes of becoming prime minister one day. Often these will be included in the Cabinet in an effort to win their support and loyalty.

The prime minister can also dismiss ministers on the grounds of failure, personal feeling, or simply a desire for change. In 1962 Harold Macmillan sacked a third of his Cabinet, and earned himself the nickname of 'Mac the Knife'.

The prime minister's power to promote people to important jobs is sometimes referred to as **patronage**. This power of patronage extends beyond political leaders. It includes the power to nominate civil servants who head government departments, the chairmen of public corporations, archbishops, bishops, and senior judges. Much advice is given on whom to appoint to these positions, but there have been occasions when the prime minister's own view was decisive.

(ii) Leading a team Richard Crossman, who was a Labour minister, described the prime minister as 'the spider in the centre of the web.' This is a good description because the spider must be sensitive to any disturbance in any part of the web. The prime minister's own position may depend on the success of his ministers. If ministers fail, the government is likely to be defeated at the next general election. Yet it will be the prime minister who will be blamed for defeat.

(iii) Chairing the Cabinet Important issues should be brought to the Cabinet for discussion. The prime minister is able to do this because he decides what is to be included in the Cabinet **agenda**. Cabinet discussions are guided by the subjects and issues on the agenda.

The prime minister chairs the Cabinet meeting and announces what the Cabinet has decided. The Cabinet does not vote on many issues. Usually the prime minister sums up a discussion by saying what he thinks the general opinion has been. Naturally this gives the prime minister an opportunity to steer any decision the way he (or she) wants it to go. In the last resort, however, the prime minister must maintain the backing of the Cabinet.

(iv) Leadership in Parliament and the country In

most people's minds, the government is linked with the personality of the prime minister. The mass media underline this by giving more attention to the prime minister's personality and actions than to any other minister. For example, the media portrayed the Falklands conflict of 1982 as 'Mrs Thatcher's War'. The success of the British Task Force was linked to her tough personality. Mrs Thatcher had already gained the reputation of sticking with the same economic policies even when unemployment was reaching record levels.

The **personalisation of politics** has its advantages and disadvantages. When things are going well, it makes the position of the prime minister very secure. The popularity of prime minister will mean that no one can topple him. When things go badly, however, an unpopular prime minister may find that most of his support has disappeared. The task of leading the country is then very much more difficult.

The prime minister's staff

Unlike most ministers, the prime minister does not head a large department. Apart from the Cabinet Office (see chapter 14), only a small number of personal advisers work at No. 10 Downing Street. These include (i) personal secretaries who organise the Prime Minister's daily schedule, (ii) a press secretary who provides information for newspapers and television, and (iii) a political secretary who keeps the prime minister in touch with opinion.

The importance of this staff depends on the use that is made of it. Under Harold Wilson, for example, his political secretary Marcia Williams (now Lady Falkender) was thought to exercise much influence. Mrs Thatcher appointed an academic, Professor Alan Walters, as her personal adviser on the economy.

Arguments for and against a prime minister's department

As we have seen, the prime minister has the task of making sure that the government's many policies work together. In other words, the prime minister has to **co-ordinate** policy-making. This is a very difficult task. Some people argue that more help is needed to do this. They point out that individual ministers have large departments of civil servants to advise them, but that the prime minister is helped by no such organisation. They argue that the prime minister should have his (or her) own department for support. Other people oppose this idea. They fear that the prime minister is already very powerful, and having a separate department would bring even more power. Nevertheless, the beginnings of a prime minister's department was set up by Mrs Thatcher. Taskpage 13.2 explores the origins of this development. It was argued that had Mrs Thatcher been given better advice the Falklands war could have been avoided.

Terms used

Agenda A list of items or business to be dealt with at a meeting.

Co-ordinate To bring together in one general direction; to remove conflict and disagreement.

Patronage The right or power to award office to others.

Personalisation of politics The treatment of politics in terms of personality clashes rather than policies or issues.

Summary

1 The prime minister is the head of government. Individuals with very different personalities have become prime minister. What they have in common is usually long experience in politics and experience as ministers in one or more of the Departments of State.

2 The prime minister's main task is to co-ordinate government. He (or she) has to decide which issues have top priority and to make sure that each department is working towards the same overall goals.

3 The prime minister has the power to 'hire and fire' Cabinet colleagues. In practice, the prime minister's choice of Cabinet members is restricted by political factors.

4 The prime minister draws up the Cabinet agenda and chairs its meetings. The Cabinet rarely

votes on issues, and the prime minister has considerable freedom in determining Cabinet policy.

5 The prime minister has relatively few staff. Some people feel that a Prime Minister's Department ought to be established. Others feel that a separate Prime Minister's Department would give the prime minister too much power.

Questions for discussion

1 'The personality of the prime minister counts for nothing in the way he performs his duties.' How true is this statement?

2 Outline the main tasks facing a prime minister once he has formed his Cabinet. Comment on the problems he is likely to face when attempting to do these tasks.

3 'The prime minister is so important that he should be elected by the people in the same way as the American president is.' Discuss this suggestion in class.

4 Collect newspapers for one week. Cut out all the items which refer to the prime minister, and try to build up a picture of the prime minister's activities during the week in question. Discuss whether or not we expect too much of our prime ministers.

5 Do the media give too much attention to the prime minister? How much do you know about other members of the Cabinet and leading members of the opposition party who form the 'Shadow Cabinet'? Discuss these points in class.

14

The Cabinet

This chapter examines the nerve-centre of government in Britain: the Cabinet. Efficient government depends on policies being co-ordinated. Making sure that all the government's policies fit together is one of the Cabinet's main tasks. How does the Cabinet work effectively in a society which is extremely complex and difficult to govern? The Cabinet Office, the Central Policy Review Staff (until 1983), and Cabinet Committees all contribute in different ways to the efficient running of the Cabinet. In political terms, it is a team of politicians who form the apex of government. The Cabinet works according to a number of rules which sometimes seem to contradict each other. All members of the Cabinet accept responsibility for decisions the Cabinet has made. Yet each individual minister is responsible for the decisions reached in his department. Finally, we consider the relationship between the Cabinet and the prime minister. Where does power really lie in British government?

The nerve centre of government

The government of Britain is made up of about one hundred politicians. This group is elected by the people and can usually depend on the support of the House of Commons. The members of the government are appointed to their positions by the monarch, on the advice of the prime minister. The prime minister is the elected leader of the party which controls the majority in the House of Commons. With rare exceptions, the government will be made up of people who are themselves Members of Parliament or members of the House of Lords.

The government consists of the prime minister, secretaries of state, ministers, ministers of state, parliamentary secretaries, parliamentary under-secretaries of state, law officers and government whips. The different titles for ministers reflect their importance. Many large ministries are controlled by a small team of ministers. The **Secretary of State** will be a member of the Cabinet. Other ministers, including ministers of state, may be in charge of small departments and are not members of the Cabinet. Below them are the parliamentary secretaries who are sometimes referred to as 'junior ministers'. The law officers include the Solicitor-General and the Lord Advocate. Some ministers have unusual names such as Lord President of the Council or Lord Privy Seal –

the most important of these is the Chancellor of the Exchequer, who in other democracies might be called the 'Finance Minister'.

As administering Britain has grown more complex, so the size of the government has grown. Table 14.1 shows the growth between 1900 and 1979. You can see that the numbers in the government have risen from 60 to 107, but that the size of the Cabinet has remained much the same. The Cabinet is simply a committee. It is well known that if committees become too large, they cease to work efficiently. The largest Cabinet which is still effective is made up of around twenty members. This is large enough to allow many different views and interests to be included. If it were much larger, it would take far longer to reach decisions. In wartime, Cabinets have to reach decisions quickly. Consequently wartime Cabinets have had a membership of only five or six.

Table 14.1 The size of government 1900–79

	1900	1920	1950	1970	1979
Cabinet ministers	19	19	18	21	22
Non-cabinet ministers	10	15	20	33	38
Junior ministers	31	47	43	48	47
Total	60	81	81	102	107

Source: D. E. Butler and A. Sloman, *British Political Facts 1900–1979*

The Cabinet

The Cabinet is the committee which is responsible for all key decisions in the government of Britain. In making these decisions, the Cabinet will attempt to coordinate the work of various departments. If different departments work against each other, the end result is confusing and contradictory. Imagine a situation in which one department (such as Industry) was trying to build up the economy of the north whilst another department (such as Transport) decided to invest all its resources in the south. This would be poor government because the policies for the different parts of Britain would be uncoordinated.

Although the Cabinet is an extremely important committee of politicians, it is not remote from the rest of society. The Cabinet will bear public opinion in mind on certain issues, particularly if the next general election is near at hand. The Government Chief Whip attends Cabinet meetings, and he is an important link between the Cabinet and party. He can try to persuade the party's backbench MPs to support the government, and he can also let the Cabinet know what the MPs want the government to do. For example, because of backbench pressure in 1979 and 1981 Mrs Thatcher's government had to withdraw bills on local government finance even though the Cabinet had approved them. In 1969 the trade unions and PLP persuaded a Labour government to abandon trade union laws contained in *In Place of Strife* (see Taskpage 13.1).

One of the most important features of the British system of government is the idea of **collective responsibility**. This means that the government behaves as a team, with all members accepting and defending decisions which the Cabinet has taken. Collective responsibility results in Cabinet members agreeing with government policy in public, even if they have argued against in private. Cabinet meetings are less secret today than they used to be. Consequently collective responsibility has been weakened because the public can learn which ministers support the prime minister and which oppose. Ministers may 'leak' information to journalists immediately after the Cabinet has met. Some publish details of Cabinet meetings in diaries only a few years after leaving office.

Although the Cabinet accepts collective responsibility for its policies, individual ministers accept responsibility for the correct running of their departments. This is known as **individual ministerial responsibility**. In 1982 the Foreign Secretary, Lord Carrington, resigned after accepting responsibility for Britain being taken by surprise when Argentina invaded the Falklands. In 1954 Sir Thomas Dugdale resigned from office in what was known as the 'Crichel Down' affair. Land had been bought from farmers in 1937 for use as a bombing range. After the Second World War the land was passed over to the Ministry of Agriculture and not offered back to the original owners. Naturally the farmers complained and an inquiry revealed a number of blunders. The Minister of Agriculture assumed full responsibility and resigned.

Cabinet meetings

The Cabinet may meet at any time in any place. Normally it meets in the Cabinet room at No. 10 Downing Street. Occasionally it meets in the prime minister's room at the House of Commons. The Cabinet meets at least once a week when Parliament is in session but less frequently when Parliament is in recess.

The business of the Cabinet includes reaching decisions on issues which cannot be settled elsewhere. Business also includes discussion of those important issues for which the Cabinet assumes collective responsibility. Any minister who finds himself unable to agree with what the Cabinet decides must resign from the government. This means a minister needs to object very strongly indeed to government policy before he is unable to accept collective responsibility. He is not going to let a small difference of opinion with the government cause him to sacrifice his post and possibly ruin his political career.

Cabinet business is always tightly organised. This means that decisions can be reached quickly. All the items to be discussed are listed on the agenda, which is circulated to Cabinet members in advance. Traditionally this always begins with any item of foreign affairs which has come up since the last Cabinet meeting. After that the prime minis-

125

ter decides what is to be included. The Cabinet usually discusses all **White Papers** produced by government departments. White Papers contain government proposals on various issues; for example, *In Place of Strife*, referred to in Taskpage 13.1, was a White Paper concerned with trade union laws. Since 1981 the Cabinet has discussed the Chancellor of the Exchequer's **budget** policy before he announces it rather than after. The budget concerns financial policy, and this is an issue which affects the work of most government departments. Finally, the Cabinet considers bills coming from the various departments of government.

Each item on the agenda will be supported by a full briefing. Except in emergencies, papers giving the background information on each item are circulated at least 48 hours before the Cabinet meets. This means that the Cabinet wastes no time on lengthy detailed explanations. Because ministers are already well-informed when they come to a Cabinet meeting, they can concentrate their efforts on reaching a decision.

Cabinet meetings are held in private and their discussions should officially stay secret for at least thirty years. As we have mentioned, however, Cabinet discussions have often been 'leaked' to journalists and printed in newspapers. This sometimes happens when a minister disagrees with his colleagues on a decision. He or she will inform a journalist of what happened in Cabinet. The journalist will publish the story without mentioning who gave him the inside information. A famous 'leak' occurred in 1976. Labour policy planned to introduce a new child benefit scheme. But the Labour government faced financial problems and the Cabinet agreed that it could not afford the new scheme. Reluctantly, the members of the Cabinet decided that the scheme could not go ahead. The Cabinet papers recording this decision were leaked to the *Observer*, and the government was both very angry and extremely embarrassed.

The Cabinet Office

The Cabinet Office makes sure that the Cabinet is efficient in its work. The record of Cabinet meetings is kept by the Cabinet Secretary. The Cabinet Secretary, supported by a staff of 600, makes up the Cabinet Office. Working closely with the prime minister, the Cabinet Secretary prepares the agenda for Cabinet meetings and makes sure that all the appropriate papers are prepared and circulated.

The Cabinet Secretary attends all Cabinet meetings. He is responsible for seeing that all Cabinet decisions are passed on to those who need to know of them. The Cabinet Office, which includes the Central Statistical Office, has strong links with all the departments of government.

The Central Policy Review Staff

Another recent development inside the Cabinet Office was the creation in 1970 of the Central Policy Review Staff (CPRS). Sometimes it was referred to as the government's 'think tank'. When Edward Heath was prime minister he felt that the Cabinet was not suited to looking at long-term policies. The Cabinet was always occupied with discussing issues of immediate importance. There was no committee which looked at Britain's long-term future, so the CPRS took on this task. Edward Heath believed that a group of highly qualified people was needed to study Britain's future. Therefore members of the CPRS were drawn from many different professions; some from industry, some from commerce, and others from administration and the universities.

Until it was disbanded in 1983, the CPRS was rather like a permanent Royal Commission which was concerned with many different issues. Amongst the issues that the CPRS examined were energy policy, race relations, the future of Concorde, and alternatives to the National Health Service. Sometimes the CPRS recommended one policy for the future whilst the minister concerned was following another policy. When this happened, ministers were worried that the CPRS was being used by civil servants to undermine their authority. Tensions of this kind occurred when Tony Benn was Energy Secretary. He chose one type of nuclear reactor for Britain and the CPRS recommended another type.

In 1982 a Think Tank report which considered dismantling the Welfare State was leaked to journalists. This embarrassed the Government and paved the way for the abolition of the CPRS. It is likely, however, that a future government will again set up a body to examine long-term policy objectives. (See Taskpage 23.2.)

Cabinet committees

The Cabinet Office services and supports meetings of Cabinet committees and sub-committees as well as meetings of the full Cabinet. Not a great deal is known about the work of Cabinet committees since it is conducted in great secrecy but it is generally agreed that Cabinet committees are very important in the government of the country. They have grown more important as the amount of work to be done has increased beyond the limits with which the Cabinet can cope.

Cabinet committees are usually chaired by the prime minister or a senior Cabinet minister. Cabinet committees deal with more general areas, while the specific areas are dealt with by Cabinet sub-committees. For example, the prime minister chairs the Economic Strategy Cabinet Committee. Two sub-committees are chaired by the Secretary of State for Industry: the Public Sector Pay Policy sub-committee and the Micro-Economic Policy and Industrial Policy sub-committee. A third sub-committee which deals with civil service pay and the problems which might be caused by strikes in the public sector is chaired by the Lord Privy Seal. Another example of the complicated network of committees is in the area of foreign policy. The prime minister chairs the Defence and Overseas Cabinet committee, and the Foreign Secretary chairs the sub-committee which deals with the EEC.

Other Cabinet committees are *ad hoc*. That is, they are formed to deal with some particular problem which has arisen. They tend to be temporary committees, dealing with a problem only for as long as the problem lasts. The standing and *ad hoc* committees of the Cabinet share one central purpose. They help to make the Cabinet more efficient by doing much of what the Cabinet would do if it had enough time.

Inner cabinets and partial cabinets

Unlike the Cabinet or Cabinet Committees, the 'inner' cabinet is not official. The inner cabinet is an informal meeting of the prime minister with his most senior colleagues in the Cabinet. Although the inner cabinet is not official, its decisions and views are very influential.

Patrick Gordon Walker described the importance of what he called the 'partial' cabinet. He wrote that the 'partial cabinet contains influential members of the Cabinet who can be said to represent it in the sense that collectively they carry very great weight within it.' This definition sounds similar to that of an inner cabinet. But Patrick Gordon Walker argued that a partial cabinet was different from an inner cabinet. He stated, 'Typically a partial cabinet is a standing or *ad hoc* committee presided over by the Prime Minister which may – in matters of great moment [importance] and secrecy – prepare policies in detail and sometimes take decisions without prior consultation with the Cabinet as a whole.' We can say, therefore, that a partial cabinet is the inner cabinet when it meets as a Cabinet Committee.

Prime ministerial or Cabinet government?

Where does power lie in British government: with the prime minister or in the Cabinet? Richard Crossman, a Cabinet minister, said that 'the postwar epoch has seen the final transformation of Cabinet government into prime ministerial government.' Patrick Gordon Walker, who was a member of the same Cabinet, disagreed with this view. He argued that a prime minister does not have as much power as Crossman believed. Gordon Walker thought that the Cabinet was still very important. He argued that 'a prime minister who habitually ignored the Cabinet, who behaved as if prime ministerial government were a reality – such a prime minister could rapidly come to grief.'

The term 'prime ministerial government' has been used to describe a situation in which the prime minister is the major decision-maker. In some ways, the prime minister resembles a president. When he was Foreign Secretary, Lord Home ▷ p.131

The Cabinet Game

The Cabinet Game was devised by Susan Roome and was first published in *Teaching Politics* in 1980. Imagine that you are the new prime minister. You have to choose nine Cabinet members. The various posts are shown below:

Departments carrying Cabinet Office
The Ministry of Defence
The Foreign and Commonwealth Office
The Treasury
The Home Office
Ministry of Agriculture, Food and Fisheries
Department of Education and Science
Department of the Environment
Department of Social Services
Department of Trade and Industry

The eight most popular politicians in your party were elected to the Shadow Cabinet when your party was in Opposition. You also have to bear in mind that some of your most loyal friends expect to be rewarded with a Cabinet post. Finally, only five members of your party have previous experience of being in the Cabinet. All of these people are shown below:

The preferences of the party
The party voted for the following Members as 'Advisers to the Party Executive' at the last Annual General Meeting (i.e. Shadow Cabinet)

1	Leader	You
2	Foreign Affairs	Milton Wright
3	Home Affairs	Anthony Houghton-Smith
4	Financial Affairs	Dame Helen Hepplethwaite
5	Education	Lady Cheryl Forsythe
6	Land and Agriculture	Jeffrey Shallcroft
7	Trade and Industry	Laurence Goldthorn
8	Defence	Robin Currier

Your special friends are:
Reginald Hamilton-Price; Lady Cheryl Forsythe; Milton Wright; Anthony Houghton-Smith.

Experienced Cabinet members are:
Lord Charles Alexander Perriwig; Dame Helen Hepplethwaite; Lady Cheryl Forsythe; Jeffrey Shallcroft; Anthony Houghton-Smith.

(i) Read through the life histories and draw up your Cabinet. Remember that you will need a 'balanced' Cabinet in terms of young and old, experience and 'new blood', party favourites and personal friends.

(ii) Write a brief explanation for each member you include in your Cabinet.

(iii) Discuss your choice of Cabinet members in small groups in class. Examine the reasons why each of you chose different people. Were your reasons similar when you chose the same people?

Life History of Politicians

Dame Helen Hepplethwaite, 72
Roedean, Girton College, read English. Worked for British Council for 20 years, on secondment to the Indian Civil Service. MP for 30 years. Originally Liberal Democrat; Commonwealth Secretary for the Liberal Democrats 5 years; resigned over the Red Sea Affairs. Changed allegiance to Authentic Democrats; Minister of State, Board of Trade 3 years; Chancellor of the Exchequer 4 years; voted by the Party as Shadow Chancellor 5 years in succession. Definitely not a friend of yours, but she is a powerful lady with world-wide connections and popular with the older members of the party.

John Ogleby, 65
Wigan Elementary School. Articled to a Wigan solicitor. Subsequently read for the bar. Became a Barrister practising mainly in the north. Judge on the Northern Circuit 15 years. Withdrew from active judicial service to write books on Law. Became an MP ten years ago.

Lord Charles Alexander Perriwig, 60
Private tutor, Eton, Oxford. Guards 2 years; M15 12 years; Military Correspondent of *The Independent Daily Watch* 18 years; advised your predecessor on defence matters and became Minister of Defence when the former ADP Minister died suddenly. He held the post for 4 years. Voted by the party as Shadow Minister of Defence 3 years in succession before being usurped by Robin Currier.

Theodore Bauchmann, 54
Swansea Modern. Dockworker. Union man for 35 years. Rose to be President of the Union of Dockers in Wales. MP for 10 years on his Union ticket. Noisy backbencher with strong union support. Regular platform speaker at the Annual Party Conference and the Annual UDW Conference. Wants greater spread of the national wealth. Very far left of the Party. Mountaineer. Spokesman for 'Welsh heritage'.

Robin Currier, 54
Army Cadet School. Joined up and rose through the ranks of the Royal Engineers. Army 28 years. Retired from the Army as a Brigadier. Came into Parliament 10 years ago at the general election. Minister of State for Defence 4 years. Tolerates Lord Perriwig. Shadow Minister for Defence 2 years in succession.

Lady Cheryl Forsythe, 50
Guildford School, Somerville College, Oxford. Read Law and went into local government from University; small private income; part-time lecturer at London School of Economics. Zealous politician. He has been an MP for 18 years. Your closest colleague and adviser. Parliamentary Secretary, Minister of Labour 18 months; Minister of State, Education and Science 2 years; Minister of State, Home Office 2 years (not very happy there); Minister of Education 18 months. Opposition spokesman for Education 3 years.
Interests: Educational Reform. All educational/teaching pressure groups lobby her and foster good relations with her.

Laurence Goldthorn, 50
Stepney Secondary School. Left school at 15. Joined the Party at 16. Union man, shop worker (Union for Workers in Distributive Trades: UDWT); union executive at 29. Editor of *Communal Effort* for 8 years. In Parliament for 20 years. Parliamentary Private Secretary. Board of Trade 3 years. Resigned over pay policy; spell on the backbenches; Minister of State, Trade and Industry 3 years. Minister for Employment 3 months, voted by the Party as Opposition Spokesman for Trade and Industry 5 years in succession.

Reginald Hamilton-Price, 54
Recently resigned as director of a large successful city firm of Merchant Bankers after 25 years service, to stand for Parliament. It is the first time he has stood. You encouraged him into a safe seat. He has been your life-long friend. You went to primary and secondary school together. You are both Oxford men, but you went to a different college. He went to Trinity College and studied Politics, Philosophy and Economics. He played an active part in the Politics Society there. Has been a member of the Secular Society (your Party's affiliated political Society) ever since. He sits on the Board of several major finance companies. His main interest is in several major finance companies. He is a moderate, believing in a mixed economic policies. He is a moderate, believing in a mixed economy, but rejects the idea of total nationalisation of property, industry and business.

Anthony Houghton-Smith, 50
Newcastle Grammar School, Durham University, Harvard (Ph.D); Party philosopher, book *Democracy in a Mixed Economy*. Your friendship arose through party work together. Minister of State for Trade and Industry 2 years, resigned over the party's aviation policy; 6 months on the back-benches; Minister for the Environment 2½ years; Home Secretary 2 years; voted by the party as Shadow Home Secretary 5 years in succession. Rival for the leadership of the Party; strong party-following. MP for 12 years; university lecturer; interested in sport, watches showjumping, plays golf.

Walter Whitehead, 55
Salisbury Grammar School, Fishponds Teacher Training College, Bristol Primary School Teacher, Headmaster of Puddletown Middle School, MP for 10 years; Parliamentary Private Secretary to the Minister of Education 2 years; (good friend of Lady Cheryl); Minister of State, Department of Education, 6 months.

Milton Wright, 53
Personal friend of yours from primary school. Medicine scholarship to Cambridge. Postgraduate Medical School, Reading, 3 years; Hanover University 1 year, still lectures annually there on National Health; Consultant for World Health Organisation, attends two Conferences a year in Geneva. Charing Cross Hospital, consultant surgeon. Came into politics with the first ADP government 12 years ago. 2 years on backbenches. Minister of State for Health 2 years; Minister for Foreign Affairs 2 years; voted by the party as Shadow Minister for Foreign Affairs.

Barry Fortescue, 41
Australian by birth, naturalised British. Sidney School of Fine Art, photographer of high repute. MP for 10 years. Minister for the Arts, 2 years. Sits on the Board of Fine Arts Council. Speaks in the House for 'Roof Over Your Head' pressure group, and 'Rights for the Homeless'.

Angela Middleford, 45
Malton Grammar School, Leeds University. Journalist on the *Northern Gazette* 10 years; Parliament 12 years; Minister of State, Ministry of Overseas Development, 2 years; Minister of Health and Social Security 2 years; voted by the party as Shadow Minister for Employment, 3 years. Interested in abortion reform and women's rights; Speaks on behalf of the society for foetal care.

Jeffrey Shallcroft, 44
Winchester School, Oxford University where he was a strong radical. Formerly Lord Jarrow of Riflestone, renounced his title 2 years ago under the Peerage Act. Member of the Party Executive for 5 years; Chairman of the Party Executive 2 years; Stationery Office 2 years; Minister of Technology 6 months; Chief Opposition Spokesman for Trade and Industry 2 years; Shadow Minister for Land and Agriculture 2 years, does not enjoy this work. Does not get on with Hamilton-Price. Wants more nationalisation. Got to know you strictly through the party. 14 years in Parliament. Interested in streamlining trade and industrial reform generally. Far left of the party.

Grahame Barker, 35
Hammersmith Senior Boys School; University College, London. Advertising Executive. Strong party affiliation, began by doing the party's account for the election 12 years ago, when employed by Verdivision Adverts. Became a local party activist for subsequent elections and came into Parliament 5 years ago. Continued advertising the party. Imaginative but erratic.

James Brewster-Campbell, 39
Harrow and Balliol College, Oxford. Barrister. Scottish National Heritage Trust Foundation 2 years. Party Spokesman on Scottish Affairs in Opposition. On the Board of Directors of two Scottish Tourist Organisations. Rector Aberdeen University, 2 years. Parliamentary Private Secretary for Scottish Affairs 2 years. Interests: Oil, Energy, Scottish Welfare in a United Kingdom.

Mabel Dean, 30
Liverpool High School, Exeter, Ph.D Cambridge. Activist from the age of 17. President of the Union at Exeter. President of the University Party Debating Society. Radio panelist for *Your Questions, Please*. Main concerns: factory conditions and women's welfare; industrial reform; speaks in Parliament on behalf of the Society for the Greater Use of Cotton.

Lord Paul Mannheim of the Mint, 35
Educated in Switzerland, Berne University, Postgraduate at Cambridge. INSEAD Management Course, Paris. Owns telecommunications equipment business in Switzerland, but is British and resident in Henley-on-Thames. Parliamentary Private Secretary to Minister of Telecommunications 18 months.

Gordon (Chummy) McLewieth, 36
Glasgow Grammar School, Journalist on the *Northern Gazette* (Scottish edition). Contributor to the *Red Light of the Morning* and the *Evening Star* (London editions) under two different aliases, and regularly tears apart the articles he writes in the 'other' paper. He has a regular football column in his local paper. Active in the Constituency for Scottish heritage. 'Party Unity is the Road to Success' is his motto. Strong family man. Sees the breakdown of family life and bad town planning as reasons for hooliganism in urban areas. Wants Social Reform and Replanning in Inner City areas. 4 years in Parliament. President of the Pure Air Society.

Ruth Parker, 34
Plymouth High School; Cirencester Agricultural College. Farmer's wife. Active in the constituency. Lively rural following throughout the country. Regular column in *Land Stock and Good Breeding and West Country Ways*. Occasionally sits on gardening panels for radio; regularly participates on TV programme *Rural Life in Western England* – on at peak viewing time. Strongly against cruel sports and speaks for the Society Contra Cruel Sports, in the House.

Simon Macclesfield, 29
Rugby, Catholic University of Rome. Began training for the priesthood, but discontinued after three years. Went to Cambridge to read Philosophy and Theology (double first). Joined the party while doing a Ph.D on St Anthony of Padua. 2 years in the East End with the Catholic Mission to Rehabilitate the Impoverished. Always in the public eye. Great TV panelist. Strong national following. First time in Parliament, tipped as a winner by Houghton-Smith who is encouraging you to give him a post in the government.

TASKPAGE 14.2

What are the arguments supporting the idea that we have either (i) prime ministerial or (ii) Cabinet government in Britain? Write out the arguments for each case in your books. The first example (1/A) has been completed for you. Material for the answers is contained in the chapter. When you have completed this taskpage, turn back to Taskpage 13.1 How would you now modify the answers you gave in light of the additional knowledge you have of the Cabinet?

PRIME MINISTERIAL GOVERNMENT	CABINET GOVERNMENT
1 General elections are presented by the mass media as battles between the leaders of the main parties. People vote for who they want to be the next prime minister. This means that all MPs in the prime minister's party owe their positions to him.	A There is no evidence that people vote for a party because they want its leader to become prime minister. In 1970 Heath became prime minister although he was less popular than Wilson. People vote on political images, not just the personalities of leaders. Therefore MPs do not owe their positions to the prime minister.
2 The prime minister has power over Cabinet and party because he alone decides the date of the next general election. If party or Cabinet opposes the prime minister, he can end their opposition by threatening to call a snap election. The thought of this is likely to bring them back into line.	B
3	C The prime minister does not have a free hand in selecting his Cabinet. He cannot surround himself with ministers who are 'yes men'. Each shade of opinion in the party must be represented in the Cabinet. There will be a number of politicians that the prime minister has no choice but to include in the Cabinet.
4 'Every Cabinet minister is in a sense the prime minister's agent – his assistant. There's no question about that. It is the prime minister's Cabinet, and he is the one person who is directly responsible to the Queen for what the Cabinet does.' (Lord Home as Foreign Secretary)	D
5	E The prime minister draws up the Cabinet agenda. This does not mean that he can leave off items which he does not wish to discuss. In practice it would be impossible to keep an item off the agenda if ministers wanted to discuss it.
6 The prime minister can ignore or by-pass the Cabinet. The decisions to manufacture atomic weapons and to invade Suez were made by the prime minister and not the Cabinet.	F

(later Sir Alec Douglas-Home), revealed the power that the prime minister wielded over other ministers. He stated that 'every Cabinet minister is in a sense the prime minister's agent – his assistant. There's no question about that. It is the prime minister's Cabinet, and he is the one person who is directly responsible to the Queen for what the Cabinet does.'

It is argued that the prime minister has more power than the rest of the Cabinet because the prime minister can sack ministers who disagree with him. There is another argument which suggests that the prime minister does not really have the power to fill the Cabinet with 'yes men'. In order to satisfy the various party factions, the prime minister has to include people of all shades of party opinion in the Cabinet. Also there will be a number of senior party figures who have ambitions to become prime minister themselves. The prime minister is likely to include these rivals in the Cabinet in order to win their loyalty and support.

It is said that the prime minister is so powerful that he can ignore or by-pass the Cabinet. For example, it has been suggested that Prime Minister Attlee decided that Britain should manufacture atomic weapons and that Prime Minister Eden decided that Britain should invade Suez. But there is evidence that the decision to make the A-bomb was discussed in a Cabinet Committee and that the minutes were seen by the whole Cabinet. Because every minister in the Cabinet agreed with the decision, it was not discussed further. With the case of the Suez policy, it was discussed by Cabinet and Cabinet Committee.

Does the power to call a general election give the prime minister power over a rebellious Cabinet and party? Some argue that it does not. They point out that many MPs will be in safe seats and a general election is no real threat to them. In contrast, a general election means a great deal of work for the prime minister. He has to campaign throughout the country, whereas a backbench MP has only to campaign in his constituency. The prime minister risks losing the prestige and influence of his office if his party loses the election. Thus a general election can be a bigger risk for the prime minister than it is for MPs.

Does the power of drawing up the Cabinet agenda give a prime minister power over his Cabinet colleagues? In reality, it gives him very little power for it would be politically impossible for him to keep an issue off the agenda if a minister was determined to discuss it.

Is, then, the prime minister no more than *primus inter pares* – that is, the first amongst equals? Do we have government in which the major policy decisions are made by the Cabinet? The job of the prime minister is simply to chair the Cabinet, not to make big decisions by himself or with one or two close colleagues. It has been argued that ministers have large departments of civil servants to support them, whereas the prime minister has little support. He cannot think of the Cabinet Office as 'his department'. This is because the Cabinet Office serves the whole Cabinet, and not just the prime minister.

The prime minister may try to push a particular policy through the Cabinet, but in the end he has to obtain Cabinet agreement if he is to succeed. He is rarely a 'one-man band'. Harold Wilson described the job of the prime minister as the conductor of the orchestra – and not someone who plays all the instruments himself. Another prime minister, Sir Alec Douglas-Home, agreed with this. He said 'a good prime minister, once he had selected his ministers and made it plain to them he was always accessible "for comment or advice", should interfere with their departmental business as little as possible.' Previously Sir Alec, as Lord Home, had expressed a different view (see Task-page 14.2). At that time, he was Foreign Secretary in Harold Macmillan's government and not prime minister himself. Harold Macmillan was interested in foreign policy and probably kept a close eye on the work of the Foreign Secretary. Thus the view Lord Home held at that time, of the prime minister's power, was not typical.

Terms used

Budget The Chancellor makes his budget speech in March. In it he outlines his financial policy for the following year. Often he adjusts income tax rates, changes the rate of VAT, or alters excise duty. The Chancellor may make a 'Financial Statement' in November, which is really a 'mini-budget'.

Collective responsibility This doctrine recognises that the Cabinet is a team which must show a united front in public. The whole Cabinet accepts responsibility for its decisions. Ministers who disagree with Cabinet policy must either accept the decision, or resign. In reality collective responsibility has been weakened because some ministers 'leak' Cabinet discussions to the press.

Individual ministerial responsibility This doctrine recognises that ministers are responsible for what is done by their departments. As government has become more complex, some people have argued that it is unrealistic to expect a minister to be responsible for every decision.

Secretary of State The senior member of the ministerial team which heads a major government department. He will be a member of the Cabinet.

White Papers These are publications which contain government proposals for a policy. White Papers are discussed by the Cabinet and by Parliament. A Green Paper is a publication containing ideas and information on an issue. The government publishes it before it decides which proposals will be put forward as policy.

Summary

1 Each large department of government is headed by a team of ministers. The senior minister is usually called the Secretary of State and sits in the Cabinet.

2 Although government has grown more complex during this century, the size of the Cabinet has stayed much the same. One of the main tasks of the Cabinet is to co-ordinate government policy.

3 The Cabinet works as a team and accepts collective responsibility for its decisions. At the same time, ministers are responsible for decisions taken in their departments.

4 The Cabinet is supported by the Cabinet Office. Much of the work of the Cabinet is done by Cabinet Committees and sub-committees.

5 Cabinet ministers are generally occupied with trying to solve today's problems. They can rarely look far ahead in policy-making. The Central Policy Review Staff was set up to consider long-term issues in Britain's future.

6 The Cabinet is still important in decision-making. However, some people feel that the prime minister's power has grown and that he is now able to dominate the Cabinet.

Questions for discussion

1 What is the best size for a Cabinet? Give reasons for your answer.

2 Does collective responsibility still exist in British government today?

3 What is the role of Cabinet committees in government?

4 'Today we have prime ministerial government in Britain.' How true is this statement? Provide examples in your answer.

5 Organise your class into a Cabinet with top civil servant advisers. The Chancellor of the Exchequer faces a severe financial crisis. He argues that he must do one of two things: he can increase government revenue by doubling the rate of income tax or he can make massive savings in government expenditure. He prefers the latter option, and has suggested that the school-leaving age should be reduced to 14. Discuss this in Cabinet. Propose new alternatives to the Chancellor. Set up Cabinet committees if necessary. The prime minister is concerned that the next general election is only a year away.

15

The House of Commons at work

Parliament is made up of three parts: the 'Queen in Parliament', the House of Commons, and the House of Lords. In the following chapters we examine all three. Some people feel that Parliament is not worth such a detailed study, claiming that it is just a 'talking shop', and that it has less power than the mass media or big pressure groups. The following pages help us judge whether or not this view is accurate. The first part of Parliament that we look at is the House of Commons. This chapter examines the role played by the Commons in the government of Britain; the next chapter looks at change and reform. We begin our study of the Commons by considering how MPs discuss problems and issues. We will see how debates influence the actions of the government. Next we examine the important part played by the Commons in making laws. In particular, we look at the opportunities for backbench MPs to propose new laws. Finally, we look at the ways in which the government is investigated by the House of Commons. For in order to keep its support, the government has to defend its policies on the floor of the House.

Government and opposition

The House of Commons consists of 650 MPs, each elected to represent a constituency in England, Wales, Scotland and Northern Ireland. With rare exceptions, all MPs are members of political parties. The House elects one MP as Speaker, and he acts as chairman for debates and other proceedings. The Speaker gives up his party membership so that he can be a fair chairman. It is a tradition that an existing Speaker has no opponents in his constituency at a general election. But in recent years this practice has been breached from time to time. There has been the suggestion that once he has been appointed, the Speaker should be thought of as being the MP of the imaginery constituency of St Stephens. Another MP would be elected in his original constituency. This would mean that the party to which the Speaker belongs would not lose a vote in the House of Commons.

As we have already seen, government cannot be carried out without the support of a majority of MPs. This means that the largest party controls and supports the government. If no single party has a majority, several parties will join in a **coalition**. If parties find it impossible to form a coalition, one of the largest may attempt to form a minority government. For most of the time, post-war Britain has had governments formed by one party which has an overall majority.

The division between government and opposition is reflected in the way the chamber of the House of Commons is laid out. The fore-runner of Parliament met in the choir stalls of a church, and the chambers are still based on this plan. Today the House of Commons is arranged so that government and opposition face each other. This emphasises **confrontation**. The major parties confront each other in physical terms, as well as opposing each other politically. Many other elected assemblies are laid out as a semi-circular arena. This does not emphasise confrontation in the same way. But perhaps seating arrangements are not really important. The arguments in many legislative assemblies are just as fierce as those in the House of Commons.

The functions of the Commons

The House of Commons has three distinct functions. They are to debate, to legislate and to scrutinise the work of government. We shall now examine each of these important tasks in turn.

(i) The debating function

The House of Commons is a debating chamber where members may discuss any subject they choose. Although the government is generally supported by a majority of MPs, it does not control all the business of the Commons. Time is set aside for the opposition to choose what subjects will be debated. Also there are opportunities for individual MPs from all parties to raise issues which concern them.

Most debates follow party lines, with the government supporting its policies and the opposition opposing them, but there are some issues which cut across party lines. This is particularly true with moral issues such as divorce, abortion or the death penalty. The House will usually have a **free vote** on these issues. This allows MPs to vote according to their consciences.

All debates are based on a **motion** put before the House. It may simply be to pass a bill, or it may be to express support or criticism of a particular policy. It may be, as was the case in 1979 when the government was defeated, a motion 'that this House has no confidence in Her Majesty's Government'. It may even be a motion that the House should **adjourn** – a technical way of allowing MPs to discuss any subject they wish. Sometimes MPs call for an *emergency debate* under standing order No. 9. If this is permitted, it means that the House of Commons will abandon its planned business for the day to debate a motion 'That this House do now adjourn to consider a matter of urgent public import, namely ... [whatever the issue may be].'

All debates must have a conclusion, when the motion is passed or rejected. At the end of a debate, the Speaker puts the question and calls for all who support it to say 'Aye' and for all who disagree to say 'No'. Then after listening to the strength of support on both sides he will declare that the 'Ayes' or the 'Noes' have it. If a silence follows this, that is the end of debate and the result is accepted. But if there is a further shout, the Speaker will call for the **lobbies** to be cleared so that a **division** may take place. This means that the votes on either side will be formally counted. When a division is called, bells are rung; this gives all MPs who are not present in the Chamber the chance to take part in the vote. They have six minutes to get to the voting lobbies. There are two long galleries known as the Aye Lobby and the No Lobby. After six minutes the entrance doors are closed and MPs then file out the opposite end. They give their names to clerks who record the vote. Two **tellers** are appointed for each side to make sure that everything is done fairly. The tellers take the voting figures back into the House, where the Speaker declares the result.

Many of these customs are ancient, and they may seem out of place in the 1980s. Do debates serve any useful function when we know that the government has already made its mind up about the policies it is going to follow? Is the lengthy voting process worthwhile, when we know that the government is going to win?

In answering these questions, we must make sure that the odd ways in which the Commons works do not distract us from seeing what is really being done. For example, free debates are important. Through debate, the government is forced to defend and justify its policies. The opposition is able to expose the failings and weaknesses of the government. Voting is important. There are occasions when the government is defeated and has to think again about its policies. The government may be forced to consult backbench MPs in order to produce a policy which finds majority support.

(ii) The legislative function

Making law is a vital part of the work the Commons does. Law-making, however, does not take up as much Parliamentary time as might be imagined. Only 40% of Parliamentary time is spent on passing legislation.

Laws made by Parliament remain in force until Parliament itself decides to **amend** or repeal (cancel) them. Unlike those countries which have a written constitution, such as the United States, Britain has no court which has the power to overrule what Parliament does.

The origins of legislation

Most proposals for new legislation come from government. A government is elected to office with a programme or set of policies and to implement this will require new laws. Also the government, backed up by the civil service, is in a position to identify where problems have arisen and where new laws are needed. In this case, a proposal for a new law may emerge from a government department. The minister may take the initiative. If it is to be supported by the government, it will be put before the Cabinet for its approval.

Any proposal for important changes in the law is published as a **White Paper**. The problems can be discussed in Parliament, and by pressure groups and the public, before any final decisions are taken. This gives an opportunity for people to evaluate the proposals. Also they have an opportunity to try to influence the shape and detail of the new laws. From the government's point of view, the publication of a White Paper shows what public reaction to the proposals are. If need be, a government might decide to make changes in light of the response to the White Paper. In 1981 the Environment Secretary, Michael Heseltine, introduced a White Paper containing the idea that local councils should hold a referendum before they could raise rates. This idea was very unpopular with MPs from all parties, and the proposal was dropped.

Some proposals for legislation come from individual MPs who have either produced them themselves or have taken them up on behalf of an interest group outside Parliament. These are known as Private Member's Bills, which we will look at later.

Finally, some proposals are presented by public bodies such as local authorities or public corporations. These bodies often require legislation to perform their own particular functions. These proposals are known as Private Bills, which should not be confused with Private Member's Bills.

Drafting a bill

A bill is the name given to a proposal for law put before Parliament up to the time it has completed all its stages. It then becomes an Act of Parliament or Statute. Because it is to become part of the law of the land, it is important that it should be written in precise language. It should not be vague or capable of being interpreted in different ways. Within each government department, and particularly within the Treasury, legal experts are employed to put the ideas behind a bill into legal terms.

Passage in the House

When a bill is ready for presentation to Parliament, it is introduced for what is called its First Reading. This is shown in Fig. 15.1. At this stage, only the title of the bill is given, and the House gives it formal approval. There is no debate at this stage. The bill is then printed in full so that copies are available to MPs. When a suitable time has passed, the bill is presented for its Second Reading. If the bill is controversial, it will not pass this stage without a debate. Discussion will be about general issues surrounding the bill, and not particular details. MPs who oppose the bill may force a vote at this stage. If they were to win, that would put an end to the bill. If the government supports a bill it is unlikely to be defeated at this stage. The government whips will instruct MPs to support the bill. Thus party discipline usually ensures that government bills go through.

Following the Second Reading is the Committee Stage. The Commons has a number of Standing Committees whose task is to examine bills in detail. At this stage MPs give close attention to the bill's individual sections and clauses and even, if need be, to the wording.

The membership of each Standing Committee is divided on party lines. This is done in proportion to the balance in the full House. Thus, the discussion is likely to continue on party lines. But governments nevertheless take the opportunity of the Committee Stage to make alterations in light of the criticisms made. **Amendments** will be made to improve or change the bill. Occasionally, the Committee Stage is held on the floor of the House with all MPs attending. This is referred to as a Committee of the Whole House.

Any amendments which are agreed in Standing Committee must be put before the full House at ▷ p.140

Fig. 15.1 From bill to statute

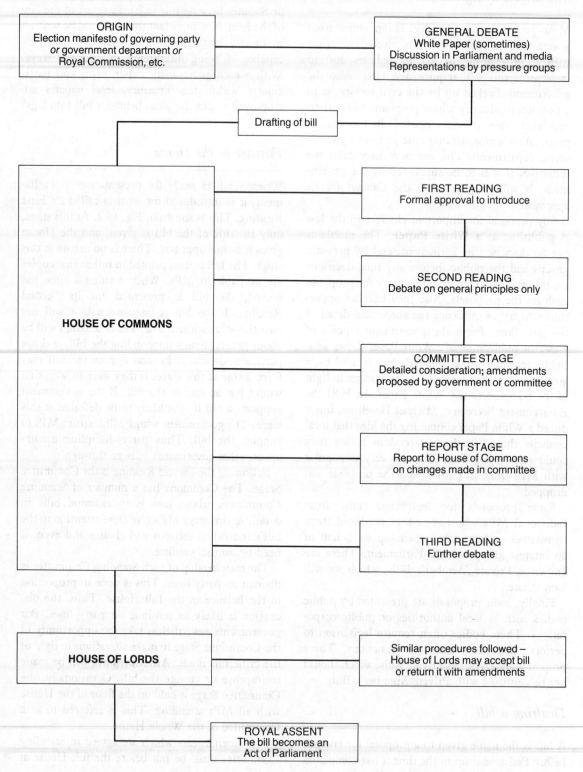

ORIGIN
Election manifesto of governing party
or government department *or*
Royal Commission, etc.

GENERAL DEBATE
White Paper (sometimes)
Discussion in Parliament and media
Representations by pressure groups

Drafting of bill

FIRST READING
Formal approval to introduce

SECOND READING
Debate on general principles only

HOUSE OF COMMONS

COMMITTEE STAGE
Detailed consideration; amendments
proposed by government or committee

REPORT STAGE
Report to House of Commons
on changes made in committee

THIRD READING
Further debate

HOUSE OF LORDS

Similar procedures followed –
House of Lords may accept bill
or return it with amendments

ROYAL ASSENT
The bill becomes an
Act of Parliament

Private Members' Bills

*Proportions of Conservative and Labour bills dealing with certain subject categories**

Study this bar graph. It shows the proportion of Conservative and Labour Private Member's Bills which deal with certain issues. On which types of issue do Labour and Tory MPs focus roughly equal attention? On which issues do Labour MPs focus most attention, and on which do Tory MPs focus most attention? In the section below, Alfred Morris MP writes about his bill. Which category on the bar graph does his bill belong to?

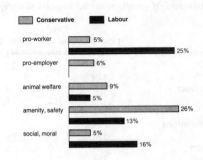

*Five other subject categories – criminal law, constitutional and local government, professional regulation, social security and miscellaneous bills – revealed no significant inter-party difference.

Source: Dick Leonard and Valentine Herman (eds), *The Backbencher and Parliament*

ALFRED MORRIS MP TELLS THE STORY OF THE CHRONICALLY SICK AND DISABLED PERSONS ACT 1970

Virtually all MPs who do not hold a government post put their names forward ... and 20 names are drawn out. The first six have a reasonable chance of successfully completing the course, providing all the other factors are favourable. I was particularly lucky. As my name was drawn out first, I had a full year of parliamentary time in which to turn my bill into law. My bill quickly attracted a great deal of publicity and support from pressure groups, from the media and from both sides of both Houses of Parliament. This was an important factor in the Treasury's decision to move a Money Resolution in support of the bill. If they had not done so, then the bill would have failed. On 29 May, the Chronically Sick and Disabled Persons Bill, which amended 39 other Acts of Parliament and which legislated in fields where previously there was no legislation of any kind to amend, was signed by the Queen. The whole process took up six busy months and I must confess there were times when I thought my bill would fail through lack of time or government support. Even if your name comes first in the ballot, there are many obstacles on the course to be surmounted. I tend to agree with

Roy Jenkins whose own Private Member's Bill became the Obscence Publications Act in 1959. He believes that the rare event of a successful Private Member's Bill needs the following combination of circumstances: 'First, a certain amount of luck; second, a great deal of time and even more patience; third, some all-party support; fourth, a minister who will be personally sympathetic at crucial times; fifth, some well organised and determined allies both inside and outside the House of Commons; and sixth, an articulate and impressive body of extra-parliamentary support.' Since my Bill needed *twelve* ministers to be 'personally sympathetic at crucial times', I sometimes think that I must have been about the luckiest Private Member of them all.

Teaching Politics, vol. 10, September 1981

If you were a backbench MP who was lucky and had his or her name drawn out the ballot, what new law would you try to get passed? What groups might help you? Discuss your ideas in class.

Question Time: numbers of questions tabled to particular departments

Departments	Oral			Written			Totals		
	1964–65	1968–69	1969–70	1964–65	1968–69	1969–70	1964–65	1968–69	1969–70
Agriculture, Fisheries and Food	601	499	393	317	389	351	918	888	744
Attorney-General	77	53	53	27	102	58	104	155	111
Aviation	429			208			637		
Church Commissioner	0	0	0	0	1	0	0	1	0
Civil Service		102	34		68	58		170	92
Colonies	215			91			306		
Commonwealth Relations	227			61			288		
Defence	538	624	519	427	599	411	965	1 223	930
Duchy of Lancaster	87	0	8	22	5	2	109	5	10
Economic Affairs	394	333		121	118		515	451	
Education and Science	576	659	547	530	602	462	1 106	1 261	1 009
Foreign (later 'and Commonwealth')	507	853	628	190	457	265	697	1 310	893
Health	712			625			1 337		
Home	633	679	559	455	667	505	1 088	1 346	1 064
Housing (and Local Government)	704	730	789	435	698	788	1 139	1 428	1 577
Kitchen Committee, etc.	15			10			25		
Labour (later Employment and Productivity)	385	660	621	283	762	443	668	1 422	1 064
Land and Natural Resources	186			40			226		
Lord President of the Council		60	61		65	53		125	114
Overseas Development	218	179	195	106	115	62	324	294	257
Paymaster-General	54	24	0	3	14	2	57	38	2
Pensions	274			218			492		
Minister without Portfolio	20	0	5	13	0	6	33	0	11
Posts, etc.	565	493	181	420	501	128	985	994	309
Power	329	510		165	317		494	827	
Prime Minister	1 146	1 207	865	156	173	124	1 302	1 380	989
Public Buildings and Works	308	280	266	139	181	98	447	461	364
Scotland	612	906	812	412	944	722	1 024	1 850	1 534
Social Services		958	685		1 196	1 041		2 154	1 726
Technology	250	407	866	80	356	495	330	763	1 361
Trade	738	911	700	476	734	529	1 214	1 645	1 229
Transport	1 048	761	630	814	840	552	1 862	1 601	1 182
Treasury	745	941	710	623	1 005	833	1 368	1 946	1 543
Wales	83	149	118	93	210	232	176	359	350
Totals:							20 236	24 097	18 469
Sitting days in Session:							178	164	122

Note: Blank spaces indicate non-existent departments
Source: Leonard and Herman, *op. cit.*

This table shows the number of oral and written questions asked over a number of parliamentary sessions. The different lengths of each session are shown at the foot of the table.

(i) In which session did the prime minister answer the highest total of oral and written questions?

(ii) In which session did the prime minister answer the highest number of oral questions each day on average?

(iii) In which session did the Minister of Education answer most questions which were in written form?

(iv) Which session had the greatest average of oral and written questions answered each day?

On 28 January 1970, the *Guardian* carried the following story headed 'Ministry denies killing old people after experiment'. It was written by John Kerr, and said that the Ministry of Defence had described as 'ludicrous' a suggestion that old people had been used as 'guinea pigs' for experiments, and quietly put to death afterwards. The allegation was made by Monsignor John Barry, the Rector of St Andrew's Roman Catholic College, Drygrange, Melrose, Scotland, in a speech about the problems of the aged, made to the Edinburgh City Business Club. He claimed:

I have seen evidence which I think is genuine, although I cannot guarantee this, that there is a certain section of the Ministry of Defence which uses elderly people as guinea pigs for experiments, and quietly puts them to death afterwards. It is carefully hidden by the Official Secrets Act.

Monsignor Barry said he was sure that the evidence that he was shown was an official document. He could not name the source of his information, or say where the alleged experiments were carried out; but he knew, and that it was in the British Isles. He firmly believed the document to be genuine, its contents being 'sufficient to convince me of its authenticity'. The incidents to which it related had apparently occurred within the previous two years, from 1968 to 1970. He said that he had seen the evidence recently and 'hadn't known what action to take'.

On 6 February 1970 the *Guardian* reported that David Steel (Liberal MP) had met Monsignor John Barry, who gave him the documents to which he had referred in January.

David Steel said that there were certain disquieting aspects of the case which needed investigating. The article continued: 'Mr Steel spoke yesterday to the private office of Mr Healey (Secretary of Defence) and as a result has passed the documents to him with a covering letter raising queries which Mr Steel has offered to discuss further.' Despite repeated follow-ups, there the matter rested.

In the House of Commons on 19 February 1970 Harold Wilson said: 'Claims that the government was putting to death old people after experimenting on them were completely without foundation.' Harold Wilson was answering a question by William Hamilton who asked if the Prime Minister had inquiried into 'the monstrous accusations' made by Monsignor Barry.

Wilson said:

Any government department may from time to time undertake scientific research involving human beings as subjects, in accordance with the volunteer principle. It is the responsibility of the Minister in charge of the department to see that there are fully adequate safeguards for the health and wellbeing of those taking part.

He said that the fullest inquiries had been made into this matter.

Harold Wilson's answers to William Hamilton were ambiguous in the extreme and one can only hope that the hospital in south east England was deterred by Monsignor Barry from pursuing the alleged experiments.

Elizabeth Sigmund, *Rage Against the Dying*

Imagine that you are a Conservative MP for a constituency in Kent. You have received a visit from a left-wing trade unionist. He gave you a copy of the document shown above. He asked what you are going to do about it. You do not quite know what to make of the document but it worries you. What actions could you take as a backbench MP to investigate the issue? Write a paragraph outlining what steps you might take.

the Report Stage. After this, the Bill is ready for its Third Reading. If the bill is controversial, a full debate will take place. The opposition will argue against the proposals and a vote is likely to take place. The Bill would be lost if the government was defeated at this stage. But because of party discipline, this is rare.

After a successful Third Reading, the Commons has completed its work on the bill. But the bill is not yet law. Unless it is a bill dealing with financial matters, it must also be passed through similar stages by the House of Lords. Some less controversial bills actually pass through the Lords first, but most start in the Commons. Since 1911, bills dealing with finance are passed by the Commons only. Any amendments made in the Lords are referred back to the Commons for approval. If the Commons do not agree with amendments made by the Lords, the wishes of the Commons normally prevail.

After completing all its stages in the Lords, the bill is then ready for its final stage; the Royal Assent. The Queen, in a message to both Houses, gives her assent to the bill which then becomes an Act of Parliament. No monarch since 1707 has refused assent to a bill. The Royal Assent is simply the formal way of bringing a bill into effect.

Private Member's Bills and Private Bills

The procedure for Private Member's Bills is similar to that for public bills. But an individual MP does not have the resources of a government department to help him. He may not receive very much support from other MPs. An individual needs a great deal of luck in getting his bill through Parliament.

Only a limited amount of time is set aside for consideration of Private Member's Bills. In order to decide which MPs will be given the chance of sponsoring a bill, a ballot is held. The first bit of luck an MP needs is for his name to be among the 20 winners. Taskpage 15.1 gives an example of a successful Private Member's Bill sponsored by Alfred Morris MP - the Chronically Sick and Disabled Persons Act.

Private Bills are sponsored by public bodies for their own regulation. They are seldom debated in the House. They are normally dealt with by two committees on Private Bills. One deals with Unopposed Bills and the other with Opposed Bills. Questions and problems are sorted out by the committees before the bill receives formal passage in the House.

(iii) The supervisory function

The third vital function of Parliament is that of watchdog. It must watch carefully all the activities of government. Almost all who work in government are convinced that they know best and that their opinions are always correct. It is the duty of Parliament to throw a searchlight on all that government does, so that ministers and civil servants can explain and justify what they do. Keeping a close check on the actions of government is a difficult task for Parliament. The House of Commons can and does peer into all sorts of corners and sometimes calls into question the actions of even the less important civil servants. Parliament can sometimes appear to be a 'busybody'. But it is only this degree of scrutiny which maintains the relatively high standard of administration that exists in Britain.

There are numerous ways in which the Commons can carry out its supervisory function. For example, detailed questions about particular policies can be raised in the course of normal debates. However, there are three other ways in which MPs can raise questions and examine the workings of government:

(i) Letters to ministers

MPs may write to ministers in order to raise an issue. The minister, together with his civil servants, knows that if the reply does not satisfy the MP the matter will be taken a stage further. Therefore careful attention will be given to the MP's letter and the minister will try hard to provide a satisfactory answer.

(ii) Question Time

One hour each day, from Monday to Thursday, is devoted to questioning ministers about the activities and policies of their departments. Taskpage 15.2 shows the number of questions and the type of questions that are asked on average. On Tuesdays and Thursdays, the last quarter of an hour of Question Time is set aside for questions to the prime minister.

Broadly speaking, questions are of two sorts. First there are those which are genuinely seeking information. Second there are those which are being used to make a political point. Often the first type of question is answered in writing and published in **Hansard**. The second type of question may involve two stages. The first question to the minister or prime minister has to be given in advance before the MP actually asks it. But the MP is allowed to ask an extra, or supplementary question. This second question does not have to be given in advance. A typical example might go something like this:

Question: Is the Secretary of State satisfied with the arrangements made for security in prison hospitals?
Secretary of State: Yes, Sir.
Supplementary Question: Is the Secretary of State aware that there have been no fewer than sixteen escapes from such hospitals in the past year and does he really think that this is satisfactory?

The minister is thus put under immediate pressure. An experienced civil servant will have guessed what the supplementary question is likely to be. He will have drafted out an answer for the minister just in case it is asked. In this example we can see that the purpose of the question is not to obtain information. The purpose is to embarrass the minister. Question Time, therefore, is a test of a minister's debating skill and his quickness of thinking; it is not always a test of how good he is as a minister in running his department.

(iii) Select Committees

Select Committees have existed in the House of Commons for over a century. They must not be confused with Standing Committees, which scrutinise bills. Select Committees are investigating bodies. We will examine the growth of specialised select committees further in chapter 16. At this stage we need only note the work of three Select Committees.

The first of these is the Public Accounts Committee (PAC), which is responsible for checking the accounts of all government expenditure. It is important not only to check what the government *intends* to spend, but also how it actually is spent. This committee provides such a check. The chairman of the PAC is usually a senior member of the Opposition. He is assisted by a permanent official of the House, the Comptroller and Auditor-General. In going over the books, the committee can uncover unnecessary and wasteful expenditure. The wasted money can never be recovered, but the reports of this committee help to ensure that the waste is not repeated.

The second committee to consider is the Select Committee on Statutory Instruments. Often Acts of Parliament are very general in nature. They give powers to ministers to make the detailed regulations. These regulations are known as *statutory instruments*. This type of law-making is known as **delegated legislation**. Even though MPs are not responsible for shaping each detailed regulation, they must nevertheless check them. The task of the Select Committee on Statutory Instruments is to review all regulations of this type which are issued by government departments.

The final committee to look at here is the Select Committee on European Legislation. Since Britain joined the EEC in 1973, it has been governed by many economic regulations issued by the European Commission in Brussels. This Select Committee has the difficult job of keeping an eye on the numerous directives from the EEC. If there are issues which members of the committee feel concerned about, then they bring them to the attention of the House.

The role of Parliament today

Some people criticise Parliament today for being weak and ineffective. Certainly the press and television appear to challenge government policies as successfully as Parliament. One writer argued that 'a television commentator in a one-hour interview with the prime minister has more chance to challenge him than the whole of the elected chamber in a week'. Others have argued that the views of trade unions, the CBI and other pressure groups have a greater influence on government policy than the views of the House of Commons.

Perhaps these views underestimate the power of the House of Commons. We must not forget that it is the one place where the government *must* defend its policies. Ultimately the government depends on the support of the House for its existence. In 1979 support for Mr Callaghan's government was withdrawn by the House, and the government fell from office. There have been many other occasions when the government has not been defeated, but opposition in the House of Commons has been so great as to persuade the government to change its policies.

In recent years the House of Commons has increased its authority. The introduction of the new Select Committee system has increased the power of the Commons. There have also been many signs that backbench MPs, regardless of party, are less willing to be 'lobby fodder'. In other words, they are not always the loyal sheep that party Whips would like them to be.

Terms used

Adjourn The Adjournment Debate is the last debate to be held each day before the House adjourns [suspends its activities and goes home]. The topic for the debate is raised by a back-bencher, who is selected by the Speaker. If MPs wish to discuss an issue at short notice, a member can move the adjournment under Standing Order No. 9. If the Speaker agrees, an *emergency debate* can be held on the following day.

Amendment A change or alteration to an original proposal.

Coalition government A government formed by more than one party in order to gain an overall majority in the Commons.

Confrontation Confrontation politics emphasises the policy differences between parties rather than the similarities. Confrontation is about conflict, not cooperation.

Delegated legislation Parliament often gives law-making powers to ministers, local authorities or public corporations. This gives Parliament more time to consider major policies rather than submerging MPs in the details of minor rules and regulations. Delegated legis-

lation can often allow departments to act quickly. For example, import duties can be raised without a great deal of prior warning. If Parliament dealt with this, there would be time for many goods to be rushed into Britain in order to avoid paying extra duty. *Statutory instruments* is the name given to delegated legislation. About forty statutory instruments are issued each week. These statutory instruments give ministers powers to make new rules and regulations where necessary.

Division a vote in the House of Commons or the House of Lords

Free votes In a free vote, MPs are under no pressure from their party leaders to vote in a particular way. In other words, the Whips are not applied. MPs are free to vote according to their own views or conscience. Free votes are usually allowed on Private Member's legislation.

Hansard Parliamentary debates are recorded in shorthand and published. Hansard is the permanent written record of Parliament.

Lobbies The lobbies include various spaces in the Houses of Parliament, which may be halls, corridors or ante-rooms. When individuals or organisations wish to influence an MP, they seek to meet him in the central lobby. This is known as 'lobbying'.

Motion This is the term used in Parliament and meetings for a formal proposal.

Tellers MPs who count the votes in a division and report the results to the House

White Paper This document contains government proposals for a particular policy. It will be debated in Parliament.

Summary

1 Parliament is made up of three parts: 'the Queen in Parliament', the House of Lords and the House of Commons.

2 The House of Commons has three main tasks: to debate, to legislate, and to scrutinise.

3 The government is forced to justify and explain its policies in debates. Occasionally governments are defeated in the House of Commons. They are forced to think again about the policies that are being put forward.

4   Making law is a complicated process. There are opportunities for backbench MPs to propose new laws. But they need a great deal of luck and strong support if their ideas are going to be successful and end up on the Statute Book.

5   Parliament acts as a watchdog. An MP has a number of opportunities when he can question the action of government. These include the opportunities to ask questions, write letters, or be a member of a committee which investigates what government does.

Questions for discussion

1   'MPs are powerless today – they are simply lobby-fodder.' Do you agree with this view?

2   In what ways can Parliament check the actions of government?

3   Does Private Member's legislation offer backbench MPs a regular opportunity to make new laws?

4   'Question Time in the Commons tests a minister's ability to debate skilfully: it does not test his efficiency as a minister.' Discuss this view.

5   Organise your class to debate an issue on which there is disagreement. This might be on an issue such as capital punishment, private education, or nuclear disarmament. Elect a Speaker. He or she must limit speeches to one minute and generally keep order. Discuss the difficulties of making speeches afterwards.

6   Appoint a small group of four or five students to represent the government front bench, and appoint a Speaker. The rest of the class are backbenchers. The government has decided to ban the sale of fireworks altogether. Sales of fireworks to children or even to organised groups of adults are no longer to be permitted. Firework displays will be allowed only on national celebrations, when they will be supervised by the army. Members of the government must defend this policy (regardless of what students might really think on the issue). Backbenchers must attack the policy (again, regardless of students' private views). After the debate, sum up which side came out best. Discuss whether or not you found it easy to argue for something you did not believe in.

16

Change and reform in the House of Commons

What sort of people become MPs? How has the composition of the House of Commons changed during recent years? There is evidence that people from a different variety of backgrounds are getting elected to Parliament now compared with even a generation ago. The changing membership of the House of Commons has had an influence on the way in which the House is organised and run. MPs are no longer happy to be loyal and obedient, and do exactly what their party leaders tell them. There is evidence that MPs are more determined to express their own opinions than they were in the past. This new mood has been a major reason behind recent reforms in the House of Commons. MPs want more influence over government. A new system of Select Committees has been set up to enable backbenchers to specialise in different areas of policy-making. But how successful have these committees been in giving power back to Parliament?

MPs in profile

MPs are elected to represent the electorate in the House of Commons. Strictly speaking, each MP represents the electorate within a geographical area. He or she will represent *all* who live in that constituency. In other words a Conservative MP represents his constituents including all those who voted for other parties at the election. But how representative are MPs of the population at large in other terms? It is well known that women are poorly represented in Parliament. But are MPs even typical of the ordinary 'man-in-the street' in terms of their social backgrounds?

(i) The age of MPs

MPs are not representative of the electorate in terms of their ages. Going into the House of Commons is very much a middle-aged profession. You can see from Table 16.1 that three-quarters of all MPs since the Second World War were between 30 and 49 years old when they first entered Parliament. There have been two small

Table 16.1 Age distribution of all members, 1945-74, on the occasion of their first election

Age	Conservative		Labour		Other		Total	
	No.	%	No.	%	No.	%	No.	%
21–29	67	8.4	38	4.5	8	10.0	113	6.6
30–39	337	42.1	266	32.2	33	41.3	636	37.2
40–49	285	35.5	334	40.3	25	31.3	644	37.6
50–59	96	11.9	155	18.7	9	11.2	260	15.2
60–69	16	2.0	35	4.2	5	6.2	56	3.3
70+	1	0.1	1	0.1	–	–	2	0.1
Total	802	100.0	829	100.0	80	100.0	1711	100.0

Source: Colin Mellors, *The British MP: a socio-economic study of the House of Commons*

but important trends which are not shown in the table. Colin Mellors's study of MPs shows that

(a) Conservatives have recently begun electing more MPs in their thirties, and

(b) although Labour tends to elect a more elderly group of MPs than the Conservatives, there has also been a similar trend of electing more MPs in their thirties in recent years.

(ii) Educational background

There is a big difference between the two major political parties in terms of the educational background of their members. In his book, Colin Mellors writes that for Conservatives:

> Breeding and educational attainment are customarily seen as the two most important qualifications in this party for recruitment to the political elite. The former is normally demonstrated by a public school background and the latter by graduation from one of the two ancient universities of Oxford and Cambridge.

We saw in chapter 2 that roughly 7% of the population had a private education. In fact, only 4% went to a public school. Yet just over three quarters (77.8%) of all Conservative MPs came from the public schools. Colin Mellors concludes that 'the "old school tie" remains the most important qualification to prospective Conservative MPs'.

In recent years there has been a very slight increase in non-public school Conservative MPs who had a university education. The leadership contest between Edward Heath and Margaret Thatcher (see chapter 7) was between two politicians who went to grammar school. The last leadership contest before that in 1963 was between Lord Home and Lord Hailsham, both of whom went to **Eton**.

The last thirty years has seen a trend towards better-educated Labour MPs. As time passes, the number who went to school before **the 1944 Education Act** gets fewer and fewer. This means that more and more Labour MPs have had a secondary education together with opportunities for a higher education. You can see from Fig. 16.1 that the proportion of MPs who attended university

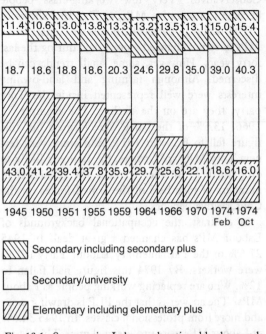

Fig. 16.1 Some major Labour educational backgrounds (percentages) (based on a figure in Mellors, *op. cit.*)

has grown steadily. The proportion who received simply an **elementary** education has fallen rapidly.

The contrast between the two major parties is striking – nearly 80% of Conservative MPs came from public schools; over 80% of Labour MPs did not. Yet Labour MPs still fail to reflect the population at large since the percentage of Labour MPs coming from public schools (18.7%) is still much higher than the 4% of the general public who went to such schools.

(iii) Occupational background

More than four-fifths of all Conservative MPs are drawn from professional and business occupations. Over half of them come from just three professions – barristers, company directors and farmers. Barristers form the largest single profession inside the Tory party, while the number of Conservatives with a business background is growing. Of the 273 company directors elected to the House of Commons between 1945 and 1974, 245 were

Conservatives. Very few working-class people become Conservative MPs, as Fig. 16.2 shows.

The occupational backgrounds of Conservative MPs have not changed a great deal during the last forty years. However, some small trends can be discerned. Although farming and land-owning interests were well represented inside the Tory party, they are on the decline. For example, in 1966, 13.6% of the party were farmers but this figure fell to 8.1% in 1974. And since very few new Tory MPs are farmers, the figure is likely to drop further. Another trend is the reduction in numbers of members of the armed forces on the Conservative benches.

In contrast, the occupational backgrounds of Labour MPs has changed a great deal. In 1945 27.6% of the Parliamentary Labour Party (PLP) were workers. By 1974 this figure had fallen to 12%. Who are replacing working people as Labour MPs? The answer is that the PLP is drawing more and more from professional classes. In 1945 34.6% of Labour MPs were professional men. This figure had risen to 50.8% by 1974. The single group of

professionals that has increased most is teachers – from 12.1% of the PLP in 1945 to 28.1% by 1974.

There are far fewer MPs in the Labour Party with business backgrounds. This is clearly seen in Fig. 16.2 where less than 10% of Labour MPs are shown as businessmen.

The changing nature of MPs

(i) Professionals and amateurs

Colin Mellor's study of MPs shows that approximately two-thirds of all who enter the Commons become 'professionals'. These are 'long-stay' MPs in terms of the years they spend in Parliament. In other words, they make a career out of being a politician. The professionals tend to get elected to **safe seats** and spend at least ten years, often much longer, in the Commons. They become office-holders and are chosen to sit on committees.

The 'amateur' MP usually spends only a brief period in the House of Commons. His will be a 'short-stay' in Parliament. He may get elected in a **marginal** constituency; a seat which he loses in the following election. Consequently amateurs may stay in the Commons for five years or less. They tend not to hold important offices or build up political reputations.

(ii) Part-time and full-time MPs

Some MPs have two jobs. They continue their careers while, at the same time, sitting as an MP. Some argue that their occupations, which may be in law, commerce or industry, keep them in touch with the 'real world' outside the House of Commons. These 'part-time' MPs tend not to have the time to serve on committees or take on additional parliamentary responsibilities. Other MPs are 'full-time' and argue that being an elected representative is a full-time job. Full-time MPs are usually the ones which serve on committees and accept additional responsibilities in the Commons.

(iii) The rebel MP

We expect political parties to disagree with each

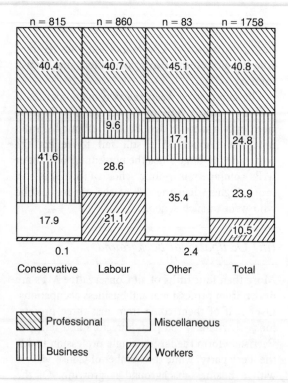

Fig. 16.2 Occupational backgrounds of MPs, 1945–74 (percentages), based on Mellors, op. cit.

other. But today in the House of Commons there is much disagreement *within* the political parties. We examined reasons for this conflict in chapter 8, where we looked at party factions. Some people may expect to see disagreement inside the Labour party. This is because there has been conflict between left-wing socialists and moderate party leaders throughout the history of that party. They do not expect to see disagreement inside the Conservative party. Yet the evidence today shows that discord within the Conservative party is as common as discord within the PLP.

Philip Norton has studied the behaviour of rebellious MPs. He has shown that until 1970 MPs in each major party tended to agree with each other. However, after 1970 disagreement inside the parties became common. Table 16.2 shows this increasing trend of **dissension**. You can see that there was more disagreement inside the parties after October 1974 than in the whole period from 1945 to 1970. The government of the day had only been defeated in Commons voting on *ten* occasions between 1945 and 1970, yet in 1971–2, Conservative MPs joined Labour to defeat a Conservative government on *six* occasions.

There appears to be a 'new breed' of MP in the Commons today. Normally he supports the leadership of his party and votes the same way as the leaders, but it is not an automatic loyalty. Neither Labour nor Conservative MPs are content to be loyal 'lobby fodder'. They appear to be more independent in their thinking and more determined to vote according to their own views.

New demands for reform

From the late 1960s there has been a new mood among backbench MPs. The 'new breed' of better educated and more professional MPs were not happy with their lot in Parliament. They wanted to play a bigger part in influencing government. Many people felt that the House of Commons had lost too much power, and that the government had gained too much. Because of increased party discipline, both government and opposition **Whips** could instruct MPs how to vote. Party leaders expected unswerving loyalty from their respective backbenchers. It is no surprise that backbench MPs were dissatisfied with this situation, for the more obedient they became, the weaker they appeared.

The remedy was for Parliament to regain some of its power. It was felt that if MPs were to have more influence over government, they needed to become more informed about policies and issues. ▷ p.150

Table 16.2 Divisions witnessing dissenting votes

Parliament (number of sessions in brackets)	Number of divisions witnessing dissenting votes*			Number of divisions witnessing dissenting votes expressed as a percentage of all divisions
	Total	Lab.	Con.	
1945–50 (4)	87	79	27	7
1950–1 (2)	6	5	2	2.5
1951–5 (4)	25	17	11	3
1955–9 (4)	19	10	12	2
1959–64 (5)	137	26	120	13.5
1964–6 (2)	2	1	1	0.5
1966–70 (4)	124	109	41	9.5
1970–4 (4)	221	34	204	20
1974 (1)	25	8	21	23
1974–9 (5)	423	309	240	28

* As one division may witness dissenting votes by Labour *and* Conservative Members, the Labour and Conservative figures do not necessarily add up to the totals on the left.

Source: Philip Norton, *Dissension in the House of Commons 1974–1979*

TASKPAGE 16.1

Occupations of Conservative MPs 1900–74 (percentages)

| Occupation | Elected at general elections between | | |
	1900–10	1918–35	1945–74
Professions	48.6 (263)	47.9 (498)	34.3 (279)
Business	30.5 (165)	38.1 (396)	53.1 (432)
Workers	—	1.1 (11)	0.5 (4)
Miscellaneous	4.6 (25)	6.1 (64)	9.0 (73)
Private means	15.3 (83)	4.6 (48)	2.9 (24)
Not known	0.9 (5)	2.1 (22)	0.2 (2)
Total	99.9 (541)	99.9 (1 039)	100.0 (814)

Occupations of Liberal MPs 1900–74 (percentages)

| Occupation | Elected at general elections between | | |
	1900–10	1918–35	1945–74
Professions	42.6 (222)	43.0 (153)	40.0 (14)
Business	37.6 (196)	37.3 (133)	51.4 (18)
Workers	1.5 (8)	3.4 (12)	—
Miscellaneous	8.8 (46)	10.4 (37)	5.7 (2)
Private means	6.5 (34)	3.1 (11)	2.9 (1)
Not known	2.9 (15)	2.8 (10)	—
Total	99.9 (521)	100.0 (356)	100.0 (35)

Occupations of Labour MPs 1900–74 (percentages)

| Occupation | Elected at general elections between | | |
	1900–10	1918–35	1945–74
Professions	2.3 (2)	18.6 (74)	32.5 (279)
Business	4.6 (4)	8.3 (33)	10.8 (93)
Workers	89.5 (77)	56.2 (223)	37.1 (319)
Miscellaneous	3.5 (3)	14.6 (58)	18.9 (162)
Private means	—	1.0 (4)	0.3 (3)
Not known	—	1.2 (5)	0.3 (3)
Total	99.9 (86)	99.9 (397)	99.9 (859)

Source: S.A. Walkland (ed.), *The House of Commons in the Twentieth Century*

(i) Analyse the changes in numbers of MPs from 1900–74 who have a private income.

(ii) How similar are the Liberal and Conservative parties in terms of occupational backgrounds of MPs?

(iii) Draw a graph which shows the decline of workers in the Labour party.

(iv) Draw a graph which shows the increase in MPs in all parties who come from a business background.

Du Cann's Case

Mr Du Cann's elegantly presented but not unfamiliar case, was that the reforms had become necessary through changes in the work of the House of Commons and its relationship to government: rigid party discipline virtually ensured the majority party of victory in the lobbies; pressure groups now bypassed Parliament and made policy direct with departments of state; the Prime Minister exerted formidable patronage, not least over the one hundred or so MPs holding government office, whilst the power of the civil service had expanded enormously as the scope of government had increased. Fifty years ago Parliament produced 450 pages of legislation; now, using largely the same methods it processed 3000 pages plus 10,000 Statutory Instruments, not to mention the EEC regulations and directives. Huge areas of government like the Nationalised Industries, the National Enterprise Board and the BNOC had grown up virtually free of effective Parliamentary scrutiny. Too often Parliamentary debates and Question Time were ritual exchanges of information and assertions of party positions; nowhere was found the sort of day-to-day supervision one might find in the commercial world. Yet the all party consensus behind the results of the June 1979 debate was a watershed, proving that 'parliament is not in decline, is not ineffective'.

The committees had engineered a transformation, completing over 150 reports into a wide variety of subjects attracting wide publicity and in many cases influencing government thinking and practice: the Home Affairs Committee report on the 'Sus' law, for example, had led to its reform whilst the Treasury and Civil Service Committee reports on the economy had made a substantial impact. The committees had provided a new and sought-after forum in which MPs could advance their ideas and their careers. And they were cheap: part-time experts gave advice as good as their government counterparts at a fraction of the cost. Du Cann blanched at the thought of committees as large and expensive as those of the US Congress but he looked forward to substantial further development of the new system. An 'honest start had been made'; for the future he urged televised debates, a wider remit for the Public Accounts Committee, and greater influence for the committees over public expenditure. This once crucial power had disappeared in the late nineteenth century since when debates and scrutiny on proposed expenditure have tended to become mere exchanges over policy. Du Cann wished to see estimates made 'negotiable' so that select committees could not only summon ministers and ask them to justify estimates but could propose different changes of emphasis under the major expenditure headings.

After he had sat down to appreciative applause a member of the audience expressed the opinion that Mr Du Cann was currently the 'foremost champion of parliamentary democracy in this country'. To this he smiled bashfully but not ungratefully. Having been passed over, for a variety of reasons for political office since 1963, Mr Du Cann has poured some of his formidable energies into developing these committees. One wonders if this enthusiasm for the cause would have been so vehement had he held regular ministerial office in Conservative governments: an unworthy thought perhaps. Equally unworthy is the thought that ambitious MPs who expect in the not too distant future to exercise ministerial power do not wish for it to be inhibited by interfering parliamentary committees. Mr Kilroy-Silk's talk, however, gave no hint of such Machiavellian calculations.

Kilroy-Silk's Case

In a less formal but scarcely less persuasive presentation he argued that the new committees, however useful they might be proving to be, were a distraction from the floor of the House, where the real action should take place. According to him, Opposition MPs should not be cooped up in committee room ante-chambers but should be crowding into the House, prosecuting the party political debate with greater energy and effectiveness. The job of the Opposition was to oppose and ultimately to defeat the government.

Apart from emptying the Chamber the committees inflicted heavy work loads on MPs: precious hours were diverted, mastering documents, absorbing information of dubious utility. As a member of one of the most successful committees this charge might seem curious but Mr Kilroy-Silk does not deny their achievements. As an energetic member he is proud of the 'Sus' law success, and, following another report, the changes made in police practice towards people held in custody, but he pointed out that most committee 'successes' are of a special kind. They were achievements in areas of bipartisan (or multi-partisan) agreement. Too often these committees scoured their particular political terrain, looking for ground upon which all members could stand. Consequently, their work was undertaken in politically 'neutral' areas. The really important areas of political debate were skirted around and on the occasions when they were addressed the committees were often unable to agree. 'We therefore have the position', he continued, 'in which Select Committees are absorbed with matters of secondary importance instead of freeing their members to conduct the real struggle on the floor of the House. My view is that as Labour MPs we should be doing everything in our power to question, criticise, embarrass and harry the government in order to persuade the electorate to vote them out. Once in power we would then be able to legislate comprehensively in the areas where committees are able to work only piece-meal. I am not saying Select Committees do not do a great deal of good – this is unquestionable – what I am saying is that we could be doing *more* good through concentrating our efforts on the party struggle.'

Finally, he argued that the new committees had not changed the fundamental distribution of power in the House which was still controlled by the front benches of the big parties. Chairmen were selected by the whips, and in some cases deliberately chosen for their respectability. The Home Affairs Committee initially elected its own chairman but Labour members were brusquely told by Jim Callaghan (then leader of the Opposition) that they had to accept Sir Graham Page as this was part of an agreement reached with the government. Furthermore, ministers might complain about the time consumed by giving evidence that they did not run scared of the committees. Their reactions were conditioned not by the committees themselves but by their particular member-ship: the Treasury and Civil Service committee which had become a refuge for Conservative critics of government policy was a case in point. Mr Kilroy-Silk concluded by suggesting that it was no coincidence that a Conservative government should have devised a scheme which took so many energetic opposition MPs out of the firing line in the House. If he had any influence regarding the committees come the next Labour government, he would get rid of them.

Bill Jones, 'Select Committees and the Floor of the House',
Teaching Politics, vol. 11, September 1982

Two MPs, Edward Du Cann and Robert Kilroy-Silk, are debating the value of Select Committees at your local university. Imagine that you are a reporter on your local evening paper. Your car broke down on the way to the university and you did not arrive in time to hear the speakers. However, one of the lecturers took the notes which are shown above, and said that you may use them in writing your article for the paper. Write an article of 200 words which reports the debate and which clearly brings out the different points of view. But remember that most of your readers do not have a deep knowledge of politics. Therefore do *not* copy out large chunks from the lecturer's notes. When you have finished, provide your article with a short headline.

If they became *experts* on issues, then they would become more effective both in scrutinising and influencing government policies. In the late 1960s three new Select Committees were set up on Agriculture, Education, and Science and Technology. This experiment was not wholly successful. It was felt that if specialised Select Committees were to work properly, they would have to cover all areas of government.

In December 1979 a new system was set up with fourteen new committees. One hundred and forty-eight MPs sat on these committees. These Select Committees were:

Agriculture	Home Affairs
Defence	Industry and Trade
Education, Science and Arts	Social Services
Employment	Transport
Energy	Treasury and Civil Service
Environment	Welsh Affairs
Foreign Affairs	Scottish Affairs

To these new Select Committees must be added the ones which were already in existence, namely, the Public Accounts Committee, the Select Committee on Statutory Instruments and the Select Committee on European Legislation.

These committees are able to question ministers much more thoroughly than is possible at Question Time. They are able to question civil servants – which is impossible at Question Time. The MPs on these committees can call for evidence and information to be shown to them. They can invite outside experts to discuss issues with them. Ordinary backbench MPs are thus able to specialise and become experts in the area covered by their Select Committee. The increased number of Select Committees means that nearly every aspect of government policy-making is examined closely. In this way, backbench MPs have won back some influence from government to Parliament. Governments now find it very difficult to 'fob off' MPs with unsatisfactory explanations for their policies.

Not all MPs agreed with setting up Select Committees. They felt that the work of the Commons should be done on the floor of the House, not in some committee room upstairs. They also felt that two classes of MP would be created since not all MPs would be invited to sit on a Select Committee. They were concerned that there would be 'super-MPs' who sat on these important new committees, and 'inferior MPs' who did not.

Supporters of the Select Committee experiment feel that they have been successful. The committees write reports on the issues they investigate and often these attract publicity. Sometimes they influence government policies – for example, the Home Affairs Committee report led to the reform of the 'Sus' law. Finally, if the opposition party should fail in its task of scrutinising and attacking government policies, then the Select Committees are there to do it instead.

Terms used

Dissension Disagreement. MPs can show their disagreement with their party leaders by disobeying the party Whip and voting against them.

The 1944 Education Act, sometimes known as the Butler Act, established the Ministry of Education. The Act coordinated education into a national system with primary, secondary and further levels of education. It introduced the idea of 'secondary education for all'.

Elementary schools These schools were eliminated by the Butler Act. Elementary education referred to the earliest stage of state education. At the time when they disappeared, elementary schools took pupils between the ages of 5 and 14.

Eton Many people believe this to be Britain's top public school. Inside the Conservative party some public schools are more important than others in educating MPs. Among the Conservative MPs drawn from public schools, 21.7% come from Eton. The next most important public school is Harrow, which provides 5.4%. Third is Winchester with 3.6%.

Marginal seats These are seats which are likely to change hands at a general election because the major parties have roughly equal support. Which party will win the seat depends on the size and direction of the 'swing'. There are fewer marginal seats today than in the past.

Safe seats These exist where one party has such an overwhelming level of support that rival parties have no real chance of defeating it at an election.

Whips These are MPs who are responsible for organising voting support, discipline and communication with leaders of the respective parties in Parliament.

Summary

1 The social background of MPs has changed considerably over the last forty years. In particular, more Conservative MPs have a business background now than in the past. Labour MPs are better educated and are more likely to come from the professional classes than in the past.

2 MPs have become less obedient and less loyal to their party leaders since 1970. This is equally true of both Conservative and Labour members.

3 A new mood of reform has led to the setting up of a system of Select Committees. This has increased the expertise of MPs and enabled them to scrutinise government policies more effectively.

4 Opponents of Select Committees believe that they are having a bad effect on the House of Commons. In particular, they create an elite of MPs who are members of Select Committees.

Questions for discussion

1 In which ways do MPs represent their constituents? How do they fail to represent them?

2 'Neither the Labour party, Conservative party nor SDP/Liberal Alliance represent the largest social class in Britain.' Discuss.

3 'When I vote for a candidate at an election, I expect him to be loyal to the party's leaders. I do not expect him to be a rebel.' How justified is this voter's view of party loyalty?

4 How successful have Select Committees been in restoring power to the backbenches?

5 The meetings and reports of Select Committees are reported in the four 'serious' papers – *The Financial Times, The Times,* the *Daily Telegraph* and the *Guardian.* Try to collect copies of these papers and cut out the clippings which report on their activities. Design a poster for your classroom wall on which to display the information you have collected about these committees.

17

The House of Lords

It is surprising that the House of Lords has survived into the mid-1980s. Although the Lords has been reformed, it is still undemocratic. None of its members are elected; indeed, some are there through the 'accident of birth'. Until 1911, the Lords had roughly the same powers as the Commons. But these powers have largely been taken away. Now that the House of Lords is weak, some argue that it might as well be abolished altogether. After all, New Zealand and Sweden recently got rid of their second chambers and the government of neither country has suffered because of this. In this chapter we examine the arguments for and against having a second chamber. We then examine the arguments for and against keeping the House of Lords as Britain's second chamber. This involves looking at the work that the Lords does in governing Britain. We conclude by considering how the House of Lords might be reformed.

Why have two Houses of Parliament?

Most countries which have a parliamentary type of government have a **bicameral**, or two-chamber, system. In other words, they have not one but two houses of parliament. In Britain, the lower chamber is the House of Commons and the upper chamber is the House of Lords. But why does Britain need a second chamber when it already has the House of Commons?

(i) A second chamber prevents erratic government. In countries such as the United States, Canada and West Germany there are second chambers which have some control over the first chamber. Because power is shared, there is less chance that the lower chamber will act in an irresponsible or unreasonable manner. The history of Britain's Parliament has led to its second chamber being unique amongst European second chambers. When democracy began to appear in Britain, those in power feared that it would lead to poor and erratic government. They worried that a government made up from directly elected representatives would be forever changing course. It would, they feared, swing first one way then another as it followed whatever course was popular at the moment.

The weakness of this argument in favour of the House of Lords as the second chamber is that the Lords is not democratic. To have agreed, first, that Britain should have a government controlled by the people, but then to say that the people cannot be trusted to behave responsibly, is contradictory. Unlike the House of Lords, the second chambers of Western European and American democracies are elected to office.

(ii) A second chamber can strengthen democracy by representing minorities as well as majorities.

Second chambers can represent people who are not represented strongly in the first chamber. For example, the US Congress has two chambers. The lower chamber is the House of Representatives and the upper chamber is the Senate. The number of members any state has in the House of Representatives is based on its population. Therefore California, with over 2 million inhabitants, is more strongly represented than Alaska which has only 300 000 inhabitants. But in the Senate, California and Alaska each have two Senators. The upper chamber is able to protect the special interests of small states such as Alaska.

Can this argument for having a second chamber be used to defend having the House of Lords? The House of Lords does not set out to represent the special interests of thinly populated areas such as Wales, Cornwall or the Scottish Highlands. So who does the House of Lords represent? Some argue that it represents no special interests and is therefore fair and impartial (not favouring one side or the other). Others argue that the House of Lords represents the small minority of people in Britain made up by the wealthy and already powerful.

(iii) A second chamber helps to cope with the burden of government. Modern government is extremely complex and the amount of work that parliaments have to get through is great. A single chamber could not cope with the workload by itself. The second chamber provides the extra help which is necessary. There is little doubt that the House of Lords is a busy second chamber. If it were abolished and no other changes made, the House of Commons would be put under enormous strain.

Reform of the House of Lords

You will see from Taskpage 17.1 that the House of Lords is still at the centre of controversy. This is nothing new. At the beginning of the century there was a major conflict over the part the House of Lords should play in politics. The Parliament Act of 1911 made it (a) impossible for the House of Lords to interfere with bills which were to do with money, and (b) allowed the House of Commons to overrule the opposition of the Lords on any bill if the Commons passed it on three successive occasions.

The Parliament Act of 1949 reduced the powers of the House of Lords still further. The power to delay bills passed by the Commons was limited to one year. Members of the 1945 Labour government made it clear that if the Lords tried to meddle with their policies or use the power of delay against them, the House of Lords would be abolished altogether. In addition to these acts, two further changes have been made.

The first change concerns the award of peerage. This was given as a reward for long and distinguished public service. But many people were unwilling to accept it because it was **hereditary**. In other words, when the peer died the title would pass on to the next male relative. This could be a burden to the son if he wished to have a career in politics as an MP. The Peerage Act of 1958 created a new category of peerage which was

awarded for the lifetime of the holder only. This act also allows women to be appointed as life peeresses and so the House of Lords ceased to be an all-male assembly. It was hoped that these measures would inject some 'new life' into the House of Lords.

The second change affected existing Lords. The 1958 Act did nothing to help those people who inherited titles but did not want them. One man with strong political ambitions who found himself in this position was Tony Benn. When his father Viscount Stansgate died, Tony Benn was excluded from the House of Commons where he was an MP. He won his fight against this in 1963 when a further Peerage Act was passed. This allowed anyone who inherited a peerage to renounce (give up) it for his lifetime. Lord Home renounced his title in order to enter the Commons and become prime minister after the resignation of Harold Macmillan.

Membership of the House of Lords

The membership of the House of Lords has no fixed limits. Well over a thousand people are entitled to be present if they wish. In practice, only a few hundred attend on a regular basis. These members can be divided into four groups:

(i) *Hereditary peers*
All peerages awarded before 1958 were hereditary. The hereditary titles, in order of rank downwards, are Prince, Duke, Marquess, Earl, Viscount and Baron. When the holder of a title dies, the title passes on to the nearest male relative. This person inherits the title and automatically becomes a member of the House of Lords. Peers are appointed by the Crown, but in modern times this is done on the advice of the prime minister. Hereditary peers are by far the largest group in the House of Lords. At present they number around 800.

(ii) *Lords Spiritual*
Since early times, the leading clergy of the Church of England have been entitled to sit in the House of Lords. The two archbishops, of Canterbury and of York, and twenty-four senior bishops sit in the Lords. Their appointments are not, of course,

hereditary. New archbishops and bishops are appointed by the Crown on the advice of the prime minister.

(iii) *Law Lords*

As we shall see, the House of Lords serves as the highest court in the land. Law Lords are chosen from the most senior and experienced judges. They are appointed by the Crown on the advice of the Lord Chancellor.

(iv) *Life peers*

Since the 1958 Act, over 300 men and women have accepted life peerages. They are appointed by the Crown on the advice of the prime minister. But, as already mentioned, their titles die with them.

By no means all peers take their seats in the House of Lords. This is shown in Taskpage 17.2. At the beginning of each session of Parliament, peers are required to say whether they are going to attend or not. Many turn down the opportunity to attend. Those who do attend receive no salary, but 'they are entitled to claim a daily allowance and expenses. In 1980 this was fixed at a minimum of £44.60 a day.

Functions of the House of Lords

Whether or not the House of Lords will survive is an interesting question. But it is not the only question. In fact there are three points of view which we need to examine. They are:

(a) that there is no need for a second chamber, and that the House of Lords should be abolished;
(b) that there is a need for a second chamber, and that the House of Lords should be kept as it is;
(c) that there is a need for a second chamber, but that the House of Lords should be replaced by a more up-to-date chamber.

In order to assess these different points of view, we need to look more closely at the work which is done by second chambers in general, and by the House of Lords in particular.

The first and strongest reason for having a second chamber is that it provides a second **forum** or meeting place. This provides an opportunity for further discussions on important public issues. The House of Commons is already overloaded with work. There is always more work for the Commons to do than time available to do it in. Having another chamber increases the amount of time available for discussing important issues. It means that *more* issues can be debated in Parliament. The House of Lords is extremely useful in getting more issues debated.

Having a second chamber also increases the *variety* of debates. The House of Commons tends to discuss issues on which the political parties are strongly divided. The House of Lords is able to hold debates on subjects which do not cause bitter party quarrels, but which are still very important. Such subjects as conservation of the environment fall into this category.

Supporters of the House of Lords might add another point. They claim that the atmosphere in the Lords is very different from that in the Commons. As a result, the standard of debate in the Lords is often higher than in the Commons. This is because (i) there is not the same degree of party rivalry in the Lords as in the Commons. This leads to a calmer atmosphere in debate. There is a greater effort to examine issues and fewer attempts to attack personalities, (ii) the Lords contain many experts who raise the standard of debate through their speeches.

The third function of a second chamber is that it can have a further look at the work of the first chamber. Because the first chamber is so busy, some of the bills which are passed receive little attention from MPs. Sometimes bills are not as carefully thought-out as they might be. The House of Lords has a **revising function**. It is able to make improvements in bills, which are then reconsidered by the House of Commons.

Supporters of the House of Lords argue that this job of revising the work of the Commons is done well by the Lords. Critics of the House of Lords argue that the Lords improve legislation on some occasions, but can produce shoddy bills on other occasions. Sometimes the Lords can make poor legislation even worse.

The fourth function concerns the amount of work that has to be done. Modern democracies have to get through an enormous amount of complex legislation. A second chamber can help ▷ p.

If you elect it, it will be a mirror image of the lower chamber. If you elect it from a different electorate, which elaborate is the right one? If you elect it by a different method of election – which method of election is a better one? (One has to be better and the other worse; one has to be more authoritative and the other non-authoritative.) If you appoint it, it will be no better than those who appoint it. There is no limit to the number of methods of producing a House of Lords by appointment that have been or could be suggested. The trouble is that an appointed chamber always tends to mirror, at an interval of five, ten or twenty years, whatever conglomeration of people, from Prime Ministers downwards (or upwards!), appointed it. So either you get a totally unsatisfactory second chamber, for whom nobody can have any respect, because of the people who appointed them, or alternatively you produce one on a basis which gives it parity with the other or lower chamber, and the result of that is going to be deadlock. Any attempt to reform the House of Lords in our circumstances is foredoomed to frustration.

Enoch Powell, MP in *Teaching Politics*, vol. 11, May 1982

The battle between the people and the Lords is an old one. Painfully, stage by stage, the Lords' Veto was ended in 1910 and the delaying power cut again in 1948. Changes in composition have also been carried through. Now the time has come to develop the work of the Commons so that it can replace the Lords without any loss of Parliamentary scrutiny. This is not an argument based on the political balance as it exists in the House of Peers. It is because it is inherently wrong that the Laws of this land should be submitted for approval to a body of men and women who lack any democratic mandate at all. It is not just that an inherited seat in Parliament is an anachronism – though it is. It is that the powers of patronage which are used by Prime Ministers to place people into Parliament by personal preferment are equally offensive.

Let me illustrate my argument with figures. The 635 MPs elected to the Commons in 1974 were put there by an electorate totalling just over 40 million people. By comparison 639 peers were put in the House of Lords by the last seven Prime Ministers. It cannot be right that seven men – however distinguished – can wield the same power to make legislators as do forty million voters. The simplest way to cut out this patronage is to end the Chamber which lives on it. I believe there would be strong public support for Parliamentary democracy to be strengthened in this way, and the day will come when it will be done.

Tony Benn, MP in *Teaching Politics*

Imagine that you are a reporter on a local evening newspaper. The editor has given you the extracts of two speeches shown above. He has asked you to write a 500-word article based on them. Do not copy out large chunks from each speech. You should contrast the different viewpoints using whatever parts of the speeches are necessary to do this. Make sure that your article has a short but accurate headline.

TASKPAGE 17.2 The House of Lords

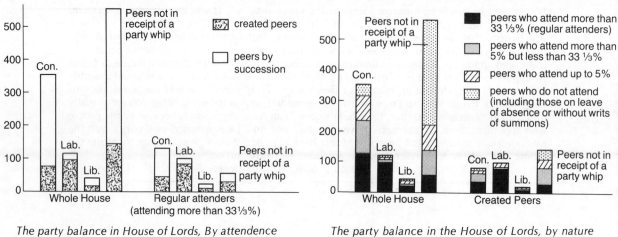

The party balance in House of Lords, By attendence (attending more than 33⅓%), 1967–8

The party balance in the House of Lords, by nature of Peerage, 1967–8

Source: Based on graphs in J.P. Morgan, *The House of Lords and the Labour Government, 1964–70*

(i)   It is often said that the House of Lords has a permanent Conservative majority. How far does the information shown in the left-hand graph bear this out? Does the Conservative party have a majority in terms of the 'whole house'? Does the Conservative party have a majority in terms of 'regular attenders'?

(ii) Which group of peers takes its responsibilities most seriously by attending most regularly (Consult left-hand graph.)

(iii) Which group of peers has the greatest proportion of 'non-attenders'?

(iv) Examine the right-hand graph. Roughly what proportion of peers never attend the House of Lords?

(v)   How frequently does a peer have to attend the House of Lords in order to be counted as a 'regular attender'?

(vi) Using the scale on the vertical axis, work out the approximate number of peers you would expect to see in the House of Lords during an 'average' debate. Roughly how many Conservative, Labour, Liberal and cross-benchers (peers not in receipt of a party Whip) would you expect to see? How many of these would be life peers?

by sharing the workload. The House of Lords helps by doing much detailed work on **non-controversial** bills. Indeed, the Lords deal with much of the general business of Parliament on which the major political parties agree. If the House of Lords was abolished, the system would break down under the strain.

The fifth function of a second chamber is that it can act as a check on the first chamber. However, it is now increasingly rare for the House of Lords to restrain the programme of the government. Some of the rare occasions it did so were during 1974–79. The Labour government did not have an overall majority in the House of Commons. The House of Lords rejected some measures that had been passed in the Commons. The Lords knew that the government would not be able to raise enough support to overrule them. In normal times, however, the Lords are unable to do more than delay legislation for a period of a year. Members of the House of Lords realise that if they did delay or obstruct the work of the government, they would probably lose the limited powers that they still have. The Lords did once 'meddle in the affairs of government'; they no longer do so to anything like the same extent.

Finally, the House of Lords has its legal function; it is the highest court in the land. In other democracies it is rare for this to be part of Parliament. For example, in the United States the Supreme Court is not part of Congress. In Britain a different situation has arisen because of the history of Parliament. Parliament was used as a court as well as a body which advised the king.

Today the House of Lords hears **appeals** against the decisions of the Court of Appeals. The Court of Appeals deals with appeals from lower courts. To reach the Lords, a case must be of special legal importance or of great public importance. When the Greater London Council introduced its 'Fares Fair' policy for cheaper tube and bus fares, it was challenged in the courts. Because other local authorities were considering similar transport policies, the final decision on 'Fares Fair' was made in the House of Lords. When acting as a court, the House of Lords sits in a special session and only the Law Lords actually attend. The House of Lords is 'rearranged' to form a court-room. The Law Lords hear the argument

of the lawyers appearing in the case and later announce their decision. Because there is no higher court, this decision is final.

The future

There is little doubt that the House of Lords will change, and possibly before very long. Both major political parties have produced plans for change. Many members of the House of Lords also feel there is a need for reform.

First of all, the hereditary idea is not one which has many supporters. The inheriting of a title is seen by many as a sign of social privilege. There are certainly no strong arguments for allowing those who happen to inherit to a title to sit in Parliament. The Lords are accountable to no one but themselves. It is true that some believe this is an advantage. They argue that because the Lords do not have to please voters this enables them to speak their minds without fear of losing their seats.

Secondly, people are concerned that the power of deciding who sits in the Lords is concentrated in the hands of the prime minister. As we have seen in chapters 13 and 14, some people think that the prime minister has too much power. Total control over all the honours is an example of this power. There is a feeling, therefore, that membership of the House of Lords should be decided differently. But how it should be decided is still a problem. Most people accept that some or all members should be elected in one way or another.

Having an elected second chamber is more democratic than the present House of Lords. But it does lead to two further questions. First, what would be the point of having a second chamber which was a duplicate of the first chamber? The second chamber might well end up trying to compete with the first chamber. In order to make the second chamber different from the first, it would have to be elected in a different way. Second, would an elected second chamber be content with the limited powers now held by the House of Lords? It is unlikely that it would. So the reform of the House of Lords could alter the power of the House of Commons.

The Labour party has voted at its annual conference to abolish the House of Lords. The

Conservative party favours a second chamber which would be partly elected by a system of proportional representation and partly nominated, like the present life peers. The SDP has proposed that new regional assemblies would elect representatives to the second chamber. Hereditary peers would not sit in the new second chamber: life peers would continue to do so but would not be allowed to vote. The delaying powers of the reformed second chamber would be increased to two years for bills other than money bills.

It seems likely that reform of some sort will eventually come. But governments seem to find much more urgent things to do. There is general agreement on the need for change, but little agreement on the precise changes to be made. As a result the highly complicated business of reforming the House of Lords continues to be postponed.

Terms used

Appeals Hearing a case in a higher court after a decision has been reached and challenged in a lower court.

Bicameral A parliamentary system made up from two chambers, such as the House of Representatives and the Senate in the US Congress. Some systems are unicameral. Denmark, Finland, Sweden, New Zealand and Israel have only one chamber.

Forum A meeting place or place for public discussion.

Non-controversial Unlikely to cause disagreement.

Revising function The House of Lords cannot revise or suggest changes in financial or money bills. But on every other aspect of the Commons' work, the Lords can examine proposals and suggest changes. Bills may be amended, improved, or changed for the worse as the House of Lords performs its revising function.

Hereditary peerage Title and membership of the House of Lords which is passed on from father to eldest son.

Summary

1 There are a number of arguments in favour of having a second chamber. For example, a second chamber can strengthen democracy by representing minorities which are not represented in the first chamber. Also a second chamber can help the first chamber by sharing the work of Parliament.

2 Some people argue that the House of Lords is no longer suitable to be Britain's second chamber. Although it has been reformed on a number of occasions, it is still not democratic.

3 Some members of the House of Lords are appointed and some inherit the right to sit in the Lords. None are elected.

4 Despite its undemocratic nature, the House of Lords performs useful tasks in helping the House of Commons. It is often said that the quality of debating is higher in the Lords. Also the House of Lords provides the opportunity for a greater variety of debates.

5 The House of Lords can initiate [start] legislation.

6 The House of Lords functions as the highest court in the land.

7 All the major political parties have plans for reforming the Lords, but none regards it as an urgent issue. As a result, it may be many years before really basic changes in the composition and functions of the House of Lords are made.

Questions for discussion

1 'Because the House of Lords is so weak, Britain has a one-chamber system of government.' How accurate is this judgement?

2 'Britain will not be a true democracy until the House of Lords is reformed.' Do you agree with this statement?

3 What role does the House of Lords play in the government of Britain?

4 What are the arguments in favour of keeping the House of Lords as it is?

5 In what ways do the political parties differ in their proposals for reforming the Lords?

6 Divide your class into three or four groups. Each group should spend 15–20 minutes discussing how the Lords should be reformed. One person from each group should report his or her group's suggestions to the class. Discuss the merits and disadvantages of each group's proposals.

18

The monarchy

The final part of our study of Parliament deals with the Queen in Parliament. The monarchy is an ancient and complex institution which has changed a great deal during this century. Yet the powers and the influence of the monarchy are still argued about. Is the monarch simply a ceremonial figure who opens hospitals, lays foundation stones and launches ships? Or does the monarch still have real power? The effect of having a monarchy in Britain is also discussed. There is no doubt that the relationship between the Queen and her people is a complex one. We examine the arguments of those who say that the monarchy provides a moral lead for the nation. We consider also the view that the Royal Family is simply another source of entertainment. Finally, we examine opposition to the monarchy.

The evolution of the monarchy

It may seem very strange that a modern democratic country like Great Britain still has the institution of monarchy. The existence of an hereditary ruler appears to be the complete opposite of all that democracy stands for. Nevertheless, it is true to say that the Queen has an important role to play in the government of Britain today.

The reasons for the survival of this ancient institution are found partly in the way in which the monarchy has developed. But they are also due in part to the skilful way in which monarchs during the last hundred years have carried out their responsibilities and duties.

The main feature of the development of the monarchy in Britain has been the complete loss of any power over the decisions of government. This was not a sudden change but a gradual process, and took several centuries to complete. By the end of the last century, the monarch had lost almost all the power that was once wielded by the kings and queens of these islands.

Monarchy was the traditional type of government in England, Wales and Scotland from the Dark Ages onwards. It was generally accepted that one man should rule and that his decisions should be final. But it was also true that a good king always took the advice of other important men in his kingdom. The king who was a strong leader was respected. The one who did not listen to his advisers was liable to make bad judgements which could weaken his position.

Thus, in Great Britain, there has evolved a monarchy which is controlled by Parliament and has lost all governmental powers. As Ivor Jennings once wrote, 'The Queen reigns but she does not rule'. But, as we shall see, she has an important part to play.

The Head of State

The main function of the monarch is to act as Head of State. Every nation in the world has a Head of State. The position has at least two important tasks:

(i) The Head of State is the person who represents the whole nation on important public occasions and in receiving important visitors from abroad.

(ii) The Head of State is responsible for the continuity of the government. The Queen appoints the person who is to be prime minister. As we have seen in earlier chapters, she does not have any personal power in who is appointed: she must appoint the person who has the support of a majority in the House of Commons. Also, when a prime minister wishes to hold a general election he asks the Queen to **dissolve Parliament** and call an election. The new session of Parliament does not begin until the Queen declares it open. But the Queen does not personally decide when an election should be held or when Parliament should meet. The Queen's consent should be seen as a **formality**. In other words, the Queen is obliged ▷ p.

What my children have taught me

BY

PRINCESS MICHAEL

She can seem the most Royal of the Royals; the fairytale Princess, tall, blonde and stately, sparkling with jewels. But take off the tiara and you'll find a mother—one filled with the same wonderment at, and worries about, her children as any of us. In a rare interview, Princess Michael talks to Gabrielle Donnelly about the problems and pleasures of being a mother

A mother worries about her children. And that holds true whether the mother is you, or me, or ... one of the Royal Family. Take, for example, Princess Michael of Kent. Now, on the surface, Princess Michael might seem to be the woman with everything. Married to the

Queen's first cousin, she has two homes — one in London, and one in the country — two bright, beautiful children, Lord Frederick Windsor, three and a half, and Lady Gabriella, one and a half, both of whom she unabashedly adores and, as if that weren't enough, she is also president — and a very active president — of the Tufty Club, the national club affiliated to the Royal Society for the Prevention of Accidents, for young children and their parents.

But when I met her at her country home recently to talk about child safety and the prevention of accidents, she revealed that, Princess or no Princess, she worries about her children every bit as much as the rest of us do.

COURT CIRCULAR

BUCKINGHAM PALACE

June 9: The President of the United States of America and Mrs Reagan, with the American Suite in attendance, left Windsor Castle this morning upon the conclusion of the Visit to The Queen and The Duke of Edinburgh.

The President visited No 10 Downing Street and had talks with the Prime Minister.

The Queen, Patron, was present this evening at a Thanksgiving Service in Westminster Abbey to mark the Centenary of the Church Army.

Her Majesty was received by the Dean (the Very Reverend Edward Carpenter) and the Chairman of the Church Army Board (Admiral Sir Horace Law).

KENSINGTON PALACE

June 9: The Prince of Wales visited the Isle of Wight today.

His Royal Highness, attended by the Hon Edward Adeane, travelled in an aircraft of The Queen's Flight.

KENSINGTON PALACE

June 9: The Princess Margaret, Countess of Snowdon, was present at the Friend's Meeting House, Euston Road, this afternoon, at the Annual Council Meeting of the National Society for the Prevention of Cruelty to Children.

Mrs Jane Stevens was in attendance.

KENSINGTON PALACE

June 9: Princess Alice, Duchess of Gloucester was represented by Miss Jean Maxwell-Scott at a Memorial Service for Dr Charles Frankland Moore at the Church of All Hallows-by-the-Tower, Byward Street, London EC3 this evening.

REPORTING THE ROYALS

It is sometimes said that the mass media in the USA has Hollywood to gossip about, and British has the Royal Family. The Royal family is the sort of subject that can be reported in ways to suit all taste. The monarch's performance of ceremonial duties may be reported in a serious and dignified way in one paper. In another paper, the life of a prince or princess might be reported in a very sensational way.

(i) Attempt to identify the type of publication that the extracts on this Taskpage were taken from.

(ii) Which members of the Royal Family are treated with respect by the mass media? Which members tend to get treated in a sensational way?

(iii) Imagine that you are editor of a daily newspaper. Describe the type of readers who buy your paper. What do they like reading about? Outline your paper's policy on reporting the Royal Family, making sure that it meets the needs of your readers.

to do as she is asked. But the monarch's part in these decisions provides an important safeguard. For example, should a prime minister try to stay in office without support in Parliament, the Queen could, as a last resort, dissolve Parliament.

The entire government is carried on in the Queen's name. Indeed, the government is often referred to as 'Her Majesty's Government' and all its official business is conducted 'On Her Majesty's Service'. Even the opposition in Parliament is 'Her Majesty's Loyal Opposition.' The armed forces owe their allegiance to the Queen. Similarly, all criminal prosecutions in the law courts are made in the Queen's name. The Latin word for queen is used; a case would appear as 'Regina v Brown'. Finally, the Queen is Head of the Church of England. The Church of England is officially supported by the state.

In carrying out all these duties, the Queen acts on the advice of the prime minister. She accepts the advice of the prime minister, no matter which party he happens to lead. Because of this, the Queen is above party politics. She is not involved in any political argument or dispute. Since the Queen is not identified with any particular policies or party, it is possible for someone to express loyalty to the Queen whilst vigorously condemning her government.

This contrasts with some countries where the Head of State is a political figure. In most countries where there is no monarch, a president is elected. In some countries, such as West Germany, the president is simply the formal figurehead of the state in the same way as the Queen. In others, such as the United States and France, the office of President is combined with that of Head of Government. Such presidents have to run the country as well as perform many of the ceremonial and formal duties of a Head of State.

The modern monarch, therefore, does not exercise any real power in government. But it is easy to be confused by reference to the **prerogative powers** of the Crown. The monarch has retained a wide range of powers in government. For example, the right to appoint ministers and ambassadors, the right to summon and dissolve Parliament, the right to declare war and make peace, the right to pardon someone of a criminal offence, and the right to award titles and honours. If the Queen really did exercise these rights, she would be very powerful indeed. In practice, however, all of these prerogative powers are exercised by the prime minister or by other ministers in the Queen's name. For example, the Foreign Secretary selects ambassadors, the prime minister decides when Parliament is to be dissolved, the Cabinet decides on war and peace, and the Home Secretary recommends pardons. In other words, the prerogative powers add up to the power of government, not the power of the Queen.

There have been occasions this century when the monarch influenced events. In 1923 the prime minister, Bonar Law, died suddenly. George V had to choose between Stanley Baldwin and Lord Curzon for the new prime minister. Some people think that the King used his own judgement when making the choice: others think that he chose according to the advice he received from senior politicians. In 1945 George VI advised Clement Attlee, the new Labour prime minister, on the appointment of ministers. Attlee was thinking about making Ernest Bevin Chancellor and having Hugh Dalton as Foreign Secretary. The King thought that neither was suitable for the job Attlee had in mind. Attlee accepted this advice and swapped them around.

Some people feel that the Queen might have as great a role to play in politics as her predecessor in 1923. They point out that if Britain develops into a three-party system, future general elections may produce complex results. For example, there may be no single obvious person who would command majority support in Parliament. Under these circumstances, the Queen might use her own judgement in calling for the leader most likely to lead a successful coalition government.

The Privy Council

One of the reminders of past royal power is the Privy Council. This was once the meeting between the king and his ministers where policy was decided. By the beginning of the eighteenth century, it had become customary for a small group of trusted ministers to meet separately. The

Privy Council became a formal and a ceremonial body.

Many of the prerogative powers are exercised by means of Orders in Council. These are regulations issued by the Queen and approved by her Privy Council. Whenever such orders are required, the Privy Council meets with the Queen present.

All senior members of the government are made members of the Privy Council. This entitles them to be addressed as 'Right Honourable' and write PC after their names. One senior minister is appointed by the prime minister to be Lord President of the Council. His job is to organise the business to be placed before the Council. Once appointed, Privy Councillors tend to remain members. But since as few as three members need to be present at a meeting, being a Privy Councillor is not a heavy burden. The main feature about being selected to serve as a Privy Councillor is that it is an honour. MPs who are Privy Councillors have certain rights in being called to speak in the House of Commons.

The Privy Council has a committee of judges, known as the Judicial Committee, which acts as the final Court of Appeal for certain colonial territories and Commonwealth countries.

The social influence of the monarchy

Does the monarchy strengthen the authority of government? Or does the monarchy simply provide entertaining gossip in the same way as the private lives of Hollywood movie stars? Or does the monarchy have a bad effect on the country, because it represents social snobbery and the class system which sets people apart? Let us consider the arguments.

Some people argue that the monarchy brings stability to Britain, particularly during periods of change or crisis. They point to the Watergate scandal in the United States which led to the downfall of President Nixon. The Watergate affair shook American voters, and many of them lost confidence in their method of governing. Had the Watergate affair happened in Britain, then the prime minister would have been dismissed. The chances are that the British people would have condemned the actions of particular politicians, but they would have kept confidence in the monarchy and the parliamentary system of government. It is argued that the existence of the monarchy helps Britain through periods of national crisis or emergency. It provides a symbol of continuity, national unity and a focus for the people's allegiance.

It is also argued that the monarch represents tradition and order. The Queen is at the very top of the social pyramid and stands for the old values. For example, the monarch represents solid belief in the value of family life. Edward VIII **abdicated** because he wanted to marry a divorcee. Princess Margaret was persuaded not to marry Group-Captain Peter Townsend because he also had been divorced. Even when Britain suffers big problems (such as war, general strikes, massive unemployment, or high inflation) there is never serious social unrest. This is because respect for the monarchy 'holds the country together'.

Other people argue that the monarchy no longer has such strong emotional links with the people. The public no longer accepts the old values associated with it. For example, the public has become more permissive despite the Queen's example. Even members of the Royal Family seem out of step with the monarch. Princess Margaret eventually became divorced from Lord Snowdon. Prince Andrew's friendship with a film starlet, Koo Stark, who had appeared naked in some film sequences, made headlines. It is argued by some that the monarchy no longer holds the country together. Britain is experiencing more and more unrest, be it on picket lines, on the football terraces, at carnivals or in the shape of inner-city riots. In other words, the monarchy no longer has an effect on people's behaviour.

The monarchy has many images and means different things to different people, as is shown in Taskpage 18.1. For most people, it is argued, the monarchy has become part of 'show business'. People celebrated the Investiture of Prince Charles in 1969, the Queen's Silver Jubilee in 1977 and the Royal Wedding of Prince Charles and Lady Diana in 1981. But they celebrated these events in the same way as they celebrated Britain's football team winning the World Cup in 1966. It is argued that the monarchy provides a harmless distraction or escape from the dreariness and problems of everyday life.

Opposition to the monarchy

Because of the popularity of the Queen, opposition to the monarchy in Britain is very slight. Only one MP is regularly heard to speak against it. This was not always so. When Queen Victoria was alive many people believed that she would be Britain's last monarch. This was because she withdrew from public life after the death of her husband, Prince Albert. In the 1860s **republicanism** had much support in Britain. It was only after the Queen was persuaded to enter public life again that the monarchy regained support. It was fortunate, too, that King George VI became a popular figure after the abdication of his brother, Edward VIII. At the time many people felt that the monarchy was threatened. This situation might have become even more serious had Edward remained king in the years leading up to the Second World War. This is because Edward VIII had in earlier years been represented as an admirer of Adolf Hitler.

Critics of the monarchy point to the undemocratic situation of someone enjoying a position of importance simply as a result of accident of birth. Hereditary rights, they argue, have no place in a modern democratic society. All positions should depend upon merit or election. Although the situation has changed quite a lot during the present Queen's reign, there is still some truth in the criticism that a monarchy encourages privilege and social snobbery. It may be argued, though, that social snobbery may flourish just as much in a republic such as the United States. Therefore it is unfair to blame the monarchy for the way other people behave.

Terms used

Abdication Giving up of power

Dissolution of Parliament Dismissal or ending of Parliament with a view to holding a general election

Formality Carrying out the rules although decisions have already been made. For example, someone who has been promised a job might still be asked to apply for the job, 'as a formality'.

Prerogative powers Those powers held by the Queen in which she is able to act without consulting Parliament

Republic A form of government not dependent upon a monarchy but which is carried out on behalf of the people. Republicanism is the idea or support for having a republic.

Summary

1 The monarchy has lost almost all the power that it once wielded. This process took several centuries to happen.

2 The Queen is Head of State, but not Head of Government. She has a number of prerogative powers which she exercises on the advice of the prime minister. The monarch is above party politics.

3 The social impact of the monarchy is hotly debated. Some feel that the monarchy provides moral leadership whilst others feel that the monarchy today simply provides glamorous entertainment.

4 Republicanism does not exist as a major political force in Britain.

Questions for discussion

1 'The Queen reigns but she does not rule'. Explain this statement.

2 What are the prerogative powers? How are they exercised?

3 'The monarchy is a valuable national institution, particularly during times of crisis when it keeps people united.' ... 'The monarchy represents snobbery and the social class system, which divides people from each other.' Evaluate these statements.

4 Imagine that you have an American penfriend who lives in Chicago. He or she has written to you asking if Britain is as democratic as the United

States. Your penfriend cannot understand how a monarchy can exist in a democracy. Write a reply explaining the position in Britain.

5 Divide the class into two and organise a debate on whether or not the monarchy should be retained.

19

Administration in Britain

The main aim of this chapter is to examine the influence and nature of the civil service. In the past, the top civil servants were unknown to the public. Today this is less true because of the work of Select Committees and the Parliamentary Commissioner for Administration. They can interview civil servants and thus draw publicity to the work of the civil service. Some people firmly believe that civil servants 'run the country'. They argue that ministers are controlled by their civil servants, that policy is made by senior administrators who walk the corridors of power in Whitehall, and not by the elected representatives in Parliament. We examine this argument. We also look at the different levels of administrators in the civil service. It has to be remembered that the civil servants we are likely to meet do not hold senior positions. How do the 'men at the top' differ from the civil servants that we come into contact with at the DHSS or Inland Revenue? There have been attempts to increase opportunities for promotion for lower level civil servants. How successful have such reforms been in increasing the efficiency of the civil service? We try to answer this question by considering the impact of the Fulton Report. The second aim of this chapter is to examine administration in Britain which is not done by civil servants. Here we look at what has become known as quasi-government. Much administration is now done by the so-called 'quangos', and we assess their growth and importance.

The civil service

Civil servants exist to help ministers administer the complex work of government. As the work of government has grown, so too has the number of civil servants. In 1900 there were 50 000 civil servants: today there are around 700 000. Civil servants are the permanent staff who work inside government departments. You can see from Table 19.1 that some departments are much larger than others. Also some civil servants are concentrated in one place, whereas others are spread around the country. For example, the Department of Education and Science (DES) is small and many of its two thousand or so civil servants work at Elizabeth House in London. On the other hand, the Department of Health and Social Security (DHSS) is large, with many of its civil servants employed in hundreds of local offices throughout Britain. The Foreign and Commonwealth Office (FCO) provides yet another contrast. Many of its civil servants are spread around the world in British Embassies, High Commissions and Consulates.

Ministers and civil servants

In theory voters elect a government by voting for the party whose policies they prefer. The prime minister chooses ministers to lead government departments and put these policies into practice. To help each minister in this task, there is a team of civil servants. The top civil servants may offer a minister advice on a decision, but the minister can overrule this advice if he disagrees with it. This is because the minister is more powerful than the civil servants. It has been said that 'the minister is on top, and the civil servants are on tap'.

The minister has to take final decisions and is answerable for them in Parliament. Because of this he is likely to prefer his own judgement on decisions to the judgement of others. Some people have argued that ministers will tend to dominate their civil servants because of their background in politics. To get to the top in politics means that ministers have survived a tough climb. They have had to defeat the enemies who exist in their own parties whilst winning support from backbench MPs. This experience is in contrast to the careers

Table 19.1 Civil service statistics

Department	Staff in post at 1 October 1980	Target numbers for staff in post at 1 April 1984
Ministry of Agriculture	13 406	11 600
Chancellor of the Exchequer's departments	115 938	102 600
Defence	235 226	200 000
Education and Science	2 571	2 200
Employment Group	50 912	49 000
Energy	1 222	1 100
Environment and Ordnance Survey	49 360	41 400
FCO/ODA	11 605	11 100
Health and Social Security	97 917	87 700
Home Office	34 924	34 900
Industry	9 120	7 300
Lord Chancellor's departments	16 370	16 000
Lord President's departments	12 289	9 100
Scottish Office	10 911	10 000
Trade, Office of Fair Trading and Export Credits Guarantee departments	9 458	8 400
Transport	13 291	10 700
Welsh Office	2 388	2 200
Other departments	10 167	9 700
Totals (rounded)	697 000	615 000

of civil servants. They have enjoyed job security and steady promotion. As a result of these different backgrounds, ministers are likely to be dominating whilst top civil servants are likely to be respectful.

Does this theory explain what really goes on inside government departments? Do ministers make all the important decisions, with civil servants merely carrying out their orders? Let us consider the arguments which see civil servants as having far more power.

The first point to note is that ministers come and go but civil servants are permanent. Most ministers are at the top of the same department for two or three years at most before moving to another. The political career of Anthony Crosland illustrates this:

1964–5	Minister of State, Economic Affairs
1965–7	Secretary of State for Education and Science
1967–9	President of the Board of Trade
1969–70	Secretary of State for Local Government
1974–6	Secretary of State for the Environment
1976–7	Foreign Secretary

Even gifted politicians such as Anthony Crosland, who held six different posts in nine years, cannot become experts overnight. It takes at least six months for a new minister to 'settle in' to his department, and much longer before he has developed any **expertise**. For most ministers, just as they are mastering their department they are moved on to head another. There are exceptions, such as Denis Healey. He served as Minister of Defence in the years 1964–70 and gained a worldwide reputation for his detailed knowledge of military issues.

In most government departments the 'experts' are the permanent top civil servants. Naturally this gives them considerable influence over ministers who do not share their expert knowledge. There have been ministers who have been totally controlled by their civil servants. This has not happened because the ministers concerned had weak personalities, but because they could always be beaten in an argument by civil servants who had all the facts and information.

Civil servants have the information which ministers need when making many policy decisions. Therefore ministers will seek advice from their civil servants. Is this advice biased? This is a difficult question to answer. Civil servants are expected to be politically neutral and to be able to work for a minister regardless of which party he represents. Yet top civil servants come from upper middle-class backgrounds. They reflect the views of well-off professional people, who might normally be expected to vote Conservative.

Sometimes the civil servants within a ministry develop particular attitudes, or certain ways of looking at the world. Economists often talk of the 'Treasury view' of financial policy. The Foreign Office is said to have a 'pro-Arab/anti-Israeli' view of problems in the Middle East. Political parties have worried that ministers might become too influenced by these departmental attitudes. They worry that the civil servants might control or manipulate the minister, or persuade him to drop the policies contained in the party's manifesto. In order to prevent this, specialist **political advisers** have been appointed since 1964. They are appointed by political parties and go into ministries with the minister. They are able to offer 'non-civil service' advice to the minister. However, many people feel that civil servants have found that these advisers do not fundamentally threaten their influence.

Inside a ministry

Ministries are **bureaucracies**. That is, they are organisations which have layers of officials with different degrees of responsibility. At the top of this 'power pyramid' is the minister. He is assisted in policy-making by civil servants in the Administrative class. At the very top of the civil service are the Permanent Secretary, Deputy Secretary and Under Secretary. You can identify these posts in Fig. 19.1, which shows the organisation inside the Department of Education and Science (DES). The department is divided into different groups of civil servants – or divisions – to deal with various tasks. These divisions will be broken down into smaller sections, each of which deals with a particular part of the division's work. Each division is led by an Under Secretary; each group of divisions by a Deputy Secretary, with the Permanent Secretary in overall charge of the department.

The civil servants fall into two other broad categories: generalists and specialists. The generalist is an 'all-rounder'. He is capable of taking a practical view of any problem, no matter what it is about. Under Secretaries, Deputy Secretaries and Permanent Secretaries are generalist administrators. Specialists have the more narrow outlook of experts. Top specialists will include the Chief Planner, Chief Architect and Chief Medical Officer. Specialists provide information and advice to the generalists, who take it into account when giving the minister advice.

Recruitment

The civil service is often criticised because its top administrators come from the upper classes. For example, between 1957 and 1963 83% of **graduate** entrants at the top level were either from Oxford or Cambridge University. Well over half of them had *arts* degrees in subjects such as History or the Classics. Few have *applied* degrees in relevant subjects, such as Public Administration.

Nearly half of top civil servants come from Social Class I. In this sense, the civil service is not socially representative. But does this matter? Some people argue that the fact that top civil servants ▷ p.17

A Minister's time

A vivid picture of the demands on a minister's time is given in a recent analysis by Tony Benn, then Secretary of State for Energy, of the way he spent 1977. During that time he:

(a) Fulfilled fifty public engagements in his constituency, made twelve general speeches in Bristol, held sixteen constituency surgeries, had handled more than 1000 personal cases.

(b) Attended four General Management Committee meetings of the Bristol South East Labour Party; attended twenty ward meetings, and five Labour Group meetings to discuss policy.

(c) Attended twelve meetings of the Parliamentary Labour Party, and made fourteen speeches to various sub-group meetings of MPs.

(d) Dealt in parliament with three Energy Bills, produced fifty-four statutory instruments; presented thirty-three explanatory memoranda to the House re European Community Energy matters; answered fifty-one oral questions and 171 written questions; had 154 meetings with non-governmental groups; produced 1821 ministerial minutes on papers taken home in the official red box; made 133 appointments to various bodies, etc.

(e) Attended forty-two Cabinet meetings and 106 Cabinet Committee meetings; submitted four Cabinet papers and forty-five Cabinet Committee papers; received 1750 Cabinet papers covering the whole range of government policies.

(f) Made nineteen visits abroad, and received in his office thirty-two Foreign Ministers and Ambassadors.

(g) In the first half of 1977 presided over the Energy Council of the European Community. This involved taking the chair at six Council meetings and having sundry other official meetings on European Energy questions.

(h) Attended fifteen meetings of the Labour Party National Executive and sixty-two committee meetings.

(i) Made eighty speeches up and down the country, gave eighty-three radio interviews, fifty-seven television interviews, gave thirty-four press conferences, wrote sixteen articles, had thirty interviews with individual journalists, and received or answered 1000 letters which did not involve constituency casework or ministerial work.

That is a killing and intolerable burden of work by any standards – and there must have been occasions when even the inexhaustible Mr Benn accepted on trust recommendations from his civil servants without being able to give them the thoughtful scrutiny that might otherwise have been the case. Now Benn is in many ways no ordinary cabinet minister. His devotion to Labour Party duties outside government business has not always been appreciated by his colleagues. But the general picture of a minister hemmed in by political demands outside his department is by no means unusual. An analysis of the working weeks of fifty ministers – covering the 1964–70 Wilson administration and the 1970–74 Heath administration – found that ministers spent a minimum of sixty hours each week (excluding weekends) working; of this at least forty-five hours each were spent in cabinet and cabinet committee meetings, Parliament, interviews and discussions with people outside the department, formal receptions and lunches, official visits, and constituency

responsibilities. In other words, every minister has a strenuous full-time job as politician and as ambassador for his department *before* he can deal with the direct task of running his department – reading departmental papers, considering official advice, discussing and deciding policy options with colleagues and officials inside his ministry. No wonder most ministers prefer short briefing papers with clear advice on all but a few issues.

Peter Kellner and Lord Crowther-Hunt,
The Civil Servants: an Inquiry into Britain's Ruling Class

Civil service influence in practice

I have seen this process of civil service containment successfully practised against both Conservative and Labour governments over the last thirty years.

The bold challenge of the 1964 Labour Government, with its 'new Britain' manifesto, was absorbed and defused by July 20, 1966, when the Treasury persuaded the then Chancellor to insist upon a package of economic measures that killed the national plan and instituted a statutory pay policy. It happened again when the 1970 Conservative Government was driven off its commitment to the philosophy developed at Selsdon Park and the then Prime Minister was persuaded to do a U-turn which took him back to the same policies that Macmillan had developed from 1962 to 1963, and that Wilson had been persuaded to follow from 1966 to 1970.

It happened again after the referendum in 1975, when the Labour Government was persuaded to abandon its 1974 manifesto and was diverted back to the policies of 1972–1974, as pursued by Heath. It will be interesting to see how long it is before the same pressures are successful in guiding Mrs Thatcher back to the well-trodden paths followed on the advice of the civil service by Macmillan, Wilson, Heath and Wilson.

It would, of course, be quite wrong to attribute all these policy changes to civil service pressures alone. All Ministers must take responsibility for what they do and all are subject to a wide range of other pressures besides those which come from Whitehall. But it is not a coincidence that governments of both parties appear to end up with policies very similar to each other, and which are in every case a great deal more acceptable to Whitehall than were the manifestos upon which they were originally elected.

It is also true that the central theme of consensus, or Whitehall, policies which have been pursued by governments of all parties for the last twenty years or more have been accompanied by a steady decline in Britain's fortunes, which has now accelerated into a near catastrophic collapse of our industrial base. The governments which followed these policies – especially 1964, 1970, 1974 and 1979 – have paid a heavy price in electoral terms, whilst those who furnished the briefing for the ministers concerned have continued to power, subject only to the normal wastage occasioned by retirement at 60.

Tony Benn, 'Manifestos and Mandarins' in
Policy in Practice: the Experience of Goverment

One of the extracts above is about Tony Benn, the other is written by Tony Benn. To what extent does the first extract explain the second? In other words, does Tony Benn's view of the civil service's influence result from the fact that he was overworked? Is this true for other ministers as well as Tony Benn? Study the two passages and write a short essay which
 (i) assesses whether or not ministers are overworked, and
 (ii) examines how far the workload of a minister makes him depend on his civil servants for advice.

Marks and Spencer and the civil service: a comparison of culture and methods

It is a well-worn theme that the civil service – and indeed the government as a whole – would gain in effiency if it were run more on the lines of private enterprise. The more grandiose variations on this theme – the notion of 'Great Britain Limited' – have never carried much credibility, but the work of Sir Derek Rayner has underlined the scope for applying in the public sector certain basic disciplines associated with a successful commercial operation. There nevertheless remains a good deal of scepticism among civil servants about whether the approach of private enterprise is really applicable on a wide scale to the management of public operations.

Comparisons between the private sector and the civil service (or more strictly, between the marketed and non-marketed sectors of the economy) are usually couched in general terms, and the main points of comparison are familiar enough: measures of effectiveness, patterns of accountability, and incentives to efficient behaviour. There is, however, a lack of more systematic comparisons based on direct experience. This paper is one contribution to filling that gap. It attempts a detailed comparison between the civil service and Marks and Spencer in three main respects: decision-taking; systems; management, leadership and motivation. Under each heading the main characteristics of the two organisations are described and an explanation suggested for some of the differences between them ...

SOME FEATURES OF MARKS AND SPENCER

Although it is a large organisation, the structure of Marks and Spencer is so simple and uniform that its main features can be outlined quickly. There are just over 250 stores employing about 40 000 people, full-time and part-time. There is a single head office in London employing over 3000 people and consisting of buying departments together with a range of ancillary services – building, transport, accounts, etc. The regional (or divisional) tier is small and is more a means of communication and quality control than a link in line management.

Systems are strongly centralised and controlled from Baker Street, which determines in detail what stores will sell and at what price. The business is mainly the retailing of textiles and foods, accounting respectively for about two-thirds and one-third of sales. Traditionally there has been little movement of staff between the sales floor and management. Managers have been recruited as trainees; after an initial period in stores they either move to Baker Street or progress in store management. Almost no managers are imported from outside. Although M & S is much less of a family company than it was, the Chairman and Vice-Chairman are still from the founding families, and in many respects the company still bears the stamp of Lord Marks and the first Lord Sieff and of the principles they established.

DECISION-TAKING

Marks and Spencer

Although the style of decision-taking naturally varies with individuals, some generalisations are possible. First and foremost, there is a comparative lack of written policy analysis. Debate tends to be conducted orally; policy papers, such as they are, tend to be short and factual; they point to a particular conclusion rather than highlight choices. The general disinclination to reasons things out on paper also extends to an avoidance of many conventional management techniques – e.g. formal investment appraisal. The result is that decisions tend to be personalised, informal, contingent on events and *faits accomplis* rather than the products of systematic analysis. Equally important, the volume of paper is small by comparison with the civil service and consists largely of progress reports and sales records (which are kept and used manually).

Speed of reaction is critical in retailing and the effectivenes of decisions is usually apparent over a short time-scale – a matter of weeks for particular lines of merchandise. Speed of communication is equally important. Thus a telephone cascade system and daily notes (privately delivered to stores) are used for factual messages; changes of mood are also communicated swiftly through the Baker Street grapevine, the divisional executives and the numerous visits to stores by head office personnel.

Employees are generally less at home on committees, especially when authority and policy is not clear-cut, than in informal or individual decision-taking. Skills of chairmanship and note-taking are less developed than in Whitehall. Similarly, people are happiest in dealing with the immediate and concrete, especially if it can be related to sales; they are less ready to focus on long-term problems, especially those such as computer development which are not easily resolved by applying traditional company principles.

Finally, it should be stressed that senior directors, notably the Chairman, have a marked influence on decisions at all levels. In part this is formal – through Board meetings, department reviews and so on. But decisions are just as likely to result from a chance meeting or visit, from a small directorial statement or from some event which happens to come to senior attention. Anything in Marks and Spencer is liable to become 'political' at any moment, especially at Baker Street. In this sense a distinction between the strategic and the operational is difficult to maintain – an interesting point of similarity with the affairs of government.

Civil service

Within the civil service there are naturally wide differences in the procedure and style of decision-taking. But the essential contrasts with Marks and Spencer are still clear enough.

The proceedings and the culture of the civil service are centred on the written word. Most issues of note are subject to written exposition, frequently exhaustive, before the point of decision. At its best, this approach can mean cogent analysis, a display of options, a clear recommendation and a generally more disciplined treatment of problems than would be likely in oral discussion. At its worst, the result can merely be an accumulation of paper and a tendency for analysis to become a surrogate for action ...

A further critical contrast is that a higher proportion of decisions in Whitehall are taken by consensus. This applies both to decisions between departments and to decisions within departments which effect more than one interest. Failure to consult gives rise to righteous indignation. One result is the proliferation of committees, with all the associated apparatus of papers, minutes and reports.

These extracts are from an article by David Howells in *Public Administration*, vol. 59, Autumn 1981. In it he contrasts two organisations: the Civil Service and Marks and Spencer.

(i)   Describe the organisation of your youth club or school. Who makes the important decisions? How are they made? Are committees important? On what grounds are individuals 'promoted' or given extra responsibility?

(ii)   How do individuals communicate with each other inside the organisation? What use is made of the spoken word? What use is made of written communications (on notice boards, memos, letters)?

(iii) Contrast the organisation you have described with the civil service in terms of three differences.

TASKPAGE 19.3

Oxbridge and non-Oxbridge top civil servants

Department	Principal and above			Deputy Secretary and above		
	Oxbridge grads.	Non-Oxbridge grads.	Oxbridge as % of all grads.	Oxbridge grads.	Non-Oxbridge grads.	Oxbridge as % of all grads.
Foreign & Commonwealth	630	170	79	42	7	86
Treasury	110	51	68	10	3	77
Cabinet Office	55	46	54	7	3	70
Education	42	50	46	6	2	75
Civil Service Department	70	89	44	3	2	60
Overseas Development	98	141	41	2	0	100
Energy	49	100	33	3	2	60
Environment/Transport	299	668	30	14	2	87
Home Office	97	230	30	5	2	71
Trade/Industry/Prices	293	897	25	16	3	84
Northern Ireland	20	66	23	1	1	50
Defence	349	1254	22	13	9	59
Employment	154	598	20	5	3	62
Health & Social Security	127	538	19	10	2	83
Agriculture	109	499	18	5	2	71
Wales	21	112	16	1	1	50
Scotland	48	375	11	3	5	37
Total*	2582	6056	30	146	51	74

*Includes some small departments not itemised above – e.g. Privy Council office
Source: Kellner and Crowther-Hunt, *op. cit.*

This table shows some general information about the universities attended by graduates in the higher levels of the civil service. An administrative Principal will work on problems connected with policy-making. He or she will be a relatively young person who has been picked out as a 'high-flyer' who can expect quick promotion. Details about Deputy Secretaries and above are contained in the chapter.

(i) Some departments are more 'glamorous' than others and still attract more Oxbridge (OXford and CamBRIDGE) graduates. From the data which refer to 'Principal and above', identify these high prestige departments.

(ii) Several studies of the civil service have shown an Oxbridge bias at senior levels. In 1950, R. K. Kellsall found that 62 out of the 96 Permanent and Deputy Secretaries had been to Oxford or Cambridge. Is the percentage of Deputy Secretary and above who had an Oxbridge education, given in this table, higher or lower than Kellsall's figure?

TASKPAGE 19.4

WHAT THE CIVIL SERVICE IS

Important to recognise what the civil service *is* and *does*
● is only a small part (10%) of the public sector work force not a mysterious mass of bureaucrats but real people doing jobs because the country wants them done
● providing services to firms (export credit guarantees), to farmers (drainage engineers), above all to the public generally (social security benefits, finding new jobs for the unemployed)
● thankless but necessary jobs (tax collectors; prison officers; driving test examiners; Customs Officers; Immigration Officers)
● backroom boys sometimes (research scientists – e.g. on road safety; the weathermen)
● about a quarter blue collar workers (printers, carpenters, welders); the Royal Ordnance Factories export more than half their annual sales of around £300m
● not 'Head Office'; of non-industrial civil servants: 83% work outside Inner London, 73% outside head offices
● not a 'bowler brigade': 46% of non-industrial civil servants are women and about one-third are younger than 30.

PAY

1 Ministers, not civil servants, authorise civil service pay rates.
2 What essentially determines a particular rate is what is currently being paid outside the civil service for broadly comparable work.
3 The basic principle of fair comparison was recommended by the Priestley Royal Commission in 1956, and accepted by all governments since, as the only principle which is both fair to the taxpayer and fair to civil servants.

PERKS

1 There are virtually no perks in the civil service – people's rewards are the published and taxed salaries. Civil servants pay for their pensions.
2 Allowances or facilities are available only when essential for work purposes, and their use is governed by detailed regulations.
3 The payment of boarding school fees for children of diplomats, the armed forces and other civil servants posted abroad simply reflects the fact that boarding school education which is entailed by the absence on duty of their parents is not normally available in the state system. The rates allowed are strictly controlled.
4 There is no equivalent in the civil service of 'the company car'. No civil servant has a car provided for private or domestic use. The use of government pool cars for official purposes is strictly controlled.
5 There is no equivalent in the civil service of 'expense account living'. The occasions on which hospitality is possible at official expense, and the levels of that entertainment, are strictly controlled.

HONOURS

Civil servants get too many honours. It is true that civil servants receive a large share of the honours, because honours have always been designed to give special recognition to servants of the Crown (whose achievements must otherwise be, for the most part, anonymous). Honours are, after all, simply public recognition, in a form involving virtually no cost to the taxpayer.
Only a small proportion of honours go to civil servants. Their proportion of honours has deliberately been reduced from over 35% in the late 1950s and early 1960s to about 20% in the last few years.
Only a small proportion of civil servants receive honours. The proportion of civil servants who receive these honours is tiny. For example, 148 out of some 726,000 home civil servants were so honoured in the 1979 New Year Honours List.
The small proportion honoured get their honours on merit, not automatically. While a very few civil servants – about 200 in the highest two ranks in the civil service – are almost bound to receive honours, there is nothing automatic about reaching this level in the service, and the honours – like the posts – go to those who have proved their ability in a full civil service career.

JOB SECURITY

1 In times of recession civil service jobs are no doubt more secure, by and large, than those in the private sector. But that is not the full story.
2 In times of full employment it is doubtful if there is much practical difference in security between jobs in the civil service and the great mass of jobs outside.
3 Where services cease to be required and those providing them cannot be redeployed, civil servants are as liable to redundancy as private sector people in the same position. But many civil servants are required to do whatever job they are given and to go wherever sent; and in recession the demand for their work increases (social security payments, unemployment benefits, finding new jobs, assistance to industry).

These extracts are from *The Quarry*, an underground publication circulated amongst top civil servants. It was published in Peter Kellner and Lord Crowther-Hunt, *The Civil Servants.*

  Draw up a questionnaire which will record a person's impression of the civil service. Use the headings contained in *The Quarry*. For example:

What percentage of the public sector workforce is employed in the civil service? 10%; 50%; 90%

Ask your friends and parents to fill in your questionnaire. What is the general impression of the civil service? Compare your answers with *The Quarry*.

What the government plans to spend in 1983/4

Defence	£15 900 million
Housing Environment	£6 644 million
Industry	£1 124 million
Transport	£3 314 million
Law & Order	£4 014 million
Education	£12 548 million
Health	£14 634 million
Social Security	£34 121 million
Other	£25 766 million
Total:	**£120 065 million**

Guardian, 9 November 1982

Civil servants, particularly those working in the Treasury, help the government of the day to plan public expenditure. Each year the Public Expenditure Survey (PESC) reviews government spending. Until recently each department worked out its own Programme Analysis and Review (PAR). This review listed the department's priorities for future spending. PESC and PAR helped the civil service to plan and coordinate policy. Today, however, the PAR review no longer takes place. Treasury approval is important in planning public expenditure. This is because it finances departments. It can, to some extent, control other departments' policies by controlling their finances.

(i)   Which government departments are the 'big spenders'?

(ii) Which departments are likely to need more money in the future?

(iii) In which ways are government policies likely to affect future expenditure (i.e. privatisation or expansion of particular service).

(iv) Prepare two brief reports: the first argues that more should be spent on public transport, and the second argues that transport should not be subsidised. Give your reasons for and against.

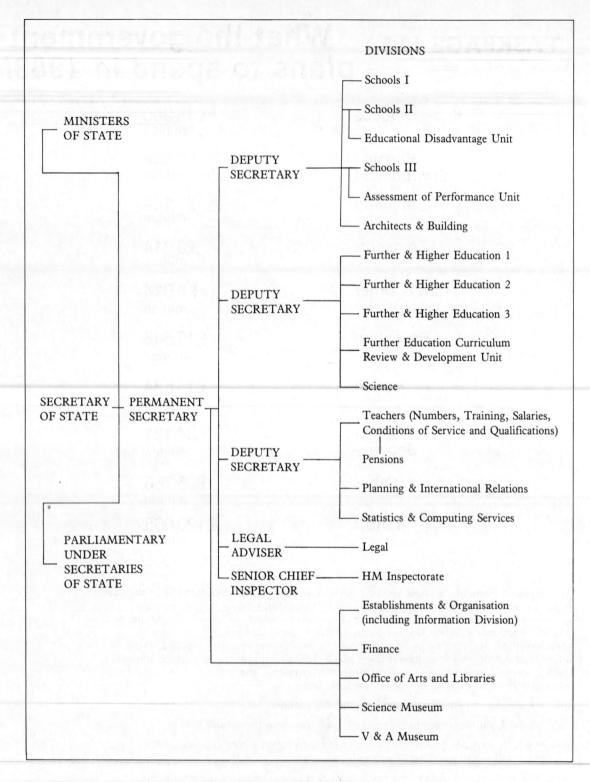

DIVISIONS

— Schools I
— Schools II
— Educational Disadvantage Unit
— Schools III
— Assessment of Performance Unit
— Architects & Building

— Further & Higher Education 1
— Further & Higher Education 2
— Further & Higher Education 3
— Further Education Curriculum Review & Development Unit
— Science

— Teachers (Numbers, Training, Salaries, Conditions of Service and Qualifications)
— Pensions
— Planning & International Relations
— Statistics & Computing Services

— Legal

— HM Inspectorate

— Establishments & Organisation (including Information Division)
— Finance
— Office of Arts and Libraries
— Science Museum
— V & A Museum

MINISTERS OF STATE

DEPUTY SECRETARY

DEPUTY SECRETARY

DEPUTY SECRETARY

LEGAL ADVISER

SENIOR CHIEF INSPECTOR

SECRETARY OF STATE

PERMANENT SECRETARY

PARLIAMENTARY UNDER SECRETARIES OF STATE

Fig. 19.1 Organisation of the Department of Education and Science, July 1981

come from upper classes does not affect their efficiency. Others argue that top civil servants are out of touch with the ordinary man-in-the-street. There is a feeling that top civil servants will defend the interests of upper-class rather than working-class people.

Reform in the civil service

There have been two major reviews of the civil service:

(i) The Northcote–Trevelyan Report in 1854

This report written in the middle of the last century introduced a number of reforms. It recommended that recruits should be selected by examination, and should be promoted according to merit. It also believed that the work of the civil service could be divided into (a) the intellectual jobs done by graduates and (b) the routine clerical work done by less qualified workers.

(ii) The Fulton Report of 1968

The Fulton Report made a number of criticisms of the way in which the civil service was organised. These were reflected in Fulton's main recommendations:

(a) The complex class structure of the civil service should be abolished and replaced by one structure covering all civil servants from the top to the bottom. Fulton felt that the class system that existed at the time hindered the efficiency of the civil service.

(b) Graduate recruits should have relevant degrees rather than arts degrees. Fulton rejected the 'generalist' philosophy of the civil service. He favoured the idea of having more specialists in top posts. For example, graduates who had studied international relations and foreign policy should be recruited to the Foreign Office rather than students who had studied Latin and Greek.

(c) A Civil Service Training College should be set up to train civil servants as managers. Fulton felt that top civil servants did not have management skills.

(d) A Civil Service Department should be set up under the authority of the prime minister. This would keep a close watch on developments within the civil service.

(e) There should be greater ease of transfer of employees between the civil service and other jobs in industry and commerce.

How far were the Fulton recommendations put into practice? Fulton's main proposals were accepted with the exception of recruiting graduates with relevant degrees. But of those proposals that were put into effect, many were changed from what Fulton had in mind. For example, a new grading system was set up; but it was not like the one Fulton had recommended. Figure 19.2 shows the old system and the new. In 1971 the Clerical and Executive classes were merged with the bottom three grades of the Administrative class to form 'the Administration Group'. Above this there is still a top layer made up of nearly 800 civil servants who are Permanent Secretaries, Deputy Secretaries and Under Secretaries. In other words, there is still not one structure to cover all civil servants. Also, generalists (who are found mainly in the Administration group) are separated from specialists.

A Civil Service Department was set up to look at pay, efficiency and recruitment. This department was abolished in 1981 when the Treasury and Cabinet Office took over its role. A Civil Service College was opened in 1970. It had centres in Sunningdale, London and Edinburgh. Because of expenditure cuts, the Edinburgh centre was closed in 1976.

Efforts to recruit top civil servants from a wider section of society have not been very successful. A new scheme was set up to recruit new people into the Administrative class. It is known as the Administrative Trainee Course. It was hoped that many people already employed at the lower levels of the civil service would be promoted through this course. However, only a quarter on the AT scheme came from the lower levels. The rest came on to the AT scheme directly as graduates. Many

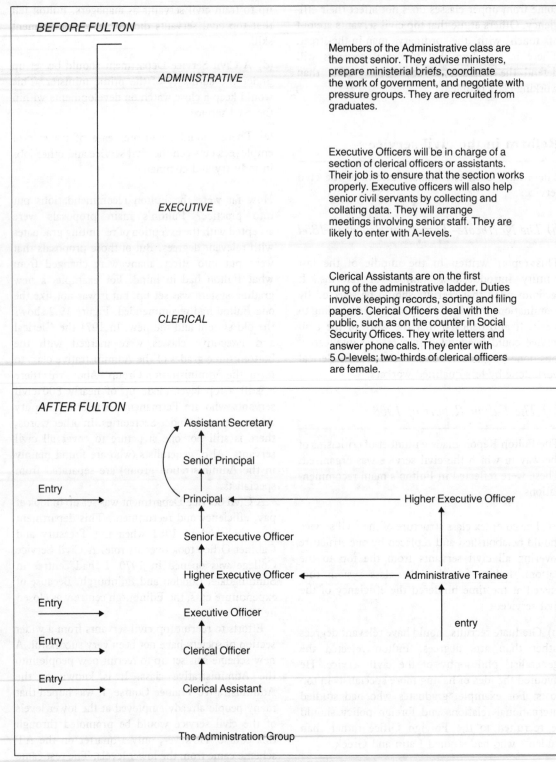

BEFORE FULTON

ADMINISTRATIVE

Members of the Administrative class are the most senior. They advise ministers, prepare ministerial briefs, coordinate the work of government, and negotiate with pressure groups. They are recruited from graduates.

EXECUTIVE

Executive Officers will be in charge of a section of clerical officers or assistants. Their job is to ensure that the section works properly. Executive officers will also help senior civil servants by collecting and collating data. They will arrange meetings involving senior staff. They are likely to enter with A-levels.

CLERICAL

Clerical Assistants are on the first rung of the administrative ladder. Duties involve keeping records, sorting and filing papers. Clerical Officers deal with the public, such as on the counter in Social Security Offices. They write letters and answer phone calls. They enter with 5 O-levels; two-thirds of clerical officers are female.

AFTER FULTON

Assistant Secretary

Senior Principal

Entry → Principal ← Higher Executive Officer

Senior Executive Officer

Higher Executive Officer ← Administrative Trainee

Entry → Executive Officer

Entry → Clerical Officer

Entry → Clerical Assistant

entry

The Administration Group

Fig. 19.2 The civil service before and after Fulton

of them had graduated in the Arts, and nearly two-thirds still came from Oxford and Cambridge.

The growth of quasi-government

Although there has been a 'growth of bureaucracy' in the last thirty years, the civil service has remained roughly the same size. Growth can be clearly seen in the numbers of administrators in local government, the National Health Service and quasi-government.

The best known organisation in the world of quasi-government is the quango (quasi-autonomous non-governmental organisation). Some people feel that the growth of quangos represents 'creeping bureaucracy' and an increase in 'indirect government'.

Why are quangos set up by the government? They are usually set up by a department and provided with money to do a particular job. The department concerned will not wish to do the job itself. Because the quango does the job, the minister is not responsible. He will, however, appoint people to serve on the quango.

Defining the term 'quango' is very difficult because individual quangos vary a great deal. Some have been temporary because the job they had to do was short-term. For example, the Decimal Currency Board was set up to administer the change-over in Britain's currency in 1971. Other quangos disappeared because Britain's circumstances had changed. For example, the Colonial Empire Marketing Board disappeared as more countries joined the Commonwealth. The best known quangos today include the Sports Council, the Arts Council, the Commission for Racial Equality and the Equal Opportunities Commission.

From time to time governments have attempted to reduce the number of quangos in existence. They have not succeeded. It is easy for politicians to point a finger at quangos and accuse them of wasting public money. In reality, quangos are very useful to governments. This is why the number of quangos increases, even under governments that say their number should be reduced.

Terms used

Bureaucracy A bureaucracy is made up of all the white-collar workers or officials who are responsible for administering an organisation. The administration is tightly organised, with each person having clearly-defined responsibilities. People who work in bureaucracies are sometimes referred to as bureaucrats. The terms 'bureaucracy' and 'bureaucrats' have become associated with 'red tape', 'delay' or 'inefficiency'. Thus some people use the words as terms of abuse.

Expertise This is specialist knowledge. The person in an organisation who has most knowledge on an issue often becomes most powerful in making decisions.

Graduate A graduate is a person who has obtained a degree. Generally that degree will be a Bachelor of Arts (BA) or a Bachelor of Science (BSc). Arts degrees are in subjects such as History, English or Classics. A degree in Politics would count as an arts degree, whereas a degree in Public Administration would be an applied degree. Applied degrees prepare students for a particular type of job rather than being a purely academic qualification.

Political Advisers are brought into government from outside the civil service. Basically a political adviser thinks about policy in political terms. He advises the minister, and keeps the minister in close contact with the thinking of his party.

Summary

1 It is hard to generalise about the civil service, or about civil servants. Departments vary in terms of size and situation. Civil servants differ at the extremes from the men at the top who help make policy and the clerical workers at the bottom who do routine office jobs.

2 The careers and experience of ministers are very different from those of senior civil servants. Some argue that this results in tough ministers who are in charge of their civil servants and policy-making.

3 Ministers swap departments every two or

three years on average. This means that top civil servants will know more about the affairs of the department than the minister. Some argue that this results in civil servants making most of the important decisions because they can control the minister.

4 Recruitment to the senior levels of the civil service still has a strong bias towards individuals from well-off backgrounds. Attempts to 'open up' the higher levels to individuals who have not enjoyed a privileged education have generally failed. Other attempts to reform the civil service have met only with limited success. Fulton's recommendation to have more specialists in top posts was rejected altogether.

5 Not all administration in the public sector is done by civil servants. For example, people who work in local government or Health Service administration are not civil servants. Nor are all the people who work in the area of quasi-government. Governments have from time to time attacked quangos as being a waste of public money, yet those very governments have created new quangos to do certain jobs.

Questions for discussion

1 'The minister is on top, and the civil servants are on tap.' Assess the accuracy of this statement.

2 Do top civil servants form an elite which is out of touch with the citizens they are serving? Would there be advantages in having a more socially representative civil service?

3 Did the Fulton Report lead to any major reforms inside the civil service?

4 Has the growth of quasi-government assisted or undermined the working of democratic government?

5 Build up a file on the civil service by collecting relevant magazine or newspaper cuttings. Note the events that lead to various departments being in the news.

6 Organise (i) a class discussion or (ii) the production of rival posters on the usefulness of 'bureaucracy'. One side must argue that government bureaucracies are vital for the welfare of the population and explain the work done. Describe what might happen if the size of the civil service etc. was drastically reduced. The other side must argue that bureaucracies waste the country's resources. Explain what the advantages would be in having far fewer administrators. You must argue your side's view as best you can no matter what your private opinion is.

20

The organisation of local government

This is the first of two chapters which examine how local government works. Except when something sensational happens, the affairs of local government tend to be neglected by the mass media. News reporters generally give much more attention to Parliament, yet what local government does affects people's lives in a very practical way. In this chapter we examine the organisation of local government. In Britain there has been a great debate about how local administration should operate. Some people wanted each area to have one body to be responsible for all services. Others wanted different levels of local government to deal with different services. We look at the important issues which affect the efficiency of local government. We also look at efficiency within each individual council. Councillors make decisions which provide new homes, leisure centres or better roads. But where does the money to pay for all this come from? Surprisingly, most of it comes from central government. This can cause tension between central and local government, particularly when central government wants to save money at a time when local government wants to spend more on services which are needed at community level. The chapter concludes with an examination of this troublesome relationship between central government and the local authorities.

Local democracy

There is an important difference between *local government* and *central administration at local level*. Some services provided by central government have local offices throughout the country, such as the DHSS. Also public corporations such as British Gas provide a local service. But neither the local social services office nor the gas showroom are part of local government.

Local government is based on the idea of representation. This means that local people are involved in deciding what services will be provided. Local democracy involves the election of representatives who make decisions which reflect local needs. For example, councillors representing an inner-city area will respond to local needs in a different way from councillors representing a seaside resort containing many retired people. Central government would not be in a position to meet local needs as efficiently as local government.

But how democratic is local government? It has been pointed out that turn-out in local government elections is very low (see Table 11.5). This, it is argued, weakens the authority of local government. Others disagree with this point of view. They accept that the percentage voting in local elections is lower than that in general elections; but, as in the case of the parish council meeting, a low poll does not reduce the degree of participation. In addition local government elections normally occur more often than general elections. In light of this, they argue that local government is just as democratic as central government.

Despite the latter point of view, concern over low levels of interest and participation led to the reform of local government. In the 1950s and 1960s the lack of democracy was reflected in the number of non-contested seats. These are seats in which only one candidate is nominated. Roughly half of all seats on the older county councils (which covered the more rural areas) were not contested.

The reform of local government

Many people were concerned about the organisation and efficiency of local government. There was a need to match competent administration

179

with the traditions of local democracy. In 1966 a Royal Commission under the chairmanship of Sir John (later Lord) Redcliffe-Maud was asked

to consider the structure of Local Government in England, outside Greater London, and to make recommendations for authorities and boundaries, and for functions and their division, having regard to the size and character of areas in which they can be most effectively exercised and the need to sustain a viable system of local democracy.

Redcliffe-Maud defended the idea of local government. But to be effective local government should have four qualities:

(i) to be efficient in looking after the well-being of people in different localities
(ii) to attract and hold the interest of its citizens
(iii) to be strong enough to form a partnership with central government, and
(iv) to adapt to change in the way people work and live.

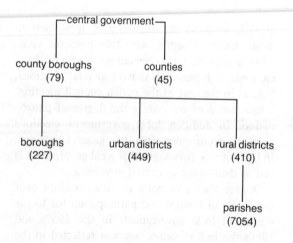

Fig. 20.1 Structure of local government in England and Wales before 1974

The old structure of local government shown in Fig. 20.1 failed to do these four things. This was because:

(i) the division of England into 79 county boroughs and 45 counties each having responsibilities within its own boundaries caused problems. It divided 'town' from 'country',

and made the proper planning of development and transportation impossible.
(ii) the division of responsibility within each county between county councils and district councils meant that services which should be in the hands of one authority were shared out among several. This was made worse with the position of county boroughs as 'islands' within the counties.
(iii) many local authorities were too small in both size of population and revenue received. This prevented them from doing their work as efficiently as they would wish.
(iv) local government areas did not, therefore, fit the pattern of life and work in modern England.

The Maud Report stated that local government should be organised according to a number of principles or rules. These principles included the idea that all services concerned with the environment (such as planning and transport) should be in the hands of one authority. Also all personal services (such as education and housing) should be in the hands of one authority. The report also argued that areas of local government should be large enough to meet the needs of a growing population. They should be bigger than most county boroughs in order to have the manpower and resources to provide efficient services. A minimum of 250 000 people should live in an authority. But authorities should not be so big that local councillors cannot keep in touch with the people. In areas of England where areas needed for effective planning contain too many people for effective personal services, responsibilities should be divided between two levels.

The pattern of local government recommended by Maud was based on those principles (see Fig. 20.2). England should be divided into eight 'provinces', each with a provincial council which would be concerned with the overall planning of the environment. Members of these provincial councils would be indirectly elected by lower authorities. England should also be divided into 58 'unitary' authorities. These authorities covered town and country and would be responsible for all services. It was also proposed that within these authorities, local councils should be elected to

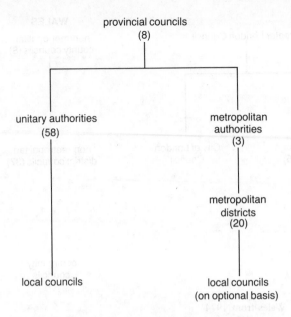

Fig. 20.2 Structure of English local government recommended by The Maud Commission

represent the wishes of local communities. These local councils would be consulted on matters of special interest to their citizens. They might also provide certain services, such as the preservation of trees and buildings.

Reactions to the Maud proposals

Although people felt that there was a need for local government reform, many opposed the particular proposals made by Maud. It was felt that there would be too many practical problems with the single-**tier**, all-purpose authorities which were being recommended for all areas except the major conurbations. But there was also the political perspective on Maud.

Conservative strength in local government lies mainly in the counties, and Labour's strength lies in the urban areas. It might be expected that Conservatives would favour a two-tier system which gave the counties some power. It is not surprising that Labour favoured the single-tier, all-purpose authorities based on towns.

The Labour government accepted the Maud proposals, although it made some changes. These included shelving the idea of having provincial councils until the idea of regional government had been discussed in more detail.

Local Government Act, 1972

The Conservatives rejected the Maud recommendations. Instead the Local Government Act, 1972, came into operation in 1974. It provided a two-tier system throughout the country, which is shown in Fig. 20.3. The idea of metropolitan areas was kept and there were to be six of these: they are shown, together with the non-metropolitan counties, in Fig. 20.4. In both metropolitan and non-metropolitan areas government was divided between *county* and *district* councils. Local government provides many different types of services – these include *protective services* (fire, police, consumer protection); *environmental* (highways, transport, planning); *personal* (education, housing, social work); *recreational* (sports facilities, museums, camp sites), and *commercial* (markets, smallholdings). Who provides what under the new system of local government? This is shown in Table 20.1.

It was argued that this new structure provided a balance between (i) efficiency, which needs large scale units of government and (ii) democracy, which works best with smaller units of government. Existing rural parishes were kept, with some new ones being created.

In a White Paper, *Streamlining the Cities*, a later Conservative Government outlined plans to abolish the GLC and the six metropolitan councils. It was argued that there was no real role for the 'mets'. Most of their functions would become the direct responsibility of the borough or district councils. Such functions would include planning, highways, waste disposal, housing and trading standards. Functions not passed to the boroughs or districts, such as fire, police and public transport, would be run by joint boards. These boards would be composed of members nominated by borough and district councils from amongst their elected members.

Who does what in local government

Local authorities do their work under legislation

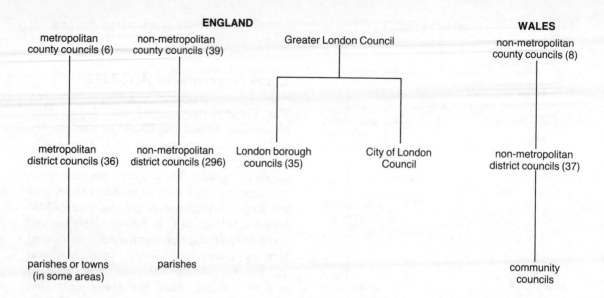

ENGLAND

WALES

metropolitan county councils (6) ── metropolitan district councils (36) ── parishes or towns (in some areas)

non-metropolitan county councils (39) ── non-metropolitan district councils (296) ── parishes

Greater London Council ── London borough councils (35) / City of London Council

non-metropolitan county councils (8) ── non-metropolitan district councils (37) ── community councils

Fig. 20.3 Structure of local government in England and Wales from 1974

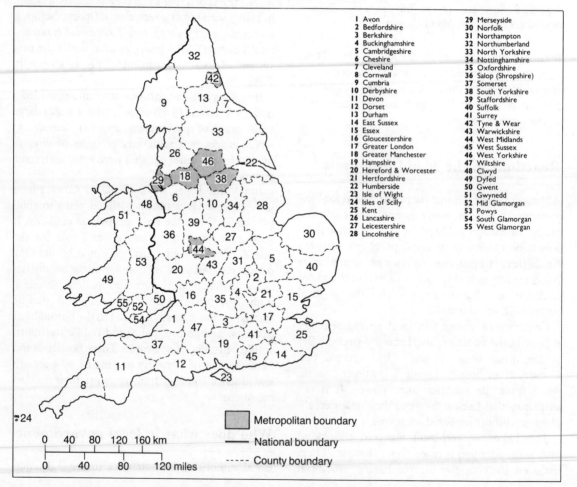

1 Avon	29 Merseyside
2 Bedfordshire	30 Norfolk
3 Berkshire	31 Northampton
4 Buckinghamshire	32 Northumberland
5 Cambridgeshire	33 North Yorkshire
6 Cheshire	34 Nottinghamshire
7 Cleveland	35 Oxfordshire
8 Cornwall	36 Salop (Shropshire)
9 Cumbria	37 Somerset
10 Derbyshire	38 South Yorkshire
11 Devon	39 Staffordshire
12 Dorset	40 Suffolk
13 Durham	41 Surrey
14 East Sussex	42 Tyne & Wear
15 Essex	43 Warwickshire
16 Gloucestershire	44 West Midlands
17 Greater London	45 West Sussex
18 Greater Manchester	46 West Yorkshire
19 Hampshire	47 Wiltshire
20 Hereford & Worcester	48 Clwyd
21 Hertfordshire	49 Dyfed
22 Humberside	50 Gwent
23 Isle of Wight	51 Gwynedd
24 Isles of Scilly	52 Mid Glamorgan
25 Kent	53 Powys
26 Lancashire	54 South Glamorgan
27 Leicestershire	55 West Glamorgan
28 Lincolnshire	

0 40 80 120 160 km
0 40 80 120 miles

▨ Metropolitan boundary
── National boundary
---- County boundary

Fig. 20.4 England and Wales: metropolitan and non-metropolitan counties

Table 20.1 The responsibilities of local authorities

	Responsible for:
ENGLAND	
Metropolitan areas:	
6 counties	Overall planning, transport, police, fire services
36 districts	Education, personal social services, housing, local planning, environmental health, leisure services
Non-metropolitan areas:	
39 counties	As metropolitan counties, *plus* education and personal social services
296 districts	As metropolitan districts, *minus* education and personal social services
Over 7000 local (parish and town) councils	Local amenities
LONDON	
Greater London Council	Transport, overall planning, some housing
Inner London Education Authority	Education in inner London
32 London boroughs	Housing, social services, leisure, public health, education (outside inner London)
WALES	
8 county councils	Much the same as non-metropolitan authorities in England
37 districts councils	
About 800 community or town councils	Local amenities
SCOTLAND	
9 regions	Overall planning, education, social work, transport, water, police, fire services
53 districts	Housing, local planning
Over 1200 community councils	Local amenities
3 island areas	All regional and district powers

Source: Tony Byrne, *Local Government in Britain: Everyone's Guide to How It All Works*

passed by Parliament. They must not act outside the powers that are granted to them. Most services are **mandatory**. This means that the local authority *must* provide them, such as police and education. Others are **permissive**. This means that local authorities *may* provide them, such as museums and art galleries. Local authorities may gain additional powers under local Acts of Parliament. For example, Hull has its own telephone service, Doncaster has a race-course and Birmingham has a municipal bank. Local authorities may

also have powers taken away by Act of Parliament. For example, water and sewage services were transferred to ten regional water authorities in 1974 when the new local government system came into being.

You can see from Table 20.1 that some powers are concurrent. That is, one part of the service is provided at county level whilst another part of the service is provided at district level. This occurs in planning. Some services are provided by both types of authority. This is the case with museums ▷ p.187

The fuse is LIT

The Government is now considering the various responses to The Green Paper on Alternatives to Domestic Rates. Our depressing premonition is that it will do nothing to overcome the main problems of local government finance, for the very simple reason that the green paper itself did not deal with the fundamental issue of the dependence of local authorities for most of their income on grant and non-domestic rates rather than on taxes that bear directly upon the local electorate.

The process of consultation has, however, led to a major advance. The green paper, by raising the topic of new sources of revenue, even in a limited context, opened up opportunities for comment and debate on the wider issues. Many of the responses to the green paper rejected the Government's narrow focus and deliberately set out to deal with the critical issues.

It is important that, whatever the Government's immediate conclusion, these wider issues are not lost sight of. In particular, a local income tax has been put on the political agenda. All concerned with the welfare of local government should ensure that it remains there.

The objective should not be hard to achieve. In all three opposition parties active consideration is being given to a local income tax. The Government itself has indicated that many of the measures it has introduced recently in Parliament are only interim, awaiting the permanent settlement of the problems of local government finance. That settlement will not be attained until central government focuses on the main issue.

The answer lies within the grasp of determined local authorities ready to campaign for a new source of revenue, a local income tax.

Local government will have only itself to blame if it does not achieve it because it failed to campaign for it.

That a local income tax is possible was shown by the Layfield Committee. That judgement has been confirmed by the green paper, but the difficulty it raises is that, because of computerisation of PAYE, the method favoured by the Layfield Committee could not be introduced before the end of the decade.

That simple statement has been by many even in local government as ruling out a local income tax from practical consideration. Rather it should be an incentive to probe the assertion, and for local authorities to assert the case for a local income tax.

Even if it were true that the only viable local income tax is through PAYE, and that it could not be introduced before 1990, that would not be a reason for rejecting a local income tax. It would be a case for a commitment to a local income tax before yet more time slipped away. If a commitment to introduce a local income tax had been made in 1976 when recommended by the Layfield Committee, it would now be in operation.

Once this commitment is made, attention can be turned from listing administrative obstacles to finding ways of overcoming them. There are more types of local income tax than that recommended by the Layfield Committee, which had neither the time nor the resources to explore all possible methods. What it set out to show, and did

show, was that one method – and it chose the PAYE-based system – was practicable.

Among other options we are particularly interested in are those which involve direct collection of the tax by a local authority on the basis of income assessments produced by the Inland Revenue. Such a proposal involved no industrial or commercial costs. It is significant that even in the green paper its public costs, which are in this instance the total costs, are £220 million, which is the same as the total costs, public and private, of the PAYE-based version. It is also significant that the costs associated with the proposal have not been subjected to the same critical appraisal as the Layfield Committee applied to the PAYE-based approach, which led to a marked reduction in the costs initially put forward. Similar appraisals applied to the other methods might well lead to similar reductions.

If a clear commitment were made to a local income tax, then a short and focused investigation would establish the most practicable method. Expertise on many of the issues involved lies not in central government but in local government. For direct local collection the expertise is not within central government but in local rates offices.

One key issue underlying a local income tax (as it would also a local poll tax) is the need for an authoritative register of residence. The expertise for compiling it lies again not in central government but in local government, experienced in the parallel but not identical task of electoral registration.

Local Government Chronicle, 23 April 1982

It would be practicable to introduce a local income tax provided it were accompanied by some administrative changes in the system of national income tax. We have therefore concluded that there are now two main possibilities: to continue with the present combination of rating and grants or to introduce LIT as an additional source of revenue for those authorities responsible for the services that account for the most expenditure. In either case it would be practicable to reduce the burden of rating, in the one case by increasing grants and in the other by substituting LIT for part of the yield of rating. The resulting change in the incidence of taxation would depend in the first case on how the government chose to raise the revenue to finance increased grants and in the second on the adjustments in the national tax system which would be required to accommodate LIT. In either case the changes would be determined by the government's overall taxation policy. There is therefore likely to be little to choose between the alternatives we have suggested in terms of the resulting overall incidence of taxation. Whether LIT should be introduced therefore depends on a decision as to how much of that taxation should be levied by the government and how much by local authorities. That decision in turn depends on their respective responsibilities for expenditure. Although the present crisis has been seen by many as a financing crisis, changing the sources of finance will not prevent similar crises from recurring in future unless the new arrangement is founded on a clear definition of responsibility for expenditure.

from The Layfield Committee Report, 1976

These two extracts are concerned with the idea of a local income tax (LIT). Mention is also made of the Government's Green Paper, published in 1982, which considered LIT as an alternative to rates. Write an article for the general reader explaining briefly how local government is financed. Outline the advantages and disadvantages of

(i)   the present rating system;
(ii) a local sales tax (not discussed in the extracts above);
(iii) LIT.

Your conclusion should mention any reforms you might like to see take place. Make sure that your conclusion is in line with the rest of your arguments. For instance, it would look odd if you attacked the present system and praised the advantages of LIT yet concluded that no reforms were necessary.

Audit under scrutiny

The new Audit Commission is welcome although all the conditions attached to it are not. Its establishment is welcomed for the very reason that the Layfield Committee recommended strengthened independent audit arrangements. 'We see no contradiction between the recommendations we make for extending the functions of external audit and the greater local accountability which we advocate throughout our report. Any large organisation can only benefit from the objective and constructive advice which external auditors are in a position to give'.

External audit is a necessary part of public accountability because accountability depends upon the provision of information to the public so that they can exercise an informed judgment.

But public accountability for a local authority is, and should be, *local* accountability, which entails the accountability of the officers to the council and the accountability of the council to the electorate.

The Audit Commission is welcomed in as far as it sustains an informed view of local accountability, as other measures such as the publication of comparative information and statistics have been similarly welcomed.

The obligation of Parliament to set for local government the framework of local accountability is acceptable. Indeed, there is a case for a further strengthening of that framework. It is always important to distinguish measures that strengthen local accountability from the long series of measures that have weakened it.

Yet the key point about external audit if it is to enhance local accountability is that it should be independent of central government or else it becomes a means of central control.

It is wrong that the Environment Secretary appoints all members of the commission, well-balanced though the first members may be.

It is wrong that the Secretary of State appoints the chairman and deputy chairman, whatever the merits of the individual appointments.

It is wrong that the Secretary of State appoints the commission's first full time chief officer.

It is wrong that the Secretary of State has the power to issue directions to the commission.

Together these powers seem to compromise the independence of the commission and to make it a potential instrument of central government.

Two of the actions of the Environment Secretary raise apprehension about the Government's attitude to the commission.

He is supposed to appoint its members after consultation with a variety of associations, but he first publicly announced his choice and then sought consultation afterwards on his names — a strange reversal of usual practice. Also, he appointed the commission's first chief officer not only before it had held its first meeting but also before it had even been properly appointed.

Nevertheless, by demonstrating its independence the Audit Commission can do much to remove anxieties that it may be a creature of the Environment Secretary. The important point for local government is that it should show that it also welcomes the commission and avoids defensiveness and hostility towards it.

The Audit Commission can assist itself and win support by adhering to certain principles and practices, particularly when it comes to consider general issues.

● It would be wise to show that, while it can and should criticise local government, it can also praise good practice when it finds it. Local government learns more easily from good practice tested than from general condemnation;

● It must at an early stage turn its critical attention to the controls and influence of central government over some aspects of local government. Thus, it would be of interest to have the Audit Commission's considered verdict on whether the operation of Government policies and controls over capital expenditure had encouraged value for money....

Local Government Chronicle,
11 February 1983

The Local Government Finance Act 1982 changed the way in which local authority accounts are examined. In the past, *District Auditors* scrutinised local authority spending. The district Auditor could be appointed by the authority. Now an *Audit Commission* is appointed by central government to make sure that local government spends its revenue economically. As you can see from the extract above, more private auditors are being used. This is in line with Conservative 'privatisation' policy.

Local authorities differ very much in the way they spend their money. For example, in 1982-3 London spent £76.71 per head on social services compared with £28.36 in East Anglia. Barking and Dagenham spent £323.04 per head on education compared with £143.45 in West Sussex. Your task is to find out how much your local authority spends on its different services. Many authorities have leaflets or newsletters which give these details. Using your own knowledge of your area and its needs, try to conduct your own 'audit'.

Three lies about local government

'We frequently meet councillors and officials who are reluctant to defend local government because they feel the centre has a good case for its controls and interventions. Time and again they tell us that central government is justified in dealing with general overspending by local government, that there is a large problem with particular authorities which overspend, and that in any case the centre is sustained by a stronger electoral mandate than local government. These three themes of conventional wisdom need to be countered.'

1 ACTION IS NEEDED TO DEAL WITH GENERAL OVERSPENDING BY LOCAL GOVERNMENT

There is no general problem of overspending by local government:

Table 1

£m at November price base			%
	Expenditure	Outturn	Deviation
1975-6	8,610.4	8,754.5	+ 1.7
1976-7	9,819.5	9,741.9	-0.8
1977-8	10,709.8	10,423.4	-2.6
1978-9	11,923.4	11,738.4	-1.5
1979-80	13,853.6	13,748.9	-0.7

In 1980-81, the Government agrees that the overspend is likely to be between 0.5% and 2.9%, which is very much within the order of overspend and underspend in previous years and much better than the normal record of central government in keeping to the targets it has set for itself – for which no penalties are imposed.

Even in 1981-82 the Secretary of State considers that overspending is likely in practice to be no more than 3.5%, and we will not even know if that is accurate for more than a year. There is no evidence that an alleged overspending of that order creates any problems for the Government's handling of the economy. The additional expenditure is financed out of local taxes and does not affect the borrowing requirements.

2 THERE IS A PROBLEM OF OVERSPENDING LOCAL AUTHORITIES

The fact that some local authorities are regarded by the Secretary of State as overspending is not in itself a problem requiring action by the Secretary of State. For the Secretary of State to say that certain authorities are overspending is merely to state that the views of those authorities on the proper level of expenditure for their areas differ from the views of the Secretary of State.

That is not a fact to be regretted. It is not a sign of a conspiracy against the Government. Local authorities are constituted to make their own decisions about expenditure levels and not to make the Secretary of State's decisions.

Some local authorities will be spending more and others less than the Secretary of State considers appropriate. They will be judged by that imperfect and varying standard – the opinion of Secretaries of State – both overspenders and underspenders. Because the Secretary of State's judgment is expressed in a figure of grant-related expenditure based on a formula, it may appear objective. But the appearance is superficial. The weight given to each factor is a judgment. Grant-related-expenditure for each authority merely gives expression to the judgment of the Secretary of State. Change any factor weight and the figure changes. A future Secretary of State might believe in massive subsidisation of public transport, and some of today's overspenders could well become average or even underspenders. . . .

3 THE WEAKNESS OF THE LOCAL MANDATE

The Government's actions against local authorities have been justified as necessary because of the weakness of the local mandate.

The local mandate is described as weak because: the percentage voting in local elections is normally much lower than those voting in national elections: and those voting in local elections normally vote not on local but on national considerations.

These points can be exaggerated: the facts require elaboration.

A considerable number of people vote for the same party in local elections as in national elections. Thus in Durham most Parliamentary elections are dominated by the Labour Party because the electorate are predominantly Labour. That fact alone does not invalidate the local mandate which is also overwhelmingly Labour. It merely means that many Labour voters tend to vote for the Labour Party both in local and in national elections.

Although the percentage voting in local elections is considerably below that in national elections, in certain authorities – metropolitan districts and over a third of other districts – the elections occur much more frequently (every year except when the county is elected). To that extent these authorities are much more subject to electoral pressure than Parliament.

Although it is correct that local electoral change has been largely influenced by the performance of national governments, there are signs that local factors have been playing a greater part in local elections since the mid-1970s.

Local Government Chronicle, 2 April 1982

This is an extract from a learned article written by two Professors of Government. Your task is to rewrite it as an article for your local newspaper. Bear in mind that your readers will not be specialists in local government. You will have to (i) *summarise* the main arguments into a 150 word article, and (ii) *simplify* the contents by using ordinary language. Finally, do not forget to provide a brief but suitable headline which is different from the original.

and recreation facilities. There is often disagreement between the different types of authority over who is responsible for what. In England county councils have overall responsibility for strategic planning but district councils have responsibility for local plans. Often the two tasks overlap and cause muddle and conflict. Refuse *collection* is a district responsibility but refuse *disposal* is a county function. Obviously, dealing with refuse requires cooperation between the different authorities.

The responsibilities of parish councils include allotments, cemeteries, crematoria, and mortuaries, public conveniences, launderettes, bus shelters, footpaths and rights of way, war memorials, litter control, recreational facilities and clearing ponds.

Internal organisation of local government

In 1971 the government set up the Bains Committee to consider preparations for introducing the new local government system. The Bains Committee thought that the new authorities should develop a **corporate** approach to their affairs. In other words, local authorities should be aware that one social or economic problem is closely related to other problems. It is better to solve these different problems through one approach, rather than through separate approaches. It is best to plan and coordinate the resources of local government as a whole to solve these problems. In the past, different departments in local government had tried to solve the problems one at a time in an uncoordinated way.

In order to achieve corporate management, the Bains Committee emphasised the importance of having a strong central body called the Policy and Resources Committee. This was set up to help the council to (i) define its objectives [what it wants to do], (ii) decide priorities [which tasks are the most important to do], (iii) exercise overall supervision of the council's activities [coordination and control]. The management arrangements suggested by the Bains Committee are shown in Fig. 20.5. You can see that the Policy and Resources Committee should have three powerful sub-committees.

These should deal with the major resources of finance, personnel and land and buildings.

The Bains Committee recommended that the Chief Executive in a local authority should be appointed to lead the officers. The Chief Executive would also act as chief adviser to the council on general policy. He would be free of departmental responsibilities. It was also recommended that each authority should set up a management team of Principal Chief Officers. This management team should be led by the Chief Executive. The team should prepare plans to meet the long-term objectives of the council. It should also coordinate council activities when carrying out these plans.

Local government finance

Expenditure by local authorities can be divided under two main headings:

(i) *revenue expenditure*, which covers the day-to-day costs of services provided, and
(ii) *capital expenditure*, which covers the costs of investment in assets such as buildings, roads, sewers or vehicles.

The cost of building a new school for a local authority would be capital expenditure. The costs of heating it and providing the income for the staff employed would come from revenue expenditure.

To pay for capital projects, such as building a new school, local authorities usually borrow money. They repay the loan together with interest over a period of years. Interest charges and repayments are included in revenue expenditure.

Money revenue comes from three sources – *grants* from central government, *rates* which are raised locally by local authorities on the services they provide, and *receipts* from various charges made. To simplify the explanation only rates and grants are dealt with here. The revenue from these sources in 1980–81 was

Domestic rate	£ 3 430 m	15.8%
Non-domestic rate	£ 4 277 m	22.3%
Government grant	£11 504 m	59.9%

(i) Government grant

Nearly 60% of the money spent by local author-

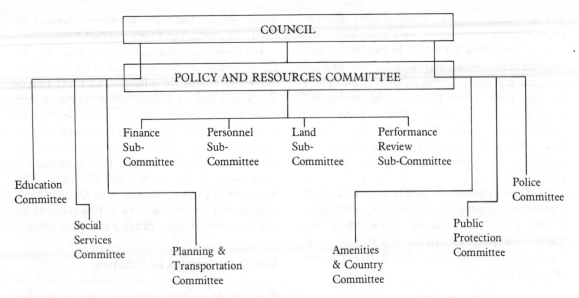

Fig. 20.5 Committee structure for a non-metropolitan county recommended by the Bains Committee

ities comes from central government. Ministers have argued that some local authorities are too eager to spend money because so little of what they spend comes from the pockets of their ratepayers. The way in which government grants are paid to local authorities has varied over the years. Until 1981 there were two main types of grant. First, the *Rate Support Grant* which was a general grant designed to cover expenditure. It was made up from three elements; (a) the needs element, which took into account the number of children of school age, the number of old people, density of population and road mileage; (b) the resources element, paid to councils whose rateable value fell below a certain level; and (c) the domestic element which compensated authorities for charging a lower rate to householders than to commerce and industry. Second, there are *specific grants* which are designed to cover the cost of particular services, such as the police.

In 1980 the Rate Support Grant was replaced by a new 'block' grant. Instead of being based on what a council had spent in previous years, the block grant is based on what central government thinks is necessary for that particular area. The purpose of the new block grant is to help central government control the spending by local authorities. There are stiff financial penalties for local authorities who overspend.

(ii) Rates

Rates are a tax on property. The domestic rate is paid by householders. The non-domestic rate is paid by local commerce and industry. The rate charged by the council varies from year to year according to its expenditure. The charge made is calculated quite easily. Each property has a rateable value based on what its rent might be. Suppose a house had a rateable value of £200 and the rate was 70 pence in the £. The amount due for that year will be $\frac{£200 \times 70}{100} = £140$. If the rate was 120 pence in the £, then the amount due would be £240. Some properties, such as churches and agricultural property, do not pay rates.

There has been a great deal of debate about the fairness of the rating system. The *advantages* of rates are:

1 There is certainty about the amount of money which rates will produce, and they can be easily adjusted.
2 They are easy to collect.
3 They are cheap to administer.
4 They are a type of tax which is easy to understand.
5 It is difficult for people to avoid paying rates.

The *disadvantages* of rates are:

1 It is difficult to value property based on the rent that would be produced.

2 Improvements to or extension of property lead to an increase in rates. People may be put off improving their homes because they will have to pay more rates.

3 Rates are not 'hidden' like VAT. They are a 'visible' form of taxation and not popular.

4 Rates tend to hit poorer householders hardest. This is not because they pay higher rates than wealthy people, but because the *proportion* of their incomes paid in rates is greater than that of wealthy people.

5 Rates are not directly related to the use made of services. For example, individuals in the 18–30 age group tend to make great use of local authority services but generally fail to contribute to rates.

6 Rates are often based on the assumption that urban areas are wealthier than they actually are.

The alternative methods of raising local revenue are (i) a local income tax, (ii) a local sales tax, (iii) a poll tax, (iv) a combination of a local income tax and a local sales tax together with a modified rating system.

Central-local relationships

If a local authority acts beyond the powers granted to it by Parliament, the doctrine of *ultra vires* ['beyond the powers'] will be invoked. The action by the local authority may be declared unlawful by the courts. Sometimes the powers over local authorities given to ministers by Act of Parliament are very broad. For example, the 1944 Education Act provides that it is the duty of the minister 'to secure the effective execution by local authorities under his control and direction, of the national policy for providing a varied and comprehensive educational service in every area'.

Many Acts of Parliament give ministers a strong *reserve* power over authorities which fail to carry out their duties. If a local authority fails to perform a particular task, the minister concerned may issue an order to do what is required. He may transfer the powers to another type of authority to get the task performed, or he may take over the powers himself. Clearly there is scope for much argument

and disagreement between central and local government. An interesting case arose in Norwich in 1981. Under the Housing Act 1980, most local authority tenants were given the right to buy their houses. Many Labour-controlled authorities were very slow in selling their council houses. The minister announced that he would send commissioners into one such authority – Norwich City Council – to administer the sale of houses. From the minister's point of view, if some local authorities were refusing to sell council houses then he needed to make an example of one of them. He chose Norwich. But Norwich decided to challenge the minister and go to court to settle the affair. Norwich Council argued that it was selling council houses to tenants, but not as quickly as the minister wanted. It was argued that the council has many statutory duties, and selling council houses was only one of them. Norwich argued that it gave a higher priority to other statutory duties.

Political scientists have studied the relationship between central government and local government. They have outlined three types of relationship:

(i) *Agency* This approach sees local government as an 'agency' for central government. In other words, local government is simply the servant of central government. Local government implements the policies that central government lays down.

(ii) *Partnership* This approach sees the central-local relationship in terms of a partnership. Both sides work together for common ends, though the two 'partners' might not be equal in power. But local government would not be totally inferior to central government.

(iii) *Power-dependence* The new approach sees that central and local government are independent of each other, and yet both depend on each other. The result is that neither has total control over the other. They bargain and negotiate with each other. Local authorities may use the mass media as a way of applying pressure on central government. Central government may supply finance to get local authority to do something that central government has no authority over. The power-dependence relationship is more equal than the 'agency' approach, but more competitive than the 'partnership' approach.

It must be stressed that relationships between central government departments and local authorities are not the same everywhere. They vary from department to department from authority to authority, as well as changing over time.

Nevertheless, central government has attempted to increase its control over local government in recent years. This has been inevitable. Local government accounts for about one-third of all public expenditure. The government's responsibility for the economy forces it to try to control local spending. When there is a cutback on expenditure at the national level, it must also be felt at the local level. But the question arises, if central government has such great control over the local authorities 'what has happened to local democracy?' Some people have argued that if central government takes any more power away from local government, then local government might as well be abolished. It would then be replaced by central administration at local level.

Terms used

Corporate decision-making Decisions are made by a central body rather than by unconnected bodies. For example, the British Rail Board makes decisions concerning rail transport which are corporate decisions. At one time these decisions would have been made by the separate regions of British railways, such as the Southern or Western.

Mandatory Compulsory.

Permissive Having permission to provide a service, but not having to provide that service.

Tier A level which has another level above or below it. It is a word that lends itself to puns: 'As the Chancellor outlined his Budget, MPs sat around him in tiers.'

Summary

1 Local government is very different from central administration at local level. Local government is based on democracy, and is best suited to meeting the needs of the local community.

2 Local government underwent major reform in 1974. The reforms did not follow the Maud recommendations. In particular, the ideas of provincial government and of single-tier, all-purpose authorities were rejected. The response to Maud was based on political considerations as much as on administrative practicability.

3 The Bains Committee recommended that the new system of local government should have councils making decisions in a modern way. It was recommended that the corporate approach should be adopted. In particular, councils were urged to set up powerful Policy and Resources Committees.

4 Local government revenue comes from two main sources: rates and government grants. Rates have been criticised as being an unfair way of collecting local revenue. It is likely that the rating system will be reformed within the next ten years. The way in which the grant from central government is paid has already undergone change. The Rate Support Grant has been replaced by a block grant. The block grant includes heavy penalties for local authorities who 'overspend'. Some people feel that these tighter controls mean the end of independent local government.

5 The relationship between central and local government is complex. There has been a trend in which central government has obtained more and more control over local government. If central government power increases much more, some people feel that it will kill democracy at local government level.

Questions for discussion

1 Do we need local government in Britain? Discuss the best ways in which various services can be provided at local level.

2 Why was local government reformed? Were those reforms successful?

3 'Local government cannot be efficient unless it has corporate decision-making.' Outline your reasons for agreeing or disagreeing with this statement.

4 'Local government is under attack by central

government.' How true is this? Examine the relationship between central and local government.

5 Read about your local council in your local evening or weekly newspapers. Collect cuttings in order to make some posters for your classroom. You may be able to show the variety of council decisions. Try to follow one decision through all its various stages.

6 Divide your class into the 'Pro-Rates' party and the 'Anti-Rates' party. Each party has to produce a two-minute party political broadcast. It can be presented 'live' or on tape. Remember that you may have to ignore your own opinion and argue on the side that you really do not agree with.

7 If you live in Scotland or Northern Ireland, then you live under a system of local government that has not been examined in this book. Write an essay which outlines your system of local government. Details can be found in books such as Tony Byrne's *Local Government in Britain* or Alan Alexander's *The Politics of Local Government in the United Kingdom*.

21

People in local government

This chapter looks at local government in terms of its personnel and examines the roles of people in different parts of the organisation. Councillors are the first group of people on whom we focus. What sort of people become councillors? What tasks do they perform in carrying out their duties as local representatives? Most are 'part-time'. Does this mean that local government relies too much on full-time officials to keep the machinery working

effectively? What is the relationship between the democratically elected councillors and the professional local government officers? We examine this in the context of the work that councils do. Much time is spent in committees, where members and officers discuss problems and policies and arrive at decisions. But is this a good thing? Are there too many committees wasting too much time? The chapter concludes by considering people in conflict at the local level. Over recent years, local government has been run much more along party lines. Some feel that councillors on all sides are more 'extreme' than in the past. We examine why party politics has become more marked in local government since it was reorganised in 1974.

Councillors

Being a councillor takes up a great deal of time. You can see from Fig. 21.1 that the average councillor spends 79 hours a month on council work. Councillors who have retired from work tend to spend even more time than this on council affairs. Above average time is also spent by leading councillors, such as mayors. The fact that being a councillor takes up so much time is one reason why many people are unwilling to be candidates at local elections.

Attending council and committee meetings are not the only time-consuming tasks. Councillors have to prepare for meetings by doing considerable reading. For example, they have to read reports and **minutes** of various committees. Councillors spend time discussing issues with **local government officers**. Time is taken up meeting local citizens and dealing with their problems. In addition to all this, there are many other duties to be performed. Councillors are expected to serve on bodies such as the water authorities or on boards of school governors. They are expected to attend school speech days, conferences and various public meetings.

Until the reorganisation of local government, councillors received no payment. They simply

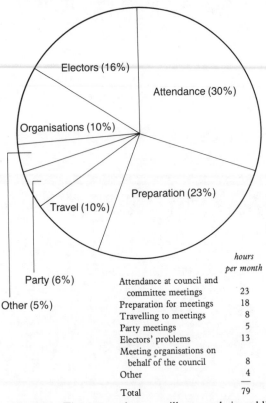

	hours per month
Attendance at council and committee meetings	23
Preparation for meetings	18
Travelling to meetings	8
Party meetings	5
Electors' problems	13
Meeting organisations on behalf of the council	8
Other	4
Total	79

Fig. 21.1 Time spent by councillors on their public duties (based on diagram in Tony Byrne, *op. cit.*)

received expenses and a 'loss of earnings' allowance for attending meeting. After reorganisation, ▷ p

192

Read this extract about councillors, *The Sunday Times,* 19 September 1982 together with the appropriate section in the chapter. Your tasks are to:

(i) write a letter to the editor for publication on the 'letters page'. Either congratulate the paper for the accuracy of the articles, or criticise them for being misleading.

(ii) draw a diagram which shows the differences in councillors' attitudes towards local government. Only include what you think are the most important party differences.

(iii) Councillors are not paid a salary and yet some are 'full-time'. Using material from the cutting and the chapter, argue the case for or against councillors being paid a full salary.

Labour's new (non-manual) breed of councillor

A dramatic portrait of the new breed of Labour councillor is revealed by a Sunday Times national survey of councillors and their views. Labour councillors, the survey shows, are now:

• Overwhelmingly left-wing. Asked whether they were on the left, centre or right of the party, 44 per cent said 'left' and a further 24 per cent said 'left of centre'. Only five per cent said they were 'right of centre' or 'right'.

• Non-manual workers. Less than 10 per cent of the councillors worked in skilled or unskilled manual jobs.

• Employed in the public sector. Five Labour councillors worked for a public sector employer for every one who worked in the private, profit seeking sector.

• Surprisingly young. The average age was 39; and there are more La-

bour councillors aged under 30 than there are over 65.

For the survey, The Sunday Times sent questionnaires to more than 300 councillors on six councils in England. In London, we surveyed Islington borough councillors as well as members of Greater London Council. Elsewhere we covered four authorities — Liverpool, Newcastle-upon-Tyne and Norwich city councils, and Somerset county council. Replies came from 176 councillors, with Labour noticeably more forthcoming than the Conservatives. We received replies from only 17 Liberal-SDP Alliance councillors.

The survey tended to confirm an old saying among political scientists: "What you think depends on where you sit". Applying this to councils, one would expect Labour councillors to work more often in the public sector and thus to be keen to expand

public spending and Conservatives to come from the private sector and to be concerned chiefly about rates. And so it proved.

Forty-eight per cent of the Labour councillors worked in the public sector – some in nationalised industries, but most as civil servants, teachers or council officers.

Although the law prevents an employee of a council sitting as a member of that council, many Labour councillors get round that by working for one council while sitting on another.

Of those Labour councillors not working in the public sector, the largest number are in the voluntary sector, primarily as full-time trade union officials or with housing associations – leaving only one in 10 in the profit-seeking private sector. By contrast, two of every five Conservative councillors work for a private employer.

Among labour councillors, a growing minority have given up the struggle to combine council with

other work. They have become full-time councillors, surviving off their allowances for attending meetings.

As Diana Wilson of Somerset puts it: 'It is not really possible to be employed if one is to fulfil one's full and fair quota of commitments. In many ways this is unfortunate, since it does limit the categories of people coming forward.'

The effect may be particularly serious for Labour. What struck home most forcibly from the study was the decline of the traditional working-class Labour councillor.

Surveying the survey, it is hard not to be impressed by the devotion most councillors show to their largely unsung, largely unpaid work.

The real question is whether they are now properly representative of the voters who elect them. To judge by their expressed opinions at any rate (see table), the old model of the local burgher carefully weighing every issue on its merits, irrespective of party consideration, is as dead as the dodo.

Two worlds: a major and a bureaucrat

When Major Roland Ingleby-MacKenzie is asked how long he has been a member of the Conservative Party, he replies, simple, 'Always.' Similarly, Bob Crossman, deputy chief whip of the London borough of Islington, has been a member of the Labour Party for all the 19 years since he became eligible to join.

The two contrasting figures, questioned by The Sunday Times as part of its unique survey of local councillors, present a cameo of the great political divide which is now the dominant fact in the lives of the men and women who run the town halls.

Ingleby-MacKenzies (on left), of Somerset county council, a 67-year-old married farmer with one son, describes himself as 'Right. Traditional Conservative.' He's against increasing rates to pay for local services, believes that council tenants should have the right to buy their own homes, and worries about local bureaucracy.

Crossman (right), 'disagrees

strongly' with the view that councils are too dominated by party politics, as indeed he would disagree with almost everything for which Ingleby-MacKenzie stands. At 35, Crossman is divorced, with a child and a 'stable homosexual relationship'. He himself works for a council, Haringey.

His politics, he says, are 'Bennite left – if you must have a label.' He strongly favours improving council services, even if it means higher rates; and he disagrees with allowing tenants to buy their own homes.

THE stark divide between the parties is shown by the response of councillors to some commonly expressed views about local government. They came near to agreement on only two points out of nine: that councils do a good job in providing services, and that one of the present two tiers (county and district) of local government should be abolished.

But on the core political issues, the divide is almost complete between Labour and Conservative (Alliance

councillors have contrasting responses on these issues, and on some others).

Almost all Labour councillors are against the government's policy of cutting local spending below current

levels, and very few join with the overwhelming number of Conservatives in favouring the right of council tenants to buy their homes – an issue, incidentally, that divides the Alliance.

What councillors believe – the party gulf

Figures show percentage saying they 'agree strongly' or 'tend to agree' with each statement

	Lab	Con	Alliance
This government is interfering too much with local government freedom	98	26	82
Local authority services should be improved, even if it means increases in rates	88	16	24
By and large, local government does a good job in providing services	88	62	77
There is too much bureaucracy in local government	55	74	82
One of the present tiers of local government ought to be abolished	47	54	53
Local government wastes a lot of money	19	72	77
Councils today are too dominated by party politics	15	54	82
Council tenants should have the right to buy their own homes	12	93	76
Local government spending ought to be cut below current levels	3	79	53

The Ombudsman: Watchdog Without a Bite

Under s31 of the Local Government Act 1974, if a local ombudsman has issued a report in which he has found injustice as a consequence of maladministration and is unsatisfied with the action the authority has taken, he is required to issue a further report setting out that fact.

The language used in these further, or "second reports", is invariably tough and uncompromising. They are issued in about 8% of cases in which maladministration and injustice had been found, so that on average a further report is issued by a local ombudsman once every three weeks.

To receive not one but five further reports in the same post is a serious matter.

The five cover fields of local government well known for ombudsman involvement.

In one of them, the ombudsman criticises Bournemouth Borough Council for not apologising to a complainant for its inadequate handling of a housing application.

Criticised council

In two others, concerning Liverpool City Council, the ombudsman criticises the council for not compensating a married couple for a mistake which led to delay in the completion of the complainants' house purchase, and for not compensating another complainant for loss she suffered as a result of the council's breach of an undertaking given to her regarding the purchase price of a house which she had occupied for the previous 42 years.

In the fourth the ombudsman criticises Bristol City Council for not compensating and apologising to 16 complainants who suffered injustice as a result of the council's handling of applications for various house improvement grants.

The fifth report, concerning Newark District Council, criticises the council for its reluctance to compensate the complainant for loss suffered through the way in which it had disposed of a listed building and adjoining land.

Although Liverpool City Council has been quick to respond in a positive way to the two further reports which concern them, so that the ombudsman is now satisfied with the action the council has taken, the fact remains that only a minority of authorities alter their position after considering a further report.

While the reports are strong on rhetoric, they may in fact encourage authorities to entrench themselves behind their earlier publicly declared positions.

The majority of cases in which further reports have been issued will ultimately find their way into the statistics as being unsatisfactory. These cases now number 62, or about 7% of all cases in which there has been a finding of maladministration and injustice.

There are two matters which are raised from this. First, whether authorities might be more ready to remedy injustice if the ombudsman were to follow more closely the procedures used by the parliamentary ombudsman, so that the first report would not only contain the ombudsman's findings of fact and conclusions, but also where appropriate, the remedy the authority had agreed to provide.

It may be that the constitutional position of local authorities, where decisions are made by the authority or its authorised delegate, would prevent the parliamentary ombudsman procedures being adopted in toto in local government.

Nevertheless, it is interesting to note that in some cases the ombudsman is now suggesting in his first report the remedy that the authority should provide if he is to be satisfied with his response.

The second matter, of much greater importance, is the growing percentage of cases where after a further report the ombudsman is still not satisfied with the authority's response.

Although within the limitations of his statutory powers the ombudsman is a useful watchdog for the citizen aggrieved by the actions of a local authority, he is a watchdog with a bark but not bite.

The parliamentary ombudsman's role is similarly limited, but his position is buttressed by national opinion and a supportive select committee. Neither can operate in local government.

The failings of the ombudsman system in this regard led to the lawyers organisation JUSTICE to propose in 1980 that the ombudsman's findings should be enforceable in the courts. More recently, the National Consumer Council has given its support to that proposal.

There is a risk that once one authority ignores the findings of an ombudsman, others will follow. Ombudsmen seem alert to this danger.

In the further report concerning Newark, the ombudsman makes the point that in considering the action to be taken on his report, the council are to some extent judges in their own cause.

He adds that he does not favour the adoption of a similar system to that in Northern Ireland which provides for the judicial enforcement of an ombudsman's findings, preferring to rely on the general and welcome readiness of local authorities to accept the umpire's verdict and carry out appropriate remedial action without fuss.

"But", he says, "reliance upon that kind of informal system will only hold good if all parties are prepared to play the same game".

Bureaucratic nightmare

In one of the further reports concerning Liverpool City Council he says: "On the rare occasions when authorities fail to respond satisfactorily to an ombudsman's report, increasingly there are explosions of support for the proposal that some legislative change should be made in order to ensure that a local ombudsman's findings will lead on to satisfactory action. Hitherto, I have had reservations about such proposals, believing that my office exists to support and not to undermine the fair and effective working of local democracy. Unfortunately the unhappy saga of this justified complaint leads to the inescapable concern about the working of local democracy in Liverpool ... the extended and unsatisfactory consideration of my (first) report bears the marks of a bureaucratic nightmare".

No one can deny the impact the ombudsman system has had on local government activity since it was established eight years ago. It may be, however, that the institution has now reached a watershed in its development.

Perhaps, local authorities have learned to live within the system, treating the ombudsman as an equal rather than as first among equals. The pity is that in an era when local government is unloved by public opinion and deeply concerned that it should be held in greater esteem it loses sight of the fact that the exercise of power includes the exercise of responsibility.

Heed might be taken of the words of the ombudsman in a further report concerning Bristol City Council. In it he says: "When a council declines to accept an ombudsman's finding that there has been maladministration on their part causing injstice, they are in effect resisting the will of the public they are there to serve who, through the proper democratic procedures of Parliament, decided that there should be an independent person to find on such matters, and in doing this a council brings discredit upon themselves".

Local Government Chronicle, 14 January 1983

We looked at the workings of the ombudsman system in chapter 5. Taskpage 5.1 contained details of the local government commissioners. The article above returns to the same topic, but it introduces new arguments. You will see from Victor Moore's article that at local level the ombudsmen sometimes make little impact on administration.

(i) What incidents involving maladministration occurred in Liverpool and Bristol?

(ii) Why does the PCA have more influence than the local government ombudsmen?

(iii) What remedy for the system's faults is proposed by JUSTICE and the National Consumer Council?

(iv) Write a brief essay which *either outlines reasons for* retaining the local government commissioners *or* argues for abolishing these local ombudsmen.

councillors could claim an 'attendance allowance' for undertaking their duties. The Robinson Committee rejected the idea of paying them a full-time salary, but it urged that payment to councillors should be increased. Some people argued that paying councillors more would attract more women, more working-class individuals and younger people on to Councils. Others argued that paying councillors could attract the 'wrong sort of person'. They thought some councillors would be attracted by the salary rather than the idea of public service.

Councillors are not typical of the population at large in terms of their social make-up. Only 17% are female. Only a quarter of councillors have working-class jobs. They tend to be better educated and earn more than the average person in Britain. Finally, councillors tend to come from older sections of the population. Only 8.5% of councillors are aged between 21–34 years, yet 28.5% of the population is in this age group. People between the age of 55–74 years form 29.5% of the total population, yet 47.5% of councillors are in this age group.

The work that councillors do in performing their duties is varied. Tony Byrne has listed these duties. Every councillor is:

(i) a representative – he is elected to represent his ward
(ii) an 'ombudsman' – he has to deal with his constituents' grievances
(iii) a manager – he must oversee the work of local government officers
(iv) a policy-maker – he must help shape policies in council and committee meetings
(v) a politician – he will seek to solve problems by trying to persuade others to accept his point of view.

Local government officers

Local authorities employ officers to help them carry out their duties. The Town Clerk used to be thought of as the council's senior officer. Today the senior officer is known as the Chief Executive. He is responsible for coordinating the work of council departments. A legal background is most common for Chief Executives.

Local government officers and council members differ in many ways. Officers are professionals and councillors are amateurs. This occurs because the officers are *selected* for their specialised knowledge or expertise. Senior officers are recruited by authorities with great care. Members are *elected*. Often candidates for the opposition party are elected because of a national swing against the government. There have been cases where people have been persuaded to become candidates in local elections on the understanding that they would lose. It would be an embarrassment for the parties if they could not produce candidates. But a surprising swing at the elections resulted in their victory, and these candidates became rather reluctant councillors.

The difference between the professional and the amateur can lead to tension. The officers may believe that their policies are superior because they are based on specialised or technical knowledge. On the other hand, members will be considering the electoral impact of policies. Councillors may reject the 'best' policy because it will be unpopular. Some councillors will want policies in line with their party's philosophy. Officers are likely to oppose such policies unless they are practical.

The final difference between officers and members is that officers are 'permanent' and members are often 'temporary'. A big swing in local government elections can result in great changes in council membership. But such a swing will have no effect on the officers. Some fear that these factors result in officers being able to control or dominate members. That is why some feel that councillors should be full-time and receive a salary. Councillors would then build up their expertise and be a match for the professionals.

The most important officer–member relationship is between the **leader of the council** and the Chief Executive. This is the main channel of communication between officers and members. As we shall see, local government today operates in a more political atmosphere than in the past. In this changed atmosphere, it is necessary for the leader of the council to provide political direction to the work of the officers. In authorities where the political atmosphere is less intense (because of many safe seats and less electoral pressures on members) the relationship between leader of the council and Chief Executive may be less close.

Councils at work

Councillors spend much of their time sitting on committees. These committees report their discussions back to the full council. Councils which have implemented fully the Bains recommendations have a committee organisation as shown in Fig. 20.5. However, some councils have 'unscrambled' Bains and moved back towards the old committee and department organisation. In these councils the Policy and Resources Committees no longer co-ordinate policy. They are simply 'rubber stamps' for decisions taken by the separate committees. Some councils have even dismissed their Chief Executive Officers.

The full council has to approve the recommendations made by committees. Except for certain financial issues, committees may be given power to make decisions. The exceptional issues where committees cannot make policy include setting the rate and raising loans for the authority. If a committee does have the power to make policy, then it merely informs the full council. It does not seek its approval.

There are many different types of committee to be found in local government. Some committees concentrate on the work in a given department, such as education. Other committees deal with a service which affects the work of many departments, such as finance or staffing. *Statutory* committees are those which councils have to set up by law. Police, education and social services are among the most important statutory committees.

When councillors meet in committee they may be joined by **co-opted** members. These members are not elected but are invited on to the committee because their special knowledge or experience allows them to make valuable contributions. The atmosphere in committees is usually less formal than that in the full council. Chief officers report to the committee on a variety of council matters, and then answer questions. Copies of committee minutes are circulated to all members of the council.

Members of the public are able to attend committee and council meetings. Occasionally the public may be excluded if confidential issues are being discussed.

In his book, *Local Government in Britain*, Tony Byrne reviews the advantages and disadvantages of using committees in local government.

Advantages

(i) Committees take the pressure off the council by doing some of its work. This allows the full council more time to consider overall policy because it does not get bogged down with detail.

(ii) Committees save time for councillors. This is because different issues can be considered by different committees, which all meet at the same time.

(iii) Committees can use what expertise councillors have to maximum effect. Committees can co-opt outside experts to give advice. This leads to efficient decision-making.

(iv) Committees are small and informal. This encourages councillors to speak their minds freely.

(v) Committees are a useful way of bringing together officials and councillors. Frequent contact with members keeps officials in touch with public opinion.

Disadvantages

(i) Committees may waste time. They may encourage councillors to go into too much detail. This may delay decisions. There may be too many committees. This may slow down the work of local government. This would be true particularly when one committee has to wait for the decision of another committee before it can decide on policy.

(ii) Committee members may specialise in a subject and become expert, but specialisation can make councillors very narrow-minded. They may end up by viewing local affairs just in terms of the effect on their own specialist concern. They may lose the broad view of what the council is trying to achieve.

Local politics in local government

Local government functions in a more political atmosphere than used to be the case. Local government is now run much more on party lines. There are a number of reasons behind this development. First, there is the consequence of reorganisation. The two-tier system often introduces political conflict. If the same party dominates both tiers, then disagreement is unlikely. But if different parties dominate the county and district level, disagreements will be common. This political conflict can intensify if there is also disagreement about the areas for which each tier is responsible.

Most councils are organised along party lines. The changes that took place within the space of five years are shown in Table 21.2. In his book, *The Politics of Local Government in the United Kingdom*, Alan Alexander says of councils:

> Most are now local versions of the parliamentary models, with a majority controlling group in charge of the determination of policy, and a minority group or groups whose principle task is to scrutinise, criticise and oppose the policies put up by the majority.

Table 21.1 Authorities with Labour or Conservative control, before and after reorganisation (percentages)

	Before reorganisation 1973	1974-5	After reorganisation 1977-8
England and Wales	53	70	79
Scotland	34	48	58

Source: Alan Alexander, *The Politics of Local Government*

The 'controlling group' is in a position similar to that of the 'majority party' in the House of Commons. It can be argued that the party group makes all the important decisions. The council is little more than a 'rubber stamp' which makes these decisions official policy. Parliament is rather like this. All the important decisions are made by the Cabinet. The House of Commons too, in the end, is a 'rubber stamp'.

The decline in consensus politics at national level has influenced politics at the local level. We have already mentioned the conflict between Labour-controlled Norwich and the Conservative minister over the sale of council houses. Another example occurred some years earlier in 1972. Clay Cross Urban District Council refused to implement the Housing Finance Act 1972. The Conservative government's policy was that all council house rents must be raised to a 'fair level'. Labour-controlled Clay Cross council refused to do this.

The idea of party politics in local government is not new. Elections in many areas, especially the cities, were fought along party lines from the time that local authorities were created. However, since reorganisation the party political element has intensified. Now many more local elections are contested by representatives of the major political parties. There are few independent candidates. Thus local elections are very much influenced by national politics. It is rare for local issues to be taken into account by the electorate in local government elections.

Party politics influence the affairs of the local authority associations. These associations discuss and represent the interests of local government. There are three major associations in England and Wales: the Association of Metropolitan Authorities (AMA); the Association of County Councils (ACC) and the Association of District Councils (ADC). The Conservatives control the ACC. However, the control of the AMA and ADC changes according to the swing of the national political pendulum.

The final development which has made local government more political is the disappearance of aldermen. Under the old system of local government, about a quarter of all county and borough councils were made up of aldermen. They were appointed because of the valuable contribution they could make. Usually, alderman were ex-councillors. They served six years in office. Since aldermen did not have to face elections, they were free from political pressures. It was sometimes argued that they provided councils with continuity, particularly when large voting swings changed elected members. Others felt that the existence of aldermen was undemocratic. Regardless of whether or not they provided continuity, it was felt that aldermen had no place in a modern system of local government.

Terms used

Co-opt Co-opted members of a committee are invited to serve on it. Other members of the committee are elected to it.

Leader of the Council The chairman of the council, elected by the councillors. Some leaders become well-known politicians, such as Ken Livingstone who became leader of the GLC in 1981.

Local government officers These are the 'civil servants' of local government.

Minutes These give an account of the proceedings of a meeting. They record who attended the meeting and what decisions were made.

Summary

1 Councillors are not typical of the population at large in terms of their age, gender, income and education. They perform a complicated set of duties, which include being a representative, policy-maker and politician. They are not paid a full-time salary, but receive an attendance allowance.

2 Local government officers are professional bureaucrats. The senior officer is the Chief Executive Officer. The most important relationship between members and officers is that between the Leader of the Council and the CEO.

3 Other contacts take place in the numerous committees of local government. There are many advantages in using committees. But some people feel that committee members become narrow-minded and lose touch with wider policy issues.

4 Local government now operates in an intensely political climate. There are a number of reasons for this development. Some result from the way in which local government was reorganised. Others result from the breakdown in consensus politics at national level.

Questions for discussion

1 Does it matter if councillors do not reflect the rest of the population in terms of age, gender and social class?

2 Why might officers prefer different policies from those preferred by councillors? What are the different perspectives that officers and members bring to decision-making?

3 'The Council makes no decisions at all. They are all made in private behind closed doors.' Does this mean that such decisions are undemocratic?

4 'Committees are the motor of efficient decision-making. They enable the correct decisions to be made in an efficient and democratic way.' 'Committees waste much time and often arrive at the wrong decision. The camel is a horse designed by a committee.' Outline the case for and against having committees to make policy.

5 What controversial issues are being discussed in your area? Follow the debate about one or more of these issues in your local newspapers. Do councillors divide along party lines? Can you relate the differences of opinion to party philosophies?

6 Attempt to find out what future development has been planned for your area. Share the responsibilities among your group: someone will have to write to the Planning Department, whilst someone else might seek information in your local library. Collect your information and present what is relevant on a poster for your classroom.

Policies and issues

22

Economic policy

This chapter considers the different ways in which governments manage the economy. During the 1950s and 1960s there was not so much disagreement between Labour and Conservative on economic policy as there was during the 1970s and 1980s. But what is going wrong with the economy? Why does Britain's economy do less well than the economies of other industrial countries? This chapter examines some of the faults in the economy which cause such problems. We look at the different lessons learnt from the Great Depression of the 1930s and the recession of the 1980s. Some politicians argue that the government has to have greater control of industry if it is to manage the economy successfully. Others argue that the economy works best when government intervenes less. We consider the arguments about nationalisation and privatisation. Finally, we examine the growth of 'corporatism' in Britain. After defining what corporatism is, we try to assess how far Britain has moved towards becoming a 'corporate state'.

Politics and the economy

The health of the economy is an important factor in British politics. Every government recognises its first and most pressing job as that of 'putting the economy right'. This is partly because the performance of the economy influences voters at elections. One calculation that voters make before going to the polls is 'which party will provide me with the highest standard of living?' This is one reason why politicians focus on economic issues during election campaigns.

There is another reason why the economy gets so much attention. This is because Britain's economy is performing less successfully than many of her industrial rivals. Although the standard of living in Britain has risen since the Second World War, it has risen much faster in Japan, France and Germany.

There are many views on what is wrong with the economy. Different governments have diagnosed different 'diseases' and prescribed different 'medicines' to cure it. Richard Bailey and Brian Snowdon have listed the main diseases that have been diagnosed. They are:

* *Low level of investment in British industry*
  Some feel that British investors have been on 'strike' for many years. If private firms and individuals will not invest in new machinery and factories, then the government will have to do so. The National Enterprise Board (NEB) was set up to invest in British industry.

* *'Stop-go' policies*
  If the economy expands too fast, it has to be slowed down. Firms find it difficult to plan ahead under these circumstances. Some argue that a planned economy would be better than 'stop-go' policies. Economic growth could be planned. In 1965 the Labour government published a 'national plan'. This plan was never implemented.

* *Trade union militancy and strikes*
  Some argue that strikes have ruined the British economy. British firms are not reliable and often fail to deliver the goods on time. Customers turn to foreign firms which can deliver on time. In fact, many of our competitors have worse strike records than Britain. The working days lost in Britain between 1976 and 1982 are shown below:

	Working days lost
1976	3 284 000
1977	10 142 000
1978	9 405 000
1979	29 474 000
1980	11 964 000
1981	4 266 000
1982 (Jan–Nov)	7 852 000

Many strikes were settled within one or two days. For example, in 1981 a third of strikes lasted less than one day. Nearly a half were settled in less than two days. Despite this both Labour and Conservative governments have attempted to limit the power of trade unions. Labour abandoned the proposals in the White Paper, *In Place of Strife*, because of union opposition. Edward Heath's government passed the Industrial Relations Act. This act led to chaos and was abandoned. In 1982 Margaret Thatcher's government passed the Employment Act which attacked the **closed shop**.

- *Poor management*
Some have argued that trade unions have been blamed for what were really the faults of management. 'Outsiders' have been brought in to manage large firms in the public sector. For example, Michael Edwardes at British Leyland and Ian MacGregor at the British Steel Corporation and National Coal Board.

- *The British class system*
Managers and workers come from different social classes and have little contact with each other. Because of this they see each other as the enemy and are unable to work together. There have been experiments in the educational system which have tried to solve this. Comprehensive schools are an attempt to get children from different social classes to mix together. However, private education has continued to exist.

- *Balance of payments problem*
Britain has to export goods in order to eat. This is because roughly half of the food we eat is imported. If Britain's economy grows too fast, people import more than is exported. This can be solved by slowing down the economy, so that Britain imports less and exports more. It is possible to use *quotas* or *tariffs* to limit imports. But if Britain limits imports from other countries, those countries might limit Britain's exports. This would cause problems because Britain has to export in order to eat.

- *Our industry is not as modern as our competitors'*
American industry has overtaken British industry in terms of advanced technology. Indeed, America has overtaken most other European countries. In order to close the 'technology gap' there have been joint projects in which a number of countries share the cost. For example, Britain and France cooperated to build Concorde. This airliner is the world's most advanced passenger jet. Unfortunately it was not a commercial success.

- *Shortage of workers in manufacturing industries*
In other words, there are not enough people are in jobs which 'make things'. Too many work in *service* industries, such as education, banking, leisure, local government, or retailing. In 1967 a Labour government introduced a Selective Employment Tax (SET). Certain employers had to pay SET, whilst others did not. The idea behind this was to move workers out of service industries into manufacturing industries. SET was an unpopular tax and was abolished.

- *Lack of incentives because of high taxation*
Some feel that people do not work hard because much of the extra wages earned would be taken away as tax. As Chancellor of the Exchequer, Sir Geoffrey Howe lowered income tax and raised Value Added Tax (VAT). But he was forced to let taxes rise because the economy had to pay out much more in unemployment benefits.

- *Too much government intervention*
Others feel that the government should not 'meddle' with the economy. They believe that the 'free market' should be left to solve economic problems. The Heath government announced that it did not intend to support 'lame ducks' with public money. These 'lame ducks' were firms or companies that were nearly bankrupt. They needed money from the government if they were to survive; if they were left in the free market they would disappear. Yet the same government did a **U-turn** and spent much public money in saving loss-making firms. For example, the Heath government nationalised Rolls Royce and Harland and Wolff.

- *Too little government intervention*
Labour believes that leaving the fate of the economy to the free market will end in disaster. Government plays a large role in the economies

of many of Britain's competitors. In Britain, there have been prices and incomes policies. These policies have attempted to regulate wage negotiations, and to protect weaker groups of workers. There have been bodies set up by the government to *restructure* and *revitalise* industry. They include the National Enterprise Board and the Industrial Reorganisation Corporation, which are discussed below.

What is wrong with Britain's economy?

The two economic problems that make most impact on British people are *inflation* and *unemployment*.

(i) Inflation has been defined as 'too much money chasing too few goods'. Prices rise as supply and demand get back into balance. As the price of goods in the shops rises faster and faster, so the real value of people's savings and wages fall. Even when the rate of inflation is falling, prices are still rising. High rates of inflation – sometimes called **hyper-inflation** – causes uncertainty and fear about the future. Conservatives regard inflation as the bigger economic evil for Britain.

(ii) Unemployment has risen dramatically over recent years. While the Labour Party recognises the danger of inflation, it regards unemployment as a greater evil. In June 1982 the labour force stood at 25 754 000. This figure is just over half the population. It includes those people in work and those who are looking for jobs.

People in employment	20 498 000
Self-employed	1 856 000
HM Forces	324 000
Registered unemployed	3 076 000
Total	25 754 000

Some have argued that government figures underestimate the extent of unemployment. The Trades Union Congress and the Manpower Services Commission believe that in 1982 nearly 4 million were unemployed. Others argue that the true figure was over 5 million. School-leavers are hard hit by unemployment. About 20% of young people between 16 and 19 years old are unemployed. Special Employment Measures (SEMS) by the government try to limit unemployment. There have been 18 SEMS since 1975 and they have been administered through the Manpower Services Commission (MSC). They include *job creation schemes*. The Youth Opportunities Programme (YOP) involved 270 000 school-leavers. This has merged into the larger Youth Training Scheme. It has been calculated that SEMS have created or maintained over half a million jobs.

When the level of unemployment is high and rising at the same time as inflation is rising, we call this 'stagflation'. Some economists say that inflation and unemployment are only symptoms of Britain's economic illness. They are not the illness itself. The illness is something that is happening deep in the heart of the economy known as **de-industrialisation**. In simple terms, de-industrialisation involves the declining output or employment in manufacturing industry. In other words, 'making things' is becoming less and less important in the economy as a whole. This can be shown in employment and trade figures. The number of people employed in industry fell by 25% from 1966–80. In the period 1955–76 Britain's share of world trade in manufactured goods fell from 30% to 9%.

What can governments do to bring about recovery?

The Great Depression of the 1930s was the first major economic crisis of this century. The main problem of the Great Depression was unemployment. A British economist, John Maynard Keynes, wrote an influential book called *General Theory of Employment, Interest and Money*. He argued that unemployment could be reduced if more money was spent in the economy. But since private individuals and firms might not spend enough, it was up to the government to spend. We can see that if a government decides to invest in new motorways and airports, it would have far-reaching effects. Not only would more workers be employed in building motorways and runways, ▷ p.20*

Where taxes hit hardest

The average British family is paying at least 10 per cent more in tax today than it did when Mrs Thatcher took office in 1979. Despite that, it is about three per cent better off: wage increases over the past four years have been sufficient to counteract the combined rises in mortgage interest rates, taxation and inflation which together go to make up that almost indefinable quality – the standard of living.

The complex figures which form this equation have been worked out by Michael Mcacher, Labour MP for Oldham West.

There has been, he says, a substantial increase in taxation over the past three years. According to the latest figures just published in the chancellor's autumn statement, total taxation as a proportion of national income rose from 34 per cent in 1979 to 40 per cent in 1982.

This, together with the other ups and downs in living standards over this period, has affected people at different income levels in very different ways. It can best be shown by selecting typical families at five different income levels from the government's family expenditure survey (see charts). Their living standards reflect three quite separate factors:

- The pay rises each category has received on average over the last four years
- The way that tax increases have affected them
- The movement of inflation over the same period

It has been assumed that the lowest-paid category (those at half average earnings) is paying council rents, while the remainder have mortgages. The families are assumed to be a paid worker, married, with two children.

The family at half average earnings received pay rises in the first two years of this three-year period of 20 per cent and 18 per cent, including the Clegg award, which kept it just ahead of the inflation rate. However, last year's rise of only seven per cent, combined with large council rent rises and national insurance increases, has more than reversed that pattern. Overall it has ended up, at £77 weekly gross pay this year, four per cent poorer in real terms than it started.

The family on average earnings has done better. Despite a 21 per cent pay rise in 1979, its real income fell slightly over the next year because of inflation generally, and the steep rise in mortgage interest in particular. Since then, pay rises of 17 per cent and 13 per cent average has kept its real income rising slowly and it has finished, with £154 weekly gross pay now, about three per cent better off.

The family of a skilled manual worker at 1½ average earnings (now at about £230 gross a week) has not fared so well. High pay increases in 1979 kept real net income rising very slowly despite the mortgage interest decrease. But since then, rises of 15 per cent and 11 per cent have not been enough to keep pace and the family ends up three per cent worse off over the period.

The family at three times average earnings and above (over £450 a week today) has seen big increases in living standards as a result of both higher pay rises (according to a retail survey of leading UK companies) and also, particularly, very generous tax concessions. Thus, at three times average earnings, annual pay rises of 25 per cent and 15 per cent combined with the abolition of the high tax bands in the 1979 budget to produce an 11 per cent real rise in this family's living standards.

The family at five times average earnings (about £750 gross a week today) shows that these same factors have produced even bigger real net gains. Annual pay increases of 20 per cent. 17 per cent and 20 per cent have been compounded by the even larger tax handouts concentrated at this level in Howe's first budget in 1979. It has ended up 22 per cent better off.

What these cases demonstrate is that, whatever tax cuts the government introduces next year, they will not be sufficient to compensate for the very substantial increase in taxation that has been imposed since 1979. Almost all families would still find their tax liabilities had increase, not decreased, over the previous four years. None of the options realistically available could eliminate the average 14 per cent increase in personal taxation at a stroke.

Moreover, it is clear that many families on either side of average earnings, even after a hefty package of tax cuts, could still end up poorer than in 1979. Whether they do or not may well depend more on the level of pay increases they secure in the 12 months to next April than on the hand-outs of a pre-election budget.

Changes in the living standards of the five typical families (above) are based on: (a) average pay; (b) taxation; (c) rents or mortgage changes; (d) inflation. Sources: government family expenditure survey; NUPE statistics; DoE Gazette; retail survey of UK companies

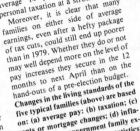

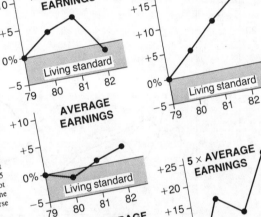

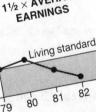

The Sunday Times, 28 November 1982

(i) Are British taxpayers paying more or less tax in 1982 than they were in 1979?

(ii) Which type of family has done best over the three years?

(iii) The article claims that a family with average earnings was 'better off' in 1982 than in 1979, while a family with 1½ times the average earnings was 'worse off'. How can both these statements be true?

Inflation and unemployment

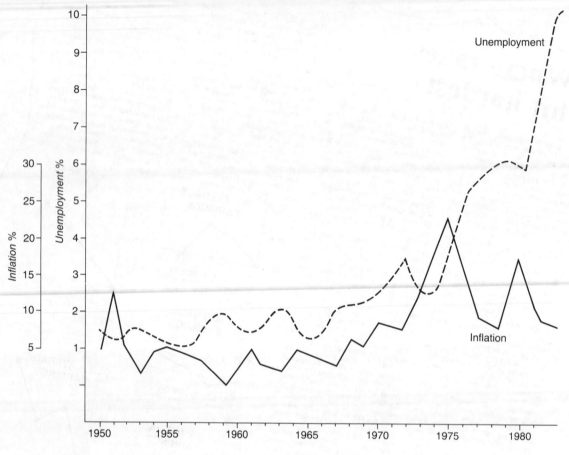

Source: Howard Elcock (ed.), *What Sort of Society?*

(i) Copy the graph of inflation and unemployment. Extend the graph as far as you are able by adding the current unemployment figure and rate of inflation.

(ii) During which periods were unemployment and inflation rising together rapidly?

(iii) Which periods suffered from the highest inflation?

(iv) During which period was unemployment at its highest levels?

TOMORROW IT COULD BE YOU

Unemployment in the 1980s means that no one can feel totally secure

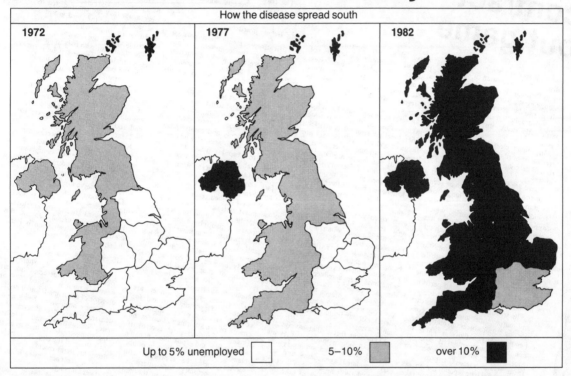

How the disease spread south

1972 · 1977 · 1982

Up to 5% unemployed   5–10%   over 10%

TWENTY years ago, unemployment was a Northern, local blight. 'Supermac' sent government ministers, as to a far country, to plan the salvation of the Tyne and the Clyde.

Ten years ago, unemployment – threatening to top one million – barely touched the rich South East. It was Glasgow, not Brixton, whose social tensions persuaded the Heath government into its famous economic 'U-turn'.

Today's unemployment is very different. It is not just that it is three times as high as in 1972.

The national dole queue has also entirely changed its character. Unemployment in 1982 is:

- No longer confined to the fringes of Britain
- No longer a threat only to manual workers
- No longer suffered mainly by men
- No longer a disease of the unqualified
- No longer a short-term problem
- No longer confined to older workers in dying industries

The Sunday Times 9 May 1982

(i)   Which area of Britain was least affected by unemployment in 1982?

(ii)   What sort of workers were hardest hit by unemployment in 1972?

(iii)   Were people in managerial and professional jobs affected by unemployment in the 1980s?

The winners of the contract-out game

Always, it seems, when privatisation is discussed, the chairman or speaker will go through the ritual motions of denouncing the word itself.

It is usually denounced as "jargon," "ugly," or, when a particularly vicious insult is needed, "American".

One thing is clear, however. What-ever name or phrase eventually takes root to describe the process, it is here to stay.

There are two reasons to say that with confidence. First, it can be seen as part of one of those long term trends which give history a cyclical appearance. The long period which saw steady growth of government has clearly given way to one in which the tide flows from government back to the individual. The demise of quangos, the eclipse and ultimate dis-posal of state industries are just as much a part of that process as is the use of private businesses to perform local government services.

The second reason is less abstract and more compelling: it is that con-tracting out produces too many bene-ficiaries. Any activity is likely to maintain a momentum if most of those who are involved in it perceive themselves as winners. It provides a very good starting point for an ex-amination of contracting out to take a look at it from the point of view of the winners.

When local government services which have been provided by in-house labour are contracted out, there are generally six classes of winners. Ratepayers, businesses, consumers, employees, councillors and council officers all gain in different ways as a result of the process.

A seventh group might be added to take account of those who benefit when local government is efficiently financed and when inflationary pres-sures on national government are lessened; but this group consists of the entire body of citizenry, and does not need separate consideration.

Ratepayers provide the main impe-tus behind the move towards privati-sation. There clearly are limits to what ratepayers will pay for their local services. More to the point, there are limits on what they should be asked to pay.

The spectacle of horrific rate bills being sent out to cover no more than a continuation of existing services or sometimes even a reduction, is one that most councils wish to avoid. Yet conscientious councillors and offi-cials can look over the budget in fine detail without finding areas of pos-sible saving.

The blunt fact is that savings are practically impossible while they are locked into a direct supply system. Accumulated agreements and self-imposed rules governing all aspects of operation conspire to take away freedom of movement, and leave no choices where cuts can be made.

The failure of the much-vaunted programme of cuts from central government illustrated this. Intended to make savings out of "wastage," they elicited proposals from local authorities to cut essential (and popular) services, proposals which were quickly whittled down under the impact of pressure groups, media coverage, and the basic powerless-ness of councillors to control major budget factors.

The reasons why contracting has ratepayers among its winners are many.

No archaic practices

Privatisation means starting with a clean slate: the contractor is not locked into archaic working practices and manning agreements. Secondly, and of course, the contractor has had to keep his capital equipment up-to-date. He has not seen it depleted by years of financial stringency.

Then again, the contractor has to face competition. Unprotected by a public monopoly and captive custo-mers, he has to seek efficiencies in order to keep his prices keen, his trade high and his profits secure.

All of this adds up to the one great fact about privatised services: they are cheaper.

When a council contracts out, the ratepayer ends up paying less for the service because he no longer has to support the panoply of inefficiency which encrusts the municipal depart-ment. When in-house services bid against commercial outsiders, with properly audited, full-cost tenders, the size of that extra burden is revealed. It is always huge and sometimes staggering.

The second group of winners are businesses. Opportunity to bid for council services offers them the chance of extra business. Despite the financial scrutiny, strict control of standards and possible penalty clauses which are involved in public service work, the contractor still finds opportunity for enterprise, development and profit in the new activity.

Some of them have faced years of undercutting by subsidised services; now, with full costing of tenders, they have the chance to show how much more efficient they are, and how much they can save for the

ratepayers.

We are sometimes told that private contractors cannot possibly cut costs and make a profit, as we used to be told that there were no contractors who could perform the service.

In both cases the solution has been to invite tenders and see both claims refuted. The National Union of Pub-lic Employees' leaflet on priva-tisation is most eloquent on this point. It tells members "We can't and shouldn't try to outbid the con-tractors."

Union officials issue dire warnings of a decline in service standards, but once again they are contradicted by the facts because the third group of winners are those who are on the receiving end of the service.

The contractor who tries to please, needs satisfied customers if he is to avoid the penalties which should be written into his contract. Where sur-veys have been done – and priva-tisation is so new here that these tend to be overseas – they show that consumers prefer the private service and feel they have more power to influence it.

It is significant that, whereas many penalty clauses in contracts are activated by customer complaints, rare indeed is the municipal work-force which loses money if those whom they serve are dissatisfied.

Quite contrary to much of the union propaganda which is heed-lessly sloshed around, the employees themselves are usually among the winners when privatisation is intro-duced.

US experience

In one American city where refuse collection was contracted out pro-gressively until it reached 50%, the director of cleansing found himself in the happy position of being able to demand unprecedented levels of ser-vice. The contractor and the in-house operator were determined to increase their share of the city. He merely laid down his requirements.

In a sentence, privatisation lets officers manage.

The only real losers among so many groups of winners are the officials of public sector unions. They deserve to be losers. After all, hubris is followed by nemesis.

Michael Forsyth

This double Taskpage is concerned with the policy of privatising local government services. Many of the arguments also apply to privatisation of state assets. Read the extracts, which come from the *Local Government Chronicle*.

(i) Write three paragraphs which outline the most important differences between Labour and Conservative arguments.

(ii) What can we learn about privatisation from the United States?

(iii) Which author do you feel argues the better case? Explain the reasons for your choice.

Flaws in the privatisation argument – the Labour party view

In *LGC*, 10 September, Westminster LBC councillor, Michael Forsyth, who since January explains he has been a public relations consultant to Pritchards, defended privatisation mainly on the grounds that its strongest critics, the local authority union leaders, were self-interested.

Mr Forsyth and the Adam Smith Institute have been waging a full campaign on privatisation. A pamphlet, *Reservicing Britain*, and other documents have been sent to every councillor in the country – 20,000 of them.

Clearly, a good return on this investment is expected. To produce it, the services, workers, community and the reputation of local government is to be sacrificed.

Mr Forsyth said that privatisation is here to stay because it is "part of one of those long-term trends which give history a cyclical appearance". He added that "the long period which saw steady growth of government has clearly given way to one in which the tide flows from government back to the individual. The demise of quangos, the eclipse and ultimate disposal of state industries are just as much a part of that process as is the use of private businesses to perform local government services".

Such views have caused the present Government to transfer or plan to transfer publicly owned assets, such as British Airways, British Transport Hotels, North Sea Oil and Gas assets, the British Transport Dock Board, new town land and even motorway service stations to private ownership.

Shares in successful nationalised companies have been sold off, sacrificing years of investment for a one-off gain. When Amersham International shares were sold speculators saw an immediate increase in their investment of 14%.

The Tories will not allow local government to go untapped.

There are grave implications for contracting out services. To begin with, local authorities are still responsible, under the Public Health Acts of 1936, for removing household waste and trade waste, and are entitled to make a reasonable charge for doing so. The employment of a private company to undertake some or all of their work does not, in any way, diminish this statutory responsibility.

But a private contractor's concern is with profit not social needs, standards or legislative requirements. There is bound to be a conflict between these incompatible objectives.

Inevitably, contractors will exploit their potential monopoly once local authorities or the national health service have made themselves unable to provide their own services any longer.

There is already evidence that contractors are submitting low tenders now in the hope of breaking into what they see as an increasingly lucrative market later. Commenting on a tender for pest control services from Rentokil, Bracknell District Council's management team said that "the current offer, according to a representative of the company, is at a representative of the company and is put forward with the cost price and is put forward with the prime intention of breaking into local authority work".

Once these companies have achieved market control their prices will inevitably increase. Authorities which no longer have the direct labour and capital equipment to enable them to do the job will find themselves held to ransom.

Promised land

For the prophets of privatisation, Southend is the promised land.

Exclusive Cleaning claim savings from the cleansing contract of £500,000. But a number of doubts have been raised about this figure (*LGC*, 27 August).

A number of other councils have considered and rejected private contractors for similar reasons, including, Three Rivers, Chiltern, Luton, Greenwich, Slough, Hillingdon and Fareham.

Two other examples are Barnet LBC and Bracknell DC. Barnet considered privatisation but rejected it on the grounds of:

- The existing labour force's local knowledge and experience.
- The need to preserve 216 local jobs.
- The danger of a contractor going bankrupt and leaving the authority without a service.
- The threat of industrial action; and
- The fact that no domestic refuse collection service in London had been undertaken by contractors for many years.

Bracknell had a simple reason for rejecting Exclusive Cleaning Group's tender for its refuse collection service. As the Government-commissioned *Report on Service Provision and Pricing in Local Government* put it: "Exclusive saw no opportunity for the type of savings made at Southend and returned a tender to Bracknell well in excess of the council's own estimate of the present method of working".

Acceptance by Bracknell of the tender would have increased the cost of their refuse collection from £473,000 to £500,000 a year.

In Rochford the use of private contractors was considered in 1979–80, but rejected in favour of a direct workforce with a new bonus scheme and different methods of collection. Manning levels were reduced from 42 to 34 and the number of vehicles from 13 to 10. The number of rounds also decreased, from 10 to 7.

At the same time better working conditions and new equipment were introduced. Rochford estimated their savings to be £124,000 in 1981–82, equivalent to 20% of total costs.

In Slough, the number of direct labour staff was cut by five, and the number of vehicles and rounds were also cut. But "task and finish" was retained. The savings in 1981 were estimated at £140,000 on expenditure of £680,000.

Hillingdon LBC contemplated contracting out in 1981 but eventually accepted a joint GMWU/NUPE/TGWU proposal even though it cost £100,000 more than the private contractor's tender. The workforce was reduced from 154 to 132 and a new bonus scheme introduced.

US contracts-in

Even in the US public employees still perform more than 75% of local government work.

Again, according to Public Services International, study carried out by the German Public Services Trade Union, the CTV, reveals similar problems.

A case study of privatisation in Gottingen and Hildsheim demonstrated that those employed in privatised areas had to accept worse conditions of employment and remuneration. "The community received a lower quality of service than that previously provided and the cost of the privatised service either did not represent any financial saving or did not give the saving which had been promised".

It was found, after the contract had been awarded, that private companies were not quoting for the same service that had been provided previously. In cleaning services, for example, important areas were omitted which made the costing unrealistically low.

Local government prides itself on fair treatment of staff and, indeed with its responsibility for the general welfare of the community, and its role as a substantial employer it could not do otherwise. But contractors rely on lower wage costs and these may be achieved through poorer conditions even when quoted wage rates are higher than local authority rates.

Barbara Turner

but more would be employed in producing cement, bricks, tarmac, and so on. All these workers would be spending more money in the shops. Therefore workers in consumer industries would be busier producing more clothes, electrical goods, cars, etc. These workers would, in turn, start spending more, with the result that even more people would be employed.

In Britain the years between 1945 and 1961 were the 'Keynesian' years. The government maintained the highest possible level of employment through what is known as 'demand management'. There was a high rate of economic growth together with a low level of unemployment and inflation. The Conservative prime minister, Harold Macmillan, was able to tell the population that they had 'never had it so good'.

The second major economic crisis started in the 1970s. Oil prices quadrupled in 1973-4. Oil is one of the basic forms of energy used in industry. As the increase in costs was passed on, so inflation rose to well over 20% a year. The American economist Milton Friedman (not Milton Keynes) argued that *monetarism* could reduce inflation. Monetarism is an economic philosophy based on belief in the free market. Monetarism involves controlling the money supply. This is done by discouraging borrowing, limiting wage increases and cutting back on government spending. Government spending is controlled through *cash limits*. Through controlling the money supply, inflation would be squeezed out of the economy.

It was also argued that if the government spent less, resources would be released for private industry to use. Others argued that government spending had increased in the past because private industry was not using these resources.

Does ownership matter?

In 1956 Anthony Crosland's influential book, *The Future of Socialism*, was published. Crosland was an economist and university lecturer who was later to hold several important posts in Labour governments. He argued that it was no longer important who owned companies, firms and industries. This was because decisions taken in large firms were taken by managers who did not own the firm. In the last century the manager of a firm was also likely to be the owner. So if the government wanted to control a firm, it had to own it. Today firms are owned by shareholders. Shareholders vary from private individuals who own a few hundred shares to insurance companies and pension funds which own millions of shares. Therefore it is no longer necessary for a government to own a firm if it wants to influence its decisions.

In 1975 Stuart Holland published *The Socialist Challenge* which argued a different case. He believed that ownership was still important because much of British industry is owned by **multi-national** corporations. These multi-national corporations might make decisions which are against Britain's national interest. For example, car-workers are paid less in Spain than in Britain. A motor manufacturer might decide to close factories in the Midlands and open new ones in Madrid. To stop firms from doing this sort of thing, argued Stuart Holland, the government must take over leading companies.

(i) Public ownership and the nationalised industries

Public ownership is a vague term. In discussing 'public ownership' some people would include roads, hospitals and schools whilst others would not. Even when it comes to saying which industries have been nationalised there is disagreement. Some argue that hospitals were nationalised when the National Health Service was set up. Others argue that it is misleading to use the word 'nationalisation' in this context. Again, some argue that atomic energy is a nationalised industry whereas others say that it is not. Another term, 'public corporation', is just as controversial. Some define the water authorities as public corporations whilst some say they are simply 'public services'.

The control of industry, or at least the most important sections of it, was seen by many people as essential for effective economic management. If the nation's prosperity depended upon the success of its key industries, then this was not something which could be left entirely to chance. In 1945, Labour was returned to power with a substantial majority. For the first time, there was an opportunity to put the idea of nationalisation into practice. In a series of major acts of Parliament the state took over the railways, coalmining, gas, electricity, water and drainage, civil aviation, heavy goods road transport and iron and steel manufacturing. The last two were partly returned to private ownership by subsequent Conservative governments. Iron and steel, however, was renationalised in 1967. The extent of public ownership grew steadily until 1979. The Post Office, which was previously a government department, became a public corporation in 1969. In 1981 it was split into two parts: one part dealt with postal services and the other with telecommunications. Other concerns that had come into public ownership included the British National Oil Corporation (BNOC), British Petroleum, the National Bus Company, the National Freight Corporation, British Aerospace, British Leyland, British Shipbuilders, Rolls Royce and British Waterways. By 1978 the nationalised industries employed 1 700 000 people. They contributed about 10% of Britain's economic output.

The early *nationalised industries* were criticised for being too bureaucratic. They were run by civil servants. Civil servants are accountable, through ministers, to Parliament for everything they do. They tend, therefore, to be cautious and unadventurous. But often these qualities are not the right ones for successfully running a commercial or industrial enterprise. To solve this problem the *public corporation* was used more frequently. The BBC was an early public corporation. While still under public ownership, the public corporation enjoys greater independence than the old nationalised industries. Public corporations tend to be run by industrialists rather than civil servants. They aim to be self-supporting in financial terms and are free from direct Treasury control. However, the government still has a degree of control over public corporations because it appoints the corporation's governing board. Also the government has to support those which make a financial loss with public money. But generally the corporation is free to take normal commercial risks in its day-to-day working. Thus public corporations combine public responsibility with independent commercial freedom.

This is not to say that there is not disagreement between the chairman of public corporations and the government. For example, the British Gas Corporation may wish to increase the charges made to consumers. But if the government is nearing a general election it may not allow the price rise. Or British Rail may seek to close a branch line which is making heavy losses. The government may order the chairman to keep it open because the service is essential to the particular area. There is often a conflict between the general interests of government and the commercial interests of public corporations. This is a basic problem in the running of public corporations and services. It is a problem which has not been solved.

(ii) Privatisation

Industries are brought into public ownership for a number of reasons. Sometimes it is to save them from collapse, as in the case of Rolls Royce and British Leyland. Socialists in the Labour party want public ownership for another reason. They believe that capitalism is based on the profit motive. In other words, it is greed that makes capitalism work. They want to see capitalism replaced by a society based on cooperation rather than competition. The first step along this road to socialism is the public ownership of industry. Clause IV of the Labour party's constitution says that one of its goals is the 'common ownership of the means of production, distribution and exchange.'

Until 1979 Conservative governments accepted the need to nationalise certain industries. Indeed, it was a Conservative government that nationalised Rolls Royce. However, when Mrs Thatcher's Conservative government came to power, it proved to be very hostile to public ownership. The Conservatives had moved to the right in political terms. Some believed that the policies that had been followed by both Labour and Tory governments since 1945 were leading to totalitarianism.

The policy of *privatisation* (or denationalisation) has therefore been followed. Conservatives have argued that returning public assets to the private sector increases economic freedom and efficiency. Critics of privatisation argue that firms like British

Leyland and Rolls Royce collapsed in the private sector. It was only when in the public sector that they did better.

The privatisation policy has caused some embarrassment to the government. Shares in Amersham International were sold very cheaply. In other words, the government was giving away public assets. On the other hand, sales of BNOC shares flopped. The public was clearly not interested in this company and did not welcome it into the private sector.

Is Britain a corporate state?

We came across the term 'corporate management' when we looked at the Bains Report on local government. In this chapter we are examining a rather different concept but one which is concerned with the centralised control of decision-making. In the corporate state, the government intervenes in the economy and makes the important decisions. Trade unions and managers give up their freedom to make decisions. They do this in exchange for participating with the government in making economic policy. The idea of the 'corporate state' has a bad image. This is because Fascist Italy and Nazi Germany were regarded as extreme types of the corporate state.

It has been argued that the close links between firms, trade unions and the government strengthen trends towards corporatism. The Labour party has strong links with the trade unions. Many Labour MPs are sponsored by the unions. Labour's Conference is dominated by block votes from the trade unions. The Conservative party has close links with firms. Table 22.1 shows how strong the connections are between three prominent Conservatives and private industry.

Some have argued that this **tripartism** has produced a bad situation in Britain. For example, the trade unions in some ways have a privileged position in law. Sometimes the activity of trade unionists falls outside the law. On the other side, private industry often gains most benefit when the government spends public money. Transport policy provides a typical illustration of this. Investment in private transport, such as motorways, benefits private road haulage firms and private motor firms. This investment has been much greater than that in public transport, such as the railways and buses.

Are we, as some have suggested, moving towards a corporate state in Britain? It is certainly clear that in recent times governments have intervened more and more in the economy. This is in contrast to the last century when governments left the economy to itself. Having to manage the economy through two major wars involved governments in making economic decisions. But most intervention has taken place in the last forty years.

A Conservative government, led by Harold Macmillan, showed mild interest in planning the economy. Conservative leaders were impressed by the progress made in the French economy which was based on planning. A Conservative government set up the National Economic Development Council (NEDC, sometimes referred to as 'Neddy'). Trade union leaders, the CBI and members of the government sat on the NEDC. It was hoped that their meetings would arrive at solutions to economic problems that Britain was facing. Later a Labour government set up Economic Development Councils (EDCs or 'little Neddies'). These bodies discussed problems in particular parts of the economy, such as vehicle building or textiles. The important point about the Neddy-system was that decisions were being made *outside* of Parliament. Some MPs feared that the NEDC was becoming more important than the House of Commons. They worried that Britain was drifting away from being a parliamentary democracy to becoming a corporate state.

Another form of government intervention has

Table 22.1 Directorships in the 1978 Conservative Shadow Cabinet

Sir Geoffrey Howe	Lord Carrington	James Prior
Alliance Assurance	Barclays Bank	United Biscuits
Associated Business Programme	Cadbury Schweppes	Avon Products
EMI	Rio Tinto Zinc	IDC Group
The London Assurance	Hambros Bank	Norwich Union Insurance Group
Sun Alliance and London Assurance	Amalgamated Metal Corporation	
Sun Insurance		

Source: Howard Elcock, op. cit.

been in the shape of 'incomes' or 'prices and incomes' policies. The first incomes policy came from a Conservative government in 1961. The Chancellor, Selwyn-Lloyd, introduced a nine-month 'pay pause'. The idea was extended under a Labour government in 1965. A National Board for Prices and Incomes (NBPI) was set up to administer government policy. A Conservative government returned to a prices and incomes policy in the years 1972–4. Some prices and incomes policies were *statutory*. In other words, they were compulsory. Others have been *voluntary*. The Labour government headed by James Callaghan struggled with a voluntary policy. It broke down during the 'winter of discontent' in 1979. Mrs Thatcher's government stated that it was not going to have an incomes policy. However, her ministers operated an informal incomes policy in the public sector.

Other bodies set up by the government which intervene in the economy included the Department of Economic Affairs (DEA). This department was set up by Labour to plan Britain's long-term economic future. It was meant to balance the Treasury's view of the economy, which is always more concerned with short-term problems. Labour also created a Ministry of Technology to oversee research and development. The Industrial Reorganisation Corporation (IRC) was set up to encourage mergers and take-overs so that small firms could survive against foreign competition. Small companies joined to form the British Computer Company, ICL. This enabled them to compete with the American Computer giant, IBM.

The DEA and the IRC have been abolished, but they have been replaced by other interventionist bodies. For example, the MSC works in the area of employment. The Advisory, Conciliation and Arbitration Service (ACAS) intervenes in industrial disputes. The most important body to have been set up recently is the National Enterprise Board (NEB).

The NEB was established in 1975 to help regenerate British industry. It invested in manufacturing industry, especially those which contribute to exports, or lead to advances in technology, or which help areas of high unemployment. A major example controlled through the NEB is British Leyland. The role of the NEB has been reduced in recent years.

In the past there has been close cooperation between government, the CBI and the TUC. This sometimes resulted in government policies being *announced* in Parliament rather than there being *consultation* with Parliament. It was this type of relationship between the government, the unions and industry which produced unease amongst MPs. Some MPs saw the coordination between government and the major interest groups as evidence of 'corporatism'. But this was a long way from the corporatism of Fascist Italy or Nazi Germany. The major interest groups, the CBI and TUC, retained their independence and the government retained the right to act as it saw fit.

Any trends towards corporatism ended with the election of the Conservatives to office in 1979. The government ignored the trade union movement. Nor did it seem greatly influenced by the CBI. Mrs Thatcher's government wanted to intervene less in the economy, not more.

Terms used

Closed shop A closed shop is made up from jobs which are open only to members of a trade union.

De-industrialisation This is measured by the falling output or employment in manufacturing industry.

Hyper-inflation This is sometimes called 'galloping' inflation because prices rise so fast. Germany experienced hyper-inflation from 1920–3. Some people feel that the uncertainty and fear that hyper-inflation caused paved the way for Hitler's rise to power.

Multinationals These are companies which own and control production in different countries. In other words, multinational companies produce and sell their goods in different countries.

Tripartism Made up from three parts.

U-turn This occurs when policies are changed so much that they finish by going in the opposite direction. A notable U-turn was done by Edward Heath in 1972. When Rolls Royce collapsed, the government he led was forced to spend public money and nationalise Rolls Royce. Until then, his policy had been one of letting bankrupt companies go out of business.

Summary

1 Economists and politicians have given many explanations why Britain's economy is doing less well than many of our rivals abroad. These faults include low levels of investment; too many strikes; poor management; de-industrialisation; too much tax; too much government intervention; and too little government intervention.

2 Inflation and unemployment are the two major economic evils that affect people's lives. Generally speaking, Conservatives see inflation as the greater evil, while Labour sees unemployment as the greater evil.

3 In the past, governments managed the economy in the way outlined by John Maynard Keynes. This involved increased public spending in order to control unemployment.

4 Since 1979 governments have followed monetarist policies recommended by Milton Friedman. This involves cutting public spending in order to control inflation.

5 There is disagreement over the place of nationalisation and privatisation in the economy. In the past, all parties in Parliament favoured a mixed economy with public and private industry existing together. Socialists currently want more public ownership and nationalisation. Conservatives favour more private ownership and privatisation.

6 There has been increasing government intervention in the economy by all governments since the Second World War. However, the Conservative government elected in 1979 was determined to reverse this trend.

Questions for discussion

1 What are the two most serious economic problems faced by Britain? What measures have recent governments taken to solve them?

Here are some fictitious quotations which could be associated with the views of some famous economists.

2 **Economist-K:** The economy is like a balloon. If the government cuts spending and takes air out, the whole balloon shrinks. When the government stops the building of a new hospital, it also cuts the profit of building firms. They buy less cement and bricks. Workers are made redundant. This causes problems for the local supermarket, corner shop, and pub.

Economist-F: The economy is just like a fruit cake. A bigger slice for you means a smaller slice or me. If the government takes too big a slice, it leaves only a small slice for private industry. If the government takes a smaller slice, then private industry can expand.

Draw a cartoon which illustrates the different economic philosophies suggested by the quotations.

3 What are the arguments for and against
  (i) more nationalisation
  (ii) more privatisation?

4 What is corporatism? To what extent could Britain be called a 'corporate state'?

5 Read your local newspapers and find out what the local economic problems are. Is there one issue which is being discussed more at the moment than the others? Is there disagreement between the local political parties on the issues? Are trade unions or other pressure groups taking a part in discussing the problems?

6 What is the major national economic issue at the present time? Make notes from the TV or radio news on this issue. Collect newspaper cuttings. Follow events and make a small file on how the issue developed.

23

Social policy

This chapter examines some of the problems which exist in social policy. Britain is a country where great differences separate the rich from the poor. Many poor families seem to be 'trapped' by poverty, and find it impossible to raise their standard of living. We will examine the poverty trap. Social policy is closely linked to economic policy. This is because economic resources have to be found to pay for the welfare state. The welfare state has not been paid for by taking away money from the rich and giving it to the poor. It has been paid for by the extra wealth produced by economic growth. We see that when the economy stops growing this causes great problems in social policy. We examine housing policy and find that there is a growing problem of homelessness. We see that some of the problems in health care have been caused by the success of the National Health Service in the past. Finally we consider the problems in educational policy. Important politicians have said that schools have failed to produce the right type of pupil.

The welfare state

The origins of the welfare state are to be found in the measures introduced by the Liberal government at the beginning of this century. These measures included old age pensions and an insurance scheme which provided help during times of sickness, industrial injury and unemployment. The basis of the welfare state as we know it today was conceived by Sir William Beveridge and his colleagues during the Second World War. The five areas of social policy in Britain were outlined in the Beveridge Report. Five social evils were identified: want, disease, ignorance, idleness and squalor. The Beveridge Committee agreed that these evils could be eliminated through the government's economic and social policies.

In the years following the war, the various governments tackled these evils through their policies. *Want* was met with schemes to maintain a person's income through difficult times. Supplementary benefits were available to people who fell into poverty, and child benefit was available to all young families who had the expense of raising children. The National Health Service was set up to fight *disease*. *Ignorance* was to be eliminated as people benefited from the 1944 Education Act. Conditions of *squalor* could be reduced through social work. Social workers could help their clients cope with the problems they faced, and show them how to overcome such problems in the future. Finally, *idleness* could be reduced by governments following the Keynesian economic policies that we examined in chapter 22.

Forty years after its birth the welfare state is in a crisis. For some, the very words 'Welfare State' are a term of abuse in politics. They blame Britain's poor economic performance on the welfare state. They argue that the welfare state has produced generations of people who lack initiative, and who have never learnt to stand on their own feet. They would like to see the welfare state abolished.

Others believe that the welfare state is beneficial. They believe that it should be kept and expanded. It is argued that spending on the welfare state is a way of investing money in people. It will produce a healthy, well-educated and well-housed population. For this reason it is argued that spending on social policy should have top priority in government policy-making.

The services which form the welfare state are costly and the money to pay for them must come from somewhere. As we have seen, there are many pressures on government to provide money for a great variety of goods and services. Although social services are seen as important they may not command top priority in competition with other demands on the public purse. Successive governments have tended to see defence as the top priority. This means that governments will keep

Britain's military forces as strong as possible. This includes nuclear weapons, which are very expensive. In the end this might mean that the welfare state suffers in order to maintain or increase spending on defence.

The government can make social policy outside of the welfare state. Through giving **tax reliefs**, the government can encourage people to provide for their own housing, pensions, and assurance. There is a feeling that the welfare state is being undermined by private schemes. In addition to private pension schemes, there is private health care and private education.

Thus decisions made in the Cabinet about the level of tax relief or about public spending affect millions of lives. The standard of living of people is altered by government decisions to raise pensions, cut unemployment benefit, or reduce the number of students in universities and polytechnics.

Poverty in Britain

We examined the importance of social class in chapter 2. The distribution of *wealth* shows how far apart people are in terms of financial resources:

- the richest 1% of the population own a quarter of all personal wealth
- the richest 2% of the population own nearly a third of all personal wealth
- the richest 5% of the population own nearly one half of all personal income
- the poorer half of the population own 5% of all personal wealth.

The picture is repeated when we consider the distribution of income. The richest 20% earn 38.8% of the total income: the poorest 20% earn 6.8% of the total income.

But do these *inequalities* mean that there is poverty in Britain? After all, over three-quarters of British homes have phones; well over 90% have fridges and televisions; and over 60% of homes are centrally heated. However, poverty exists alongside these symbols of affluence.

The *Child Poverty Action Group* believes that about 15% of all households live on or below the poverty line. Families with children under the age of 5 years are amongst the worst hit. *Age Concern* has revealed how pensioners can suffer in Britain. The rising price of fuel (electricity, gas, coal) causes pensioners much hardship. Poverty is not spread evenly across Britain. It is more common in Scotland, Northern Ireland, and the north of England than in the south of England. Even people still in jobs can experience financial hardship. The *Low Pay Unit* found that well over 30% of the full-time, adult work-force were **low paid**.

Low paid workers can get caught in the *poverty trap*. This happens when a worker receives a wage rise, but ends up worse off. It occurs because some of the wage rise goes back to the Inland Revenue in income tax. Also the wage rise might bring the worker's wage above the level at which benefits are paid. When the wage increase is worth less than the benefits which are lost, the worker is worse off.

Forty years of a welfare state in Britain have not eliminated poverty. It seems that it is really true that 'the poor are always with us'. In fact the recession of the 1970s and 1980s is making poverty more serious. The rich are getting richer whilst the poor get poorer. For example, the share of income earned by the richest 20% has increased by 3.5% between 1976 and 1980. During the same period the share earned by the poorest 20% fell by 10.5%. In addition to the poverty trap, there is a *cycle of deprivation* which keeps people poor.

The cycle of deprivation is a vicious circle. It involves poor people who, through ignorance and an unhealthy environment, suffer more illness than others. The schools in such areas have problems and their pupils leave without qualifications. The children grow into adults, suffering from the same ignorance and poverty as their parents.

People's attitudes towards poverty are complex. On the one hand there is sympathy towards the poor. On the other hand, poor people can be despised. We can see this contradiction in attitudes towards the unemployed. Most of those who are unemployed do not enjoy being unemployed. Many firms have gone bankrupt because of the recession. Workers find themselves out of work for reasons that are beyond their control. Yet there is still an attitude that unemployed people are 'lazy' or are 'scroungers'. This attitude does not blame the economy for producing unemployment, but blames the workers for being unemployed.

Public spending on welfare

The Labour party has a strong belief in the welfare state. As we saw in chapter 8, the right wing of the party is more interested in developing the welfare state than is the left. The left is more interested in changing economic policy. The record of recent Labour government is one of trying to limit the growth in spending on welfare. In 1974 government spending was £5.8 billion more than had been planned for that year. Labour therefore restricted spending on hospitals, housing and education.

When we examined Conservative attitudes towards the welfare state we found disagreement. Conservative 'wets' believed in the welfare state, whereas the right saw it as a burden. The early years of Mrs Thatcher's government saw social spending rising quickly. This was because of pay increases in the public sector and the rising costs of unemployment. There was no growth in the economy to pay for this increase in social spending. So the Central Policy Review Staff (the 'think tank') suggested that savings could be made in other parts of the welfare state. In particular, the CPRS proposed privatising parts of the National Health Service and the introduction of student loans to replace grants.

We saw in Taskpage 19.5 how the Public Expenditure Survey Committee (PESC) attempts to plan public spending. We also saw in the last chapter how cash limits are now used by government to limit public spending. On occasions public spending has been influenced by bodies which have lent Britain money. In particular the International Monetary Fund (IMF) and foreign banks have caused Labour governments to restrict welfare spending.

Housing policy

One area of social policy that has suffered from recent cutbacks is housing. But only part of the reason for this was the need for savings. Another reason was the failure of experiments with 'high-rise' developments, which resulted in large and expensive blocks of flats having to be knocked down. Also local authorities with large numbers of council houses found them more and more difficult to administer.

Government is nevertheless heavily involved in housing. At both local and central levels, government influences the provision of houses. Central government can encourage people into the private sector with mortgage relief. Central government can produce new laws which affect the rights of tenants, the rights of landlords, or the principles on which rents should be fixed. Local government can increase the supply of new houses by actually building them.

Peter Malpass and Alan Murie have pointed out that housing policy is different from other aspects of social policy, such as education or health. They argued that nearly everyone turns first to the state-run National Health Service when they are sick. Nearly all parents send their children to state schools. But most people choose to buy a house or rent privately, rather than rent a council house.

The 1950s, 1960s and early 1970s were the years of high housing output. This was the period of extensive slum clearance. During the 1950s most new houses were built by local authorities. During periods of Conservative government in the 1950s and 1960s local authority building was restricted and the private sector expanded. Public sector housing outstripped private sector again under Labour in the late 1960s.

The changing pattern of ownership is shown in Table 23.1. The growth of owner-occupied housing is dramatic in the post-war years. The change is even more startling if 1918 is the baseline. Ninety per cent of homes were then privately rented.

Government intervention has influenced these changing patterns to a considerable extent. For example, the Rent Act 1965 introduced the idea of 'fair rents' in the private sector. The Housing Finance Act 1972 introduced the idea of 'fair rents' to council houses. The Rent Act 1974 gave security of tenure to tenants in furnished dwellings. The Housing Act 1980 gave council tenants the 'right to buy' their homes at discount prices.

Table 23.1 Housing tenure in Great Britain, 1945–79 (percentages of all households)

	Public rented	Owner- occupied	Private rented*
1945	12	26	62
1951	18	29	53
1961	27	43	31
1969	30	49	21
1971	30.8	52.7	16.5
1979	31.9	54.6	13.5

*Including housing associations

Source: Malpass and Murie, *op. cit.*

The politics of housing policy has caused bitter disagreement in recent years. Labour has been concerned with the rights of tenants. Conservative policy has pursued privatisation with council house sales. Selling council houses is a policy which is popular with the electorate. Between 1971 and 1973 90 000 council houses were sold.

Selling council houses has an interesting political impact. There is some evidence to show that when people change their vote from Labour to Conservative, for many it happens when they become owner-occupiers. Moving from rented houses to owning their own homes causes changes in some people's view of themselves. They see themselves as now being more middle-class. This causes a change in voting behaviour as they vote the way they understand middle-class people to vote.

Health Care

The National Health Service (NHS) was established in 1948. It was the first comprehensive and free health service in the world. But its very success has caused further problems. For example, people in Britain are now living longer, and this partly because of improved health care under the NHS. However, old people are more expensive to look after than young people. A patient aged 75 or over costs more than six times as much to care for as a patient of working age. In 1982 each man aged between 25 to 44 cost the NHS on average £82 per year: that sum rose to £507 for a man of 75 years.

The NHS is a huge organisation and very difficult to administer. There have been two major reorganisations of the NHS within ten years. Although it employs twice as many people today as it did in 1949, waiting lists for treatment are still long. For example, suspected cancer patients have to wait an average of six weeks for their first hospital appointment.

Despite the success of the NHS, Britain is not a healthy nation. This sounds like a contradiction, but it is not. Because the proportion of old people in the population is increasing, chronic illness is more common. Changing moral values have led to medical problems. There are now many more people suffering from sexually transmitted diseases and alcoholism than in the past. Increased affluence brings new diseases, as people change their diets and take less exercise. The new technology in medicine can now keep alive patients who would have died in the past. Finally people's views on what illness is have changed. A complaint that a person thinks is 'serious' enough to go to the doctor with today may have been shrugged off as 'nothing much' by that person's parent.

All these changes mean that the NHS is extremely busy. Absenteeism from work because of sickness has risen by 7% a year since the beginning of the NHS.

During the 1970s doctors increased the number of prescriptions they wrote out by a quarter. This increased load has given the DHSS the reputation of being a 'big spender'. The government has insisted that the NHS spends within its cash limits. In order to limit the growth of public spending on the NHS, the government has ordered 'efficiency savings' to be made. But some people feel that 'efficiency savings' is another term for 'expenditure cuts'.

The reputation of the DHSS being a 'big spender' is not justified if we look at spending in other industrialised countries. Table 23.2 shows that only Japan spent less of its national wealth on health care than did Britain. In terms of social security benefits, only Japan and the USA spend a smaller proportion than Britain. Britain spends 16.3% of its national income on social security benefits. West Germany spends 22.4%. At the top

Table 23.2 Expenditure on health as a percentage of Gross Domestic Product (1974)

	%		%
Japan	4.0	West Germany	6.7
Britain	5.2	Canada	6.8
Norway	5.6	France	6.9
Finland	5.8	Sweden	7.3
Italy	6.0	Netherlands	7.3
Australia	6.5	USA	7.4

Source: Howard Elcock, op. cit.

of the spending league is Sweden with 29.7% of its national income paid out in social benefits.

The biggest failure of the NHS is that it does not care for all the population equally. There are different standards of healthcare which the architects of the NHS never planned for:

(i) *Types of illness* Patients who suffer from a short-term illness which can be cured get a higher standard of care and more resources than patients with chronic illness. Looking after geriatrics and the mentally ill are known as the 'Cinderella' services. The standard of care is lower than in the more 'glamorous' areas of the NHS. Even amongst the medical profession, some areas of care are more prestigious than others. Specialising in organ transplants is more prestigious than specialising in geriatrics.

(ii) *Social class* The biggest difference between social classes is found in infant mortalities. For every death in the first year of life of children with professional parents, there are four deaths amongst children with manual working-class parents. The effects of poverty on health are reflected in other statistics. For example, twice as many men in poorer social classes suffer long-standing illness than men in the professional class.

(iii) *Regional differences* There is not 'equal access' to the NHS. In other words, health care facilities vary from region to region. Such differences involve the number of doctors per thousand people, the number of specialists, the number of hospital beds, and the number of dentists.

(iv) *Public and private medicine* Many middle-class people who feel that the quality of NHS care has diminished have joined private health schemes. In addition, some trade unions have made private health care a benefit for their members. At the end of 1980 there were 1 647 000 people in private health schemes. With their families, this amounted to 3 557 000 people – or 6.4% of Britain's total population. The growth of private health care means that the original goals of the NHS will never be achieved. Some people worry that the NHS will become the dumping ground for illnesses which are not 'profitable' for the private sector. Britain could follow the American example, spending more on health care and yet getting less value for money. An American professor of health administration pointed out the contrast in the USA of 'the bright, cheery, well-equipped private hospitals with affluent patients in need of minor treatment coming and going with public hospitals with poorer, more chronically-ill and socially-depressed patients coming in and staying'. Is Britain beginning to be like that?

Education policy

The period from the late 1940s to the early 1970s was one of great educational expansion in Britain. The number of pupils in primary schools rose from 4 to 5 million in the years between 1955 and 1975. The number of secondary school pupils rose from 1½ to 4 million. The increased school population led to a doubling in the number of teachers to 435 000. In **higher education** there was an explosion in the number of students. Numbers rose from 86 400 to 462 000.

Despite this growth in education, many other countries educate their young people more than Britain. For example, there are fourteen other countries with a greater proportion of 20-year-olds in higher education than Britain.

The 1980s have seen a decline in education. The number of pupils is falling. It has been estimated that they will have fallen from a maximum of 9 million to 7 million by 1990. Universities and polytechnics now enrol fewer students. ▷ p.224

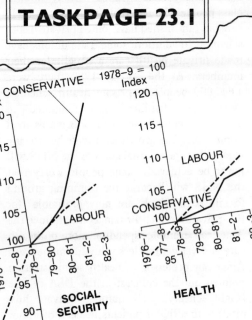

SOCIAL SECURITY — 1978–9 = 100

HEALTH

HOUSING

The dotted line represents Labour spending up to the election and its planned spending after it

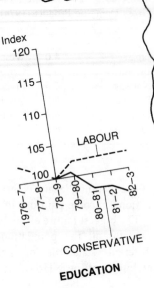

EDUCATION

Social security now accounts for 29 per cent of all government expenditure. This year's expenditure – about £32 billion – is 22 per cent higher in real terms than in 1979. Hidden within the rising total however are cuts worth about £2 billion per year.

The abolition of the old index for pensions – which linked pensions to either earnings or prices whichever was higher – has meant a married couple on a pension is £3.25 a week worse off this year. Families with dependent children, however, have been hit hardest of all. The support which working families receive – child benefit – has dropped under this government to a 30-year low and is now only equivalent to the frugal level achieved in the Fifties. Sick, disabled and unemployed families have had national insurance benefits have had the support which they are given for the children cut by 23 per cent in the last four years.

These cuts have coincided with increased taxes on all but the very richest of families. A married couple on average earnings with two children is paying 16 per cent more tax in 1982 than in 1979. Couples with less than average earnings are suffering even higher tax increases. A couple with two children earning 75 per cent of average earnings is paying 18 per cent more tax.

The apparent increase in expenditure in the graph on health requires several qualifications. Firstly, the increase in spending includes the increase in charges. Prescriptions, for example, have gone up five times since the last election – from 20p to £1.40 – which accounts for about one-fifth of the 5.5 per cent real increase in spending since 1979. Secondly, the graph only measures increases in spending, not the increase in demand. When the increase in demand – particularly the increase in the over-75s who make disproportionate demands on the NHS – is taken into account, the increase in public expenditure has roughly allowed the NHS to stand still.

The argument from the left that this Government only cuts subsidies to the well-off but protects the subsidies to the better off is sustained by the biggest cut of all – the 50 per cent reduction in housing subsidies. In 1979, subsidies to council housing were running roughly in line with mortgage interest but by this year, mortgage relief was costing the Treasury four times as much as council housing subsidies – £2,000 million compared to £550 million.

The government would reply that it has helped workers to buy their own council homes through its promotion of council house sales. Of the six million plus council homes, almost 500,000 have been sold since the election. Paradoxically, the Government has cut back local council loans which were used to buy private houses – from 31,000 in 1979 to just over 3,000 last year.

The effects on families of the cuts to the education budget and the apparent increases to health are harder to measure. A cut in education expenditure does not necessarily mean a reduction in the service because the number of children is dropping dramatically — from 9.4 to eight million in the 5 to 15 age group during the Eighties.

Education, however, has suffered a cut over and above the drop in numbers. The biggest cut has been in higher education. Schools have not escaped but in higher education, for example, one out of every six of the 80,000 teaching posts in polytechnics and universities in 1981 will have been eliminated by 1985.

The degree to which individual families have been affected by these cuts depends on the local areas in which they live. Unlike social security, education is locally administered. The cuts to locally administered services — education, housing and personal social services — would have been grimmer but for the fact that many local councils refused to follow the Government's guide-lines. In 1980-81 they spent 5.5 per cent more than Whitehall wanted; in 1981-2 some 8 per cent more; and this year an estimated 7 per cent more.

Guardian, 10 March 1983

From these four graphs and comments on social spending you will see that some arguments can be used to 'condemn' the government's record on social policy. Other arguments can be used to 'excuse' or 'explain' the government's record. Using these facts and others contained in chapter 22, write:

(i) the draft of a parliamentary question from the leader of the opposition to the prime minister attacking the government's social policy.

(ii) the draft of a reply from the prime minister defending the Government's record.

Storm over secret Think Tank report

A family of four would have to pay £600 a year in health insurance and £950 a year for each child's school fees, if radical changes in public services, outlined by the Government's Think Tank were to be introduced.

It would also cost, on average, £12,000 to put a child through university, and all State benefits, including pensions, would be worth 10 per cent less than they are now.

The figures come from a discussion document circulated to members of the Cabinet this month by the Central Policy Review Staff. News of the document, which has been seen by THE OBSERVER, has caused a storm among both Conservative 'wets' and opposition politicians.

The report was drafted during the summer as a result of gloomy long-term economic forecasts drawn up by Treasury officials. Working on the most pessimistic projection for economic growth, the planning documents showed that maintaining public services at their present level would cost £12,000 million to £13,500 million more by 1990, an increase of around 10 per cent.

Since it is Government policy to reduce both borrowing and taxation, the Chancellor, Sir Geoffrey Howe, asked the Think Tank to devise ways of bridging the gap by cutting spending.

The report suggests that savings could be made by an 11 per cent across-the-board cut in all services. But this, it says, would be unpopular and impractical.

The Think Tank suggests instead a series of radical options, but warns throughout of the difficulties of carrying these through.

The opinions are set out under three headings. The first, 'Partial Change,' suggests charging for higher education to save an estimated £1,000 million and increasing and extending charges for health services, to save another £1,000 million.

Under the second heading, 'Comprehensive Changes', they suggest charging for schooling, saving £3,000 million to £4,000 million; switching to a private insurance scheme in place of the National Health Service, saving £4,000 million; and de-indexing social security benefits, saving £3,000 million.

The third heading, 'Less Resources', suggests a cut of £1,000 million in education – and abandoning the present commitment to increase defence spending, to produce a saving of £1,500 million.

If the 'comprehensive changes' were introduced, the report warns, radical changes in the taxation and benefits system would be needed and these could be costly. 'If even the poorest had to pay full charges, this would exacerbate poverty to a level which we assume Ministers would judge unacceptable.'

It also warns that while public spending would be reduced, the proportion of 'the community's wealth' being spent on education and health would not be reduced.

Of all the options the two under the heading 'partial' are thought by Whitehall to be most feasible.

For higher education, savings of £1,000 million would be made if students were charged the full cost of courses. Means tested scholarships would be available for 300,000 students, or about three-fifths of the number of students now in higher education. Loans would be available for others.

Under health, the report says charges would have to be introduced for people now treated free — children and the elderly — for visits to GPs and for hospital places to produce savings of £1,000 million.

The Cabinet did not discuss the Think Tank's report in detail at the 9 September meeting, a meeting for which there are — exceptionally — no minutes. The departmental Ministers affected by the proposals have been asked to undertake further study of the suggestions and report back to the Cabinet.

Strenuous efforts have been made to prevent news of the exercise seeping out. When the first reports of it appeared in *The Times* two months ago, all copies of the relevant documents circulating in Whitehall were called in. Some members of the Cabinet are said to be anxious about the effects knowledge of such plans could have upon the party's electoral prospects.

Observer, 19 September 1982

A CPRS report was leaked to the press just before the annual conferences of the political parties. This extract discusses the report and the way in which it became public knowledge.

(i)   Why would the government have wanted the report to be kept secret?

(ii) Was the report discussed by the Cabinet in its meeting on 9 September?

(iii) In which areas of the welfare state would cuts have been made if the think tank's report had been put into practice?

(iv) What were the differences between the 'comprehensive changes' and the 'partial changes' in the report?

'Bludgeon' protest over council-house sales

The government was accused last night of 'bludgeoning and bribing' council tenants in an attempt to make more of them buy their own homes.

According to Labour's housing spokesman, Gerald Kaufman, the bludgeon takes the form of higher council rents. Since 1979, rents have risen 117 per cent and now average £14 a week.

And the discounts of 50 per cent off the market value which tenants receive if they buy are the bribe, says Kaufman.

The average tenant pays only £9800 for his home – £7000 less than its full market value. With 100 per cent option mortgage, this need cost him only £19.83 a week. In return he will enjoy capital appreciation of his home.

This dramatic increase in the financial benefits of buying a council house has caused sales to take off sharply (see graph). The Tories believe this will boost their vote in the local government elections on May 6.

John Stanley, the housing minister, claims that house sales are now running ahead of the government's expectations. Before the May 1979 general election, it was up to each local authority whether it sold its houses. But the new government moved to the offensive, encouraging councils to sell, and increasing the discounts they could offer to tenants. In October 1980 they changed the law to give tenants the right to buy their own homes.

About 250 000 homes have been bought since May 1979, out of a total council stock of more than six million.

Sales are still patchy. One of the keenest councils, West Lancashire, had sold 639 out of a stock of just over 4000 by the end of 1981. At the other end of the scale, Tower Hamlets in London had sold just seven out of a total of 18 000.

About 30 labour councils mounted a determined rearguard action against the law giving tenants the right to buy. Only with Lord Denning's ruling earlier this year that one of the recalcitrant councils, Norwich, must speed up sales or face a central government takeover of its housing operation have the last obstacles to sales been removed.

Already, the effects are beginning to show. In South Shields, Tyneside, the Labour council is gritting its teeth and obeying the law. To its chagrin, more than 3500 applications have flooded in since October 1980 from tenants of more than three years' standing, eager to buy their homes at substantially reduced prices.

On the Whiteleas Estate, where the streets are named after painters, parts of Rembrandt Avenue and Millais Gardens are becoming little havens of owner-occupiers.

Garages, porch extensions and stone garden walls are unmistakable signs of home-ownership. The colour of guttering downpipes has become a subtle indicator of imminent purchase.

Those who have bought say there is no ill-feeling between them and those who still rent. And, they say, everybody is taking greater pride in the estate. But the potentially divisive effect of council house sales is illustrated by the fact that there are few buyers on the hard-to-let estates in South Shields, where poor families and families with social problems are concentrated. It is the cream of the houses that go.

Many families on the bad estates would like a transfer to better homes. In the short run, the fact that houses have been sold does not affect their chances. The same people live there – only as owners, not tenants. But in the long run, those people might have bought from the private sector, moved away from the area or died. Then the house would have become available to the council to re-let. The worries about creating ghettoes are strong, and wholesome local authorities – mostly Conservative – have gone beyond the legal requirement to sell to sitting tenants. Many are prepared to sell off any house that is empty.

In South London, Wandsworth council is selling, with the aid of a glossy brochure, homes in Althorpe Grove – 'Battersea's new prestige development, named after the country home of Battersea's Lord of the Manor, Earl Spencer.'

Not that it needs to drop the name of the Princess of Wales' father to sell the homes: they are built round a village green and ornamental waterways and prices start at a modest £41 000 for a three-bedroomed maisonette.

Intending purchasers should make haste, however, for if Labour is returned to power in the local government elections, it is committed to block further sales. The houses were built to rent, and rent them they will. The Social Democrat Liberal alliance in Wandsworth has also set it face against 'indiscriminate' sales.

To justify its stance, it points to the 2500 Wandsworth families with children living more than four floors off the ground.

Just down the road from Althorpe Grove, stands the notorious Doddington Estate. 'It's like a prison camp,' says 28-year-old Tom Muir, who lives with his wife, Joan, and three young children on the ninth floor. 'The lifts break down all the time, and with the pram, my wife can't leave the house.' One day, Muir hopes to buy. But with rent, rates and heating costing him £32 a week, he finds it difficult to save a deposit.

John Stanley says: 'We are giving a substantial number of people an opportunity of home ownership that they would not other wise have had.' But his opponents want to know what he is proposing to do for those for whom even 50 per cent discounts make home ownership an impossible dream.

The Sunday Times, 25 April 1982

(i) By what percentage was it claimed that council-house rents rose between 1979 and 1982?

(ii) What was the average cost to a tenant of purchasing a council house?

(iii) What price would the average house have fetched on the open market?

(iv) What is the total number of council houses?

(v) Which councils oppose council-house sales?

(vi) Why are some tenants reluctant to buy their houses?

The housing gap: demand increasing while building slumps

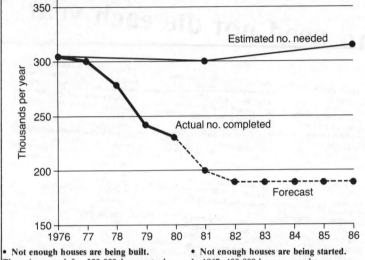

• **Not enough council homes are being started.**
In 1967, 200,000 council homes were begun. This year, building begins on only 35,000 homes.

• **3,000,000 homes need serious repairs.**
547,000 in England alone are unfit for habitation.

• **The number of unemployed in the building industry has more than doubled in the last two years.**
In August 1979 the number of building industry jobless was 153,000. Now it is 370,000.

• **850,000 homes are overcrowded.**
• **There are 50,000 homeless in England alone.**
• **There is an imbalance in the amount of state subsidy given to different types of household.**
In 1981/82, council tenants will receive a subsidy of £241 per household.
Private home-owners will receive £285 per household, through tax relief on mortgages. Private tenants, however, will receive only £21 per household.

The Times, 1 December 1981

• **Not enough houses are being built.**
There is a need for 300,000 houses to be completed this year. Only 205,000 are expected to be finished.

• **Not enough houses are being started.**
In 1967, 400,000 houses were begun. This year, building begins on only 145,000 homes.

Secret report warned about housing 'disaster'

LOCAL councils all over the country face the prospect of having to pull down thousands of system-built homes at a cost to the nation of up to £3,000 million—but the disaster could have been averted in 1969.

The National Building Agency, set up by the government to certify new building methods, was called in at that time by the London borough of Hillingdon to report on condensation and water leakage problems in its brand-new Bison system-built estates.

The agency produced a confidential report detailing fundamental faults in the system, which uses pre-cast concrete panels, assembled jigsaw-fashion. Thousands of similar flats, which should have lasted 60 years or more, continued to be built throughout the country as late as 1977. Most of these suffered identical problems to those discovered in Hillingdon, yet the Ministry of Housing (as it then was) chose to ignore the devastating findings of its own agency, and continued to push local authorities to using industrialised system building.

Moreover, the National Building Agency itself, which is now defunct, failed to take effective action against system building, despite its own damning report on Hillingdon.

Last week The Sunday Times revealed how flaws in design or in construction methods could mean water penetrating thousands of system-built homes, causing damp and mould and leading to widespread health problems. Now local authorities and tenants alike are asking how these homes, the housing hope of the Sixties and Seventies, have turned into the despair of the Eighties for so many families.

The Sunday Times, 18 April 1982

(i) Is the 'housing gap' getting smaller, staying much the same, or growing?

(ii) How many homes suffer from overcrowding?

(iii) What problems do many new system-built homes suffer from?

Thousands who need not die each year

Thousands of people die unnecessarily each year because of inadequate treatment by the health service, according to a team of medical experts. It has found that there are 20 500 avoidable deaths annually for which either poor help or the victims' slowness in seeking it are responsible.

The researchers, from St Thomas's Hospital, London, studied the incidence of deaths from 13 diseases which should be curable in young and middle-aged people. They found it varied widely from area to area.

For example, about 260 people between the ages of five and 49 die of asthma each year. In the best areas, mortality from the disease is about one-third the average and in the worst areas it is twice the average.

Professor Walter Holland, who undertook the research with John Charlton, Bob Hartley and Ruth Silver, says 'In an ideal world, these deaths should not occur.'

The team has drawn up a list of the best and worst areas. Tyneside came out as among the best, while nearby Cleveland was down among the ten worst.

In order to make the criteria of avoidable death very strict, the team limited its detailed analysis to certain age groups. The most common cause of avoidable death in people aged from 5 to 64 years is high blood pressure. This results in some 1540 deaths per year. Cancer of the cervix takes 1205, tuberculosis 461, bacterial infection 154, hernias 140, gallstones 130 and appendicitis 97.

Among people aged from five to 49, pneumonia and bronchitis were the cause of 930 avoidable deaths, acute respiratory disease 187. In people aged from five to 44, chronic rheumatic heart disease caused 240 avoidable deaths and

childbirth 72 avoidable deaths. And in the five to 34 age group, Hodgkin's disease, a form of cancer, caused 149 avoidable deaths (these are calculated for 1974 to 1978 – the latest period for which full figures are available).

The team estimates that avoidable deaths either outside these age groups or due to diseases other than the 13 it selected bring the total figure up to 10 000.

The other 10 500 are premature babies who die because of inadequate facilities at the hospitals where they are born.

Health service areas are, on the whole, equally successful in treating bacterial infections, Hodgkin's disease, gallstones, appendicitis, and in caring for mothers in childbirth. And in the case of tuberculosis and cervical cancer, social factors such as poor housing and sexual habits probably account for most of the difference in mortality from district to district rather than treatment. But social factors do not account for the large variation in the incidence of deaths from pneumonia or acute respiratory disease (severe sore throat or laryngitis) hernia, asthma, anaemia or high blood pressure.

Generally, the north and the Midlands come out poorly in the league table of best and worst areas drawn up by the St Thomas's team.

The researchers were surprised, therefore, that Tyneside did so well. North Tyneside was top of the league for treatment of the 13 avoidable diseases (as judged by fewer deaths after allowing for the age and social structure of the population). Newcastle-upon-Tyne came fourth. The team questioned colleagues who had worked on Tyneside, and discovered that the standard of health service work in the area has a high reputation.

Second on the list of the best areas came Oxfordshire, which earlier this year threatened to curtail NHS services severely if it was not given more funds. Others in the top ten are Sheffield, Gloucestershire, Bromley, Avon, Suffolk, Cumbria and Hampshire.

The common factors in these areas which lead to success are probably the medical schools in Newcastle, Sheffield and Avon (Bristol), and the relatively rural or small-town nature of the other areas.

Even so, these good areas scored low points for certain diseases. North Tyneside did badly in treating cervical cancer. Sheffield in treatment of respiratory disease and Hodgkin's disease. Avon in treating anaemia and Suffolk in treating hernias.

Professor Holland says: 'I believe that in some parts of the country medical intervention is not so effective as in others. We were very strict in choosing for examination only those diseases which can be effectively treated to give a person years of useful life.'

He does point out, however, that the survey published in the current issue of *The Lancet* is based on what is put on death certificates and might contain some bias.

The worst ten health areas, in addition to being in the north and Midlands, were also mostly towns with large immigrant populations. Bottom of the list came Walsall and Bolton.

Over the last five or more years, successive governments have tried to eliminate the differences in the health service across the country by giving more funds to the poorly-endowed areas. The investment has not clearly been sufficient to provide enough to eliminate all the inequities.

The Sunday Times, 27 March 1983

(i) What two causes lead to more people dying than need be the case?

(ii) Which area 'surprised' the researchers because it provided above-average care? Why were they surprised?

(iii) What factors helped the 'best' areas? What did many of the 'worst' areas have in common?

(iv) How has the government tried to solve the problem outlined in this article?

Frequency of involvement
in various socio-cultural pursuits (percentages)

	Often	Sometimes	Hardly ever/Never	No chance
Reading				
Maintained	23	47	25	4
Private	40	43	15	3
Sports				
Maintained	38	35	24	3
Private	46	33	17	5
Watching TV				
Maintained	65	29	5	1
Private	52	39	8	1
Dancing				
Maintained	39	31	25	5
Private	26	34	31	10
Voluntary work				
Maintained	8	30	46	16
Private	7	31	45	18

Source: Ted Tapper, in forthcoming volume of Teaching Politics

This study was based on 12 000 pupils in maintained and private schools. How do the cultural lives of pupils in the different schools vary?

(i)   Which pastimes are pursued in roughly equal proportions by pupils regardless of the type of school they go to?

(ii) In which pastimes do pupils from maintained and private schools differ from each other most?

Like the NHS, education has to work within a cash limit. For example, in 1982 leaders of teachers' unions were warned that if they won a pay rise above what the government recommended, it would have to be paid for with redundancies. Also, like the NHS, educational resources are not shared out equally. You can see from Table 23.3 that some local authorities spend much more on each pupil at school than others. The size of classes varies from one authority to another. Bigger classes are less expensive than smaller ones. Also authorities spend different amounts on books, equipment, school meals and in employing non-teaching staff in schools.

Naturally, the cut-backs in education have caused disagreement between the political parties. So too have the measures taken to 'privatise' education. It is a new development for education to be such a controversial issue. In the 1960s there was a *consensus* about education in Britain. Both parties believed that Britain's future lay in a highly educated population. Looking back it is true to say that politicians expected too much from schools, universities and polytechnics. They believed that better education would halt, or even reverse, Britain's economic decline. When this did not

Table 23.3

| Authority | Expenditure on education, 1982–3 | | |
	Unit cost per pupil £	Pupil-teacher ratio primary	secondary
ILEA	1427	18.5	14.7
Brent	1183	17.8	13.5
Haringey	1245	18.0	14.0
Harrow	1154	20.5	14.1
Newcastle	1024	17.5	15.1
Bradford	753	20.3	18.4
Wakefield	748	22.4	17.9
Essex	862	24.2	17.4
Hereford & Worcester	797	25.7	18.2
Leicestershire	884	23.2	16.5
Lincolnshire	885	24.4	17.5
Northumberland	797	22.7	18.3
Dyfed	923	18.8	16.7
England & Wales	**903**	**22.3**	**16.6**

happen, politicians grew disillusioned about the education system.

In 1976 the Labour prime minister, James Callaghan, called for a 'great debate' about education. Some felt that many school leavers did not have the skills that employers expected. In particular, school-leavers were not **literate** or **numerate** enough to become efficient employees. Since 1976 the government has indicated that it wants to control what is taught in schools. This control would be achieved through all schools teaching the *core curriculum*. Also the education of many 16- to 19-year-olds is now under the control of the Manpower Services Commission. This body is primarily concerned with training in skills needed by industry.

One of the most bitter disagreements between the political parties in the 1980s is over private education. In the same way as Conservatives accept the principle of private health care, so they accept private education. It is argued that parents should have the right to buy education for their children. This gives parents *freedom of choice* in the way their children are educated. A Conservative government set up the *assisted places scheme*. This provides financial help for some less well-off parents who want their children to be taught in the **private** sector.

Conservatives believe that choice for parents in the **maintained** sector could be increased by introducing **vouchers**. Each child would receive a voucher, which could be 'spent' at whichever school the parents chose. Good schools would survive, and poor schools would wither away.

The Labour party opposes education based on 'free market' principles. Labour argues that private schools divide society into classes. Most parents are not wealthy enough to send their children to private schools. Labour argues that private schools are a symbol of *privilege* in society, not freedom of choice. In addition, Labour believes that private schools undermine the quality of education in maintained schools. As a result, Labour's policy is to take away financial advantages enjoyed by private schools. In particular, Labour would end the *charity* status of private schools. This would mean that private schools would lose the tax advantages enjoyed by charities.

Labour believes in trying to obtain *equality of*

opportunity in education. There is a strong belief that comprehensive education is the way in which this is most likely to be achieved. Liberals and the SDP accept private education in principle. There is some disagreement among Alliance members as to whether or not public money should support private education.

Arguments and differences of view about education and other social services reflect the wider differences in British society. Much of what has been dealt with in this and earlier chapters is concerned with *quantitative* aspects of life. These are things which can be measured, such as a person's income or number of years spent at school. But equally important are the *qualitative* aspects of life which are very difficult to measure. It is not easy to separate the two for attitudes and feelings are as important to people's happiness as material well-being. Even the most generous social policy cannot guarantee human happiness, but it can contribute towards it. Politics and political decisions are by no means the whole of life. But they are closely interwoven with the nature of society and the quality of life that we enjoy.

Terms used

Higher education This part of the educational system is provided by universities, polytechnics and colleges. They offer a variety of qualifications including degrees and diplomas.

Literacy The ability to read and write. A person who can only just read simple words might be described as 'semi-literate'. An illiterate person is someone who cannot read or write at all.

Low pay Low pay is usually defined as less than two-thirds of average male earnings. It is roughly the same as supplementary benefit payments to a two-child family.

Maintained schools Schools maintained by the state. They are usually administrated through LEAs.

Numeracy A basic knowledge of mathematics.

Private schools Fee-paying schools which are not maintained by the state.

Tax relief The government can encourage people to make private arrangements for social policy of giving them tax relief. For example, until 1982 a person with a mortgage paid less tax than he would have had he not had a mortgage. Now the relief is deducted from the amount that he pays to the building society rather than the amount he pays to the Inland Revenue. But the principle remains the same.

Vouchers These are 'educational credit cards' worth an amount of money which can be 'spent' in the school of one's choice.

Summary

1 The welfare state was set up to combat five social evils: want, disease, ignorance, idleness, and squalor.

2 Despite the existence of a welfare state, there is still considerable poverty in Britain. Many poor families fall victim to the 'poverty trap'. There are contradictory attitudes towards poverty in Britain: some people blame the poor for their poverty, others blame the economic system for creating poverty.

3 As we saw in chapter 22, monetarist economists believe that cutbacks in government spending will revive the economy. They urge the government to cut the welfare state to allow economic growth.

4 Patterns of home ownership have changed considerably over the last fifty years. Conservatives support the sale of council houses to tenants. Labour opposes this policy.

5 The work load of the National Health Service has grown for a variety of reasons. Improved health care has led to people living longer. However, older people suffer from more illness. Because more people are living longer, the NHS requires to spend an extra 2.4% a year just to stand still. It is therefore difficult to cut the cost of the NHS without cutting services.

6 The consensus on education policy in Britain has ended. Conservatives support private education through the assisted places scheme. Labour supports comprehensive schooling.

7 Despite the existence of a welfare state, many other countries spend more on social policy than Britain.

Questions for discussion

1 What are the arguments for and against having a welfare state in Britain?

2 In what ways do Labour and Conservative policies differ with regard to housing policy?

3 'People receive different levels of health care in Britain.' How can this be true?

4 'Private education means that parents have freedom of choice when selecting schools for their children'; 'Private education exists only for a privileged few and destroys equality of opportunity'. Evaluate these statements.

5 Ask for a volunteer in your class to collect some welfare leaflets from the local DHSS office or post office. Are your leaflets successful in communicating their contents to those who need to know?

6 What are the arguments for and against comprehensive education? Organise a debate on this topic. Remember that you may be asked to argue a point of view that privately you do not agree with.

24

Law and order

This chapter examines an issue which has in recent years become increasingly important in politics. The debate on law and order has moved to the forefront of public debate because many people believe that Britain is becoming a more violent society. Crime statistics present some complicated problems. We explore the difficulties in measuring the extent of crime and violence in society. We see how there may well be more crime than we know about. Yet we also see how some crimes get exaggerated in newspapers and cause unnecessary anxiety to the public. The chapter examines the various courts that exist, and looks at the people involved in maintaining law and order. In particular, we look at the role of the police in society. Do the police lack sufficient strength to cope with increasing crime? Or are they too strong, operating beyond democratic control? The chapter concludes by examining party attitudes towards the police.

Is Britain a violent society?

It is very difficult to measure how much crime and violence there is in society. This is because most crimes known to the police are reported to them by the public. In other words the police discover only a small fraction of crimes committed. These tend to be mainly minor offences, such as being drunk and disorderly, motoring offences and petty theft. Some police forces look out for particular crimes more zealously than others. Changes in the law change the nature of certain offences. There are many crimes which do not get reported to the police, and there is no way of knowing how much crime goes unrecorded. Some experts feel that there are more unreported crimes than crimes which are reported to the police.

One reason for an *increase* in crime statistics may be no more than an increase in the number of people who decide to report crime to the police. For example, the number of women who get attacked may appear to increase from one year to the next. What might have happened is rather different. The same number of women may have been attacked in both years, but more of them reported the incident to the police in the second year. Incidents involving wife-battering and baby-battering seem to have increased rapidly over recent years. But is this really so? It is likely that some wives and children have always been abused. What has changed are people's attitudes. Fewer wives now, than in the past, are prepared to be beaten without complaining, and fewer accept that violence is 'normal' in family life.

Bearing in mind that we have to treat crime statistics with caution, it is nevertheless true that there has been a rise in serious offences since the 1950s. The number of serious offences recorded in England and Wales are:

$$1951 - \quad 549\,741$$
$$1961 - \quad 870\,894$$
$$1971 - 1\,660\,000$$
$$1981 - 2\,960\,000$$

The number of firearms offences have risen from 1700 in 1971 to 8000 in 1981. As a result of this, the police carry arms more frequently. It is not surprising therefore, that law and order has become a major issue in British politics.

Sociologists, such as Steve Chibnall in *Law and Order News*, have argued that people began seeing Britain as the 'violent society' in the early 1970s. You can see from Fig. 24.1 that two themes joined together in people's thinking to form this conclusion. The view that Britain was the scene of increasing *criminal* violence dated from the mid-sixties. A few years later, people saw Britain as a country of increasing *political* violence. Once these two themes joined together, people saw Britain as the 'violent society'. After they had done this, they began understanding all sorts of events in terms of violence. Industrial relations, particu-

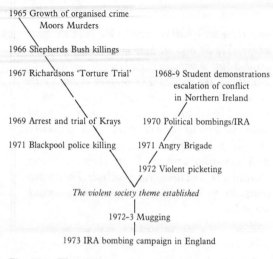

Criminal violence theme	Political violence theme

1965 Growth of organised crime
    Moors Murders

1966 Shepherds Bush killings

1967 Richardsons 'Torture Trial'   1968-9 Student demonstrations
                                          escalation of conflict
                                          in Northern Ireland

1969 Arrest and trial of Krays   1970 Political bombings/IRA

1971 Blackpool police killing   1971 Angry Brigade

                    1972 Violent picketing

The violent society theme established

            1972-3 Mugging

        1973 IRA bombing campaign in England

Fig. 24.1 The violent society: convergence of themes

larly picketing, and pressure group demonstrations were looked at in terms of violence.

Why have people become so worried about violence? It has been argued that the mass media play an important role in the way we understand what is happening in society. The fear of being mugged is an interesting example of media influence. We hear of 'little old ladies' who are frightened to step outside of their homes because of violence in the streets. If we trust the statistics, we find that mugging offences make up less than 1% of all crimes. The rise in mugging offences is less than the rise in violent crime generally. The people most likely to be mugged are between 21 and 30 years old. Assaults are more common on men than on women. Asians are fifty times more likely to be mugged than whites. By distorting news about mugging, the media create what is known as a 'moral panic'. People become unduly worried about mugging, and the police are put under pressure to deal with the muggers. Society does contain violent people, but it can be made to appear more threatening than it really is.

'Little old ladies' are in greater risk of being killed by a car than by a mugger. The press, however, is fascinated by crimes of violence. Journalists report muggings in vivid detail, but remain silent on the details of car crashes. If the horror of every crash was reported - with details of

crushed and disfigured bodies, missing limbs, brain damage, etc., few of us would ever be happy to be a passenger or a pedestrian again.

Law and justice

Complex societies produce a large number of rules and procedures to govern people's behaviour. Some rules are known as law. When a person is found guilty of breaking one of these rules, he can expect to be punished. But he may or may not get justice. This is because *law* and *justice* are not the same thing.

Law refers to the rules acted upon by the courts. Justice is concerned with ideas about right and wrong, or fairness and unfairness. Often people who have been found guilty of an offence in court will appeal against the punishment. They are not saying that the verdict is wrong, but that their punishment is unfair.

Courts administer the law as it exists, whether or not it is just. If the public believes that a particular rule is an unjust or bad law, there is likely to be an effort to change it.

Some people are worried about what they call 'negotiated justice'. It is a practice which they believe is growing in the British legal system. It involves prosecuting and defence lawyers making a bargain about the outcome of a trial. For example, suppose a person is being charged with murder but is pleading 'not guilty'. In order to speed up the trial, a 'deal' might be made. The prosecuting lawyer might reduce the charge to manslaughter if the defendant changes his plea to guilty. If such 'negotiations' do go on before and during a trial, then they interfere with both the law and justice.

Sources of law

English law has developed and grown over a very long period. It comes from four main sources.

(i) Common law, which is the oldest part of English law. In the distant past, disputes and offences were dealt with in local courts by the lords of the manor. A body of law based on custom and tradition was gradually built up. In the twelfth

century the king's justices visited all parts of the country and held 'Assize' courts. The Assize courts led to much greater uniformity in the law.

(ii) Equity, which is a system of principles and decisions, supplements the common law. It arose in the early days when the common law provided no remedy for certain wrongs. Citizens appealed to the king as the 'fountain of justice' and a separate set of rules developed. These are now administered as an integral part of common law.

(iii) Statute law is the law made by Parliament, it includes acts of Parliament, statutory instruments and by-laws.

(iv) Community law, which is a relatively new source of law in Britain. Britain joined the EEC in 1973. Since then delegated legislation coming from the Commission, the Council of Ministers and the European Court of Justice becomes British law. If there is a conflict between an existing British law and a new Community law, then the latter prevails.

Law and order personnel

(i) The police Policemen are common law officers in the service of the Crown. The number of policemen and policewomen has grown greatly in recent years – from 72 000 in 1960 to 111 000 in 1979. However, recorded crime increased at a higher rate, leaving the police undermanned. The working day of a real policeman is very different from that of a policeman in a TV series. For a start, only a small part of a policeman's day is spent pursuing criminals. Traffic duties, attending to accidents, tracing missing persons and dealing with domestic disputes take up most of a policeman's time.

Professor Michael Zander has stated that the average foot-beat in a large city covers about 180 acres (72 hectares). It will be made up of four or five miles (six to eight kilometres) of road containing a population of around 5000. A mobile car-borne beat may be three times that size. The average foot-beat results in one reported crime a day, whilst a mobile beat results in three a day.

The police have undergone a crisis in recent years. There have been inquiries into police corruption. Some people feel that the police themselves have become more violent in their methods. It is often suggested that the 'bobby on the beat' who was part of the local community has been replaced by 'tough cop' strangers in panda cars. **Chief Constables** have argued with each other in public about how to police urban areas. Some want 'tougher' police methods whilst others want more 'community' policing. Finally, there has been evidence that some policemen harass black people. After the inner-city riots of 1981, Lord Scarman reported on what happened in Brixton. Amongst other things, he recommended that racially prejudiced behaviour by police should be a dismissal offence.

Lord Scarman also recommended that the police be made more accountable to society. Parliament has surprisingly little control over the police. The Metropolitan Police is accountable to the Home Secretary. The Home Secretary has a number of other duties. These include approving the appointment of Chief Constables, providing central services such as the Police College and making regulations covering many aspects of police administration.

Outside the Metropolitan force, *local police authorities* have the duty to maintain an adequate police force. These authorities are committees; one-third of the members are unelected magistrates and there are also local councillors. In other words, the local police force is not directly accountable through local democratic control. The local police authorities provide funding for the police, and yet lack any real power over police activity. Each authority has *duties* which include appointing a Chief Constable (subject to approval by the Home Secretary); keeping informed about how the Chief Constable deals with complaints from the public, and providing rent- and rate-free accommodation for officers. The local police authorities have the *powers* of providing buildings, vehicles and equipment; determining the number of cadets, and requiring the Chief Constable to give a written report on the policing of the area.

(ii) Barristers and solicitors Barristers have

passed the 'Bar' examinations. They are members of one of the four Inns of Courts: the Inner Temple, Middle Temple, Lincoln's Inn and Gray's Inn. Barristers normally appear only in superior courts. They do not communicate directly with the general public. A solicitor will act as 'middle man' and brief a barrister. Solicitors are qualified and 'admitted' to the legal profession. They do have direct contact with the public.

(iii) *Judges and magistrates* Judges are appointed by the Crown on the recommendation of the Lord Chancellor. Before being appointed, a judge must have had at least ten years' experience as a barrister. In order to keep the *independence* of the judiciary, judges' salaries do not have to be approved by Parliament. They are paid from the Consolidated Fund. Judges are free to speak out in court without the threat of being sued for defamation. Some people have argued that judges may be independent, but they are not *impartial*. This is because they are drawn from the upper classes in society. For example, 81% of judges went to public school and 76% went to Oxbridge. As a result of this, some people feel that there is a danger in judges being anti-working class or anti-trade union without realising it. There are two types of magistrate. Most are *lay* magistrates or Justices of the Peace (JPs). They are part-time 'amateurs'. Others are *stipendiary* magistrates. They work in large cities, and are full-time paid officials. Magistrates are also drawn from the upper social classes. One study found that 77% came from social classes I and II. Roughly one-third were women. Since 1966, new magistrates have had to undergo short courses of training to prepare them for the duties that they undertake.

(iv) *Juries* In criminal cases a jury consists of twelve individuals. Before 1972 juries were made up from 'property-owners'. This meant that only 22% of voters were eligible to sit on juries. In order to make juries more representative, all people between 18 and 65 years of age on the electoral register are now eligible. Jury service is compulsory for an individual who is called upon.

Before 1967 jury verdicts had to be unanimous. In other words all the jurors had to agree. Now majority verdicts are accepted. Eleven out of 12 jurors must agree for a majority verdict. Under certain conditions, trials may proceed with a number of jurors less than the original 12. Where, for example the number is reduced to 10, nine of them must agree for a majority verdict. In certain civil courts which have juries of eight people, seven of them must agree for a majority verdict.

Courts

Crimes are regarded as offences against the community as a whole. Prosecutions are brought in the name of the sovereign. Civil law, on the other hand, is concerned with disputes between individuals or organisations. Here the state acts as umpire. Many civil disputes are settled out of court. Criminal and civil law are administered in different ways.

Magistrates' courts deal with 98% of all criminal cases. Most of these are 'summary' [or less serious] offences. In more serious cases, the convicted person may be tried in a magistrates' court or by jury in a crown court. The convicted person has the right to choose. Magistrates' courts even have a part to play in very serious cases. The preliminary hearing – or committal proceedings – takes place in a magistrates' court. This is the test to see if there is sufficient evidence for a case to be heard by a higher court. The magistrates' court will either dismiss the case or commit it to a crown court.

There are two types of magistrate. Most are *lay* magistrates or Justices of the Peace (JPs). They are part-time 'amateurs'. Others are *stipendiary* magistrates. They work in large cities, and are full-time paid officials.

You can see from Fig. 24.2 that above the magistrates' courts are the crown courts. Individuals found guilty of criminal charges in the crown courts can appeal against the verdict or the sentence. Such appeals would be heard by the courts of appeal (criminal division). An appeal on a point of law is heard by the divisional court of the Queen's Bench. The House of Lords is the highest court of appeal in both criminal and civil matters, and this was discussed in chapter 17.

Magistrates' courts deal with some civil cases. These include charges concerning public health ▷ p.23

To make the punishment fit the crime . . . . .

Some crimes are committed because the wrong-doers are sick. They need treatment.

Some crimes are committed because wrong-doers are placed under intolerable personal provocation. They may, in certain circumstances, be excused.

Most crimes are committed because of human wickedness. Those who perpetrate them should expect to be punished. This is a simple statement of what the majority of men and women believe to be true.

In recent years, however, sociologists, psychiatrists and penal reformers have sought to shame the public into thinking otherwise. Don't blame the criminal, we are told, blame his social background . . .

We are people, responsible people. Not the puppets of social conditioning.

Daily Mail, 5 June 1975

. . . We need to know more about the springs of violence. **How far** is poverty in a rich society and the misery of deprived families a cause? **How far** is educational inequality a cause? **How far** is dull and repetitive work a cause? These are problems for social political action by governments.

But the rest of us do not have to sit back and wait for that.

Trade unionists should blacklist rough necks.

Sports fans should boycott grounds where hoodlums run amok.

Parents should boycott films which exploit violence . . . .

Daily Mirror, 'Shock Issue on Violence'
19 September 1972

The two editorials above have some arguments in common. But there are differences in attitudes towards crime.

- What part do the *Daily Mail* and *Daily Mirror* feel that social conditions play in causing crime?

VIOLENT CRIME, GUNS AND THE POLICE

In the space of four days, £7 million was stolen by armed men who threatened to burn a security guard alive, a policeman was shot by a Bristol bank raider who then held a truck-driver at gunpoint for 100 miles, a schoolboy was taken hostage by a gunman in Leeds, and Chief Constable Jim Anderton of Greater Manchester announced that armed police were touring the city 'round the clock.'

More sober evaluations were scarcely less discouraging. They concluded that a huge increase in firearms offences over the past decade from 1700 (in England and Wales) in 1971 to 8000 in 1981 was causing chief officers to abandon this country's almost unique tradition of unarmed policing. There had been, said Labour MP Michael

Meacher, 'a major and unauthorised step down the road towards a permanently armed police force.'

Yet there is surprisingly little evidence for this proposition. From the maelstrom of selective data, fuzzy statistics and suspect graphs, it is possible to pluck three relevant facts:

• Although armed robbery has increased, it has done so from a much lower base than these alarming figures suggest;

• The issue of firearms to police officers in relation to the number of armed robberies has stayed pretty constant and does not appear to reflect any disturbing 'cultural change' in the attitudes of the police, among whom guns remain unpopular;

• Anderton is certainly operating on the

margin of accepted policing practice as defined by the Home Office guidelines, but his men are acting within strictly supervised limits – and he is not the first to use the same strategy.

The fuss has been created by a freakish concurrence of sensational crimes, by the delayed effect of the shooting of Stephen Waldorf in Kensington last January, and by the natural reflex response to Manchester's hyperactive police chief, who is apt to make any pronouncement on crime and policing sound like a sermon by Savonarola.

On Tuesday, as it happens, his statement was untypically terse: 'Armed police officers, travelling inside police vehicles, are patrolling Greater Manchester round the clock to deal with a serious escalation of armed robberies.'

Observer, 10 April 1983

These extracts are from an article written by Laurence Marks. You will see that he suggests that Britain is still a long way from seeing regular gun battles between 'cops and robbers'.

Draft two letters to your MP. In one, urge him to support the arming of the police. Give reasons for your view. In the other, urge him to oppose any use of firearms by the police except in exceptional circumstances. Give reasons.

The misleading use of the language of violence

In the most obvious instances, this *editing for impact* shows through simply in terms of the way the violence which is taken to characterise the football incidents is transferred to the presentation of the story. Not every clash between supporters or between supporters and the police justifies the language of 'Rampage' and 'Riot', 'Bottle Boys' or 'Thugs', which has by now become customary. Some incidents deserve dramatic language but this makes it all the more important to retain a proper sense of scale and judgement, so as to avoid presenting hooliganism as a general feature of all major football games (which it isn't), and on an ever-upward curve of escalation. It is also something of a paradox when the language of control equals, in violence and vehemence, that which it is trying contain. In such cases, it hardly matters that the 'BIRCH 'EM!' headline (*Mirror*, 30/8/76) is attributable to Tommy Docherty 'Doc slams United thug fans'; or that the 'SMASH THESE THUGS!' headline (*Sun*, 4/10/76) is a sort-of quote from 'Home Secretary Merlyn Rees .... the ex-Ulster supremo – fresh from handling terrorists in Northern Ireland ...'; or the 'TERRIFIED!' headline (*News Of The World*, 29/1/77) is quoted from a longer statement by Dave Mackay. The press often plays an active role in the campaign for tougher measures. Not in its own name, but by putting its weight behind the disciplinarians, or by 'speaking on behalf of its readers' – taking the public voice.

It's even more problematic when this kind of language – on both sides of the dividing line – is placed in the context of the general language of sport. The 'FANS GO MAD' story (*Sunday People*, 3/4/77) tells its own story: 'hundreds of fighting fans raced on to the pitch'. But, on the preceding page, the even bigger 'C-R-U-N-C-H' headline starts a story which is *not* about hooligans but about a tackle on the field that sent Howard Kendall off to 'have six stitches inserted below his right knee' in a Birmingham–Newcastle game: 'Nulty charged in like the Light Brigade ...' The *People*'s 'TEARAWAY RICHARDS!' is *not* a negative comment on some fan on the rampage but a positive description of the blinder John Richards played for Wolves .... So are a number of other headlines, reporting other hard games, in the *same* issue of that paper: 'FOREST'S BLITZ'; 'POWELL BLAST SHOCKS STOKE'; 'Hankin Makes Blues Suffer'; 'RAY'S ROUSER: But Villa make it mighty tough', and 'Doyle's Karate Gets Him Chopped'. The *People*'s report of 3/4/77 headed 'FANS GO MAD' ended with a note that – 'The other big fight – for the First Division title – swayed Liverpool's way' – thus making the equation between the two fights explicit.

If the language of football reporting is increasingly the language of thrills and spills, hard tackles and tough games, of struggle, victory and defeat, studded with images drawn from the blitzkrieg and the military showdown, it is not so difficult to understand why some of what is going on on the pitch, and recorded with such vivacity in the newspapers, spills over onto the terraces. Here, the line between the sports reporter glorying in the battle on the pitch, and expressing his righteous moral indignation at the battle on the terraces, or between the managers who drill and rehearse their lads in tough and abrasive styles of play, but who think their faithful and involved fans should be birched or caged in or hosed down –'DRENCH THE THUGS' (*Mirror*, 4/4/77) – is a very fine and wavery one indeed.

Roger Ingham, Stuart Hall, John Clarke,
Peter Marsh and Jim Donovan,
Football Hooliganism

This extract criticises the use of 'violent' language in news stories where it is not appropriate. Write a fifty-word article describing a football match or other event (i) in appropriate language (ii) in exaggerated language of violence. Which story is the most compelling to read? Would you agree that newspapers are partly guilty of causing the hooliganism that they condemn?

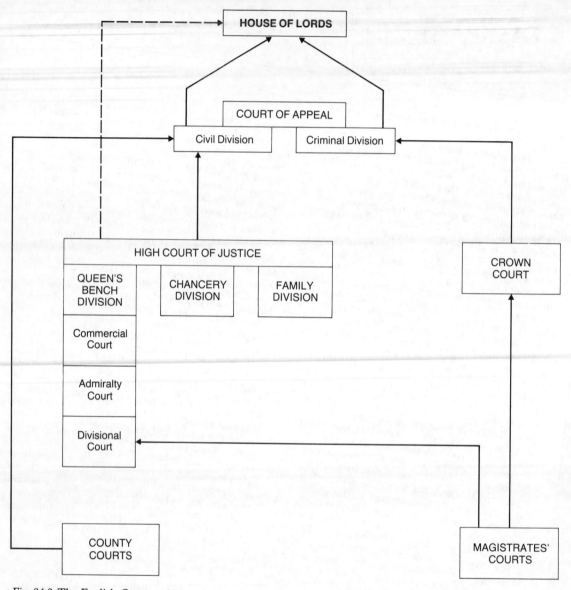

Fig. 24.2 The English Courts
Arrows indicate direction of appeals

and matrimonial proceedings such as separation and maintenance orders. Civil disputes which involve disputes over the dissolution of partnerships, bankruptcies, hire purchase, divorce proceedings, and complaints brought by the Race Relations Board are heard by county courts. The cases are usually heard by a judge sitting alone. Sometimes there is a jury of eight people. Appeal from the county court lies with the court of appeal.

The High Court is made up of three divisions; the Queen's Bench Division, the Chancery Division and the Family Division. The Queen's Bench Division has wide **jurisdiction**. For example, with the Queen's Bench Division is an admiralty court which deals with cases involving collisions at sea and salvage. There is also a commercial court which deals with matters such as insurance and banking. There is also an election court which considers disputed results in parliamentary and local elections.

The Chancery Division deals with matters including winding up companies, bankruptcies and taxation. The Family Division considers matters including divorce, adoption, maintenance orders and property disputes between spouses.

The politics of law and order

The major political parties have differing views on law and order. Conservatives see themselves as the 'law and order' party. There is strong support for the police. There is also strong belief in punishment as an effective way of deterring crime. Many Conservatives would like to see the return of capital punishment.

Labour is concerned with bringing the police under democratic control. There is Labour support for a new method of investigating complaints against the police, disbanding the Special Patrol Group, and giving policemen the right to join a trade union.

There is a long tradition of protecting civil liberties within the Liberal party. Liberals support the policy of more community policing.

Terms used

Chief Constable A Chief Constable is at the head of a police force. Powers include promoting officers, appointing and dismissing special constables and cadets, and providing help to other police forces. The powers of chief constables have increased considerably since the last century. The Chief Constable of Greater Manchester, Jim Anderton, has the reputation of being tough. He was often in public disagreement with liberal-minded John Alderson, the former Chief Constable of Devon and Cornwall.

Jurisdiction To have jurisdiction over a matter is to have the authority to deal with it.

Summary

1 Measuring the extent of crime and violence in society is difficult since not all incidents are recorded. There is evidence that crimes involving violence against the person have increased by an average of 11% a year since the 1950s.

2 Much of what we learn about crime and violence comes from the mass media. The press has exaggerated the risk of mugging and caused a 'moral panic' through distorting the news.

3 There is a difference between law and justice. Bad laws generally produce injustice. There is some evidence of 'negotiated justice' coming from British courts.

4 There are four sources of English law: common law, equity, statute law and community law.

5 In the past there has been criticism of judges and magistrates. Today the police are under scrutiny. The Scarman report made a number of criticisms of policing methods.

6 Most criminal cases are settled in magistrates' courts. Magistrates' courts also deal with certain civil cases. Above the magistrates' court are the crown courts. Appeals against the verdict or sentence from a crown court are heard by the court of appeal (criminal division). Most civil disputes are heard by county courts, although many are settled 'out of court'.

7 Law and order is now a political issue. Conservatives believe in strong policing and tough punishment for offenders. Labour believes in making the police more accountable.

Questions for discussion

1 'Society is getting more and more violent'. Evaluate this statement. What are the difficulties in measuring violence?

2 a) What are the sources of English law?
b) Outline the structure of English courts.

3 'The police should be made more accountable for their actions'; 'The police are the experts, and they should be left to do the job as they see fit'. Discuss these statements.

4 'Judges are members of a small, privileged elite and are out of touch with ordinary people. They

are the very last people who should sit in judgement on the rest of us.' What are the strengths and weaknesses of this argument?

5 After you have completed Taskpage 24.2, discuss the case for arming the police in Britain.

6 Analyse the different ways in which a tabloid and quality newspaper report 'law and order' news. Measure the column inches devoted to crime and express it as a percentage of all the paper (minus advertisements). Contrast the type of language used. Show your results on a poster for your classroom.

25

Britain's borders: the external and internal problems

This chapter considers the problems involved in drawing Britain's borders. Which areas on the globe should Britain try to influence? Where should the government position armed forces in order to defend Britain? These have proved difficult questions to answer, since circumstances change so quickly. Britain has experienced a decline from being a global power to being a regional power in a very short period of time. Today Britain and her once-powerful European neighbours are dwarfed by the giant superpowers. In many ways the future of Europe will be decided by the USA and the USSR, and not by the countries of Europe. But the problems of drawing boundaries has been experienced inside as well as outside Britain. During the 1970s there was a debate about devolution for Scotland and Wales. Some wanted more than this. They wanted devolution for England. In the event, none of this was to come about. Only in Northern Ireland was there to be devolution. But is devolution sufficient to solve the problems faced in Northern Ireland? Are there any solutions to the violence and bloodshed carried out in the name of politics?

Foreign policy

Control of territory is a major factor in international politics. Sometimes wars between countries result from disputes about the ownership of territory. The war in 1982 between Britain and Argentina over the Falklands is an example of this. On other occasions war can result from disagreements about which country will influence the future of a territory. The Anglo-French invasion of Egypt in 1956 resulted from a dispute about which country was going to control the Suez Canal.

Each country has a foreign policy which is guided by that country's **national interest**. In other words, every country will follow a foreign policy which attempts to win advantages from other countries. Normally foreign policies are pursued through diplomatic negotiations and bargaining. War may break out if diplomacy fails to settle an important issue.

Foreign policy is made up from the decisions taken by the government which involve other countries. This means that foreign policy differs from other policies, such as those involving housing, education or health. Decisions taken by government on social policy can *create* new conditions. For example, a decision to build more houses will result in less homelessness or a decision to equip schools with computers will improve pupils' data-processing skills. Foreign policy, however, tends to be made in *response* to events which have already taken place. The Suez invasion was in reaction to Egypt's decision to nationalise the canal. The sending of a naval task force to the South Atlantic was in reaction to the Argentinian invasion of the Falklands.

The major trends in British foreign policy since the Second World War have been in response to Britain's weakening economy and the rise of nationalism in the colonies. The best way of analysing the changes that have taken place in the last fifty years is to start with Sir Winston Churchill's view. He described British foreign policy in terms of being based on 'three majestic circles'. These are shown as the three circles of British interest in Fig. 25.1. The changes that have taken place in each 'circle' are:

(i) *the collapse of the Commonwealth*. It is hard to appreciate that only half a century ago Britain

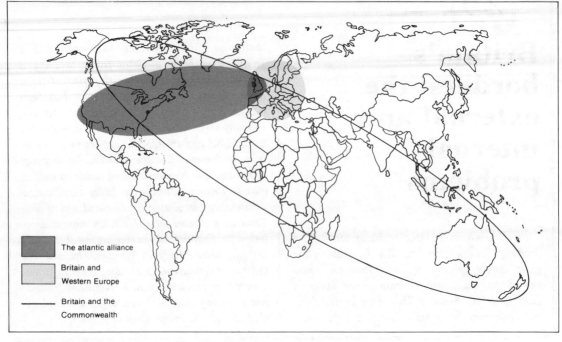

The atlantic alliance

Britain and
Western Europe

Britain and the
Commonwealth

Fig. 25.1 The three 'circles' of British interest

ruled the biggest empire the world has ever known. The British flag flew over every continent. The British Empire covered over a quarter of the world's land surface. In Africa the old dream of a 'Cape to Cairo' railway would have passed over British territory throughout the length of the continent. By the end of the 1980s the Union Jack will fly over only a handful of dependent territories. What now remains of the 'British Empire' are the islands of Hong Kong, Pitcairn, St Helena, Gibralter and the Falklands. The empire has been transformed into the Commonwealth. The Commonwealth is a free association of independent states, with the Queen as its head. In the 1950s and 1960s the Commonwealth was looked on kindly by Labour and Conservative MPs. Labour supported the Commonwealth because it provided a chance for new countries to emerge without becoming wholly capitalist or communist. Many Conservatives had strong links with the 'old' Commonwealth countries of Canada, Australia and New Zealand.

The Commonwealth was, however, to become a great disappointment for Britain. Labour's plan in 1964 to turn the Commonwealth into a trading organisation failed. Two years later the idea of a Commonwealth peace mission to settle the Vietnam war also failed. Many leaders of the 'new' Commonwealth expressed anti-British views. Even members of the 'old' Commonwealth, such as Australia and Canada, contained strong republican movements which wanted to weaken links with Britain. The weakness of the Commonwealth was revealed when members countries declared war on each other, such as India and Pakistan.

One of the most bitter blows to Britain came when Australia and New Zealand looked to the USA for protection. In the past these two countries had looked to Britain. The ANZUS pact between Australia, New Zealand and the United States actually excluded Britain. The British Government objected, but was never invited to join ANZUS.

By the 1970s it was clear that the Commonwealth would never be an important international organisation. At times it seemed to provide Britain with more problems than benefits. The transformation of Rhodesia into Zimbabwe proved to be a difficult responsibility. The long-term future of the Falklands promises to be another lengthy problem for Britain (see Taskpage 2.3 for examples of Falklands headlines). The role of the Commonwealth today is that it is a useful 'talking shop' between the rich nations of the industrialised north and the poorer developing nations of the south.

(ii) *the decline of the 'special relationship' with the United States.* The bonds of a common language and a similar culture drew Britain and the USA towards each other. The close partnership formed in the Second World War lasted on into times of peace. With its large navy and Commonwealth connections Britain was a useful ally to the United States. Britain was not powerful enough to be described as a 'superpower' during the 1950s, but she was a 'junior world policeman' alongside the United States. This partnership was referred to as Britain's 'special relationship' with the USA.

During the 1960s and early 1970s the special relationship was to be weakened. First, Britain's economic problems led to reductions in the armed forces. Britain could no longer afford to patrol large areas of the world. What became known as the withdrawal from 'east of Suez' took place after 1967. Thus Britain gave up the role of 'junior world policeman'. Second, Britain refused President Johnson's request to send soldiers to fight alongside US forces in Vietnam. Third, the Conservative victory in 1970 made Edward Heath prime minister. He favoured a special relationship between Britain and Europe rather than between Britain and America. Finally, the USA began to see Germany as more important to NATO than Britain was. The Americans saw London as the 'capital of Europe' in the 1940s; in the 1960s they looked to Bonn.

Recent prime ministers, including James Callaghan and Margaret Thatcher, were on better terms with the US government than were Harold Wilson or Edward Heath. But the UK–US relationship is now simply one of friendly allies. It is not 'special' in the sense of being a close working partnership between two global allies.

(iii) *the growing strength of the countries of the EEC.* Britain rejected an invitation to participate in the early stages of European **integration**. Britain preferred a loose association with Europe rather than the tight legal relationship of the EEC. In response to the threat posed to British trade by the EEC's customs barrier, Britain tried to set up a Free Trade Area. This would have included Britain, the EEC and any other country in western Europe that wished to join. The French undermined the negotiations and the Free Trade Area was never established. As a result Britain set up the European Free Trade Association (EFTA) of seven countries which were not in the EEC. Europe was said to be 'at sixes and sevens' during the 1960s, and the members of the rival organisations are shown in Fig. 25.3. In 1961 the prime minister, Harold Macmillan, decided that Britain should join the EEC. But the French president, General de Gaulle, refused to let Britain become a member. Harold Wilson applied to join in 1967 but received similar treatment from De Gaulle. However, De Gaulle retired from public life in 1969. The way was now open for Edward Heath to successfully negotiate Britain's entry to the EEC. Britain joined in 1973 and a referendum in 1975 confirmed that Britain should remain a member.

The EEC	EFTA
Germany	Britain
France	Sweden
Italy	Norway
Luxembourg	Denmark
Belgium	Austria
The Netherlands	Switzerland
	Portugal

Fig. 25.2 The EEC and EFTA organisations 1959–73

The economies of the six original members of the EEC – France, Germany, Italy, Belgium, the Netherlands and Luxembourg – grew rapidly during the 1950s and 1960s. Britain has not enjoyed the economic growth rates experienced by the original members. In fact Britain imported more manufactured goods than she exported for the first time after joining the EEC. Many critics of the EEC are most concerned about the Common Agricultural Policy (CAP). There was hope that CAP would be reformed after Britain joined. This, however, has not yet happened. The CAP continues to dominate the budget of the EEC. It leads to over-production of high-cost food.

Conservatives are committed to remaining in the EEC, although there is still some strong opposition to Europe inside the party. The Liberals are pro-EEC and the SDP are very strong supporters of the EEC. The Labour Party is not pro-EEC. A past Labour government 'renegotiated' the terms of Britain's entry into the EEC. Opinion in the party has swung towards withdrawal and many expect a future Labour government to take Britain out of the EEC.

In 1962 an American politician, Dean Acheson, said that Britain had lost an empire but not yet found a role. In many ways this is still true in the 1980s. Although the last thirty years have seen Britain change from being a global power to a regional power, there is still disagreement about British foreign policy. Some Labour and Conservative MPs wanted Britain to set up closer economic links with the United States. They believed Britain's future inside a North Atlantic Free Trade Area (NAFTA) would prove the best option. Others wanted to see Britain continue in the future with the policies of the past. They did not want Britain to get too involved in any organisation. They wanted Britain to 'Go it alone' – an option known as 'GITA'. Labour wants Britain out of the European Community, but it is not clear which alternative policy will take the place of EEC membership.

Defence policy

A country's foreign policy is supported by its defence policy. As an imperial power, Britain needed a large navy. But as a European power, Britain needs a much smaller navy. In 1981 the Defence White Paper proposed a big reduction in the strength of the navy. It was argued that the British navy of today only needs fighting ships necessary for operations in the NATO area. However, after the Falklands war the 1982 Defence White Paper restored the cuts made in the navy. It was agreed that the navy would have an 'out of the NATO area' role.

There has been a public debate about Britain's nuclear defences. It began in 1979 after NATO's decision to modernise its long-range nuclear forces. This involves the introduction of three new weapons systems that are vastly superior to anything previously deployed by NATO. Britain

will be the site of American-controlled cruise missiles, and Trident submarine-launched missiles will replace existing Polaris missiles. Pershing II missiles will be based in other European members of NATO, but not in Britain.

Improvements have also been made in the Soviet missiles that are targeted upon the cities of western Europe. Soviet generals believe that a nuclear war in Europe is not only a possibility, but that it could be won by the Soviet Union. This is because the improvements in the accuracy of Soviet missiles gives them a **first strike** capability. In other words the Soviets feel that if they launched only a fraction of their missiles they could destroy most of NATO's nuclear weapons. The remaining Soviet missiles aimed at large cities would force NATO to surrender.

However, NATO also has a first strike capability. Cruise missiles are slow but very difficult to detect by radar because they fly close to the ground. Pershing II missiles take only five minutes from launch to strike deep in the heart of the Soviet Union.

President Reagan described the 1980s as 'the dangerous decade'. This is true since the world is moving into an age of new nuclear technology and political mistrust. Events such as the Soviet invasion of Afghanistan, events in Poland and Soviet involvement in Southern Africa ended the years of *detente*. During detente, relations between the United States and the Soviet Union improved. Sadly, the Cold War has returned in the 1980s. What makes the current era of the Cold War more dangerous is that each side is losing faith in **deterrence**. Nuclear weapons are no longer held in order to deter the other side from launching an attack. They are now held with a view that they could be used in a European war, and that one side could win such a war.

There are endless international negotiations on the reduction of nuclear weapons. Herein lies an ultimate test for politics. Can nations find a way of living together in peace and avoid the ultimate catastrophe of a nuclear holocaust?

Regionalism and devolution

Britain has complicated borders for a country so

small in area. The United Kingdom, England, Great Britain and the British Isles overlap a great deal in terms of geography. In political terms, however, they are quite different. The task of trying to fix Britain's internal borders has been as difficult as guiding Britain's external foreign policy. We have already seen in chapter 20 that changing the boundaries of local government proved to be a controversial problem.

Questions about the internal boundaries of Britain came to a head in the 1970s. Wales became united with England during the middle ages, and the Scottish Parliament met for the last time in 1707. Yet during the 1970s some Welsh and Scottish nationalists were demanding the dismantling of Great Britain.

Many public sector services are organised on a regional basis. For example, the regional water authorities, regional health authorities, electricity and gas services, and rail and bus transport are all organised along regional lines. Independent television and the BBC also have a regional basis. But this regionalism fell far short of what was wanted by the Scottish National Party and Plaid Cymru.

The Kilbrandon Commission investigated regional needs and reported its findings in 1973. The commission considered a number of options. It examined the idea of *separatism*; that is, the idea that England, Wales, Scotland and Northern Ireland should be separate states. It also considered *federalism*. This idea involved dividing the powers now held by Parliament between Parliament and the new regional assemblies. However, the commission believed that *devolution* was the best solution. Devolution involves giving some powers to elected regional assemblies. But Parliament would keep superior powers and have the right to reject decisions made by the regional assemblies.

The Kilbrandon Commission had two views on devolution. The majority report recommended that Scotland and Wales should each have an elected assembly. These assemblies would have responsibility for policies such as health, welfare, and town and county planning. The minority report wanted five English regions to be set up and treated in the same way as Scotland and Wales.

In the event, devolution proposals came to nothing. After a stormy passage in Parliament, the proposals for a Scottish and Welsh assembly were rejected in referenda.

Northern Ireland

Devolved government is not something new to British politics. Between 1921 and 1972 Northern Ireland was governed from Stormont. As the 'troubles' in Northern Ireland approached becoming a civil war, Stormont was suspended. Once again, Northern Ireland was governed directly from London. From 1982 there has been an experiment with 'rolling devolution'.

Northern Ireland is a major political problem. It is a problem with deep historical roots. In Ireland there has been a history of persecution by the British. In the distant past, much of the best agricultural land was given to English and Scottish settlers. Catholic peasants were driven on to the poorer land in the hills and west of the country.

There are events in the histories of most countries which seem unacceptable today. Such events are kept alive in the Irish culture. Catholic and Protestant pupils are educated in separate schools. They learn different accounts of Irish history, and celebrate different historical events.

The division in Northern Ireland between Protestant and Catholic is more than a difference in religious beliefs. The Protestants come from English or Scottish families which settled in Ireland. The Catholics come from Irish stock.

They see the differences between Protestant and Catholic as hostility between colonists and native inhabitants. In other words, they see Britain's problem with Northern Ireland as a left-over from the empire. Although Ireland was colonised long before Rhodesia, in both cases the 'settlers' have most power, most wealth, and discriminate against the 'native' inhabitants.

Some people argue that the problem between the two communities is that both are the minorities. As minorities, each community has developed aggressive and untrusting attitudes towards the other. The Catholics are a minority in Northern Ireland. But the Protestants are a minority within the whole of Ireland. This is why most Protestants want to keep links with the rest of the United Kingdom, and are against links with the Republic ▷ p.244

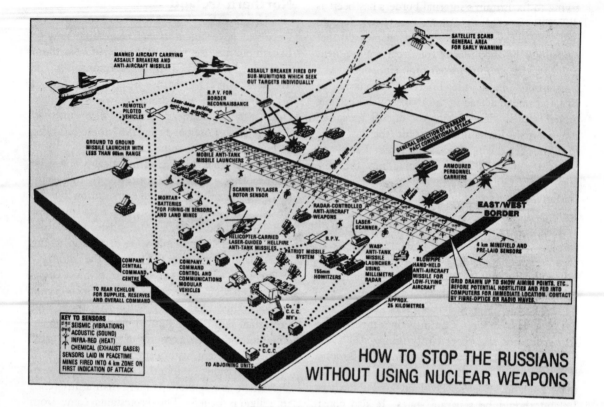

HOW TO STOP THE RUSSIANS WITHOUT USING NUCLEAR WEAPONS

Alternative to Bomb

Intense interest is being shown within the peace movement in a report to be published next week by the Alternative Defence Commission, an independent academic body that has been studying non-nuclear defence options.

Its findings are expected to include a 'provisional' recommendation that Britain should stay, at least temporarily, in NATO, in an attempt to initiate a process of nuclear disarmament in Europe.

The commission believes that a government committed to unilateral disarmament should tell NATO allies that it will leave the Alliance within a year unless NATO adopts a no-first-use policy as a signal of its commitment to move away from reliance on nuclear weapons.

The study was funded by the Lansbury House Trust and sponsored by Bradford University.

Evidence was heard from a wide variety of military and scientific experts, among them Oxford's Professor Michael Howard, Colonel Jonathan Alford of the International Institute for Strategic Studies, and Cambridge's Sir Martin Ryle.

Last week another independent body – 'Just Defence' – made a similar call for a NATO declaration of no-first-use and progressive denuclearisation.

Its members include Professor Frank Barnaby, General Sir Hugh Beach, Brigadier Michael Harbottle and the Bishop of Birmingham.

'Just Defence' says that the latest nuclear 'counterforce' weapons are no longer defensive but mutually provocative, and that the concept of balance is irrelevant to defence.

Optimistically, however, it believes that the technology which has created the nuclear threat can also provide an alternative defence. This would be by switching resources into a new range of unmistakenly defensive weapons – particularly precision-guided anti-tank and anti-aircraft missiles – and electronic warning and surveillance systems.

A 'Just Defence' projection (above) of a viable non-nuclear strategy for Western Europe envisages a deep belt of eastwards-pointing seismic, acoustic, infra-red and chemical sensors, supplemented by pilotless reconnaissance aircraft to give tactical warning of attack.

Behind this would be an in-depth defensive system based on precision-guided 'smart' weapons that because of their mass-produced electronic content, would be both deadly and relatively cheap. Some types are already in limited service.

Why US may count on Soviet 'fratricide'

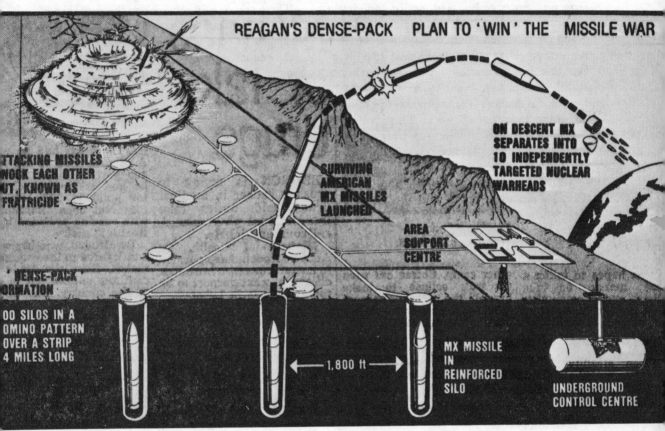

REAGAN'S DENSE-PACK PLAN TO 'WIN' THE MISSILE WAR

ON DESCENT MX SEPARATES INTO 10 INDEPENDENTLY TARGETED NUCLEAR WARHEADS

ATTACKING MISSILES KNOCK EACH OTHER OUT, KNOWN AS 'FRATRICIDE'

SURVIVING AMERICAN MX MISSILES LAUNCHED

AREA SUPPORT CENTRE

'DENSE-PACK' FORMATION

100 SILOS IN A DOMINO PATTERN OVER A STRIP 14 MILES LONG

1,800 ft

MX MISSILE IN REINFORCED SILO

UNDERGROUND CONTROL CENTRE

This double Taskpage is about ways of defending the West. Details are shown of two strategies for two different types of attack.

(i)   What are the different ways shown in which the Warsaw Pact might attack the West?

(ii) What are the differences in the ways that the West would be defended?

(iii) How could a Soviet invasion of West Germany be halted without using nuclear weapons?

(iv) How would dense-pack MX missiles survive a Soviet missile attack?

of Eire. It is also why many Catholics would like to see Northern Ireland join Eire and be governed from Dublin.

The problems faced by the British government are both short-term and long-term ones. The short-term problem is dealing with armed and violent minorities from both sides. The main paramilitary group on the loyalist side is the Ulster Defence Association (UDA). The Provisional IRA, however, is seen as the greatest threat to law and order. British soldiers have been stationed in Northern Ireland, but this gives the impression of a military occupation to the outside world. There is also the danger of incidents between the army and civilians, such as took place on 'Bloody Sunday' in 1972. There is 'internment without trial' in which suspected terrorists are picked up and detained. This is a denial of civil liberties. It is something expected to be found in South Africa or in the Soviet Union rather than in a democracy. Finally, the strength of the police and the Ulster Defence Regiment (UDR) has been increased to deal with the short-term problems.

Long-term problems include (i) bringing the two communities together to live in an atmosphere of trust and harmony, and (ii) finding agreement about the future of Northern Ireland. Efforts to increase understanding between the two communities have not met with much success. Most notable was the 'Mothers of Peace' mass movement in the 1970s. The group failed to have any lasting impact, but proved that it was not impossible for Catholic and Protestant to unite for peace.

The British government has also attempted to share power in Northern Ireland and involve the Catholic minority. The Conservative government led by Edward Heath set up a power-sharing executive. However, opposition from Protestant trade unions led to the collapse of the executive.

In 1982 the Secretary of State for Northern Ireland, James Prior, attempted another power-sharing experiment. He set up a Northern Ireland Assembly. Proportional representation was used to elect the assemblymen. The SDLP and Sinn Fein candidates announced that they would not take their seats in the assembly if elected. In the election, nearly all the Catholic vote went to these candidates. The British government was disappointed with the election. This was because electors failed to vote in a 'moderate' way. The most remarkable result was the election of five 'revolutionary' assemblymen from Sinn Fein, the political wing of the Provisional IRA. The voting figures are shown in Table 25.1.

There are no easy solutions to the problems of Northern Ireland. Successive governments have struggled to cope with the continuing terrorism and mutual suspicion between the opposing groups. It is difficult to see how these problems can be finally settled in a way which pleases both the Protestant and Catholic communities within Northern Ireland as well as the governments of Britain and the Irish Republic.

Table 25.1 Elections to the Northern Ireland Assembly, 1982

Party	% of the vote	No. of seats
Democratic Unionist	23.0	21
Official Unionist	29.8	26
Other Unionist	5.4	2
Alliance	9.3	10
SDLP	18.8	14
Sinn Fein	10.1	5
Others	3.3	0

Terms used

Deterrence This is a way of defending a country, based on the rational behaviour of a possible enemy. Deterrence in the Cold War is based on the rational thinking by NATO and Warsaw Pact leaders. The Communists know that even if they strike first and attack NATO, their countries will be destroyed by NATO's second strike missiles. Similarly, if NATO strikes first the West will be destroyed by Soviet second strike missiles. Second strike missiles are ones that are safe from attack. They may be located in deep silos, easily moved from place to place, or under the sea in submarines. If the time comes when these missiles can be destroyed by an enemy, they cease to have a second strike capability. This situation is fairly stable, because attacking the enemy also involves committing suicide. There is no point in launching an attack, since both sides will be destroyed. Each side's nuclear weapons deter attack from the other side.

First strike This occurs when one side has the ability to destroy the enemy if it strikes first. First strike missiles have to be accurate, powerful and numerous. If fired, they will not leave the enemy with any missiles to fight back. In western films, the shoot-out between the sheriff and outlaw is based on first strike. Whoever shoots first with accuracy wins the duel. First strike situations are unstable because there is always the temptation to shoot first.

Integration This occurs when countries join together and give some of their policy-making powers to the same superior body. EEC members have agreed that certain common policies will be decided by the Council of Ministers and not by their national governments. Integration would increase in the EEC should there ever be one common unit of currency in member countries. EFTA was an international organisation which did not involve integration. All decisions about trade remained in the hands of members' national governments.

National interest A vague concept often resorted to by politicians or newspapers to get people to do something which is unpopular. In international politics, the national interest of a country is what its leaders want to achieve for the country. As leaders and circumstances change, so does what is seen as in the national interest.

Summary

1 Britain's role in the world has changed dramatically since the Second World War. Having once influenced events around the world, Britain is now more concerned with influencing events in Europe. Britain's roles as close partner of the United States and centre of the Commonwealth have declined. Occasionally Britain has to deal with 'left-overs' from her world role, such as the Rhodesian problem and the Falklands crisis.

2 There is controversy in Britain over the question of nuclear weapons. The 1980s have been described as 'the dangerous decade'. This is because the idea of deterrence is losing support. Many military leaders in NATO and the Warsaw Pact think that a nuclear war could be fought and won in Europe.

3 Britain's internal borders have been discussed during the 1970s. New boundaries for local government came into existence, but proposals for devolution in Scotland and Wales were rejected by the respective electorates.

4 Only in Northern Ireland is there a form of devolved government. The attempt to share power has not been a great success.

Questions for discussion

1 Describe British foreign policy as it exists today.

2 Why did Britain join the EEC? What are the advantages and disadvantages of membership?

3 Outline the differences between separatism, federalism, devolution and regionalism.

4 Would devolution in England increase democracy or add an unnecessary level of government?

5 Should Britain have its own nuclear weapons? Should American missiles be based in Britain? Discuss these questions in class.

6 Organise a debate about the problems of governing Northern Ireland. Agree on the motion to be debated.

Index

and Liberals 56
  support 105–6
socialisation 16, 106
  agents of 106–8
social security 218
sociology 8, 16
Solicitor-General 124
solicitors 230
sovereignty 40
Soviet Union 240
Speaker of the House of Commons 133
Spence, James 112
stagflation 14
Steel, David 64, 66, 71, 139
'stop-go' policies 200
Stradling, Robert 53–4
Streamlining the Cities 181
strikes 200
Suez war 131, 237
suffragette movement 76, 87

Tapper, Ted 223
Taverne, Dick 97
taxation 203
Taylor Report 50
Teer, Frank 112
televising Parliament 21
tellers 134
Thatcher, Margaret 13, 58, 97, 118, 121, 125, 145, 201, 211
Tory Reform Group 71
Trades Union Congress 13, 23, 31, 35, 60, 81, 83, 211

Trenaman, Joseph 108
Tribune Group 71

unemployment 17, 202, 204–5
United States of America 239
U-turns 118, 201

value-added tax 201
voting behaviour 89, 93–4, 91, 98
  in by-elections 109
  and dealignment 105–6
  in European Parliamentary elections 108–9
  and floating voters 101
  in local government elections 108
  and religion 108
  swing 98
  tactical 109
  of teachers 102

Walker, Patrick Gordon 127
Walters, Alan 122
Watergate affair 163
welfare 32
welfare state 213–14
whips 150
White Papers 135
Williams, Shirley 66, 97
Wilson, Harold 22, 31, 115, 118, 122, 139
Wright, Erik Olin 106

Young Conservatives 70

Zander, Michael 229

Acknowledgements

The authors and publishers wish to thank the following who have kindly given permission for the use of copyright material:

George Allen & Unwin (Publishers) Ltd for a table from *Local Government in Britain since Reorganisation* by A. Alexander;

Associated Newspapers Group Ltd for an extract from the *Daily Mail* 5 June 1975;

Tony Benn for 'Manifestos and Mandarins' in *Policy in Practice: the Experience* of Government, published by the Royal Institute of Public Administration;

BBC Publications for an extract from *Why is Britain Becoming Harder to Govern?* edited by Professor Anthony King;

S. J. Chibnall for a figure from *Law and Order News*;

The Conservative Central Office for an extract from *The Conservative Manifesto 1983*;

The Conservative Political Centre for statistics from *The Future of the Welfare State* (1958) by Dr Mark Abrams;

The Controller of Her Majesty's Stationery Office for extracts from *Committee on the Future of Broadcasting* (CMND 6753); *Royal Commission on the Press*; *The New Local Authorities: Management and Structure* (1972); *Local Government Finance Report of the Committee of Enquiry* (CMND 6453), and a table from *Britain 1980*;

Ivor Crewe for research figures from his article 'The disturbing truth behind Labour's rout', *Guardian*, 13 June 1983;

The Economist Newspaper Limited for election results published in *The Economist* 11 June 1983;

Faber and Faber Ltd for a table from *Politics in England Today* by Richard Rose;

Gower Publishing Company Ltd for a table and extract from *The British MP: a Socio-Economic Study of the House of Commons* by Colin Mellor;

Guardian Newspapers Limited for the table 'What the government plans to spend in 1983/4', 9 November 1982, four graphs and extract from article by Malcolm Dean, 10 March 1983, and an article by Julia Langdon 25 November 1982;

David Howells for extract from 'Marks and Spencer and the Civil Service: Comparison of Culture and Methods' in *Public Administration*, volume 59, Autumn 1981;

Hutchinson Publishing Group Ltd for an extract from *The Government and Politics of Britain* by John Mackintosh;

Inter-Action Imprint for an extract from *Football Hooliganism* by Roger Ingham, Stuart Hall, John Clarke, Peter Marsh and Jim Donovan;

Peter Jenkins for an extract from *The Battle of Downing Street* (1970);

The Labour Party for an extract from *The New Hope for Britain: Labour's Manifesto 1983;*

Local Government Chronicle for articles 'Three lies about local government' 2 April 1982; 'The fuse is LIT' 23 April, 1982; 'The winners of the contract-out game' 10 September, 1982; 'Flaws in the privatisation argument' 26 November 1982; 'The Ombudsman: Watchdog without a bite' 14 January 1983, and 'Audit under Scrutiny' 11 February 1983;

London Express News and Feature Services for a news extract from The *Sun* newspaper 31 October 1982;

Longman Group Ltd for an extract and table from *The Politics of Local Government in the United Kingdom* by Alan Alexander;

The Observer Newspaper for extracts from four issues;

Oxford University Press for tables from *Origins and Destinations* by A. H. Halsey, A. F. Heath and J. M. Ridge © 1980; from *Dissension in The House of Commons* by P Norton, © 1980; from *House of Commons in Twentieth Century* by S. A. Walkland © 1979; and for extracts from *Political Studies* vols 17 and 18;

Penguin Books Ltd for tables from *Local Government in Britain* by Tony Byrne (Pelican Books, Second edition 1983). Copyright © Anthony Byrne 1981, 1983;

A. D. Peters & Company Ltd on behalf of Peter Kellner

and Lord Crowther-Hunt for extracts from *The Civil Servants: An Inquiry into Britain's Ruling Class*;

Pluto Press for an extract from *Rage Against the Dying* by Elizabeth Sigmund;

The Politics Association for extracts from articles in *Teaching Politics*;

Martin Robertson and Company Ltd for two tables from *What Sort of Society?* by Howard Elcock;

Syndication International Ltd for an extract from *Woman's Realm* magazine, and an extract from the *Daily Mirror*, 19 September, 1972;

Times Newspaper Limited for voting figures from *The Times Educational Supplement and Higher Educational Supplement*, 1974; graph and extract from *The Times* 1 December, 1981; report by Marjorie Wallace in *The Sunday Times*, 18 April, 1982; article by David Lipsey and Chris Highe in *The Sunday Times*, 25 April 1982, extract from 'Tomorrow it could be you' by Sarah Hogg from *The Sunday Times*, 9 May, 1982; article by David Lipsey 'Labour's new (non-manual) breed of councillor', in *The Sunday Times*, 19 September 1982; article 'Where taxes hit hardest' by Arnold Legh in *The Sunday Times*, 28 November 1982; article 'Thousands who need not die each year' by Oliver Gillie, in *The Sunday Times*, 27 March 1983 and *Court and Social* column, by permission, in *The Sunday Times*, 10 June 1982.

The authors and publishers wish to acknowledge the following sources for use of material in this publication.

By kind permission of Her Majesty The Queen p. 161 bottom
Associated Press p. 63 centre right
British Museum Newspaper Library/Les Gibbard p. 12
British Museum Newspaper Library/Sunday People p. 26
British Museum Newspaper Library/Times Newspapers Ltd p. 26
Camera Press Ltd pp. 33, 34
Commission for Local Administration in England p. 46
Conservative Central Office p. 63 centre left
Labour Party Library p. 63 top and bottom right
Labour Party Young Socialists p. 103 left
Liberal Party p. 63 bottom left
Photo Source p. 64
Popperfoto p. 65 and cover
S.D.P. p. 103 right
TUC p. 80
Kipper Williams p. 52
Woman's Realm p. 161 top

Her Majesty's Stationery Office for permission to use data in compiling diagrams and charts.

Every effort has been made to trace all the copyright holders, but if any have been inadvertently overlooked, the publishers will be pleased to make the necessary arrangements at the first opportunity.